Qais Akbar Omar at the Fort of Nine Towers © Thomas R. Fattori

QAIS AKBAR OMAR (whose first name is pronounced "Kice") manages his family's carpet business in Kabul and writes books. In 2007, he was a visiting scholar at the University of Colorado. He has studied business at Brandeis University and is currently pursuing an MFA in creative writing at Boston University. Omar has lectured on Afghan carpets in Afghanistan, Europe, and the United States. He is the coauthor, with Stephen Landrigan, of *Shakespeare in Kabul*.

ALSO BY QAIS AKBAR OMAR

Shakespeare in Kabul (with Stephen Landrigan)

Additional Praise for *A Fort of Nine Towers*

"The compelling firsthand account of growing up in Afghanistan over the last three decades. Inspirational, tragic, and funny, it was hard to put down." —*The Christian Science Monitor*

"*A Fort of Nine Towers* is a poetic, funny, and terrifying memoir. . . . A book of hellish encounters . . . and familial love." —*The Economist*

"Spirited . . . The story of Qais's family is the story of Afghanistan. . . . I spent almost three years in Afghanistan with the State Department and have waited a long time for a nonfiction account like Qais's, one that captures the resilience of the people amid the jagged landscape of the Hindu Kush." —John Kael Weston, *The Daily Beast*

"[Qais Akbar Omar] is one of the most compelling memoirists to emerge out of the country's troubles in recent memory. . . . He offers a forceful account of coming of age at the height of Afghanistan's civil war, becoming a man under the Taliban, and learning to rebuild amid the uncertainty of a post-9/11 world." —*Foreign Policy*

"Extraordinary . . . Here at last is a powerful, haunting memoir that does justice to [Afghanistan's] tough, tenacious, and astonishingly good-humored people." —*London Evening Standard*

"Among Omar's many achievements, his greatest is in capturing a child's world. . . . Exhilarating and unsettling because this is Omar's lived experience, and one that is far stranger than fiction." —*The Independent* (London)

"Omar's beautifully written book is an affecting account of survival in the midst of brutality and fear, and a testament to the importance of family and friendships in a place where neighbors turned on neighbors." —*The Sunday Times* (London)

"[Qais Akbar Omar] has written an autobiography that is among the best to emerge from Afghanistan. . . . It captures the chaos and depredations of the era." —*The Globe and Mail* (Toronto)

"Omar crosses the divides that make Afghans so frustratingly exotic to tell a universal story of survival and the power of family." —*The Toronto Star*

"Profoundly moving . . . As lyrical as it is haunting, this mesmerizing, not-to-be-missed debut memoir is also a loving evocation of a misunderstood land and people. A gorgeously rich tapestry of an amazing life and culture." —*Kirkus Reviews* (starred review)

"Omar's account of his childhood will humble you. . . . Perfect for readers of books like Gayle Tzemach Lemmon's *The Dressmaker of Khair Khana* and Azar Nafisi's *Reading Lolita in Tehran*." —*Library Journal*

"The first true-life memoir of growing up in Kabul, this is both a magical and a chilling book, which conveys the strength of family in truly terrible times." —Christina Lamb, author of *The Sewing Circles of Herat*

"Inscriptional: Its images carve themselves into the reader's mind. Unlike most accounts of life in exile, *A Fort of Nine Towers* never leaves Afghanistan, as a boy and his family remain trapped within the nation's borders by familial ties and by war. This book is essential reading for anyone eager to learn what more than three decades of war have cost the Afghan people." —Eliza Griswold, *New York Times* bestselling author of *The Tenth Parallel: Dispatches from the Fault Line Between Christianity and Islam*

"I know of no other book in which the complex realities of life—and death—in contemporary Afghanistan are so starkly and intimately portrayed. This brave memoir, rich in tough humor and insight, recounts an insider's view into both the suffering and the integrity of an uncompromisingly proud and courageous people. Above all, it is a powerful reminder of the extraordinary tenacity of a culture that foreigners have repeatedly and fatally misjudged."

—Jason Elliot, author of
An Unexpected Light: Travels in Afghanistan

"This is a book for those who love Afghanistan, for those who want to understand it, or simply for those who value deeply the best in the human spirit. It is a tale that deserves to rank with *The Kite Runner*."

—Ronald E. Neumann, former U.S. ambassador to Afghanistan and president of the American Academy of Diplomacy

A
FORT
OF NINE
TOWERS

An Afghan Family Story

QAIS AKBAR OMAR

Picador

———

Farrar, Straus and Giroux
New York

The Library of Congress has cataloged the Farrar, Straus and Giroux edition as follows:

Omar, Qais Akbar.
    A fort of nine towers : an Afghan family story / Qais Akbar Omar. — 1st ed.
    p. cm.
    ISBN 978-0-374-15764-7 (hardcover)
    ISBN 978-0-374-70918-1 (e-book)
    1. Omar, Qais Akbar.   2. Afghanistan—Social conditions—20th century.
3. Afghanistan—Biography.   I. Title.
CT1878.O63 A3 2013
958.104092—dc23
[B]   2012034566

Picador ISBN 978-1-250-04365-8

Picador books may be purchased for educational, business, or promotional use. For information on bulk purchases, please contact Macmillan Corporate and Premium Sales Department at 1-800-221-7945, extension 5442, or write specialmarkets@macmillan.com.

First published in the United States by Farrar, Straus and Giroux

First Picador Edition: April 2014

10 9 8 7 6 5 4 3 2 1

If sorrow settles in your heart, then where is the home of joy?
The sorrows and joys of life are all mixed together.
No one can separate them, except the One who created them.

Real men do not die of death; death finds its death in man.
Real men do not die of death; death finds its name in man.
When a man's name is respected, then death has no name.

My grandfather said

Contents

PART THREE: IN THE TIME OF SHAITAN

PART FOUR: THE TRIUMPH OF MADNESS

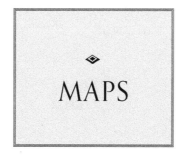

MAPS

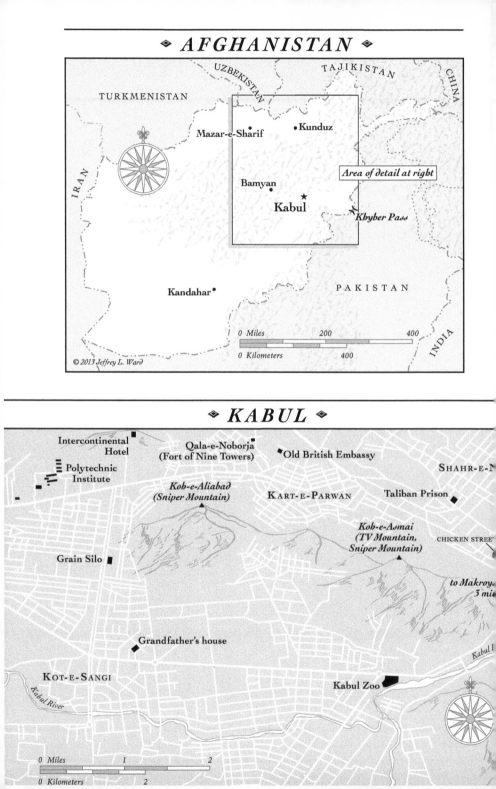

❖ AFGHANISTAN ❖

TURKMENISTAN

UZBEKISTAN

TAJIKISTAN

CHINA

IRAN

Mazar-e-Sharif

Kunduz

Bamyan

Kabul ★

Khyber Pass

Area of detail at right

Kandahar

PAKISTAN

INDIA

| 0 Miles | 200 | 400 |
| 0 Kilometers | 400 |

© 2013 Jeffrey L. Ward

❖ KABUL ❖

Intercontinental Hotel

Qala-e-Noborja (Fort of Nine Towers)

Old British Embassy

SHAHR-E-N

Polytechnic Institute

Koh-e-Aliabad (Sniper Mountain)

KART-E-PARWAN

Taliban Prison

Koh-e-Asmai (TV Mountain, Sniper Mountain)

CHICKEN STREE

Grain Silo

to Makroy 3 mi

Grandfather's house

Kabul R

KOT-E-SANGI

Kabul River

Kabul Zoo

| 0 Miles | 1 | 2 |
| 0 Kilometers | 2 |

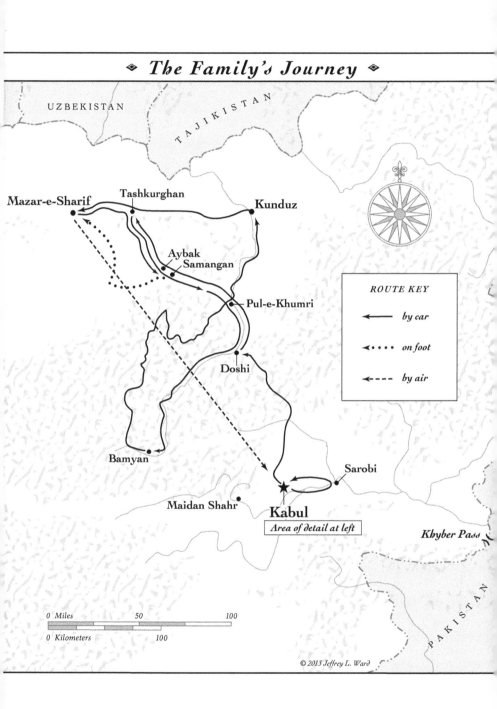

❖ The Family's Journey ❖

UZBEKISTAN

TAJIKISTAN

Mazar-e-Sharif

Tashkurghan

Kunduz

Aybak
Samangan

Pul-e-Khumri

Doshi

ROUTE KEY

◄——— *by car*

◄···· *on foot*

◄--- *by air*

Bamyan

Sarobi

Maidan Shahr

Kabul
Area of detail at left

Khyber Pass

0 Miles 50 100

0 Kilometers 100

PAKISTAN

© 2013 Jeffrey L. Ward

A
FORT
OF NINE
TOWERS

Prologue

The calls always come early in the morning. Sometimes I am still praying when I hear my mother's phone ring upstairs. I lean forward and touch my head to the carpet and make an extra effort to focus on the ancient verses streaming through my mind.

Alla-hu-Akbar. Subhanna rabbiyal A'ala . . .

Even before my mother answers it, I know who is calling.

It is my aunt, in Canada. She has just come home from a wedding party where she met a family with a daughter, a beautiful girl, very intelligent, and funny. A very good family. They are from Kabul, or Kandahar, or Mazar-e-Sharif, and our grandfather knew their uncle, or her father went to Habibia High School with the cousin of our neighbor who used to manage the Ariana Hotel before it was destroyed, or . . .

Qul Huwa Allāhu 'Aḥadun, Allāhu Aṣ-Ṣamadu, Lam Yalid Wa Lam Yūlad, Walam Yakun Lahu Kufūan 'Aḥadun.

My aunt has been in Canada for thirty years. I think she knows all the other Afghans there. She helped many of them when they first arrived, even though she herself was a young widow with a small daughter in a strange land whose language she struggled to master. Afghans never forget a kindness, though. Now, everywhere she goes, she is welcomed by those she helped and respected for the kindness in her heart. Almost every week, except during Ramazan, she is invited to a wedding.

Weddings are where my aunt keeps track of the young women whom she has known since they were babies. She has watched them grow up, and seen them taking full advantage of opportunities they would never have had in Kabul had their families stayed there over the past three decades. Through it all, she has kept a list of future husbands for them in her mind—nephews, neighbors, sons of former students from her days as a teacher—always waiting for the time when she can be of help.

Innā a'ṭaynāka al-kawthar, Fa-ṣalli li-Rabbika wanḥar, Innā ᶁhaani-aka huwal abtar.

I am twenty-nine years old. I have a university degree. I run my own carpet business and sometimes work with the foreigners. I have both arms and legs, which is an issue in mine-ridden Afghanistan. I come from a good family and am not yet married. I am a Pashtun with Hazara eyes thanks to a great-great-grandmother whose name no one remembers because she was a woman, and who was from some Central Asian tribe with Mongolian roots. I am the embodiment of this world-spanning mixture of peoples we call Afghan.

I give my aunt a reason to go to weddings on the nights she is tired, or when the snow is deep. I give her something to talk about, and someone to boast about. I sell carpets. She sells me. Her great hope is that I can live someplace where I can prosper and be safe.

How do I tell her, then, that though it sounds mad, I love Afghanistan? That I love being an Afghan? That I want to help rebuild what so many others destroyed? I know it will take a long time. I understand that. I am a carpet weaver. I know how, slowly, one knot follows another until a pattern appears.

Oh, God, can you not weave my destiny to keep me close to these people who mean more to me than any others in the world?

Ameen.

When I finish my prayers, I sit near the tall windows that look down over Kabul University and to the mountains beyond. The dust is so thick even at this early hour that I can hardly make out the outlines of the jagged peaks against the dawn.

Kabul has become a very dusty place. How many million people live here now? No one knows. When I was young, there were only eighty thousand of us. A big town with big houses that had big gardens. Now we live on the side of a mountain, like goats, on land sold to us by a squatter.

The sun rises from behind the mountains and burns through the dust with a greasy glare. I lean back on a cushion that was made by nomads who travel each year across miles of arid land in search of a patch of grass for their flocks. My people were nomads until my grandfather settled in Kabul. We have no livestock now, unless you count the cat on the roof.

My youngest sister brings me a thermos of green tea and the news that our aunt has called from Canada. I do not let on that I had already guessed that. I do not want to spoil her excitement at telling me. She has a devilish glint in her eye. I know she wants to make a joke about the girl my aunt was describing. By now, of course, my mother has given all the details to my four sisters who still live at home. My older sister, who is married, will hear everything before long. Marriage discussions in Afghanistan are a family matter, and a major source of entertainment. My youngest sister is trying to decide whether I am in the mood for jokes, or whether I will just send her away.

In the end, she walks off giggling to herself. If I ever leave this place, I will miss her more than I can bear to think about.

Sometimes I wonder whether it was difficult for Grandfather to leave the open lands of his nomad days for the confining walls of the city. I think of my teacher, Maulana Jalaluddin Mohammad Balkhi, known to the world as Rumi. He had to flee our country when the greatest teacher of our warlords, Genghis Khan, swept across our land, destroying everything.

It is time to go upstairs for breakfast. My father has already ridden off on his bicycle to teach his high school physics classes. My mother is preparing to go to her office where they coordinate relief for natural disasters. My two youngest sisters are leaving for school, adjusting their white headscarves over their black uniforms as they go out the door and head down the hill.

One of my other sisters has laid out some yogurt and fruit for me in the kitchen. She is studying agriculture at Kabul University and will soon go for her classes. My only brother, who is eight years younger than I am, is doing exercises in the room above me, sending down tiny clouds of dust as he skips a rope.

These are the things that happen every day. These are the rhythms of my family in the morning. These simple things will stay with me always; that is the one thing of which I am sure.

Uncertainty hangs thick like the dust in the air. I cannot see where the path of life will lead me. It is not my nature to sit and wait for something to happen. For the moment, though, unable to look forward, I have settled for gazing backward, to chronicle what I have witnessed in these few strange and turbulent years I have known.

Perhaps someday I will understand all these things better. Perhaps others will, as well. Perhaps this book will help.

Insh'allah.

PART ONE

◆

THE
HOLY
WARRIORS

1

❖

In the Time Before

I n the time before the fighting, before the rockets, before the warlords and their false promises, before the sudden disappearance of so
many people we knew to graves or foreign lands, before the Taliban
and their madness, before the smell of death hung daily in the air and
the ground was soaked in blood, we lived well.

We have no photos. It was too dangerous to keep them during the
time of the Taliban, so we destroyed them. But the images of our lives
before all hope fled Afghanistan remain sharp and clear.

My mother is wearing her short skirt, sitting in her office in a bank,
tending to a long line of customers. She is respected for her knowledge
of banking, and her ability to solve people's problems.

My father looks like a movie star in his bell-bottom trousers,
speeding through the Kabul streets on his motorcycle. Sometimes he
ties me to his back with a tight belt. His long hair catches the wind as
we ride off. When he turns the corners sharply, the metal guards he
wears on his knees shoot sparks into the air as they scrape the pavement. The next day I tell my classmates about that, and make them
envious.

One of my uncles goes on business trips to other countries. The other uncles and aunts study at universities in Kabul. All of them wear the latest styles. Grandfather, his thick white hair neatly combed, is elegantly dressed in finely tailored suits from Italy that emphasize his affluence. When he enters a room, he dominates it.

Grandfather is an impressive man, tall, with broad shoulders. Unlike many other Afghans, he keeps his well-tanned face freshly shaved. It is his wide, black eyes that you notice most. So deep. So commanding. So gentle.

The images come in a rush. Sometimes they play out in little scenes.

My father is calling me to get ready for school. I open my eyes and look at the clock above my bed. It is too early, but what can I say to him? He is my father. I am his son. Pashtun sons must obey their fathers.

But I am not ready to wake up. I rub my eyes. My father keeps calling, "Get up! Put on your gloves. I'm waiting for you in the ring." He wants me to exercise with him before breakfast. He has started training me to become a famous boxer like himself, and fight as he has in international competitions.

I hate waking up early, but I love exercising with my father. He always lets me beat him, even though I am seven years old.

I love school, too. I have perfect attendance. I am smart and popular. Sometimes the boys complain to the headmaster about me when I punch them in their faces. The headmaster covers for me, because he is Grandfather's best friend. But he never smiles at me.

My sister and I are in the same school. She is a year and a half older than I, and even smarter and more popular, but she never punches any girls, even though she is the daughter of a well-known boxer.

The heart of our world is my grandfather's house.

Grandfather had built it in the late 1960s, when he was the senior accounting officer in the Bank-e-Millie, the National Bank of Afghanistan. The country was prosperous, and he could see that Kabul would outgrow its twisted thousand-year-old streets along the Kabul River.

He bought about five acres on the far side of the small, steep mountain with the two peaks that for centuries had protected Kabul on its south and west sides. The land beyond them was then all farms with mud-brick villages, but not for long.

Grandfather had studied the land, talked to the farmers who knew it, and carefully chose the piece that had the best well. We had always had water even in the driest months, even when our neighbors had shortages. He enclosed most of his land with a sturdy cement wall, but set part of it aside for a school for all the kids whose families he knew would transform the farmlands into a neighborhood.

My father and six of his seven brothers, along with their wives and kids, all lived comfortably within Grandfather's wall. I had more than twenty-five cousins to play with, most of them around my age. Every family had two large rooms of its own. The rooms were clustered in a single-story building on one side of the garden. Grandfather's rooms were on the other side. Between us were sixty McIntosh apple trees. Grandfather's cousin had brought them from America as little branches that he had grafted onto Afghan apple tree roots. They were very rare in Afghanistan, and Grandfather was proud of having them.

At one end of the property was a block-long building with two floors of apartments above the shops on the street level. Grandfather rented out the apartments to people who were not relatives. All the windows in the apartments faced the street. No Afghan allows strangers to look into his family's garden.

My father set up a gym in one of the shops. Every day after school, dozens of young men would come there to train as boxers. My cousin Wakeel and I would watch them from the sidewalk pounding the punching bag, or doing push-ups, or skipping rope, while my father sparred with one or sometimes two at a time inside the ring he had built.

Wakeel was seven years older than I was. He was the older

brother I never had. I was the younger brother he always wanted. He let me use him as a punching bag when I imitated the boxers. Every time I hit him, he laughed.

Grandfather, by then retired from the bank, used one of the larger shops as a warehouse for his carpets. It had a thick door with a strong lock and was filled with the sweet, lanolin-rich smell of wool. He had thousands of carpets in there. My boy cousins and I liked to jump from one high pile of folded carpets to another.

All of my uncles had their own businesses, except Wakeel's father. He was a major in the National Army of Afghanistan. He always said, "Business is too risky. Most of these businessmen have heart attacks, or die at an early age." He was my grandfather's oldest son, and thus had a special place in the family. He and his wife enjoyed a relaxed life on his army salary with Wakeel, my favorite cousin, and their two daughters.

One day he went to his office and never came back. We still do not know whether he is alive or dead. It was in the time when I first heard the word "Communists," but I did not know what it meant then. For more than twenty-five years, his wife has been waiting for him to come home. Even now, she runs to the door whenever someone knocks.

My father was the third son. Like all my uncles, he had only one wife. It was not our family's custom to have more than one.

Our neighbors respected my father like a holy man. They came to see him and talked with him about their businesses and their problems. They called him *Lala*, "older brother," even though some of them were older than he was. They told him, "Your thoughts are older than your age." He was a man willing to try everything. He had no use for the word "no."

He was also the only one of his father's sons who was involved in carpets. His five younger brothers saw carpets as something from the past. They were looking to the future, making money in new ways.

One was importing goods from Russia. Two others were still in university but talking about importing medicine to sell to pharmacies all over Afghanistan.

Often, we all ate dinner together, more than fifty of us sitting on cushions around one cloth spread on the well-trimmed lawn that Grandfather had sown at one corner of our courtyard. Colorful little lightbulbs hung above us. After dinner, my grandfather and his sons sat in a circle talking about their businesses, or to which universities in Europe or America they should send my boy cousins and me.

The women made a separate circle to talk about their own things. It was the responsibility of the older women to find good husbands for the younger ones, such as my father's two unmarried sisters, who lived with us. His two older sisters were already married, and had moved away to the homes of their husbands' families in other parts of Kabul. Discussions on suitors could go on for months and involve the whole family until a choice was made.

My cousins and I sat in another circle, boys and girls together, telling one another scary tales, and staring at Kabul's clear night sky with the moon and stars scattered across it. When we got tired of stories, we shaped animals from the stars and laughed.

Sometimes after we had finished eating, my father or one of my uncles would take the kids around the mountain to buy ice cream at Shahr-e-Naw Park, or to one of the Kabul movie theaters for an Indian or American film.

Kabul was like a huge garden then. Trees lined the wide streets and touched each other overhead in tall, leafy arches. The city was full of well-tended parks, in which tall pink hollyhocks competed for attention with bright orange marigolds and hundreds of shades of roses. Every house had a garden with pomegranate, almond, or apricot trees. Even the mountain with the two peaks was covered in low-growing weeds and grasses that came to life with the spring rains. In both spring and fall, the sky filled with the brightly colored water birds that rested in the wetlands around the city as they flew between the Russian steppes and India. Ancient underground channels brought water from the mountains, and kept our gardens green.

Every Friday, the Muslim holy day when schools and businesses closed, we carried a large lunch to one of the gardens of our neighbors, or to picnic spots nearby at Qargha Lake or in the Paghman Valley, or sometimes even as far as the Salang Pass, high in the mountains of the Hindu Kush an hour's drive north of Kabul. This was a day for extended families to spend together, visiting and joking and gossiping.

My cousins and I climbed hills, while the elders reclined against huge pillows in the shade of willow trees or under the broad leafy branches of a *panj chinar* tree. My unmarried aunts were kept busy boiling water for the others who drank one cup of tea after another. In these long afternoons they took turns spinning some small event into a big story that made everybody laugh. They all tried to outdo one another, of course. They are Afghans. Of them all, my mother was the best.

My uncles were *tabla* drummers, and my father played the wooden flute, though he had never had lessons. We stayed until late into the evenings, singing, dancing, and cooking over an open fire.

Sometimes on these outings, the cousins held a school lessons competition. Whoever got the highest score could demand that the other cousins buy whatever he or she liked, no matter the cost. We, too, were very competitive. Our parents were the judges, and cheered loudly every time one of us got a correct answer. Sometimes the competition ended in a tie. We hated that.

Occasionally, some of the cousins fought and did not talk to each other for a day or two. But we could not maintain that for very long. Our games were more important, and never ended, whether we were playing hide-and-seek in the garden, or shooting marbles, or racing our bicycles in the park near our house, or especially when we were flying kites from the roof.

Every afternoon in the spring and autumn, when the weather

brought a gentle breeze, hundreds of kites would fill the sky above Kabul and stay there until dark. Kite flying was more than a game; it was a matter of the greatest personal pride to slice through the string of your rival's kite. The trick was to draw your kite string—coated with powdered glass—against your opponent's with speed and force.

Wakeel was the kite master, the kite-flying teacher to us all. The kids on the street had given him the title of "Wakeel, the Cruel Cutter," because he had cut so many of their kites.

One afternoon, Wakeel looked at me as we were heading to the roof with our kites and said, "Let's have a fight!" As usual, his long, dark hair fell over his forehead, brushing his thick eyebrows. And below them were his deep-set, dark eyes that sparkled, always.

I said okay, though I knew he would cut me right away. But from the earliest age we are taught never to run away from a fight, even if we think we cannot win.

The roof of Grandfather's apartment block was ideal for kite flying. Rising high above the trees that grew along the street, it was like a stage. People below—adults as well as kids—would see the kites going into the air, and stop everything that they were doing to watch the outcome. A good fight would be talked about for days after.

After we had had our kites in the air for half an hour, taunting and feinting, Wakeel called from the far end of the roof in amazement, "You have learned a lot! It used to take me only five minutes to cut you. Now it has been more than half an hour, and you are still in the sky."

Suddenly, he used a trick that he had not yet shown me. He let his kite loop around mine as if he were trying to choke it. I felt the string in my hand go slack, and there was my kite, flat on its back, wafting back and forth like a leaf in autumn, drifting off across the sky away from me.

Wakeel laughed and made a big show of letting his kite fly higher so everybody in the street could see he had yet again been the victor. I ran downstairs to get another kite.

Berar, a Hazara teenager who worked with our gardener, loved kite fighting. All the time I had been battling Wakeel, he had been carefully following every dive, envious.

Berar was a few years older than Wakeel, tall, handsome, and hardworking. His family lived in Bamyan, where the big statues of Buddha were carved into the mountains. Berar was not his real name. Berar in Hazaragi dialect means "brother." We did not know what his real name was, and he did not mind us calling him Berar.

As the suspense had built between Wakeel and me, Berar could not stop watching us. The old gardener spoke to him impatiently several times: "The weeds are in the ground, not in the sky. Look down." The gardener was always harsh to Berar.

"Give the boy a break," Grandfather told the gardener. They were working together on Grandfather's beloved rosebushes. I had just sent a second kite into the air. Grandfather nodded at Berar. "Go on," he said.

Berar ran up to the rooftop, where I was struggling to gain altitude while avoiding Wakeel's torpedoing attacks. Berar took the string from me and told me to hold the reel.

I had never seen Berar fly a kite before. I kept shouting at him, "*Kashko! Kashko!* Pull it in!" But Berar did not need my instructions; he knew exactly what to do. Wakeel shouted at me that I could have a hundred helpers and he would still cut me. Though he was tall and skinny, he was very strong and he was furiously pulling in his kite to circle it around mine.

Berar was getting our kite very high very fast, until in no time at all it was higher than Wakeel's. Then he made it dive so quickly that it dropped like a stone through the air. Suddenly, there was Wakeel's kite, drifting back and forth from left to right, floating off to Kandahar, separated from the now limp string in Wakeel's hand.

I climbed on Berar's shoulders, screaming for joy. I had the string of my kite in my hands. My kite was so high in the sky, it looked like a tiny bird. The neighbor kids on the street were shouting, too. They had not seen Berar doing it, only me on Berar's strong shoulders, cheering and shouting: "Wakeel, the Cruel Cutter, has been cut!" I kissed Berar many times. He was my hero. He gave me the title of "Cutter of the Cruel Cutter," even though it was he who had made it happen.

Wakeel sulked, and did not talk to me for two days.

———

We had another cousin who was a few months younger than I. He never really got along with any of the others. Wakeel used to call him a jerk. All the other cousins, everyone, started to call him "Jerk" as well.

If he bought new clothes, he would walk in front of us to show them off and say something stupid. "We went to a shop in Shahr-e-Naw that opened a few weeks ago. They bring everything they sell from London and Paris. The owner told my parents that I have a good taste for clothes. I don't think you guys can afford a suit like this." When I asked how much he paid, he would triple the price.

Wakeel would ask, "Hey, Jerk, do your clothes do any magic for such a price?"

Jerk could never see a joke coming, and would ask something witless like, "What kind of magic?"

"Can they make you look less ugly?" Wakeel replied, his voice cracking into shrieking guffaws.

We'd all laugh, and Jerk would run toward his house and complain to his parents. We would run to the roof, or outside the courtyard, or hide in the garage inside my father's car to escape punishment.

Once when Jerk had on his good clothes and was showing off, Wakeel filled his mouth with water, and I punched him in his stomach. That forced Wakeel to spit it all on Jerk. Poor Jerk looked at us in disbelief and asked with outrage in his voice why we had done that.

Wakeel told him, "We are practicing to be tough. We punch each other unexpectedly, so we will be prepared if we get into a fight with someone. You should be tough, too." Then we punched him in his stomach, but avoided his face so we would not leave any bruises, because we knew that would get us spanked by his parents.

Jerk had one unexpected strength: he was always a reader. For his age, he had more information than he needed. He had a good mind for memorizing, too. That turned us even more against him.

Wakeel teased Jerk all the time when we were at home playing with our cousins. Outside, though, Wakeel would not let anybody bother him. Wakeel was like an older brother to all of us. When Jerk got into fights with the neighbor boys, which happened a lot, Wakeel defended him. When we were playing football in the park, Wakeel always made sure that Jerk and I were on his team, so he could protect us.

Our neighbors were like us, quiet and educated people. When there was a wedding or engagement party in one of their houses, everyone in the neighborhood was invited, along with their kids and servants.

Every week my grandfather talked for ten minutes in the mosque after Friday prayers about how to keep our neighborhood clean, or how to solve water and electricity problems, or how to take care of the public park and create more facilities where the kids could play together. He had never been elected to any position, but people listened to him.

When a family was having financial problems, one of its older men would quietly speak to Grandfather and ask for the community's help. Then, after Friday prayers, Grandfather would explain to the other men in the mosque that some money was needed, without ever saying by whom. It was important to protect the dignity of the family in need.

One Friday after the others had left the mosque, I saw my grandfather giving the money he had collected to a neighbor whose wife had been sick for many months. The man kissed Grandfather's hands, and said, "You always live up to our expectations. May God grant you long life, health, and strength." When Grandfather noticed that I was watching him, he scowled at me, and I quickly turned away. This was something I was not meant to see.

Grandfather's house was his great pride, and the McIntosh apple trees were his great joy. He was in his late sixties when I was born, and soon after became a widower. By then he had retired from the bank, and busied himself in the courtyard, planting roses, geraniums, and hollyhocks or watering his McIntosh apple trees, always singing in a whispery voice under his teeth, or quietly reciting the ninety-nine names of God.

And for hours he would sit reading, surrounded by his books. His favorite, in two beautiful leather-bound volumes, was *Afghanistan in the Path of History* by Mir Ghulam Mohammad Ghobar. The title was embossed on the cover in gold. Sometimes he read to me from it.

He also had the *Complete Psychological Works of Sigmund Freud*, which had beautiful covers as well; but he did not read those to me. When I asked about them, he said he would give them to me when I was old enough.

In winter, he studied the poets Rumi, Shams Tabrizi, Hafiz, Sa'adi, and Omar-e-Khayyam. Sometimes he invited his friends to discuss the political affairs of Afghanistan and the world. But before long, the talk would turn to poetry. He always wanted me and my boy cousins to listen to what was being said, and to ask questions.

My sisters and girl cousins were never part of those discussions. Their lives moved on a different path from those of the boys, but they were always allowed to read Grandfather's books. Indeed, Grandfather always encouraged them to do so. "Education," he would say, stressing the word, "is the key to the future." They read lots of poetry, as well as novels by Dostoyevsky, Tolstoy, Thomas Mann, and some Afghan and Iranian novelists whose names no one knows in the rest of the world. All these books were in Dari.

Some of the older girls, including Wakeel's sisters, read Grandfather's books by Sigmund Freud long before I did. We could hear them whispering about something called "the Oedipus complex," and then laughing. As soon as any of the younger cousins got too close to them, though, they stopped talking and looked at us in a way to make us understand that we were not welcome.

One day during one of Grandfather's discussions, Wakeel raised his hand and asked what politics was all about.

A friend of Grandfather's answered, "In fact, politics is really just a bunch of lies, and politicians are very gifted liars who use their skill to control power and money and land."

"They must be devious people, then," Wakeel said.

"That's true."

"Which country has the most devious politicians?" Wakeel asked.

"Let me tell you a story, my son," Grandfather's friend said, clearing his throat. "Someone asked Shaitan, the devil, 'Since there is such a large number of countries in the world, how do you manage to keep so many of them in turmoil all the time, like Afghanistan, and Pakistan, and Palestine? You must be very busy.' "

"Shaitan laughed and said, 'That is no problem. Not for me.' He leaned back on his cushion and raised the mouthpiece of his *chillum* to his scaly lips. He drew in a sour-smelling smoke that made the water in the pipe turn black with oily bubbles, then let the smoke drain out of the corners of his mouth. 'There is one country on the earth that does a better job than me in creating problems everywhere.' "

"Really?" Wakeel asked. "Which country is more devious than Shaitan?"

" 'It is called England,' Shaitan said."

My grandfather and his friends all laughed, and then they talked about poetry again.

It would be years before I understood the bad feelings that many Afghans have for England, which three times invaded Afghanistan and three times was driven out. For nearly three centuries, the English used Afghanistan like a playing field to challenge the Russians in a very ugly game. Neither side won, and neither side cared how many Afghans they killed or how much suffering they inflicted on Afghan people.

Those days were long in the past, like the battles between the ancient kings who had fought to rule our country. Life was smooth, and easy, and full of joy, except maybe for Jerk when we played tricks on him. Time moved graciously with the pace of the seasons, and nudged us gently through the stages of life. But then one night the air was filled with the unexpected cries of *"Allah-hu-Akbar,"* and nothing has ever been the same since.

2

❖

Allah-hu-Akbar

Chill winds from the high mountains around Kabul had begun to blow down on the city. Autumn was coming. It had been especially cold the past two nights. Now my parents and my aunts and uncles were using this Friday afternoon to set up the wood-burning tin stoves called *bokhari* in every room. When flakes of last winter's soot fell out of the pipes, some of the uncles said bad words. The cousins laughed and raced to tell one another what they had heard.

Just as night fell, the electricity suddenly went out. I looked outside. It was not just our house. The whole city was completely dark. I had never seen that before. Kabul always had electricity.

My mother said, "Oh, it's as dark as a grave."

I thought for a moment. How did my mother know how dark a grave is?

"Have you ever been in a grave?" I asked her.

"Stop being silly," she chided as she went to find candles.

My older sister had been doing her homework. "There is no electricity in a grave, idiot," she said. "Of course it is dark." She went to help my mother.

I looked out the window again into the darkness. No one was in the street. Could a grave be as big as a whole city?

I could hear voices in the distance. It was like the murmurings of a thousand people from the far side of Kabul. At first, I thought that it must be *muezzins* calling people to prayer. But the prayer time had been twenty minutes ago, and the voices were not familiar like the *muezzins'*. Nor were they coming over a loudspeaker, nor from the direction of the nearby mosques. The voices kept getting louder. Now I could hear them shouting *"Allah-hu-Akbar, Allah-hu-Akbar."* God is great.

I ran to find my mother to ask her why they were saying that. She was searching through all the drawers for candles; my older sister was looking for matches.

"I don't know," she said.

"You're even more than four times older than I am," I told her insistently, "but still you don't know more than me." She finally located a candle and lit it. She held it in her right hand and cupped her left palm around it. The soft light made her look very beautiful.

She kissed me on my cheek, which made me smile, and said, "Go and ask your father. Then you will know more than I know." The wax dripped on her thin, delicate fingers. She flinched and put the candle on the table. The wind blew in through the windows, making the curtains dance and the candle flutter; the voices outside grew louder.

I found my father in the courtyard, up on a ledge of the thick mud-brick wall that separated us from the street. He was leaning over, hoping someone would pass who could tell him what was going on.

The sound grew, like a wind rising. Now we could hear people in many places yelling. They were not organized. Everybody seemed to be saying their own *"Allah-hu-Akbar,"* some louder and some softer.

Suddenly, the man across the street who owned the shop at the corner started calling *"Allah-hu-Akbar"* inside his courtyard. Then I heard his two brothers join him. A couple of more courtyards down the street began having their own voices.

My father jumped down from the ledge. He landed on one of the low wooden platforms where we sometimes spread carpets and ate dinner. He, too, started shouting, *"Allah-hu-Akbar!"*

I was very surprised. I wanted to shout, too. But I did not hear any kids' voices. It was all men, and I was a little bit frightened. I hugged my father's leg.

I put my head against his leg and heard a different voice coming from inside it. Then I pulled my head away and heard his usual voice. I did this several times, then called my older sister and told her to do the same. She grabbed his other leg and put her ear to it. We were fascinated by our new discovery. My father paid no attention to us. He was shouting louder now, and that made it more exciting for us. We were putting our ears to his legs and pulling away, giggling.

I heard some more familiar voices joining in, and even some women. I pulled my head away from my father's leg. All my uncles and my aunts were standing behind my father and shouting, *"Allah-hu-Akbar."*

"Why are they all saying that?" I asked no one in particular.

"It is doomsday," my sister said. "The sun will rise from the west during the night, and the moon and stars will disappear. The mountains will become smooth, and the whole earth will become flat." I was now eight years old and almost as tall as she, but she was frightening me. She was very good at scaring us younger kids whenever she told stories.

"From the east to the west, and from the north to the south, there'll be no mountains at all. You'll be able to see an egg from one corner of the world to the other. All the dead bodies from the beginning of time, which goes back centuries, will come back alive, and God will put the sinners in hell and the honest in paradise." I wanted her to stop, but she kept on, making grotesque faces to emphasize her words.

"Hell is full of fire and wild and dangerous animals. The sinners will die, and be reborn, and die and be reborn, and will always suffer. And that is where you are going, because yesterday you stole my pencil, and lied to Father that the pencil was yours, and then you blamed me for using your pencil. You will go straight to hell, because you committed three big sins. And you will have to stay there for a very long time." I was starting to cry.

"But I didn't mean it, and I gave it back to you. I was just joking and teasing you," I wailed.

"It doesn't matter; you made me suffer. If I don't forgive you, you will go to hell," she said, and she was very firm.

"What do you want me to do for you to forgive me?" I begged.

"You have to kiss my hands and my feet, then buy me a package of candy in school tomorrow. Then I will think about forgiving you," she said.

"But you said it was doomsday. There is no tomorrow!" I said.

"Oh, yes! I forgot. But you must kiss my hands and my feet. Hurry, or you won't have enough time!" she warned.

I hesitated for a minute and did not know what to do.

"Hurry up, if the sun rises now, then your apology won't be acceptable," she said. "Start by kissing the sole of my foot."

I looked at the starry sky and was doubtful that the sun would rise at 8:00 p.m. But when I looked at my sister, she was grimly serious. She was holding up her right foot.

I bent down to kiss her sole. That distracted my father. He looked at me kneeling on the ground getting my clothes dirty and asked, "Hey, hey, what are you doing?"

My sister shrieked and ran away. If I had been sure that this was just one of her stupid jokes, I would have run after her. But I wanted to be certain about doomsday first.

I asked my father, "Is it true that it is doomsday?"

He laughed as he ran his hand through my long hair, which was thick, wavy, and brown in those days and made me look like a foreigner.

"Why is everyone shouting?" I asked him impatiently.

"Because they want the Mujahedin to come to Kabul and make the Russians leave Afghanistan," he replied, grinning with joy at the idea, and then started yelling again.

Sometimes we had seen Russian soldiers when I was very small. The Russians had blue eyes, red hair, and white skin. They threw candy to us when they rumbled by in their huge tanks. We always yelled *"Spaseva,"* though we did not know what it meant, and they smiled.

For other Afghans, the Russians brought bombs, not candy. Whole villages and large neighborhoods in cities were wiped out by the

Russians dropping one bomb after another from their planes, which seemed to fly only a few meters above the houses. They did this if they thought there was even one person living there who was opposing them. Everyone was slaughtered, the guilty and the innocent. But how can a man be guilty when all he wants is to protect his family and his land from invaders?

Afghans had only their old hunting guns and their determination to defend themselves against the Russians. Every village in Afghanistan, however, has a council of elders called a *shura*. Once the elders have decided that the village will do something, every family in the village must do it. The *shuras* decided that all the men should form fighting groups and join with others all over Afghanistan. They did, and they called themselves Mujahedin, the Holy Warriors.

My grandfather, father, uncles, and Grandfather's guests had often talked about the Mujahedin long before they came to Kabul. In fact, people had been talking about them from the time they were formed in Pakistan and Iran. When anyone spoke of them, they often referred to them proudly as "our Mujahedin brothers, who will come and liberate this country from these religionless and Communist Russians."

As kids, we heard the Mujahedin spoken of with such respect that we could not wait to see them.

For ten years, they had fought relentlessly against the Russians. The Americans had sent them more powerful weapons, and that had helped. Finally, the Russian soldiers were driven out of Afghanistan in 1989. Their defeat was so devastating that it helped end Communism in Russia and Eastern Europe. But the new Russian government still tried to control Afghanistan. They put Afghans in charge who had been educated in Russia, and sent them lots of money, as well as food and fuel. But even with all the Russians' help, everyone knew that the Afghan government could not last for long.

My grandfather and his sons talked about it whenever we ate together. One of my uncles imported things from Russia. Like all Afghans, he wanted the Russians to stop interfering with our country. But we did not know what this would mean for his business.

Now the Mujahedin were coming to Kabul to drive away even these Afghans who were running the government for the Russians.

After twelve years of turmoil, Afghanistan would become a place of peace again.

I could not hold back any longer. I started saying *"Allah-hu-Akbar, Allah-hu-Akbar,"* first in a shy voice, then louder and louder.

About a year and a half after the night we heard people shouting *Allah-hu-Akbar*, the Mujahedin finally took control of the country in April 1992. The Russian government had stopped sending money and supplies to the Afghans they had put in charge of our government three months before. Without the Russians' support, the prices for food and everything else, such as flour, cooking oil, rice, beans, chickpeas, sugar, soap, and clothes, quickly started going up.

Until the Russians had left Afghanistan three years before, everybody who worked for the government received coupons for these items, which they could buy at the end of each month for a very low price from the government stores. When there were several people in one family working for the government, they often had so much that they could sell what they did not need in the black market, and at a price higher than they paid, but still much cheaper than the market price. Also, the quality of the Russian goods was much better than most of the other things in the market. But once the Russians had left, the coupons stopped.

Food became hard to find in the markets. Even the large food supply in our house began to shrink. We no longer had five things at each meal but only beans with bread, or boiled potato and bread, or rice and slices of tomato and onion. When we asked our mother where all the vegetables were that she usually served along with chicken or lamb, she would make a joke: "The seeds for the vegetables have not been planted yet, the lamb is still a baby, and the chicken is still an egg."

There were times when my two younger sisters would not eat breakfast, because they wanted to have jam and butter to put on their *naan*. But when my mother put two extra spoonfuls of sugar in their milk, they drank it happily with a piece of *naan*. Somehow our mother managed to keep us fed.

One day, even though there was very little food, we had a big party after my mother had given birth to my little brother.

My father was overjoyed to have a second son. To celebrate, he went out to buy a big cake. A couple of hours later he came back with a cake no bigger than a brick. As soon as we saw it, we all laughed, thinking that he was making a joke. He laughed with us as he handed the cake to my mother. Then he told us that he had gone to about twenty shops and could not find even one other cake.

My parents and sisters, with some of my aunts and cousins, stuck a few small candles on the small cake, lit them, and after a few moments everybody blew them out. Then my father cut the cake into very, very small pieces. As he handed everyone a piece, he joked, "At least it is enough to fill the cracks between your teeth." We all laughed.

I was so hungry, though, that I swallowed my piece half-chewed. I asked for another. My father looked at me and said, "Sorry, son, nothing left. Wait for next year, when you will have another brother, *Insh'allah*, then you can have your second piece." Everybody laughed. I never did have any more brothers, but in the years that followed God granted me two more sisters.

As the shortages became more severe, the government became more desperate, and the anger of ordinary Afghans increased. The government tried many things to calm the situation, but they did not know what to do. They tried to work out a deal with the Mujahedin, but it was too late. The president, Dr. Najibullah, fled to the United Nations compound in Kabul to seek asylum. The time of the Communists had ended, and the time of the Mujahedin had begun.

When I heard that the Mujahedin were coming, I had expected to see heroes in uniforms and shiny boots. But they were dressed like villagers with big turbans, the traditional baggy pants called *shalwar*, and the long, tunic-like shirts called *kamiz*. Their waistcoats were filled with grenades and bullets. They all had beards, mustaches, and smelly shoes that wrapped up stinky feet; not one was without a gun.

On TV, the female announcers now covered their heads with scarves. Women singers were no longer seen. Instead, we saw men with big turbans and long beards sitting on the floor, reciting the

Holy Koran. The male TV announcers started wearing *shalwar kamiz* instead of a pressed suit and tie. The TV programs were now filled with interviews with the men we would come to know as commanders. They were talking about their factions, and what they wanted to do for Afghanistan.

They all sounded like professors of the Holy Koran in the way they talked about Islam, and its importance for Muslims and Afghans. They all connected themselves to the Prophet Mohammad, peace be upon him, and claimed to be descendants of Arabs to make themselves sound like they were linked closely to the Prophet Mohammad, peace be upon him, even though we all know that Afghans are descendants of Zoroastrians, Jews, Greeks, Mongols, Aryans, and many other people, as well as of the Arabs who entered our history much later.

Two months before the arrival of the Mujahedin, we had been taught in school that we are related to monkeys. The teacher told us that little by little some of the monkeys changed and became more like humans. Some of them did not want to be human and civilized, because there are many problems in civilizations. We had a series of pictures in our textbooks showing how monkeys became human.

Our teacher said, "Humans are a kind of animal, and animals were created by nature."

"Who created nature?" I asked.

"Nature was self-created," our teacher said.

He took us to the Kabul Zoo to see the monkeys and to compare their faces with ours. None of the monkeys looked like anyone I knew, until I saw a cage with some new monkeys that had just arrived from India. One of them looked exactly like our teacher.

Excitedly, I raced to tell him, "There is a monkey that looks exactly like you."

My teacher was with my classmates and two other teachers. All of them laughed. He came close to me and squeezed my left ear very hard and whispered, "Students don't talk to their teacher like this."

"Maybe he was one of your ancestors," I persisted.

By then, my classmates were confirming my observation. Our teacher shouted at the other students that it was time to leave, though we were supposed to have spent the rest of the day in the zoo.

After the Mujahedin came to Kabul, our same teacher now taught us from a new textbook called *The Creation of Adam*. It did not say anything about monkeys.

We learned that we all came from Adam and Eve. Our teacher started saying things like, "The history of humans started from Adam and Eve, and the earth existed long before them. Do not let Shaitan be your guide; he misled Eve and Adam and drove them out of paradise."

I was confused. "What happened to the monkeys?" I asked our teacher, "And nature?"

The teacher sat on the edge of the desk, and for a minute he did not say anything. "The monkeys and nature are Communist perceptions." His voice was very calm, and he looked straight into my eyes as if there were no one else in the class. "The Islamic perception is: God is the creator of nature and all creatures." Now he was looking at everyone. "Adam is the father of all humans," he said.

I was still confused. I came home and asked Grandfather what all these things meant.

He told me, "Time will show you the truth. You are too young now. Wait and be patient, you will find answers to your questions."

I did not know why grown-ups always said that I was too young now. I wanted to grow up, be tall, and have a mustache and some wrinkles on my forehead, and snore when I slept and know everything.

Once the Mujahedin were in control, everything was cheap, and food became plentiful for a few months after they had opened the government food stores. For the first time in years, people could travel anywhere in Afghanistan without worrying about being caught in a crossfire if some group of fighters suddenly started attacking government cars or Russian military vehicles from their hiding places.

Grandfather was very optimistic. It was springtime, and it felt like the whole world was making a new beginning. Several times, he invited some of the Mujahedin to our house, served them good food, and treated them like his best friends. My father shared Grandfather's feelings at the beginning. But after a while, he began to have doubts. He did not like how they were running the country.

Within weeks, fighting between some of the Mujahedin factions broke out in certain areas of Kabul, small incidents at first. People said, "There must be some misunderstandings. In a family, there are always squabbles. They will solve it."

But those small fights became big fights. Chaos started spreading all over Afghanistan. Afghans who had a little money or relatives in other countries quickly left. Others who stayed were beaten up, or had their property stolen. We heard about women who were raped by the soldiers of the same commanders who had talked about Islam and its importance to Muslims and Afghans only a few months before.

My father wanted to leave Afghanistan for Turkey or Russia, where he had many friends from his days as a boxer, but my grandfather would not give him permission to go. "The borders are still open," my father said. "We should go while we can. We will come back when things quiet down."

"Afghanistan is in good hands now. We are with our own now, and we can decide what we want. Give them time," Grandfather urged. Besides, he needed my father's help. My father was the son on whom my grandfather most depended.

Slowly, one Mujahedin faction took over a part of Kabul City, and another faction took another part. They started by seizing control of a neighborhood where many people of their tribe lived, then tried to take other areas around them. Soon, each faction had its own territory. As spring turned into summer, we started hearing about "checkpoints" and the "front lines." The factions started firing rockets at each other. Now innocent people were being killed, especially in our neighborhood, which by sad chance was about as far as the rockets from each side could fly before they fell.

First it was a dozen people who were killed. Then it was a hundred. Then a thousand. It was like when a forest catches fire, both the dry and the wet burn.

One faction overran Pul-e-Charkhi prison and freed not just the political prisoners, but even those who had committed inhumane deeds against common ordinary people.

One day while two factions were firing rockets at each other over our heads, there was loud knocking on our courtyard door. I had just come out of Grandfather's room, where he was starting his prayers, and I ran to the door.

When I opened it, I saw some guys with guns, grenades, and bullets tucked into special belts and in their waistcoat pockets. The hooks of the grenades were hanging out.

One of them walked through the door without being invited and pushed me against the wall. He had an ugly scar on his face. Two others followed.

"Where is the owner of this house?" he asked loudly.

"He is inside praying," I told him.

"Where?" he asked gruffly. I pointed to Grandfather's room. He kicked open the door. Grandfather was on his prayer rug, with his head touching the ground.

"Give me the key to your carpet warehouse!" the man with the scar shouted at Grandfather, but Grandfather ignored him, and kept on praying. The man shouted again and pointed his gun at Grand-father's head. I started to cry.

My grandfather ignored him until he had finished his prayers. He quietly rose to his feet and folded his prayer rug as if he were the only person in the room. Finally, he looked at the gunman, who had been shouting the whole time.

"If you think I will be scared by your loud voice, you are stupid." Grandfather spoke calmly, like he was talking to one of his clients at the bank.

The shouting had attracted the attention of my father and my uncles. I could hear them running toward Grandfather's room. They were shouting, too, asking what was happening. The thieves took positions in the corners of the room. As my father and his brothers came rushing in, the thieves put their guns to the backs of their necks. Everyone froze where he stood.

My cousins had come racing down the long corridor that led to my grandfather's room, their mothers behind them. When they saw the thieves and the guns, there was a moment of horrified silence.

Then Grandfather spoke softly. "Go ahead, kill me, and then you will get the key. Whatever I have earned in life came from the calluses of my hands. I will not give it to a bunch of cowardly thieves."

The one in charge, with the scar, grinned at my grandfather and said, "You stupid old man, I won't even waste a bullet on you." Then he shouted at my uncles, cousins, and their mothers to move back. Everyone did. The thieves braced the butts of their Kalashnikovs against their stomachs, pointed the barrels toward us, and walked backward out the courtyard gate.

When they had gone, my father locked the door after them. My father and my uncles went to Grandfather's room. Their wives were whispering to one another in the courtyard.

My cousins came to me to ask me what had happened. I stood with them all around me and told what I had seen. They paid close attention to everything I said, even the ones who did not get along with me. Now that I had become so important, I told them, "You have to wait until I finish my explanations, then I will answer your questions."

A moment later, we heard three gunshots in the street. My father and two of my uncles ran from Grandfather's room toward the courtyard door. My mother and my uncles' wives cried to them not to go out. But they did not listen.

Grandfather came out of his room and ran after them. Nobody dared to tell him what to do. As he hurried toward the courtyard gate, he nodded at me to follow him. Grandfather always wanted me to see life as it is and not hide from it. I followed him, and my cousins followed me. Outside our courtyard gate, we found my father and my two uncles handcuffed in front of Grandfather's warehouse. Several more robbers were in the street. Two of them were again pointing guns at the backs of their necks. One of the locks to the warehouse had been shot open. One of the thieves was positioned as a lookout at one end of our short street; another one was at the far end. One more was standing in the middle of the road in front of our warehouse.

Two others were still trying to break the second lock. Sweat was dropping from their chins, though it was cold and a light cover of snow had whitened the ground. One of them wanted to blow the lock open with a grenade, but his friend did not let him.

"No!" he said. "They'll hear it. We'll have to share the carpets with the commander." Suddenly, I understood that these guys were ordinary thieves who had joined one of the factions. They were not true Mujahedin who defend their country and faith against the invaders and heretics.

The one who had suggested using the grenade stepped back and shot three bullets at the lock. On the third shot, it shattered and the door opened. The one who was standing in the middle of the road called the two others at the ends of the road to join them. They all went inside.

The warehouse was dark. The carpets were piled one on top of another, all the way to the ceiling. Over the past sixteen years, since my grandfather had retired from the bank, he and my father had gathered more than six thousand carpets. One of the thieves drew the curtains, and sunlight rushed in.

The warehouse was a treasury. Every carpet spoke through its colors and its designs. Many were very old. Each one had been selected carefully by Grandfather and my father, but we could do nothing to stop the thieves from taking them away from us.

Working quickly, three of them loaded as many carpets as they could into their old Russian jeep. Three others stood guard outside with their fingers on the triggers, ready to shoot anyone who bothered them. I saw the carpet that I had helped wash in the courtyard with the washers we hired once a month. They cleaned the old carpets that my father brought back from the villages. That was my favorite carpet, but I could not tell these thieves to not take that one because I liked it.

It took them two days to steal all the carpets. The war had now come to us, as it had to so many.

We were not the only ones who were robbed. Our part of Kabul was almost empty. Most of our neighbors had fled, some in such a hurry they took nothing with them. Soon their houses were stripped bare.

The women were no longer at their windows with their elbows on the ledges, chatting. Now, instead, unfed cats leapt from the ledges and hissed at each other.

Every time the wind blew, the doors of the empty houses started banging, windows slammed, curtains blew in and out. When there were no sounds of rockets exploding or guns being fired, the neighborhood was filled with the howling of the hungry dogs who had been abandoned.

Only a madman would try to go out in the street. Snipers had taken up positions on the small mountain behind us and might take a shot, just for fun. The twin peaks had lost their old names of Koh-e-Asmai and Koh-e-Aliabad and had become known as Sniper Mountain.

As spring brought warm days back to Kabul, it became too dangerous to move around in our courtyard. Some snipers even used Grandfather's high roof where we flew kites to shoot at those on the mountain; the snipers on the mountain shot back. Sometimes they fired rockets. A few landed in our courtyard. The rest fell in the streets around us, on our neighbors' houses, in our park, where they destroyed the trees, and on our small neighborhood school, which had been our joy until it was blasted into dust.

The grass in the courtyard began to die as the weather grew warmer, because no one dared to go outside to water it. In the end, it became too dangerous even to stay in our rooms. We had to move to a large room in the basement under the apartments, where we hoped we would be safer.

It had never been wired for electricity, and both day and night we lit oil lamps and candles. We slept on the cement floor.

We ate together, more than fifty of us sitting on the floor around one tablecloth. Each day's meal was like a little party, but a sad one. Nobody talked, nobody laughed. In fact, we were waiting for a rocket to land on us and kill us all.

All the uncles had radios with tiny earphones. They spent all day listening to news from the Dari-language broadcasts on the BBC World Service and other stations. I wanted to listen to Indian songs. Worry will not change my destiny, I thought; worry brings more worries.

One Sunday night around nine o'clock, the uncles all started telling everyone to be quiet. The BBC announced that the next day there would be a ceasefire in our Kot-e-Sangi neighborhood. It would last for ten hours starting from eight in the morning. This meant we could leave our house. Everyone began to talk at once. What should we do? Where should we go? Who would help us?

As I was falling asleep that night, I could hear rockets whining in flight; when they landed, they made the ground rock like a cradle.

Around three or four in the morning, I woke up needing to use the bathroom. We did not have one in the basement. I walked to the courtyard to pee under a tree as I had done on other nights since we had been forced from our rooms. It was very quiet, but I heard the sound of shoveling. I rubbed my eyes and looked around. In different parts of the garden, all of my uncles were digging narrow, deep holes. They dug in the dark. No one dared light a lantern. It would have been a target for the snipers.

I went to one of my uncles and asked him why he was digging a hole at this time of the night. He did not answer me. I went to another uncle and asked him the same question. He did not answer either.

I went back to the basement to ask my father. He was not there next to my mother. My mother, sisters, and little brother were all sound asleep. I quietly rushed to the corner of the courtyard where our part of the house stood. There was my father digging a hole beneath the mulberry tree we liked to climb.

"Dad, what are you doing?" I asked.

He stopped and looked at me. "Go and sleep," he said. He sounded harsh.

"Why is everybody digging holes?" I asked determinedly.

"I said, go and sleep," he almost shouted at me, but very softly as if he did not want anyone to hear. His voice made me frightened. I did not ask any more questions. But I was angry.

Instead of going back down to the safety of the basement, I went to our own rooms, and I slept in my own bed. It was so good to sleep in my own bed after so many weeks on the hard cement floor of the basement. I did not care if a rocket fell on me. A few minutes later, I was sound asleep, and had no idea of the strange new life that would start for my family and me in the morning.

3

❖

The Other Side of the Mountain

I woke up just before dawn. My father and mother were running all around our rooms, putting clothes into suitcases. My little brother was asleep on a pile of blankets in a corner.

My three sisters came in from our corner of the basement. They were rubbing their eyes and stretching their arms and yawning. Their hair was tangled. My father sat them next to me on the edge of my bed. He crouched in front of us and spoke very seriously.

"We have to leave here today. It is the only chance we may have," he said.

In about half an hour, we were ready to go. It was the first time I had seen our rooms so messy. I told my mother that if she wanted to tidy a bit, I would help her. She nodded and began picking up things that had been scattered in the hurry to pack. My father spoke sharply to her: "What are you doing? Who are you tidying for? Thieves and looters? We are leaving, for God's sake. Get into the car, everybody!"

Were we leaving all our things for thieves and looters? What was going to happen to my kites and my marbles? I started filling my pockets with my best marbles.

"Qais! The car! Now!" my father said. From the way he spoke, I knew not to argue. Several marbles slipped out of my hands and went rolling around on the floor. I left them and ran out the door.

We walked quickly across the courtyard to the garage. I looked under the tree where my father had been digging a hole last night. But there was no hole anymore. The green cucumber vine was there, just as it had been before. I wanted to ask him what happened to that hole, but I thought he might shout at me again like last night.

We got into the car while he opened the garage door to the street. As he started the engine, one of my uncles burst into the garage from the courtyard.

"Where are you going?" asked my uncle, who was a year younger than my father.

"I told you last night," my father replied, "to my friend's house in Kart-e-Parwan."

"Where are the rest of us going to go?" my uncle asked plaintively.

"You have had weeks to think about that," my father replied. There was an ache in his voice.

"Take our kids and wives with you; they want to live, too, like your own," my uncle pleaded.

"This is a small car, not a bus or truck," my father said. "It can only take four people at a time, and we are six already, plus a baby."

"Leave that part to me. I know how to do it. I'm a good packer," my uncle said.

Hardly a minute later, all six of my uncles with all of their kids and wives arrived in the garage and tried to fit themselves into our car. Two of my uncles' wives sat on the front seat, and seven of my cousins sat in the backseat. There was no space left for us. My father slammed the door near the driver's seat. "I'm not going anywhere," he said angrily.

My uncles started to argue with my father. He walked into the courtyard and kept walking slowly around the trees. I had never seen him behaving that way, or talking to his brothers like this before. It reminded me of Indian movies in which the bad brothers did not get along.

Everybody got out of the car and stared at one another. There was a deep silence.

My father came back after a few minutes and told my mother and my three sisters to take the baby and sit in the backseat. Then he ordered four of my cousins to squeeze in there, too. He asked me and three of my other cousins, including Wakeel, to sit in the trunk. Two of my uncles' wives sat in the front seat with my father. The rest would have to stay at the house and wait for him to come get them later.

He backed the car out onto the street. The bottom scraped the road from the weight of so many passengers. My father drove slowly for the four blocks through our neighborhood until we got out to the main road.

What we saw, I will never forget. Thousands of people like us were taking advantage of the ceasefire to flee from our part of the city. Thousands and thousands of people, all walking in near silence. When they spoke, they whispered as if they had been forbidden to talk normally. They were strung along each side of the roadway, moving along like lines of ants. All of them had two or three bags in their hands.

Ours was the only car on the road. When they saw our car, they all rushed toward us, asking us to give them a lift, even though they could see that our car was already fully packed. The crowd that gathered around us was so huge that my father could not move the car forward, not even one inch. Some were trying to pull my cousins and me out of the trunk so they could take our place. My father shouted back to us, "Hold on to each other, and lock your fingers together tightly."

We did what we were told, and my father rolled up his window, pressed the horn, turned on the lights, and drove slowly, then faster until one by one the people let go of us.

For the first time in the two months since the fighting had started, all of us were seeing the destruction it had caused. Things we had heard about, but had not wanted to believe, we were now seeing for ourselves.

The block-long, eight-story yellow grain silo that the Russians had built was full of holes where rockets had hit it. Small mountains of wheat lay at the base of the silo where it had flowed out through the holes.

There were big craters in the road where rockets had fallen. This had been the best road in Kabul. There were still many half-exploded rockets standing in the middle of the road, like nails that had been banged halfway through a piece of wood.

Hundreds of dead bodies were scattered all over the pavement, on the sidewalks, and in the park in the middle of the road. Some looked like they had been there for a long time. Blood was matted all over their clothes. Most were on the main road. Maybe they had been hit by a rocket while they were trying to cross it. But many of them had been shot with bullets to the head, chest, or back. This was the work of the snipers. I could not believe my eyes; I thought I was seeing an American horror movie, especially when I saw parts of bodies, like arms or legs or even heads, lying by themselves.

My father had no choice but to drive over the ones in our path. Some of the dead bodies were on their backs as if they were sleeping. When our car drove over them, the speed of the car turned their faces toward the road, and the car rose up off the pavement.

To avoid hitting a man who was running toward us, my father drove the wrong way around the roundabout in front of the Polytechnic, then gunned the car up the hill toward the Intercontinental Hotel.

Beyond the top of the hill, everything looked different. The unimaginable scene through which we had just driven suddenly vanished. In its place, we saw real life.

People were buying bread from bakeries for their breakfast. Little kids were holding their parents' hands as they were walking to their school. The dogs were not howling. The roads were not empty. People's windows were not slamming, and their doors were not banging. There was no war. None.

I saw smiles on the faces of people who showed no signs of worry. But they could not stop staring at us; they had never seen a car packed like ours before. The lines of refugees had only just begun to reach that area, and they had no idea how many thousands more were coming. The small mountain that rose between our house and this neighborhood had protected these people from the fighting. Not even the snipers had come around to their side of the mountain, though they could have. But they were fighting over our neighborhood, which lay between two factions. The people we saw acted as if they did not even know that vicious combat was going on less than two miles away, though they would have to have heard the rockets and the shooting.

We came down the hill from the Intercontinental Hotel into the Kart-e-Parwan neighborhood. There were only a few cars on the road, but many people walking. Most of them were Indians going barefoot to their temples, carrying brass bowls filled with milk. Their men were dressed in white or orange. The women wore bright-colored saris. The kids walked behind. The boys' heads were shaved except for one braid. Some of the men had stripes painted on their foreheads.

My cousin Wakeel was sitting next to me in the trunk. He laughed at the kids with no hair, but said he wished he could have one of their bowls of milk.

At the bottom of the hill, we turned sharply to the left a couple of times and drove through a pretty, small park I had never seen. All the flowers were carefully tended.

We passed a large white building that stood behind a high wall. There were guards in strange uniforms with guns out in front of its fancy gate. They stood like statues. Big dogs from Russia were next to them. A sign said "British Embassy" in Dari under big letters in some other language.

We followed a dirt road that ran for two hundred meters beside the wall. That was the bumpiest road in Kabul. It took us down into a deep ravine and then up again as loose rocks slid underneath the wheels of the car. The top of the trunk bounced down on our heads with every bump. The dust stirred up by the car rolled in on us and made us choke. All of our eyebrows and eyelashes got covered with it. We looked like the clowns that used to perform on the stage of our school for Teacher's Day.

My father stopped the car in front of a tall, rusted metal gate in a high mud wall. He blew the horn a few times. Finally, with a scraping sound, an elderly *chowkidar*, the gatekeeper, drew open a small door next to the gate, saw that it was my father, then opened the gates wide. My father drove inside. The *chowkidar* rubbed his eyes to see whether he was dreaming. He closed the metal gates behind us and rushed toward us to help us get out of the trunk. He whispered to himself, "I have never seen so many people in a Volga before."

"I bet you haven't," I said back to him with a grin.

He got red and tried to hide his embarrassment. "I didn't mean to be rude; I'm just shocked." He had not expected to be heard.

We climbed out of the car. Some of my aunts had to be pulled. But the kids were all jumping out and looking around at where we had stopped, hardly four miles from the war zone we had just left.

In front of us rose a massive wall more than two stories high. It had one small opening in its dun-colored expanse, and that was filled with a thick, unpainted wooden door studded with the flattened heads of thick spikes. At the far end of the wall was a tower with eight sides that loomed above the high walls and the tops of some very big trees. We had seen another tower like it just outside the gate, but it was damaged, and half of it was missing.

A few moments later, the thick wooden door opened with the clank of a thick chain that must have been attached to it. A man whom I recognized as my father's business partner came through it, with two house servants close behind. I had seen the man many times in his carpet shop. He had always been impeccably dressed in a silk necktie and tailored jacket, with bright eyes that poured a good feeling into his customers. But this morning, he was wearing only his pajamas and holding a cup of tea in his hand. His eyes were sleepy. He greeted my father, gave *salaam*s to the other adults, and welcomed all of us.

His name was Haji Noor Sher. Whenever my father took Wakeel, my older sister, and me to the shop, Haji Noor Sher gave us candy and put some small money in crumpled bills in our pockets. He always had foreign customers in his shop looking at carpets, but he would put his business affairs aside when we came in and give all his attention to us. He never used our real names; instead, he called us "nephew" and "niece," and he told us to call him "uncle."

If he was surprised to see us all at that early hour that morning, he did not show it. We had had no way to get a message to him to tell him that we were coming. But he and my father were close friends, and close friends help each other in times such as those.

My father took him to one side, and they talked quietly for a moment. Haji Noor Sher spoke to one of the house servants, who always stood behind him like bodyguards. The servant ran back into the house to get us some tea and something to eat. Haji Noor Sher acted as if he were accustomed to having visitors every day at this time, and to keeping those words for his servants ready in his mouth.

"Hey, everybody, welcome to my house. Do you like it?"

We really had not seen anything yet except big walls and the towers, but we nodded because we were relieved to be away from the fighting.

"This place is called the Qala-e-Noborja. Did you know that?" He held himself like a famous actor whom everybody knows, but none of my aunts and uncles had ever seen him before. "The reason we call it the 'Fort of Nine Towers' is because when it was built more than a hundred years ago, it had nine towers. It's antique, like me." He had a big smile that was contagious, so we all smiled at him.

I interrupted him: "Uncle Noor Sher, but I only see one tower." I pointed to the one full tower, ignoring the stub of the other one outside the gate.

He looked at my father, winked, and said, "Oh, he is smart." I liked hearing him say that, especially in front of all my cousins. "The other towers," he said with a twinkle in his eye, "are invisible. Just because we cannot see something does not mean that it is not there."

Even though the Qala-e-Noborja had only one tower still standing, it made me feel safe, especially since it had been there for more than a hundred years. Maybe the rockets could not hurt us here.

He handed his teacup to the other house servant and led us away from the door and down a steep, rose-lined path from the old fort to a terrace on the slope below. He and my father walked in front, and my cousins and I followed behind them, my mother and my aunts after us. The terrace was covered by a canopy of grapes. The bees were humming around them.

The sky was completely clear, and the sun was floating in a

lapis-blue space shining down at everything through the leaves. The wind gave no rest to the leaves and rustled them. I wondered whether there was still war on the other side of the mountain, or whether everything there had changed, too.

When I turned and looked behind me, I saw the old fort's one last tower rising above me. It looked even higher from where we were standing below it on the terrace. I was curious what was inside those high walls, but was too busy seeing all the new things in this large garden that surrounded them to wonder about that for long. On the terraces—there were four of them cut into the steep slope—rosebushes and vegetable gardens were laid out in neatly tended rows.

On one of the terraces a fountain shot water into the air. Near the fountain were two massive trees. Two of my cousins tried to hold hands with me around one of the trunks. We could just barely reach one another's fingertips.

Down another level, in a flat area at the lowest point in the garden, was a stream. As he led us to it, Haji Noor Sher told us that its cold water came from the Hindu Kush mountains sixty miles away. It was flowing into a pool cut into the rock. More than ten types of colorful fish were swimming in the pool.

Some parrots, canaries, and eagles were in cages near the pool, and cooing pigeons had a place of their own.

In a cage built against the high wall that separated the garden from a street, a big dog with bloodshot eyes was pacing quietly. Some bones lay in a corner. He was the kind of dog the Kuchis, nomads, keep in front of their cattle to protect them from wolves. From other cages next to it, two Russian wolfhounds glared at us.

When we got close to the cages, the dogs began barking at us, and jumping against the sides, trying to break out and tear us apart. They were fighting dogs. We ran away.

There was yet another cage, a very large one, at the base of the tower. At first we saw nothing in it and thought the cage was empty. Then something shifted in the shadows of a small doorway that led into the bottom of the tower. Slowly, the shadow moved toward us. It was very big. My older sister and some of my girl cousins took a step back.

Nobody said anything as a leopard walked gracefully out into the sunshine and looked at us. It was yellow with brown spots. We had seen leopards in the Kabul Zoo. We had been told they were very dangerous. No one dared to speak as the blood ran out of our faces. What kind of place is this that has a leopard in the garden? I wondered.

The leopard had no interest in our fear. He lay down in a sunny place and started licking himself. We all tiptoed away. This garden seemed to me like paradise, but even more interesting than the way my older sister had described it.

The house servants appeared, carrying a huge breakfast on big shiny trays; many types of fruit juices, apples, grapes, milk, tea, butter, cheese, yogurt, hard-boiled eggs, and fresh breads. They unrolled several bright red and green *sofrah*, eating cloths, on the terrace near the fountain, and began to set the trays of food on the ground. Haji Noor Sher invited us to start eating, then went back up to his rooms inside the courtyard of the old fort.

We did not know what to eat first. We had not had a proper meal for weeks. Everybody forgot all their manners as we piled our plates high. My father said, "Slowly, slowly, the food is not running away." Wakeel laughed, but the others were too busy eating.

Above the clink of the knives and forks, we could hear the birds singing as they flew from one tree to another. We had not heard birds in Kot-e-Sangi in months. Twelve baby deer that were grazing placidly in the garden around us occasionally looked up at us.

As we finished eating, Haji Noor Sher came out of the old fort and down the garden steps to the wide terrace where we were seated. Now he was wearing a white *shalwar kamiz*, a silk *chapan* coat, a *karacol* lamb's wool hat, and leather slippers. His two house servants stood behind him. They were much taller than he was.

Haji Noor Sher was so short and so portly he was almost round. My cousin Wakeel whispered to me that he could be a large marble like the ones we played with. My father overheard him and glared at him. Wakeel lowered his eyes sheepishly, but the rest of us were giggling very softly. Even though he was small, Haji Noor Sher had a big presence. I had never seen the king, except on television, but Haji Noor Sher looked like a king to me.

"Do you like my garden?" he asked us. We all told him how beautiful it was. A big smile took over his face.

"Come with me, I will show you my courtyard." Now we would see what was inside the high mud-brick walls of this Fort of Nine Towers that had only one tower. He turned and led the way up the steep path. We all rushed to find our shoes that we had taken off when we sat to eat. I wore one of my own shoes, and one of Wakeel's. He shouted at me. I had to run back and give him his.

Haji Noor Sher pushed open the heavy wood door that led from the garden into the courtyard. Finally, we could see the thick chain attached to the inside of it that made a clanking sound each time the door moved. After the first door was another, but it was at right angles so that anyone trying to invade the fort could be stopped in the passage and not just rush straight in.

Beyond it was a large courtyard half as long as a football field, and half as wide. It was surrounded by two levels of rooms with tall, wood-frame windows. On one side of the courtyard, a room with windows on three sides projected into the garden. On the other, the rooms on the upper level were set back, leaving a broad upper terrace in front of them. A perfect place for flying kites, I thought.

The courtyard was full of fruit trees and roses and many flowers I had never seen before and whose names I did not know. Grapevines covered an arbor in the far corner. A tall acacia tree dominated the end near us, and a very old, spreading *arghawan* tree reigned at the other. In between were peach and pomegranate trees, as well as two enormous thickets of lilacs. Haji Noor Sher made a special point of showing them to us. The lilacs had been a gift to his father from the king. He said that for years after acquiring the fort from the royal family, his father had always sent the first lilacs of the season to the king, large scented armloads of them.

Carefully trimmed rosebushes enclosed beds of brightly colored geraniums and lilies. Haji Noor Sher was proudest of a black rose that he had, and cautioned us against telling anybody about it. He said it was very rare and someone might come and steal it. Morning glory and honeysuckle vines climbed the wall at the far end of the courtyard, where a small door led into a *hammam*, a steam bath.

In front of the *hammam* was a large enclosure with a few deer in it that looked like they were the parents of the little deer outside in the garden. Two peacocks stood watching us with their tails spread. Haji Noor Sher made a funny noise, and they came running to him. He patted them; we all wanted to do that, too. But when we tried, they ran away and screeched, "Fanark!" We soon learned that "fanark" is the most common word in the peacock language. It is always said very loudly.

As we walked across the courtyard, I found a small peacock feather. I picked it up and kissed it, because we had been told they are holy. These many years later, I still use that feather as a bookmark for my Holy Koran.

My father walked next to Haji Noor Sher. He was much taller than Haji Noor Sher. I walked next to my father. The rest of the family walked behind us, and the servants behind them.

Haji Noor Sher showed us five rooms that faced the courtyard and said we could use them all. He was living in the old fort by himself in some rooms above the passageway into the courtyard. He had moved his family to India as soon as the fighting had started so they would be safe. Now he flew back and forth between Delhi and Kabul every couple of months. He had shops in both places. In Kabul, he bought old carpets with my father's help, and in Delhi he sold them.

The floors of our rooms were covered with several layers of carpets. Low mattresses had been placed all around the walls, with long, narrow carpets covering them. In the corner of each room was a pile of quilts and pillows. The carpets made the rooms look like the garden had come in from outside.

Haji Noor Sher told the servants to bring us more tea as we came out of the rooms. We all sat in the shade of the grape arbor and relaxed in a way that we had not done for months.

I entirely forgot about war and those dead bodies on the road. I even forgot about my grandfather and my uncles and unmarried aunts who were still at our house, until we heard the first rocket.

There is a noise a rocket makes when it is fired. You can hear it from miles away. It is not loud, but it stops all conversations instantly. First, there is the *fumf* of the launch, then the silence as everyone waits, and then the explosion as a house is destroyed or a school collapses. Then slowly the conversation resumes, sometimes with a half-spoken prayer.

For some reason, the ceasefire had ended hours earlier than had been announced. My father jumped up and looked panicked. He had been enjoying the magnificent peace in this place for a few moments before heading back to get the others. But if the fighting had started again, he could not go home now.

We were hardly four miles away from our house, but it was too far to go if the snipers had started shooting again. We could not hear the fighting, because the small mountain with two peaks separated us from it. In our mind's eye, however, we could see everything that was happening.

Over the next few days, we settled into our new rooms and worried about Grandfather and the others. We could hear the rockets, but the fighting seemed very far away. The cousins filled the days playing hide-and-seek in the vast garden, or splashing cold water on one another from the pool. The adults said we would not be here long. The fighting would end soon, and we could go home.

On the fourth day, we heard again from the BBC World Service that on the following day there would be a one-day ceasefire between the two main factions that were fighting in our Kot-e-Sangi neighborhood.

Early the next morning, my father woke me up. Then he went to my sisters to rouse them. In five minutes we all were awake, waiting to hear what my father would tell us.

My father kissed my mother first, then he came to me. I was still sitting on my bed, stretching my arms. He crouched on his heels in front of me and said, "I'm going now to bring your grandfather and the others here. If something happens to me, and I cannot come back, you have to forget that you once had a father. You will be your own father, and a good son to your mother, and a kind brother to your sisters and your brother. I leave you all the responsibility of a father. But you have to learn how to take care of your sisters and mother. Understood?"

I did not know what to say. I was now ten years old. I said, "Yes."

He went to my older sister. He sat on his heels in front of her bed and said, "You are my oldest child. You're the most beautiful and intelligent child that I have, but you have to learn how to be helpful to others, and not to feel lonely if I'm not around. You have to educate your little sisters and help your mother. Don't wait for anyone to tell you what to do. If something happens to me, you are responsible for your sisters, to keep them busy, and make them learn one new thing every day. Help with your little brother and keep your mother happy, understood?"

Tears came from my older sister's eyes as she gazed straight at my father. My father hugged her for a minute. Then slowly and gently he rubbed her back and told her to be brave. I did not feel sorry for her. Wakeel and I used to call her "fountain eyes," because she cried so easily, when she was not making stupid jokes.

He went to my two little sisters, who slept together in one bed in those days, because they were scared of the rocket sounds. "Did you have good dreams last night?" my father asked them.

The older one said "Yes." The younger one said "No." Then she changed her mind. "Yes, I had a good dream last night." They both wanted to talk at the same time. Both wanted to talk louder to be heard.

"Stop, stop, stop! One by one! Who had a good dream last night, raise your hand," my father said.

Both of them quickly raised their hands.

He pointed to the littler one. "You tell me your dream."

She thought for a second, then said, "I didn't dream last night. I will try to have a nice dream tonight, and I'll tell you tomorrow morning."

My father smiled and tousled her hair. "You naughty little girl." Then he asked the older one to tell him her dreams.

She cleared her throat, but she was silent for almost a minute. My father was waiting to hear from her. She cleared her throat a second time, but was still silent.

"Come on! Tell me your dream," my father said.

"Why are you in a hurry? Are you going somewhere?" she asked.

"I just don't want to wait till evening, listening to your throat clearings," my father said.

She cleared her throat a third time and said, "Well, it will take seven hours to tell you my dreams, because I slept for seven hours last night. Now, sit properly. You may get tired sitting on your heels."

My father asked both of them to come closer to him, then he hugged them both and kissed their heads, foreheads, and cheeks and said, "I'm going out to buy some milk for breakfast. When I come back, I will listen to your dream stories. Okay?"

They both nodded their heads and smiled at my father. The younger one pulled her blanket off and got up from the bed. The older one, suddenly cold, shouted at her. The younger one shouted back to wake up and brush her teeth. Then they started arguing with each other, as always.

My mother was standing the whole time at the corner of the room with folded arms, leaning against the wall, resting her head on her right shoulder, watching my father. My father got up and walked toward her. He stood in front of her and said, "I have to go. It will get late."

Her face looked very sad. "Be careful." She started to say something else, but her voice caught. We all looked at her. "We are waiting for you," she said softly.

I could read in my mother's face that she had a lot in her heart. She wanted to say something, but her mouth, lips, and throat refused to obey.

My father kissed her forehead and hugged her. He winked at me with a big smile over her shoulder, and I smiled back.

He stood at the threshold of the door, holding the doorknob; he took a long look at all of us and said, "I will be back soon." He looked at my older sister and me and said, "You two, don't forget what I told you." Then he went out. My mother followed him.

When she came back inside a few minutes later, she took a deep breath and told everybody to start folding their sheets. My littlest sister ran outside, but my father had already gone. She came back to tell my mother, "Father doesn't need to buy milk. His friend's servants prepare us a good breakfast every day, and it has milk, too."

"Yes, you are right; I forgot to tell him that." My mother tried to sound surprised. "But don't worry, he'll drink the milk before he goes to sleep."

"I want to drink milk, too," she said.

"Yes, of course. How can he drink it without you?" my mother said.

Later I found out that my cousin Wakeel had gone with my father. I felt very alone. Why had he gone to Grandfather's house and not taken me with him? Maybe he would bring our kites and marbles when he came back.

4

❖

To Be a Family Again

My father was supposed to come back that same day, but he did not. We had no idea what had happened to him. My littlest sister kept asking my mother, "Why is it taking Father so long to buy milk?"

"Maybe it is not easy to find milk in this part of town," my mother replied again and again. She tried very hard to be busy, and kept doing things that did not need to be done.

Since the civil war had started, I had seen my mother crying many, many times, though she always tried to hide her tears from us. Now, every night since my father had left, she cried in the dead of night. Mostly she went outside in the courtyard, and cried very softly. Sometimes she just sat on the bottom step of the stairs outside our rooms, and the tears started coming. One of those nights, my littlest sister saw her, and the next day she imitated her by sprinkling water under her eyes and pretending to be the little mother.

On the third day, my father returned with my uncles, their wives, their kids, and my unmarried aunts. Like us, they all had crammed into the Volga with the kids in the trunk, about twelve of them. They looked really dirty, so we made jokes about them. They laughed. Then we sent them one by one to bathe.

The only ones who had stayed behind at our home were Grandfather and Wakeel, the two people for whom I cared most. Grandfather was refusing to leave his house to the thieves and the warlords, but what could he do to protect it?

My father told us that four rockets had landed in Grandfather's courtyard on the day after he had arrived there. A day later, two more rockets had destroyed some of my grandfather's McIntosh apple trees and most of his flowers. Grandfather's heart was broken. He had been so optimistic about the Mujahedin.

"A broken hand can work, but a broken heart cannot," was what Grandfather had told me one day when I did not want to be with my parents, because my father had shouted at me after I had received bad scores in arithmetic at school.

At night I would think about Grandfather on the other side of the mountain, without his carpets, his beloved trees now only stumps and splinters.

A week later, early on a Friday morning when it was still dark, I heard a loud knocking on the front gate. It went on for almost ten minutes, but nobody opened the door.

The *chowkidar* was an old man, and when he slept it was as if he were dead. Someone had to sprinkle water on his face to wake him up.

The knocking continued, followed by low arguments that became louder. I slowly recognized the voices.

I woke up my father. He hurriedly put on his clothes and ran outside. I followed him. A moment later, we saw Grandfather and Wakeel and the *chowkidar* arguing. By now they were shouting. The gatekeeper would not let them in. He kept saying, "If you need some food, come back in two hours, but now everybody is asleep, go, go . . ."

The gatekeeper thought my grandfather and my cousin were desperate beggars looking for a place to stay, or a meal. He was half-deaf. They did not know that they had to shout into his ears.

Haji Noor Sher was not home either. He had gone to visit his family in India, and to check on his shop in Delhi. His *chowkidar* never let any strangers come in when he was away. He was an honest and strict man.

My father rushed and hugged his father and Wakeel, and the gate-keeper stopped talking. My father shouted very loudly in the door-keeper's left ear, which worked a little: "This is my father and my nephew." He apologized and shuffled away with his stick.

My father brought us all into the room where the rest of the family was sleeping in rows of little mattresses on the floor. He turned on the lights and shouted at everybody to wake up and say hello to Grandfather. My grandfather and Wakeel were covered in dust. Their clothes were very dirty, as if they had not changed them for months. We surrounded them and were all waiting for them to say something.

I read a great sorrow on my grandfather's face; I had never seen him so sad, or so dirty before. He had always worn expensive suits with silk ties, his shoes polished to a blinding shine. But that day, his feet and head and even his eyelashes were covered with dust. He did not talk to anyone. He asked my mother for a blanket. When she brought it, he lay on the floor and covered himself from head to toe without washing or saying a word. In five minutes, he started snoring.

We all left the room quietly, tiptoeing out to let him sleep. We took Wakeel with us into the next room. We asked him to tell us how he had gotten there. He did not want to talk. He was tired and hungry and thirsty, but when we insisted and he had been given a glass of water, he took a deep breath and started.

"We left home around one o'clock in the morning. We stayed in the shadows of the buildings in case there were snipers on the mountain. After we started walking out on the main road, we were stopped in two places," he said, and took a sip from his glass. "At the first place, there were some guys whose faces were all covered. They spoke with a Hazaragi accent. They all had guns and all kinds of other weapons hanging on their chests, backs, even their legs.

Wakeel's voice was deep. Like Grandfather's, it was always calm. He always spoke very clearly in a way that made even grown-ups pay attention to what he said. And he always chose his words very care-fully. His face was like a fast-changing sky and revealed his thoughts even before he expressed them in words. His eyes would grow large one moment and tight the next. His mouth changed shape with his emotions.

"They put us in a dark room with no windows. They stood outside talking. We could not hear what they were saying very well, but I think they were worried that we belonged to another faction, and were spying on them. After about half an hour, they came back in. They whispered to one another for a minute or so, then let us go without asking us anything.

"That was near the silo. Then we started walking toward the Polytechnic, but the Panjshiris had a checkpoint there, only we could not see it in the dark."

We had been hearing about checkpoints on the BBC, but this was the first time that they had entered our lives directly.

"Some guy shouted at us, '*Stop! Stop!*' Grandfather said to keep moving, but the guy fired at the sky and cried again, '*Stop! Stop! Stop!*'

"He wore military clothes and searched us from head to toe. He and his friend put their guns to the back of my head and Grandfather's head, and commanded us to walk forward. They led us to a small room. Another guy was there sitting on a bed with dirty sheets.

"He asked Grandfather a few questions, like why we were coming this direction, and who we work for. But Grandfather didn't answer him. He told the commander, 'You guys call yourselves holy warriors, but you are just killers and thieves.'

"The commander smiled at Grandfather and said, 'Behave yourself!'

"Grandfather didn't say anything. He just stared at the commander, and the commander stared back for a few moments, then ordered one of the other guys to search our bags. But all we had was Grandfather's books, so they let us pass."

I looked into the large cotton bag near my foot and saw the two volumes of *Afghanistan in the Path of History* by Mir Ghulam Mohammad Ghobar. Grandfather had to leave his house, but he would not leave his books or his brown leather briefcase with his diaries.

When Wakeel finished speaking, he asked for a blanket and went to the room where Grandfather was sleeping. A minute later, he was asleep, too.

The months passed. We stayed in Haji Noor Sher's house, eating the good food cooked by his servants, enjoying fresh fruits from the garden, and playing with the dogs. By then, all the dogs had become friendly. The leopard was not friendly. So we left him alone.

Every night we listened to the BBC World Service and other broadcasts, but there was no good news. Our country was being destroyed more every hour, by factions whose leaders slaughtered thousands during the day, then talked like holy men on their broadcasts during the night. They always introduced themselves as the holy warriors and said that they were fighting against evil. Day killers; night liars.

I started to hate the broadcasts. None of them gave us any good news; they were all the same. They made my grandfather, uncles, and father unhappy, which made me feel sorry for them. I decided to break all the radios. Then I thought that it would make them even sadder. The BBC was the only thing they had to look forward to all day.

Now, for the first time, there was serious talk among my father and my uncles of leaving Afghanistan. My grandfather did not say anything this time. Sometimes late at night when they thought I was asleep, I would hear my father telling my mother what the men had been discussing.

My father again wanted to go to Russia, as he had proposed the year before when we were still at home. He had been in touch with his friends there from his boxing days. They had offered to help us get settled once we arrived. But now the borders were tightly closed, so we would need a lot of money to pay smugglers to get all of us across.

My father's only income in those days came from the carpets that he had gathered from the villages before the fighting had started, and which Haji Noor Sher still sold in his shop in India.

He had not been paid in several months for his job teaching physics at Habibia High School. Though the fighting had closed the school, which had been hit by rockets, he was still supposed to be receiving his government salary.

Some Kuchi nomads had been trapped in the building during one of the times when a ceasefire had suddenly ended. They had been passing through Kabul on their way from their summer grazing lands in the mountains near Bamyan to their winter base in the lowlands near Jalalabad, but had to hide their sheep, donkeys, camels, cows, and horses in the basement of the school. Some of the local factions discovered them and took the sheep to feed their soldiers. For months after the Kuchis left, the whole school smelled like a barn.

Every morning when I woke, I was still confused for a moment until I looked around and saw my family sleeping on the floor nearby and remembered where we were. But in other ways, our lives had settled into routines.

My uncles still went to their jobs in the city when there seemed to be a break in the fighting. Sometimes it would suddenly end, and things would be quiet for weeks. Then, without anybody knowing why, it would start up as fiercely again.

My mother stopped going to the bank. She did not feel safe traveling across the city. Also, she was much busier than before going to the bazaars to buy food, which was sometimes hard to find—mostly rice and whatever vegetables the farmers could bring to the market, and not the meat that Afghans love. At Grandfather's house, she had had a lot of help from my uncles' wives, my father's unmarried sisters, and even my older sister and my girl cousins. At Noborja, my grandfather's family was still living together, but we had been shattered into small parts as we tried to survive.

Though his family was in Delhi and he had shops in both Kabul and Delhi, Haji Noor Sher preferred to be in Kabul. In Delhi, he had rented an apartment for his family in the Lajpat Nagar area, but hated living in it, he told us. He had grown up in a large house with a big garden, and the apartment felt like a prison cell to him. Even worse, he did not know many people in India and felt very lonely there.

During his stays in Kabul, his wife often called from Delhi and begged him to come there. He would put off going as long as he could, and then left only when the fighting heated up. As soon as he heard that there was a ceasefire in Kabul, though, he was back with us in the fort.

Each time he returned, his friends would start showing up at Noborja that same day. Somehow they knew he was back. Though we could sometimes hear the sounds of rockets, bombs, and rifles being fired on the other side of the mountain, they laughed and enjoyed one another's company, my father among them. Hearing the sound of their laughter made us hopeful.

Often Haji Noor Sher asked his cook to prepare special food, such as a big *qabli pelau*, with its mountains of rice mixed with shredded carrots, raisins, and nuts heaped over big pieces of meat. Or there were lamb kebabs, or lamb soup. He asked my mother to cook her famous corn bread for dessert. Every day felt like a holiday when he was at Noborja.

In the mornings, as soon as I had woken up and splashed some water on my face, I ran to his rooms, where some mullahs he had known for years were reciting verses from the Holy Koran with melodic voices. I sat in a corner and listened, or took a Koran and followed the lines the mullahs were reciting by heart.

After breakfast the mullahs left, and musicians would come and start singing sweet *ghazals* softly accompanied by a *tambour, sitar, tabla,* and harmonium. The music went on until lunch, when there was a one-hour break for naps. Then some other friends of his, who were the best storytellers I have ever heard, came and told stories about almost anything.

Haji Noor Sher always sat in his chair like a king on his throne while his guests sat on the *toshak* cushions on the floor around the room. His eyes were closed. He fingered his *tasbeh* prayer beads, moving his head gently as if in a trance. If in the middle of a story one of the servants knocked on the door, he opened his eyes and said, "Stop."

The storyteller immediately halted.

He said, "Come in."

The servant would come in with a fresh pot of tea in his hands. Haji Noor Sher looked at the glasses on the floor, which was the sign for the servant to fill them up. The servant stepped lightly from one cup to the next, then left the steaming pot on the floor in the middle of the room and softly walked out.

Haji Noor Sher turned to the storyteller and said, "Continue."

At night, he turned on his generator so that all of the kids could watch an Indian movie with him in his room. He often fell asleep in the middle of the film, half sitting and half lying on his bed. When the movie ended, we pulled his blanket over him, turned off his light, tiptoed out of his room, turned off the generator, and went to our rooms to sleep.

One day, when Wakeel and I were on the roof with our kites, we noticed that below us in the courtyard the house servants and all the other servants, who kept the gardens and looked after the animals, were doing unusual things.

They were shampooing the deer and tying pretty ribbons to their antlers. Later, they strung multicolored lights along the tops of the courtyard walls and hung paper lanterns from the graceful, bending canes of the lilac bushes. Then they hung a very large square of brightly covered cloth from the upper terrace. It draped over the windows of the rooms on the courtyard level until other servants set poles under its lower edge and raised it up to make an awning. Under the awning they built a low platform.

The servants did not stop for lunch but kept on working, washing the large, square paving stones in the courtyard floor. Haji Noor Sher said they had been part of the Buddhist *stupa* that had stood here for centuries before the Qala-e-Noborja had been built by Abdur Rahman, the king, for his *wazir*, his most important minister.

As the evening approached, the courtyard became even busier. Haji Noor Sher was ordering the servants to do this and that. Hurricane lanterns were set up along both sides of the paths around the courtyard and next to the flowerpots overflowing with blooms. Some of the flowers were bright red and tall, some wound like vines up the walls, and some were orange and gold.

Wakeel and I had long stopped flying our kites for the day, and were watching all the activity, wondering what was going on.

My father had come into the courtyard and was standing next to Haji Noor Sher, discussing something with him. When Haji Noor Sher went upstairs to his room, I ran down from the rooftop to ask my father what was happening. He told me that Haji Noor Sher was having some foreign guests for dinner, people who were working for the United Nations. I ran up and told Wakeel.

Haji Noor Sher loved having guests, especially when he could show off his garden, and his wealth, and how many servants he had.

My father went inside our rooms to take a shower. My mother started ironing his best *shalwar kamiz.* Wakeel and I went down to the courtyard to help the servants.

Two servants carrying shiny silver trays with tea and glasses entered the courtyard. They asked us to carry them upstairs, to Haji Noor Sher's rooms. I took the tray that had two pots of tea on it. I could smell the strong scent of cardamom coming from their spouts. Wakeel took the tray of glasses and walked ahead of me, climbing the stairs to Haji Noor Sher's apartment.

When we reached the top, Wakeel carefully pushed the door open with his foot and went in without knocking. Haji Noor Sher had just finished having his shower. He was standing in the middle of the room, drying his head with a small blue towel, but otherwise completely naked.

When he saw us, he gasped and hurriedly looked for something with which to cover himself. I was horrified. It is very shameful to be naked in front of someone else, and even more shameful to look at someone naked. I quickly placed the tray in front of the door on the floor and ran back down the stairs. Wakeel ran after me, laughing, and nearly knocking me over as he raced down. I started to laugh, too.

Haji Noor Sher shouted at us. We did not hear what exactly he said, but we knew that he was very angry that we had not knocked on the door before we came in. But how could we? Our hands were full.

Wakeel and I ran out of the door, across the courtyard, and back up to the roof terrace. There we collapsed into embarrassed laughter. Wakeel asked, "Did you see them?"

"What?" I asked, still giggling.

"Did you see that he had five testicles?" Wakeel asked.

"Five?" I asked in disbelief. "How could he have five?"

"I counted them very carefully," Wakeel said seriously, then fell into a heap as he exploded laughing. And each time that the laughter started to ease, we would look at each other and Wakeel would say "Five," and it started even fiercer than before. When Wakeel laughed, his eyes glowed and his brilliantly white teeth shone.

Several minutes later, we saw Haji Noor Sher, now very nicely dressed, coming out of his door into the courtyard. We peeped from behind a low wall in a corner.

Haji Noor Sher was standing in the middle of the courtyard, in a white *shalwar kamiz* and a black waistcoat, ordering his servants to lay carpets on the paths around the courtyard, and to bring the peacocks from the garden. He wore a small, round red hat with a tassel.

A group of musicians walked in through the low door and greeted him as if he were a prince. He directed them to sit on a platform in the middle of the courtyard that had been covered with an old Bukhara rug made soft and shiny from years of use.

The musicians were dressed very elegantly with beaded black waistcoats. Each wore a brightly colored turban. One started tuning the twenty-two twangy strings of a *rabab*. Another was blowing the Kabul dust out of his flute-like *ney*. The oldest one sat with a *tambour* rising from his lap, running his fingers up and down its long neck, playing silent music that only he could hear in his mind. And the fourth had a shining pair of brass *tabla* drums that he kept tapping on the sides with a small hammer to tune them, and put a snap into their sound. After a few minutes, they finished their preparations, and the courtyard was filled with their soft, sweet music.

When my unmarried aunts and my cousins heard the music, they joined us on the terrace, watching everything from there. By now, it had become dark, and nobody could see us.

For a few minutes, Haji Noor Sher left the courtyard, then returned with four foreign men. Haji Noor Sher looked too short to be standing next to those people, who were extraordinarily tall and strong, with long, yellow hair, blue eyes, and unusually white skin.

Haji Noor Sher talked to them in a strange language, showing them the carpets on the paths and talking about them. The guests asked questions in the same strange tongue.

I asked one of my aunts what language they were speaking. She said, "English." I liked the sound of it. It sounded very much like Dari, but even though I paid close attention, I did not understand a word of it.

From time to time, Haji Noor Sher would have one of the servants pick up a rug so one of the guests could inspect it more closely. He would turn it over and show them the knotting on the back side, then rub his hand across the pile as if it were his favorite cat.

Suddenly, I understood what was going on. I had seen him do this many times in his shop. He was trying to sell carpets to these foreigners. As the fighting in Kabul had become worse, Haji Noor Sher's customers had stopped coming from other countries. He still sent a few carpets to people who phoned him from Berlin or London, and he had taken many carpets to India. But he had not sold any carpets in Kabul for a long time.

My father shared in the profits with Haji Noor Sher, and he spoke about these things with my mother at night. Now the only foreigners in Kabul were the aid workers. If these foreigners bought some carpets, perhaps we would have enough money to pay smugglers to get us out of Afghanistan.

My father came out of our house and shook hands with the visitors. My father talked to them in their language. I was amazed. I did not know that he could speak English.

The servants brought tall glasses of pomegranate juice on trays filled with plates of nuts and dried fruit, as the musicians continued playing soft music. We watched as if it were all a movie. Haji Noor Sher had the servants bring several very old carpets from inside and lay the carpets out on the carefully cut grass. These were the most expensive pieces, the carpets my father had found when he had gone to the villages and knocked on doors. One of the visitors got down on his knees as he was admiring the old carpets. The discussion about prices would happen after they ate. Haji Noor Sher, like any good rug dealer, wanted the customer's excitement about a carpet to build until he could not stand the thought of leaving it behind.

Haji Noor Sher led the guests to the awning under which the servants had arranged large cushions and several layers of carpets on the platform so they could sit comfortably while they ate. Some were at ease seated, like Afghans, with one leg folded on top of the other. But one of the guests kept shifting his position, trying to get comfortable. A servant brought a pitcher of water and a bowl. He stepped carefully among the guests as they settled on their cushions and poured warm water over their hands into the bowl so they could wash. Another servant followed him with small towels.

Then the food started to come. The servants, who were now dressed in even nicer clothes, carried big rice platters heaped with *qabli pelau* covered with raisins and grated carrots and set them on the cloth that had been spread in front of Haji Noor Sher, my father, and the guests.

An Uzbek man who usually helped Haji Noor Sher in the shop had been cooking kebabs out in the garden outside the courtyard. The smoke had been curling up to us on the rooftop, making us all feel hungry. A few minutes later, the Uzbek came running into the courtyard with long swords of grilled meats, and set them down in front of the guests, where they sat under the awning. Then other servants brought dishes filled with roasted aubergines and spinach. There were bowls of salads and yogurt and large baskets piled with freshly baked *naan*. It was still warm, and we could smell it. Someone else brought all kinds of drinks.

There were only four guests, plus Haji Noor Sher and my father, but there was enough food for everyone living at the Qala-e-Noborja.

We were happy about that, because we knew that later when the guests had left, the leftovers would be offered to us.

When the guests had all eaten too much, Haji Noor Sher insisted that they eat more. They patted their stomachs, while Haji Noor Sher pretended to be offended that they had eaten so little. The servants brought them *chillums*, water pipes, and carefully lit the apple-flavored tobacco using pieces of glowing charcoal.

One of the foreigners sucked a lot of air through the embroidered tube and made the *chillum*'s water bubble. But he did not manage to get any smoke. When he breathed out, expecting to see a blue cloud as when my father had done it, there was nothing. Wakeel laughed; the foreigner heard him and looked up at us. Haji Noor Sher looked up, too, and then the other foreigners looked at us as well.

Wakeel whispered to us, "There is the man with five testicles." His disheveled hair framed his dark, shining eyes.

I burst out laughing. Wakeel laughed out loud, too. My other cousins who were hiding with us in a doorway on the roof terrace laughed without knowing why. The foreigners laughed out loud. The musicians stopped playing, and they laughed, too. Haji Noor Sher looked at us with sparks in his eyes for a second. But when he saw all his guests laughing, the frown on his face was put away, and it became a big smile with a loud laugh.

"Five," Wakeel repeated, nodding his head convincingly.

And then, somewhere to the north of us, the first rocket exploded. Perhaps it had hit Khair Khana, a Panjshiri neighborhood about five miles away. Perhaps it had been sent by Gulbuddin Hekmatyar. Perhaps by Sayyaf. It did not matter. The guests quickly got up from their cushions. They thanked Haji Noor Sher, and said good night to my father. They took lingering looks at the carpets on the grass and carefully stepped around them, as their security man hustled them to their cars without taking any carpets with them.

My father and Haji Noor Sher smiled as they saw them off. If they were feeling disappointed at having sold nothing, they were too polite to show it.

That was the last party that Haji Noor Sher ever gave in that court-yard. A few weeks later, a rocket landed in the street in front of his shop. He had seen what had happened to my grandfather and his carpets. He was one of the last carpet dealers still in Kabul. Now he knew it was time to go. The next day, he closed his shop and shipped all of his best carpets to Delhi, where he would go to join his family in the apartment he hated.

Early the next Friday, while we were still eating our breakfast, we were told that some men had come to take the leopard to a new home. All the kids wanted to go watch, but Haji Noor Sher had already or-dered his house servants to chain the courtyard gate so we would not get hurt if the leopard somehow escaped. Haji Noor Sher watched it all happen from the safety of his bedroom, which overlooked the gar-den from the window on one side, and the courtyard from the other.

Later he told us how the men had put a small cage on wheels in front of the leopard's home at the bottom of the one tower that was still standing. Being a cat, the leopard had to see what this new cage on wheels was all about. He sniffed it for a minute, walked into it, sat down, and started licking himself as the door was dropped closed and he was rolled slowly down the hill and out a rarely used gate that led through the high wall to a small street that ran beside it.

Haji Noor Sher then called out to Wakeel, my other cousins, and me from his window that faced the courtyard: "Now you can go to the garden." We ran out through the right-angled passageway in the high walls as if we, too, were being released from a cage. We jostled one an-other against the heavy wooden door with its clanking chain and down the hill to the leopard's cage. It now had one of the large dogs in it. It had been his cage before the leopard came, we had been told. Maybe he was happy to be home. We looked at the dog and at each other, and were not sure why we had run so fast to see what was no longer there.

Over the next few days, Haji Noor Sher gave away all his birds to different friends, except for the pigeons, which he could not give to anyone because they would only come back to their roost that rose at the far end of the courtyard. He made his funny noises at his peacocks one last time as they were being taken away.

As for the deer, as things worsened for us in the weeks ahead, they became food for us, and we threw their bones to the dogs in the cages.

Then the day came for Haji Noor Sher himself to leave. My father, my grandfather, and my uncles all lined up outside the courtyard gate to see him off, and to thank him for having saved us by giving us a place to stay. They all shook his hand and hugged him. All the cousins stood around, watching silently.

He asked my father to take care of the Qala-e-Noborja as he took a long look at the last remaining tower. Then he got into his car. As his driver pulled off, he waved at us kids.

His two house servants watched him being driven out the gate to the airport, and had no idea what to do next.

5

❖

The Long Road Home

Every morning before sunrise, I was awakened by the sound of water splashing in the bathroom next to the room where I slept. It was Grandfather taking ablutions before he prayed.

When the splashing stopped and I knew he had finished, I went to the bathroom and took ablutions myself. Then I went to Grandfather's room and put my prayer rug next to his while he was still praying. Before I started my prayers, I looked up at him. A smile appeared on his face and soon transferred to mine, but he continued his prayers without looking at me, and I started mine feeling his smile all around me.

After Grandfather finished his prayers, he sat cross-legged on the prayer rug. He kept his eyes closed, his *tasbeh* prayer beads in his hands, softly reciting verses from the Holy Koran. I still remember the sweet sound of his mumbling. Whenever I think of it, it brings my grandfather back to me.

After I finished my prayers, I sat cross-legged on my prayer rug, exactly like he did, kept my eyes closed with a *tasbeh* in my hands, audibly reciting the verses of the Holy Koran that I knew by heart.

Sometimes I looked at Grandfather and wondered what he thought about when he was meditating. Twice he had gone to Mecca, and as with all pilgrims to that holy city everyone called him "Haji," except for his children, who called him *Agha*, Dad. We called him *Baba*, Grandfather.

After breakfast, Grandfather usually went to the large garden outside the courtyard with a book in his hand. Haji Noor Sher had a large collection of books and he was happy to have Grandfather read them. He sat under the grapevine, but he could not read like in the old days, with full concentration. After a short while, he put the book aside and started walking back and forth under the trees, making a path in the grass of one of the long terraces below the tower. He seemed to me the way the leopard had been in the cage, restless. The sight of him made me sad.

Sometimes I went to walk with him. When he saw me approaching, he would smile, but I could see that this was a forced smile. I walked with him back and forth under the trees, without uttering a word. All we could hear was the sound of the dry leaves under our feet.

Every now and again, I looked up at him and saw a deep sorrow on his face. His face was like a mirror, accurately reflecting everything he was thinking.

Sometimes he talked to me of his business, and how hard he had tried to accomplish so many things in life. Sometimes he talked with regret of things he had not achieved. Sometimes he talked of soul, or heart, or essence, or spirit. But most of the time he talked of his carpets that had been stolen, his house that lay in ruins, his apple trees and his rosebushes that had been destroyed, and his lost peace of mind.

Grandfather hated idleness. For three months now, he had been at the Qala-e-Noborja doing nothing. Finally, he could sit there no longer. His house had been his life, and he had to go see it. He asked my youngest uncle to join him.

"With all respect, no, I don't want to go. You shouldn't go either. The house is there, no one can take it. The looters have probably plundered everything else. They might even have taken the windows and beams and cut the trees for firewood. But the land will always stay there," my uncle said.

"I brought you up for such a day to tell me 'No'? Huh? Huh?" my grandfather asked, as he stared at my uncle.

"You know I have never said 'No' to you in my entire life, Agha. Please, at least once in your life, listen to me. Let's not go today," my uncle politely said.

"If you don't want to go, just say you are a coward," Grandfather retorted.

My uncle grinned to hide his embarrassment. "I'm not a coward, but I am afraid of being killed by a coward. Those who kill thousands of innocents to make themselves rich are cowards. If we go there, they will smell money on us, even though you have lost everything. We have a little money left, we can survive for a while. Who knows what is going to happen next? They have been fighting for months; it cannot last much longer. Let's not risk the things that we buried there!"

I did not know what he meant. What things were buried there? But I knew I should not ask.

Grandfather turned away from my uncle. He looked at me, and for a moment, he did not say anything. Then, very coldly, he said to me, "Prepare yourself. We will leave in ten minutes."

I looked at my father. From his eyes, I could see that he was not happy. Grandfather looked at my father. I looked at Grandfather. My father looked at me.

"Do what your grandfather says," my father said quietly. My mother's face went pale. But it was not her place to challenge Grandfather.

I knew from my father's tone of voice that he was not pleased with Grandfather's idea. But he was too respectful to say "No."

"Are you a coward like your uncle?" Grandfather asked me.

I looked at my uncle, who was only a couple of years older than Wakeel. His face was full of hurt at having been called a coward by his father.

"I will do what my father and you say," I replied softly. But I did not want to go.

Grandfather smiled, but sadly. "You are a good boy."

We left home in midmorning. We got a bus that took us halfway. The bus had to stop before it reached the front line between the Panjshiris and the Hazaras. The front line moved from time to time as one side gained a temporary advantage over the other. No one ever knew for sure where it was.

We got off the bus and started walking. The road was empty. This was the same road that had been crowded with lines of refugees on the morning we had fled our home. It was the widest road in Kabul, so wide it had a park with big trees running down the middle. Before the fighting, young men met young women there to sit under the trees. Sometimes we saw them kissing and laughed at them. Wakeel called them pigeons.

Now the pavement was all broken. Everywhere there were holes where rockets had exploded, and craters made by bombs dropped from planes by some of the factions. Some of them were so deep that they had filled with groundwater from far below. All around us were pieces of twisted metal. It was so quiet, we could hear the sound of the bees humming.

As we were walking, my grandfather asked me whether I had ever been in love with someone. I was too shy to say "Yes," so I said "No." I desperately wanted to say, "I am in love with my classmate, Yaldda." But I was only ten years old, and boys that age are not supposed to have girlfriends.

My grandfather looked into my eyes. His voice was uncharacteristically gentle. "The person who doesn't have love in life has emptiness. I'm sure you are in love, but I know you don't want to tell me."

I had never kept anything from Grandfather. He had always advised me on everything important. Whenever I told him my secrets, I felt very light and happy.

"I love a girl in my old school," I confided to him. "She is my age, her name is Yaldda, and she is very beautiful!"

My grandfather laughed very loudly. "A woman can keep you warm like wine, or turn cold like ice. Be patient, little man. A person without patience is like a candle without wax. Sometimes love makes you very impatient. Keep control of your feelings."

We said nothing more for a while as I thought about what he told me. And I thought about Yaldda. I had never seen her again after the fighting started. I wondered where she was, and whether she was safe. Had her family left in time, or had they waited too long? Sometimes I wrote poems about Yaldda in my diary, where I kept all the important things that Grandfather told me.

Our steps were surprisingly loud as we walked down the middle of the road with not a single creature in sight, except for some sparrows occasionally flying past, making their *chuk-chuk* noises. The sky was completely blue. Had it not been for the destruction around us, it could have felt like we were going on a picnic.

"Were you impatient, too, to marry Grandmother?" I asked.

"I was in love with her. I was very lucky to have a wife like her, but I didn't know until many years later that marriage has three stages," he said, and sighed as he gazed up at the mountain with two peaks. Its bare rock rose up steeply behind the large yellow grain silo that the Russians had built.

"The first stage is that you talk, and your wife listens. The second stage is, she talks and you listen. And the third stage is, both of you talk, and your neighbors listen," he said with a grin growing wide at the corners of his mouth until it became a big and loud laugh. "The first stage is the best," he said. Grandfather had not told a joke in months. I laughed to hear the happiness in his voice.

But there was more to Grandfather's story than that. His great-grandfather, Khaja Noor Mohammad, had come from a village near Herat in western Afghanistan and had settled in the Maidan Valley about thirty miles from Kabul, where he built a large mud-brick fort with high walls, as was common all over Afghanistan. Though it was large enough to hold his extended family, it was much smaller than the Qala-e-Noborja.

From their base in Maidan, several generations of his descendants have followed the seasons with their herds. They raised sheep and camels for their wool, which they sold to carpet weavers and cloth makers.

Grandfather's father was the third youngest among his six brothers, yet he was to die before his older brothers. Grandfather was only four years old when he lost his father. His younger brother was born two months after their father's death.

Two years later, Grandfather's mother was married, but not, as was the custom, to one of Grandfather's uncles, but instead to one of his cousins, who was closer to her age. Though he was now his stepfather, Grandfather still called his cousin *Lala*, older brother, as he always had.

Grandfather's father had not left much for him and his brother, except for some livestock, a bit of land, and part of the old fort. Grandfather wanted to do more in life than raise sheep and goats. His own grandfather, Mullah Abdul Ghafor, had been a very holy man. And his oldest uncle had been the district governor for several years in Kandahar, where he had become a rich and respected man.

Grandfather wanted to earn respect like his grandfather and wealth like his uncle. He taught himself how to read and write, and told us that he always had a book in his hands. He was determined to educate himself. When he was twelve, he decided to go to Kabul. But when he first arrived, he had nowhere to live. He slept in mosques and shrines for several days until he finally got a job as a clerk in a branch of the Ministry of Transportation called Inhisarat, which transported wood and government goods to other countries.

The job became his school, though he had never gone to one. He studied other people around him very carefully and learned what they did. He learned how to dress well and never forgot the practical things of life his mother had taught him. Soon he had his first promotion and moved to an office where he became an accountant.

He got a job as a clerk in the National Bank of Afghanistan, where he continued to teach himself new things. He studied the law, and how the courts worked. He learned how to look after other people's money and talk to the king.

Despite his success, he told us, he had never felt more lonely, though he had been alone for many years. He kept looking for someone to give color to his life of carefully written columns of numbers.

One spring day, as he was coming out of a restaurant after lunch, he saw a caravan of Kuchis crossing through Kabul. The Kuchis are the Pashtuns who live as nomads. In fact, the word "Kuchi" in Pashto means "nomads." They were coming from their winter quarters near Jalalabad and heading toward their summer pastures in the high mountains at the center of Afghanistan in Bamyan. He saw a beautiful girl among them walking next to a camel.

He recognized her, because he had seen her many times years before when he was young, when the nomads had come to Maidan and stayed there for several weeks in early spring. He told us that he fell in love with her instantly. They had one brief moment of eye contact that afternoon, and that glance became the first link in the chain that connected their lives for the next fifty years.

He went back to the bank and explained to his boss that he would have to be absent for a few weeks, then he followed the Kuchis as they made their way along their usual route to Maidan, where they stopped for a month to let their herds graze. Finally, after a couple of weeks of indecision and fear, he went to the uncle of the girl, who was the lord of that caravan. He expressed his love for the man's niece. The uncle threatened to kill Grandfather, because Kuchis marry only Kuchis to bring more Kuchis.

My grandfather was frightened and almost went back to Kabul. But after a few days of thinking about his situation, he asked his mother to go and broker the deal.

His mother, a very courageous woman, explained to the uncle that our family came from a background similar to his. We, too, had been herders for generations. She told him how we were descended from the Arabs who had come to Afghanistan more than a thousand years before, and who were related to the family of the Prophet Mohammad, peace be upon him. She recited the names of the twenty-nine generations between the Prophet's family and her son, Khaja Ghulam Jallani.

The girl's uncle listened, but said nothing. Grandfather's mother was happy with his silence, because that meant "Yes." There were no threats this time. Grandfather now understood that he was engaged to his beloved, though he would not be able to see her again until their marriage.

The nomads left Maidan soon after to move on to their summer pastures in Bamyan. But in early autumn when they came back, Grandfather had made all the preparations for the wedding ceremony and was waiting for them.

He had the grandest marriage ceremony in the valley of Maidan. It went on for days. When the nomads left to go back to their winter quarters in Jalalabad, their daughter stayed behind with Grandfather and his mother.

Grandfather returned to his job at the bank and started building his house on the land he had bought in Kabul. Though we always called the place Kot-e-Sangi, after the nearby neighborhood, it was actually in Dehnaw Dehbori. He was busy for ten years constructing it and planting his courtyard. Meanwhile, his wife was giving him children. In the end, there were sixteen, though two sets of twins died before they reached six months.

Grandfather had one promotion after another at the bank until he became the head of its Accounts Reconciliation Department. It was his responsibility to review the papers of every deal the bank made. Everybody respected him highly, and after a few years they started calling him "President," even though that was not his title, because he stepped in and ran the bank when the president of the bank and his assistant went to other countries.

With his knowledge of banking and transportation, Grandfather was asked to come work as the head accountant for the Afghanistan Customs Bureau in the Ministry of Commerce. A few years after he went there, though, he uncovered a serious fraud by one of his colleagues. Grandfather went to the minister of commerce to report what was happening, but the minister defended the man who was stealing the funds. Grandfather walked away from the ministry that day and never worked in a government office ever again.

Several high-ranking officials came to him in the weeks that followed, apologized to him, and asked him to come back to his job. But he did not go back. He had lost his faith in the government.

To earn money, he started dealing in carpets he bought from weavers he had met when he was traveling as a boy with his father, who had sold them wool.

Over the years, he bought and sold thousands. Every spring and summer, Grandfather would travel to the villages. Often, he took my father with him, just as his own father had taken him as they followed their herds. It was Grandfather's way of reliving his old nomadic life.

As they went from house to house buying new carpets, Grandfather trained my father to recognize beautifully woven old carpets and *kilims*—flat woven rugs without a knotted pile—that had been made with natural dyes. He also taught my father how to bargain until the last moment to get the best price. They would sit and drink tea for hours and tell jokes and learn the names of all the sons of their hosts.

By the time I was born, Grandfather was not traveling as much. He sent my father to look for carpets while he stayed in Kabul and carefully picked the best times to buy and to sell, quietly amassing a fortune and an inventory of valuable rugs without anyone knowing how he was doing it. And then, of course, he had seen them all stolen from him by those who falsely used the word "Mujahedin."

A pack of stray dogs came in our direction, then stopped and ran away. We turned into the street that led to our house, and a few minutes later we could see the yellow apartments at the end of our courtyard that rose above the surrounding one-story houses. At least that part of the building was still there. Grandfather stopped for a moment when he saw it.

"Life is a gamble," he said as if he were speaking mostly to himself. "You may lose, or you may win. If you search for its meaning, you may never find it, and lose. But maybe you will find it, and win."

He looked at the sad evidence of war all around us. Nearly all the houses on our street had been reduced to jagged, broken walls.

As we got closer to our house he started humming something in the whispery voice he used when trimming his roses. Grandfather was happy to be back in our own neighborhood, even with so much destruction around us. Then a strange voice behind us shouted, *"Stop! Stop! Stop!"*

We turned around and saw two men pointing Kalashnikovs at us. Their faces were covered with the bandannas. I could only see their eyes, which looked like cracks in a grain of wheat. They came toward us and one of them asked my grandfather, "What are you doing here?"

"Visiting my house!" Grandfather said.

"Where is your house?" he asked.

Grandfather pointed with his right hand.

"You must be a rich old man to have such a big house!" one of the guys said. He was tall and thin. His voice was harsh. "Let's talk for a minute," he said, and then pointed his gun toward our neighbor's house.

The gunmen were Hazaras; they were in their late twenties and part of one of the factions who were trying to control that area of Kabul. They wore black *shalwar kamiz*. Each had grenades in his belt, and a knife strapped tightly to his right leg.

"I will come talk to you later, after I see my house," Grandfather said.

"Do what I said," the tall one shouted. He shoved his gun at Grandfather's chest. I heard evil in his voice.

We had no choice but to go with them to our neighbor's house. He had been a successful importer, and had built one of the most beautiful houses in our street. When one of our captors opened the door of the courtyard, I smelled blood like a butcher's shop. There was also a stink of something that had been rotting for days.

The first gate opened onto a twenty-foot corridor that led to a door into the courtyard. I remembered having been there two years earlier with my father for an engagement party. That night the grass in the courtyard had been neatly trimmed, making a green carpet. Roses were in bloom all around. A few McIntosh apple trees in the center, a gift from Grandfather, had big apples hanging from their slender branches. There were some pear, apricot, and pine trees, too. Every path around the courtyard was lined with flowerpots. The rooms around the courtyard had beautiful lamps in them that sent a glow over their fine furniture. The owner often went to London and other places, and brought back fancy things that no one else had.

Musicians had played from a low platform covered with deep red Afghan carpets. Men and women sat together around the courtyard, chatting. Some were on chairs around small tables, others on cushions spread on the grass. They all had a drink in their hands as they talked and laughed. The man's son had just come home from Harvard to meet the bride his parents had selected for him.

My father and I stayed until one in the morning. When we left, some of the guests were still listening to the soft music and talking to one another about their lives, their businesses, their families, their futures.

In those days, grown-ups were always talking about these things. The Afghan Communists were still in control even though the Russian soldiers had left, but they were being challenged fiercely by the Mujahedin in many places. I listened to them out of curiosity, but never understood why they sounded so worried. The only thing that they knew for sure was that no one could know for sure what would happen.

Now here I was standing in that place again, and finally understanding exactly what they had been talking about. These beautiful rooms had no glass in their windows, and it looked as if it had been centuries since anybody had been living in them. There was no sign of any tree in the courtyard. They had all been cut down for firewood.

In the center of the courtyard where the platform for the musicians had been, there was now a ditch filled with the heads of men and women. Dozens of them. I looked at them with their eyes open, staring at me with their shabby hair matted with blood. I started to vomit, but controlled myself.

I did not know who they were. I did not know how they had ended their days on this earth in this place. But I have never been able to forget them, though I have tried many times.

The two men pushed Grandfather and me along a pathway that ran between rosebushes that needed to be pruned. Thorns grabbed my sleeve as I brushed past. I remembered the time I had cut a rose from one of these bushes. The owner told me, "A flower looks happiest on its bush. That is where it belongs." Since then, I have never cut a flower, because he was right. But I could not imagine how anyone had cut the heads off these men and women. They belonged on their bodies, I thought.

The stench in the heat was unbearable. I did not want to be there for even a minute. I felt tears coming from my eyes, and a tightening in my throat was cutting off the air flow. Even though I closed my eyes, the pile of heads, legs, and hands with no fingers was still there in my brain, sending pictures to my eyes.

I looked at those two guys with their faces behind their bandannas. Those who carry a gun are the most cowardly of all, I thought, because they cannot protect themselves without it.

I did not have a gun for killing them. I had no shovel to cover those lost souls with earth. And I had no ability to ask for any of those things.

The two guys pushed us into a room at the end of the courtyard. It was damp and smelled of blood. He locked the door after us. The walls were covered with writing in chalk and charcoal. Someone had written, "Once you come to this room, you will not leave alive. This was my brother's fate, and it will be mine."

On one side of a wall was written, "Don't be afraid of death. You were born one day, and you will die one day."

Another person had written, "No matter how much you have prepared yourself, there is no guarantee for the future." I closed my eyes so I would not have to read any more of them.

An eerie feeling inside me was getting stronger and stronger. I wanted to scream, "If you kill me, I will be one of these heads, but it is unkind to show me these hundreds of innocents whom I did not know." I was too afraid to scream, though. My voice hid inside my chest. I did not dare to say a word.

I kept my eyes tightly closed, trying to force what I had seen from my mind. Silence filled the room until Grandfather spoke in a strange voice.

"You have to find a way to survive. And the secret of survival is to open your eyes. Closed eyes can never see the path." I slowly opened my eyes to see Grandfather down on one knee in front of me. His face was level with mine. He looked very shaken. "If they kill me and keep you, you have to promise me to find your way home."

"Why will they keep me and kill you, and why are you saying all these things? I'm not going anywhere without you," I said defiantly.

"I'm old, and they don't need me. But they will need you for work, or for their sexual pleasure," my grandfather said.

He could see the confusion in my eyes. "I don't have to tell you what that is, but when the time comes you'll know it. They may use you for a while, but you must find an opportunity to escape. I'm sure you can do that. Don't show them that you are smart. Always act stupid."

"No, no, don't tell me that you can't come with me. Please stop," I said. I never liked crying but was afraid I might start, and I did not want Grandfather to see that, because maybe he would call me "fountain eyes," the way my older sister did to get back at me for saying the same thing about her.

"Just listen to me. We may not have another chance to talk again. If these people here make you very unhappy with your life, you may think that killing yourself is the best way to overcome all your sorrows. But believe me, it is not," Grandfather sternly said. It was the first time he had ever spoken to me like that.

"You have to be a brave boy, and if they do kill you, accept the death with open arms, and never beg for your life, because in the end death gets us all one way or another."

"Before they kill me, I want to see my family once more, I want to say goodbyes to them, and I want to tell them I love them," I said. My voice choked as I spoke.

I started remembering my father's jokes, my mother's smile, and my sisters' innocent looks. I remembered sitting around one tablecloth with my parents and sisters, eating breakfast and laughing.

He stared into my eyes for a moment, then said, "The past is like water that flows in a river, you can't bring it back with a shovel. Let the past be in the past, and move on; you won't lose anything. Remember all that I told you. Okay?"

"Yes, I shall remember," I said. I was looking into his eyes, and they were getting watery. When he finished, he turned his face away and blew his nose with his pocket handkerchief. He looked at the walls and started reading what had been written on them. He said, "We need to leave our words, too." He picked up a piece of charcoal on the floor and gave it to me. "Write, 'Death only breaks the cage, but it does not hurt the bird.'"

It was a great relief to hear such a wise saying from him instead of these other despairing statements. I wanted to hug him, but his face was lost in his handkerchief.

The tall, thin guy unlocked the door and came in. He pointed his right hand at my grandfather. "Bring me four hundred thousand afghani, and I will let you go. But the boy will stay with us till you come back with the money," he said.

"I'll find you four hundred thousand afghani, but you will get none of it if you hurt my grandson!" Grandfather said.

"As long as you stand by your word, we won't hurt the boy," he said. Then he went out to talk to his friend, leaving the door open.

"How will you find the money?" I asked my grandfather.

"Don't worry about money. It is not the issue. We have to get out of this situation," Grandfather said.

"I think it is very good to be rich in such circumstances," I mumbled.

"We were rich, and that is why we are here. Being rich from now on will be like cooking a sheep for dinner and inviting wild and hungry wolves with sharp teeth to join you. When the dinner is not enough for them, then they'll invite themselves to eat you," Grandfather said with a worried tone. "For now, we just have to keep them talking."

The tall guy came back and pointed at my grandfather. "Are you Sunni or Shi'a?"

"Sunni and Shi'a are the two wings of one body, and thorns to enemies' eyes. They are both believers in God and Mohammad, peace be upon him," Grandfather said, his voice oddly relaxed. The separation of Sunni and Shi'a started with a dispute among those closest to the Prophet Mohammad, peace be upon him, over who would lead Islam in the years after his death. Both Sunni and Shi'a share the same Islamic beliefs and articles of faith.

The guy suddenly acted ashamed of his question and walked out, as if not sure what to say next.

The other guy, who had said nothing until now, came in and grabbed Grandfather's collar and pulled at him. "I'm gonna make a deal with you. How much do you have to give us now?" Then he slapped my grandfather on the face. I stood up to defend Grandfather, but the guy pushed me in the chest and knocked me backward. He rolled up his sleeves to make his hands ready for more slapping.

My grandfather recited in Arabic one of the Hadiths of the Prophet Mohammad, peace be upon him: "The Messenger of God, Mohammad, said, 'He is not one of us who does not treat our young with compassion or acknowledge the dignity of elders.'"

He stared at my grandfather fiercely for a moment, hesitated, then left the room without saying anything more. His tall, thin friend came and locked the room, leaving Grandfather and me alone again.

I looked at Grandfather. His face was red, and I saw the print of four fingers on his left cheek. If my father had been there, he would have punched those two guys brutally and changed the geography of their faces.

Grandfather smiled at me. "That was an adventure." Then he began pacing from one corner of the room to another.

I thought about my death. What if my family receives my body without my head? Will they put my body in the grave without it? What will be in the grave? Only earth under me and big stones on top of me. I would be covered with a white sheet. I thought about how lonely a grave must feel. That was even more frightening than looking at the heads and legs that I had seen in that ditch. At least the heads were together. They did not eat and chat with one another, but they were not alone.

Suddenly I wished for oblivion, to be at rest. I would drink a glass of poison if that would take away the sight of those heads and send me to sleep forever.

I heard footsteps in the courtyard. I saw a third Hazara man through the broken window of our room. He was not wearing a bandanna, or even carrying a gun except for the pistol in his belt. He was a couple of years older than the other two, but probably not more than his early thirties. He was very muscular. His little finger was halfway up his nostril.

The tall guy unlocked the door and shouted to us, "Come out and talk to our commander."

We went out. The commander was standing at the edge of the ditch, staring at the severed heads. He did not seem to mind the bad smell. He did not pay any attention to us for almost five minutes. The commander continued cleaning his nostrils, then rubbed his finger against his vest, which had little pockets and compartments for holding bullets and grenades. All his grenades had fuses hanging out. I thought for a moment of pulling one of those fuses and pushing him into the ditch.

He cleared his throat with a fake cough, still staring into the ditch, and asked my grandfather, "Do you know why I have kept all these heads here?"

"No," Grandfather said.

"Do you want to know?" the commander asked.

"Do you want to tell me?" Grandfather replied.

"Do you want to know, young man?" the commander asked me.

"No. Because it is obvious. You are a killer," I said sadly.

The commander turned toward us for the first time. He looked at me with dead eyes.

Grandfather squeezed my shoulder and hurriedly said, "He is a kid. He doesn't know what he is saying."

"Kids are honest, and they know exactly what they are saying. I like people who talk frankly. I also like to collect human skulls. Sometimes I plant flowers in them; they look beautiful that way. Do you want to have your skull become a nice pot for a rosebush?"

Grandfather said nothing.

"Your skull will turn to earth after a while anyway. Why not use it for something?" the commander asked with a smile. His little finger was still going in and out of his nose, searching for something. "A man should be happy to be turned into blossoms."

Grandfather was watching the commander, who in turn was enjoying the sight of those heads. The other two guys watched us from the side of the garden.

"And do you know what rotten human flesh is good for?" the commander asked.

"Tell me," Grandfather said.

"It makes good fertilizer. Didn't you know that?"

"No. I didn't know that," my grandfather said, almost as if he were interested. But I could tell he was afraid.

"Yeah, me neither. I just found out a few months ago when I put some in one of my skull pots. That rose blossomed like crazy; it's still in bloom. Maybe you would like to see it?" he said, smiling, and looked straight at my grandfather for the first time. He cleared his throat again. "In fact, why don't you choose which kind of rose you would like to have growing in your own skull?"

"As you wish," Grandfather said very softly. "But may I ask your permission to visit my house across the street one last time?"

The commander laughed, much too loudly. I looked at him and wondered what he found so funny. "That is not your house," the commander said.

"Actually, it is," Grandfather replied, as if he were making a point to a customer. "I built it. I lived there, and it was my hope to return to it when you all go back from where you came."

The commander narrowed his eyes and looked at Grandfather with disgust. "I told you I like people who tell the truth. I know the owner of that house, and he is not you. He is my teacher. And my trainer. I went there every day to train in his gym." He drew his pistol. "You are a dishonest man, like all these people with money."

"Are you speaking of Abdul Basir?" Grandfather asked quietly.

"Of course! Abdul Basir is a man of honor, a man of respect."

"Yes, I know that," said Grandfather.

"That is his house, not yours!" The commander was shouting now.

"Abdul Basir is my son," Grandfather said.

The commander narrowed his eyes again. "Don't try to fool with me."

"He is my father," I said emphatically. "If he were here and saw you talking to Grandfather like this, he would have broken your nose by now."

The commander looked at me. "This boy doesn't look like Abdul Basir. He looks like a Hazara, like us," the commander said to Grandfather.

"From his mother's side," Grandfather replied. Was that true, I wondered? I had never heard that before.

"Tell me about your son. Where is he a teacher?" the commander shouted.

"At the Habibia High School. He is a boxing trainer, too. He had one gym there and one gym in our house, at the corner. He used to train two hundred people in Habibia High School every day, and fifty people in this gym at home. He has been in many international boxing matches, and won most of them," Grandfather said. "What else do you want me to tell you about him? What he eats for breakfast, or what color he likes to wear, or what kind of motorbike he rides?" Grandfather was on the edge of sounding disdainful.

"Tell me about his motorbike," the commander said edgily.

"English. Four cylinders. Fifteen hundred cc. It was noisy and big. Two years ago, a tourist from Denmark came to Kabul and bought it from him. Then he used the money to buy a Russian Volga."

The commander's face changed. A small amount of life seemed to have crept into his eyes, but only just a little. "You are right," he said in a low voice. His whole body relaxed. Then he took my grandfather's right hand and kissed it and touched his eyes to it several times. This is how we were taught to kiss the Holy Koran and a holy man's hand as a sign of respect and honor.

I was not sure whether to be relieved, or more frightened. Everything that had been happening was so strange. Now, just by his having said my father's name, it was becoming even stranger.

The commander led us out of the courtyard. He seemed very embarrassed. His two friends followed. When we got outside, he asked my grandfather whether his men had treated us badly. His behavior had totally changed. He was not a bully anymore. He was acting like a servant to a king.

"Ask them yourself," Grandfather said.

"Did you treat them badly?" he asked his men with a harsh voice. They were standing behind him, staring at their feet. He asked them once again, but very quietly this time. They still did not answer. He slapped one of them so hard on the face that mucus exploded out of his nose and all over the commander's left hand.

The guy started wiping his nose, and the commander beat him on his back with his heavy fists. And as he was beating him he was saying, "Snot-filled bastard, do you know who you are dealing with? This holy man is the father of my teacher. His son was very kind to me. He has won more boxing matches than you have hair on your head!" The commander pummeled the man mercilessly, until he was on his knees wailing. The commander must have been a strong boxer.

Grandfather asked him to stop the beating.

The commander kicked his underling, then ordered the other to bring us tea. He asked my grandfather what type of tea he drank.

"Let me visit my house now; we will have tea another time," my grandfather replied.

"I'm sorry; you can't go to your house today." His voice was much calmer when he talked to Grandfather. "Your house was the front line last week, and our guys put mines all around the courtyard." Grandfather's face fell. "They are fighting in Bamyan now, but they'll be back in a few days. By next week your yard will be fully cleaned, I promise!" the commander said.

Grandfather had just survived a near encounter with death, yet he was even more devastated to know that though our house was right in front of us, we could not go in. We walked into the street. We stood there and stared at our house and said nothing.

That street had once been full of joy. I watched as two stray dogs went into the house where only a few minutes ago we had been held captive. One of them came back with a forearm in his mouth. Our neighborhood had become a fast food restaurant for dogs.

The commander insisted that we have lunch with him, but Grandfather wanted to go.

"You seem to be a good man," Grandfather said. "Did you really kill all those people whose heads were in that ditch?" His voice was very calm, like he was talking to one of his sons.

"No, Uncle. I'm not a good man anymore. I am a killer. I used to be a good man, but that seems like a very long time ago."

"What happened?" Grandfather asked.

"I used to be a student in Habibia High School. I always got the highest scores in the class. I was preparing for the university. You can ask my teacher, your son, Malem Abdul Basir. I was also one of the best boxers in the school gym. But this war has destroyed everything good in my life. It has taken everything from me." He sighed and looked at the mountain.

"It is not just you," Grandfather said. "It is everybody in Afghanistan."

"No. It is not true. For centuries we Hazaras have been treated like slaves in this country. Pashtuns and other tribes always thought of us as outsiders, and treated us like dogs. A few months ago, one of my cousins was captured. He had an air hose put in his ass, the kind you use for tires. They pumped him full of air until he exploded. Do you know who did that? Gulbuddin Hekmatyar. And who is he? A Pashtun, who hates Hazaras. Then one of my brothers had a nail hammered into his head by one of Masoud's commanders. They laughed while he screamed. Do you know who Masoud is? A Panjshiri who hates Hazaras. Everybody in this country looks down on us. What have we done to this country to be treated so badly? Name me one Hazara who is working in a high position in this government. I assure you there is none." His face was getting red with anger.

"But what you are doing is not good either. You cannot clean blood with blood," Grandfather said.

"I want revenge." He said those words very slowly. His voice was getting higher and louder. "I want revenge! My whole family has been killed by Gulbuddin, Masoud, and Sayyaf. Their commanders raped my mother and my sisters before they killed them. Do you want to know how I know that? They made me watch them! One of my sisters was only seven years old. I am the only one who survived, and I know that sooner or later I will be killed, too. But before I die, I'll kill as many of their people as I can. I will rob them, rape them, and murder them," he said, getting even louder.

"This is not a very smart way to solve the problem," Grandfather said.

"I think this is a very smart way. Other tribes should count Hazaras as Afghans, as one of them. If they think they can do all these bad things to us, now they should learn that we can do bad things, too. We tolerated too much for too long, for centuries. Now the bowl of our patience is overflowing."

Grandfather did not say anything and the commander was silent, too. The commander was looking at the mountain. Grandfather was looking at his house. The commander broke the silence. "I am sorry that you cannot visit your house today."

Grandfather nodded.

As we walked around the corner, I automatically looked for my good friend Muhammad Ali, as I always did at that place. He had lived in a nice house across the street from ours, but it looked empty now. He and Wakeel were the same age and were friends in school together. He was one of several Hazara neighbors we had. He taught me how to ride a bicycle, and he was very good with kites. I wondered where Muhammad Ali was now. Many of his relatives had gone to Germany. Was he there safely with them? Or had the Hazara-hating warlords done terrible things to him and his family?

"I can drive you halfway back from where you came," the commander offered.

Grandfather nodded. The commander walked ahead of us, and we followed him to a Russian jeep that was parked along the road. The commander climbed in, and we did, too. We sat in the car and the commander drove us along the road past the yellow silo where we had walked an hour and a lifetime before. He stopped near the bus stop, where no bus had stopped since the fighting had begun. He stepped outside. "I cannot go farther than this. This is the front line between Hazaras and Panjshiris. They will kill me if I go past here," he said.

We climbed out of the jeep. The commander did, too. He came around to our side of the vehicle. He kissed me on my cheeks and urged me to give my father his warm regards. He told us his name. His breath smelled so bad that again I nearly threw up. Once more, he kissed Grandfather's hand. He stood watching us for a long time as we walked away.

When I got home, my mother was cooking dinner. As soon as she saw me, she ran and kissed me on my cheeks. Her hands smelled of onions, and that scent meant everything that is good in the world.

She kept asking me how our house was, but I could not talk. I thought of the pile of skulls, and the dogs. My grandfather went into his room without saying anything. My uncles and aunts quickly started gathering there to hear about what he had seen. My cousins stood outside the door, watching me but saying nothing, waiting for me to say something.

My mother insisted that I tell her what we had seen, but instead I started to cry, sobbing uncontrollably, and I could not stop. My mother cried, too, but without knowing what had happened to me. My sisters cried softly also, except my older sister, who had a wicked gleam in her eyes.

My mother was one minute shaking my shoulders and the next hugging me. "What's wrong?" she asked me forcefully. I sobbed even louder to try to release the grief in my soul.

I do not remember when I stopped, but I do remember falling asleep with my mother holding my head on her chest and rubbing my back, while my older sister was smiling at me. I knew why she was smiling at me. She was planning to tease me with "fountain eyes" for the rest of my life.

The next day when I woke up, I felt so ashamed that I had cried in front of everybody that I did not want to see anyone. I tried not to look them in the eye, but everyone was nice, even my older sister. By now they all must have heard about what had happened to us.

I went to Grandfather's room, where he was reading a book. He smiled at me and continued reading. I just sat there in front of his stretched-out feet and took a book for myself. I looked at it for a long time, but I could not concentrate.

After a while, Grandfather took an apple from a dish next to him and made a few little jokes as he peeled it with his knife. He offered some of the pieces to me and talked about a few things that were of no importance. But he never mentioned what had happened to us. When we had eaten a couple of apples he said, "Okay, Gorbachev, it's time for you to go out and play while I do some writing."

"Gorbachev" was one of his nicknames for me, though I never knew why.

As I left his room, my older sister ran to me and gave me a big hug, holding me in her arms for several minutes. Then she looked at me with her eyes full of tears and kissed me several times. Taking my arms in her hands, she said, "You know I love you very much." I nodded, unable to say a word.

I went up on the roof, where Wakeel was already flying a kite, and Jerk was holding his reel. When Wakeel saw me, he took the reel from Jerk and gave it to me and told me to do a good job, because he was in a fight.

Surrounded by those who I knew loved me, I felt the pain from the day before begin to ease, at least for a time.

6

❖

Under the Earth

Now everything was different. Now we knew we would not be going back to our home. Now we understood that the fighting would not end soon. Now my father and my uncles were more open in their discussions about fleeing the country. Grandfather listened to them, but said nothing.

We had been at the Qala-e-Noborja for half a year, longer than any of us had expected. After Haji Noor Sher left, some other people who were either Haji Noor Sher's distant family or close friends moved into the fort. That made us more aware than ever that we were not living in our own home. We had lots of room at Noborja, but no Afghan wants to live in someone else's house.

A school near the Qala-e-Noborja opened sometime in the late summer but closed two weeks later, when the principal heard a report on the BBC that a faction was threatening to attack our neighborhood that afternoon. We were sent home.

The principal told us to listen to the radio. "As soon as the radio announces that the schools are open again," he said, "you must come." Some of my classmates were very happy, because they did not like school. I found their attitude very strange. I had had so much fun in our old school. What do these new classmates like, then? I asked myself.

I thought that the school would be closed for no more than a few days. But we did not go back to school for two years.

Our parents started teaching us at home. It was not fun; there was no one to compete with. I could not compete with my older sister. She knew all my lessons much better than I did, because she was two classes ahead of me.

My father often taught us. He was very strict. Sometimes in school we had joked with one another when our teachers were writing things on the blackboard. I could not do that at home. I started to lose interest in all subjects, except for astronomy, which was not then taught in our schools. I read the textbook all the way through a couple of times. At night I went out in the courtyard and stared at the sky for hours, drowned in strange thoughts. But my father emphasized math, and the more pressure he put on me to learn, the more I lost interest.

Wakeel and my older cousins, who were in upper grades, often just read novels, or magazines, or books on subjects that interested them. I felt envious of them. Nobody pressured them to study boring school subjects. Wakeel read poetry for hours and could recite line after line of Hafiz by heart. Hafiz was his favorite.

As children we had our own world. We went to the garden every day after breakfast, played with the animals that were still there, or swung from the branches of the trees. We found new friends among the kids in the neighborhood.

After lunch we flew kites. The roof of the fort was even higher than the one at home. With enough string, we could almost float our kites over the top of the twin-peaked mountain that separated us from our house. Wakeel was cutting all the other kites nearby, but nobody in our neighborhood knew it was he. For some reason, they thought it was I. Soon my name was famous, and all the kids called me "Qais the Kite Cutter."

Wakeel just smiled at me when he heard them. That made me feel a little bit small. But, still, I never told anybody that it was Wakeel who had cut them. Wakeel was my closest friend, but we were very competitive when it came to kites.

Then, strange things started to happen with my kites. I would put them up very high and look for somebody to cut. Usually, once one kid had a kite up, others would quickly rise to challenge him. But before another kite even had a chance to appear in the sky, my kite was suddenly floating free, as if somebody had cut it. Wakeel came running over to see what had happened.

"Did you cut your own kite?" he asked. He was laughing, of course.

I did not know what to say to him and just shrugged.

About two days later, the same thing happened. I told myself that the wind must have been very strong up high where the kite was, and maybe it had ripped the kite from its string. That had never happened before. But I was looking for an explanation.

I had been using the string for two years. Wakeel and I had prepared it very carefully. It had taken weeks. First we had collected old light bulbs and ground up their glass into a fine powder. Then we mixed the powdered glass into the paste we made from boiling rice down to a soggy mess. We rubbed the paste and glass into the string to make it like a razor when it went into the sky. My string had cut every kite it fought, except Wakeel's. Now it was cutting itself.

What was worse, after my kites were cut, they floated into the grounds of the old British Embassy, which had been abandoned when the Russians came, and whose walls were topped with barbed wire. There was no way to get over those walls and bring back the kites that had fallen inside them.

The next week it happened again. And then five more times. It was very mysterious. Now the kids in the neighborhood were all laughing and calling me "Qais Who Cuts His Own Kites."

At the Qala-e-Noborja, we did not often eat together as we had at Grandfather's house. There was no room large enough to hold us all. Sometimes, though, we squeezed ourselves into a couple of adjoining rooms, especially when my mother made a special meal and invited my grandfather, my uncles, and their families to join us.

The grown-ups sat at the upper end of the tablecloth, and my cousins and I sat at the bottom. Sometimes we would throw bones at one another, or rub hot peppers on bread and leave it for someone to eat without knowing. Mostly the grown-ups were silent; they were always unhappy. Whenever any of them talked, it was about how to leave Afghanistan.

Every day my father and uncles went out to look for smugglers to get us across the border to one of the nearby Central Asian countries. Most of the smugglers in those days were taking Afghans to Iran and Turkey. Those borders were easier to cross, but the smugglers demanded a lot of money because the trip was long and dangerous. We simply could not afford to go with them.

One night my father came home very happy. He made a few jokes as he took off his jacket. A few minutes later we were all sitting around the tablecloth. When my cousins and I started throwing bones at one another, my father joined us, throwing bones from the upper end. We all looked at him, wondering what was going on. He made a few more jokes that made everybody laugh. It was the first time in months that I was seeing everybody laughing.

After dinner we had tea, and my father announced that he had found a smuggler to take us all out of Afghanistan to Russia and, eventually, Germany. He was very expensive, and we did not have enough money to give him. But the smuggler was willing to wait. He knew my father had been a famous boxer and wanted to help him.

Later, there was quiet talk among the grown-ups about "the garden." My mother frowned and flatly stated, "No. You are not allowed to go there." And then they went back to speaking quietly again.

A month passed. My father tried to call Haji Noor Sher in India several times to ask him for a loan of some money to pay the smugglers, but the Afghan phone system had been completely destroyed.

Then we heard from the BBC World Service that the opposing factions who were battling for control of Kabul had agreed to a ceasefire for a week.

That night my father announced that he was going to our house the next day. Grandfather tried to stop him, but my father was the most stubborn of his sons. Once he said he would do something, no one could stop him from doing it. The next morning, he told me to get ready to go with him.

"No way. You have no idea what I saw there the last time, and I don't want to see it ever again," I said as stubbornly as I could. A look of pain crossed Grandfather's face as I said that. He studied his hands.

"You will come with me," my father said firmly. "I expect you to obey me."

In the end, I went. I would soon be eleven years old and felt nearly like a man. A Pashtun son obeys his father, no matter what the son's age. His voice softened a little, and he explained that he thought he would attract less attention if he had me with him than if he were on his own.

We took a bus from Kart-e-Parwan as far as the Polytechnic, where the Panjshiri control stopped. We got out and walked along the wide, empty avenue that led to our side of town. Even though there was a ceasefire, the Panjshiri soldiers were searching people who were coming toward them from the far side of the front line. I was wearing my jeans and a white shirt with a blue sweater on top. My father had a white *shalwar kamiz*. He was carrying a cloth sack with a shovel in it. He did not explain why.

I walked next to my father, both of us looking around and not saying anything. The leaves on the trees in the park that runs up the middle of the road had gone yellow, like the big yellow silo we were passing that the Russians had built. A wind moved a cloud of dust from one place to another place. There was no one else besides us, except for fat dogs running up and down.

We turned into the narrow streets that led to our house. We had been walking for a half hour by then. Silence hung over the neighborhood, except when a dog howled. As always at that time of year in Kabul, the sky was clear and beginning to have the glow that comes with autumn.

Finally, the high yellow wall of our house was in view. All the windows were broken. The walls had many holes from bullets that had not been there when I had come with Grandfather two months before. Some of the curtains were still in the windows, but they were dirty, and some had been shredded by gunfire. The heavy wooden door that led inside was splintered. It looked like it had been used as a target. My father pushed it gently, as if he were trying not to make it hurt any more than it already did. It swung smoothly on its strong hinges.

As we stepped into our courtyard, we heard a gunshot at the end of the street. We looked around. Two guys were coming from one end of our street, and four more from the other. One of them pointed a gun at us as he walked.

"Again!" I thought. I wanted to run into our garden, but I froze instead. My father tried to pretend he knew them. They said nothing when my father told them about the ceasefire. One of them walked up to us and handcuffed us without telling us why.

"Gentlemen, do you think that we have committed a crime?" my father asked politely. They did not answer. Instead, they kicked him in his back.

The handcuff rings were too big for my thin wrists. They slid down over my hands. I moved my hands in and out of them several times, but I never let the guys with the guns see that. In fact, I was holding the chains in my hand so they would not fall off.

They marched us all the way back to the silo. My father and I were in front. Our captors were spread out behind. Like the guys who had threatened Grandfather and me before, they were Hazaras, but not the same ones. I was looking around to see whether I could find my father's student. The Hazaras continued to control that side of Kabul. But he was not there.

These guys were wearing Western-style clothes. They had boots that were laced tightly up over their ankles. One with big shoulders wore a red headband showing that he was willing to be a martyr. Their hair was nicely combed. They were clean. If there had been no war, they would have been running shops or doing metalwork, for which Hazaras are famous. These guys did not look like bad people. They seemed like those who had been trained to do bad things.

When we arrived at the courtyard of the high, yellow Russian grain silo, they made us crouch on our knees in front of a hole in the ground with steep stairs going down almost like a ladder. The guy with the red bandanna unlocked my father's handcuffs. I slipped mine off and handed them to him. He looked at me holding out the handcuffs to him and laughed. Then he kicked my father down the muddy stairs into the hole, and then me. I rolled down the stairs and dropped onto my father's chest. My father was breathing heavily. He had a few cuts on his face, but they were not deep wounds. His clothes were streaked with dirt.

From where we had fallen, we saw that we were at the mouth of a tunnel. We heard footsteps coming toward us from somewhere inside. In a moment a man stood in front of us with a lamp in his hand. I was trying to stop the bleeding on my father's head with a piece of the toilet paper that my mother had taught us always to carry when we left the house.

"Get up! Follow me," the man said.

I helped my father to stand, then we followed. It was very dark. My father had to walk hunched over because the ceiling was so low. We could barely see our steps. We walked for several minutes. With each step, the air got heavier and damper.

When we got to the end of the tunnel, we saw in the dim light a few men and women sitting along its wall. The man told my father and me to sit next to them. Then he knotted our hands and feet to the others with rope, like slaves. When any one of us moved, the rest of us were forced to move, too. The guy with the lamp who had brought us there sat on a chair in front of us, pointing a gun at us, his finger on the trigger.

A few minutes later a couple of other ragged-looking Hazaras with guns and grenades attached to military belts came to inspect us. They were different from the well-dressed guys who had captured us. They counted us. We were eighteen. There were five women among us. One of them was pregnant, and about twenty-five years old. The rest of the women were middle-aged.

The guards talked among themselves, put a lantern on the ground in front of us, then left.

None of the captives said anything. Some were staring at their feet, some at the tunnel wall. We were all deep in our thoughts about how to get out. The faces of the women were filled with resentment, the men's with anger. It was a moment of heavy silence. Then all of a sudden the pregnant woman began screaming. She had her hands on her stomach and was shouting for help, wailing, "My dear mother, come and help me!" And she kept repeating the name Ahmad.

I asked my father, "What is happening to her?"

"A labor contraction," he said. I had no idea what a labor contraction was.

We were all staring at her, as she was howling in agony, grunting, and occasionally yelling high, piercing shrieks that were made louder by the echoing walls of the tunnel.

One of the women sawed through another woman's bindings with a piece of stone, and she in turn untied the other women. The four of them quickly made a circle around the pregnant woman. Then they asked the men to help them. Two of the women started untying our hands and feet. One of the women said to the men, "We need some hot water. She is going to give birth to her child now."

My father was freed first since he was on the end of the line, then he untied me. He patted my head and said, "I'm going to ask one of those guards to let that woman go to the hospital. Stay here and don't move until I come back." Then, bent over like a cripple, he disappeared down the long, narrow tunnel.

Ten long minutes later my father returned, followed by the commander, who had his gun at the back of his head. My father's hands were tied up with a rope behind his back again. The guy pushed my father hard on his chest against the wall and said, "You don't move from there, or I'll shoot you in your head, understood?"

My father nodded.

He pressed the button of his walkie-talkie and said, "Hey guys, come here, we have a movie without a ticket."

Minutes later, five other guys rushed up the tunnel toward us like wild dogs. They grabbed from behind the four women who were trying to help and dragged them away from the pregnant woman.

By now her cotton *shalwar* trousers were off. She was screaming for help. One of the women said, "For God's sake, she needs to be in a hospital now. She needs a doctor."

"I'm a doctor. Don't you see my Kalashnikov?" One of the men laughed as he held up his battered weapon that had probably passed through a dozen arms dealers before it reached him. "I use this to do my operations." He was about twenty-five years old, and as thin as a stick. His gun was hanging from his right shoulder, and its weight made his shoulder droop. The rest of them laughed loudly.

They were all standing around her and one of them invited me to watch. My father looked at me fiercely and whispered, "Don't go."

"No thanks, I'm fine here," I said.

"It is an order! I said 'Come,' otherwise I'll shoot you," he shouted.

I looked at my father again, and he nodded at me to go. I stood next to those guys and closed my eyes.

The guy next to me slapped me hard on my head and said, "Open your eyes and watch."

When I did, I saw that the woman had a kindly, beautiful face that was twisted by her pain. Her nostrils flared, and her voice shook as she screamed for help. She lay down on her back. Blood was coming from between her legs.

She kept taking deep breaths. Every time she breathed in, her whole body shook, and her face got redder. I knew that I should do something to help her, but I did not know what.

She kept screaming for almost an hour until finally the baby came out, and she went numb. One of the women jumped from where the guards had dragged her, grabbed the baby, and held him upside down. The baby screamed, and the woman told the new mother, "It is a boy."

The guys with guns cheered and said, "It's a boy! It's a boy!" as if he were their nephew. Then one of them said, "Let's go, the movie is finished." They all left.

The other women made a circle again around the new mother and did what they could to help her. The men, sitting shoulder to shoulder, were deeply embarrassed.

The young mother woke up after half an hour. When she opened her eyes she started saying "Ahmad! Ahmad!" again.

We did not know who Ahmad was. We all looked at one another to find whether there was an Ahmad among us. But there was no Ahmad there. A woman who had torn her scarf in two, and wrapped the baby in half of it and tied the other half around the young mother's head so she would not feel ashamed at being uncovered, asked her gently, "Who is Ahmad?"

"Ahmad is my husband. Who are you? Why am I here? Why is it so dark here?" She sounded confused, as if she did not remember what had happened to her. She asked all those questions in one breath.

The men and women all looked at one another and did not know what to say.

She repeated, "Why am I here? Where is my husband? Who tied up my head with this cloth? Oh, I'm feeling dizzy. What is wrong? Why is everyone staring at me?"

"Calm down, calm down, sister! You just gave birth to this child. He is a boy. We are here because we are in the captivity of those warlords, and we don't know what is going to happen to us next. Don't you remember anything?"

The new mother touched her stomach, then looked up at the woman next to her, not really understanding what she had just heard. She grabbed her child from the woman and started kissing his bloody face. Then she looked around her once again and asked, "Did I give birth in the presence of all of you in here?" She was looking at everybody's eyes, one by one, to hear an answer. Then she fainted. The woman next to her caught the baby just before he hit the ground. He cried from the shock.

The men and women looked wearily at one another. There was no water to give her.

The woman who had torn her scarf left us and disappeared up the dark space of the tunnel. She came back in ten minutes with a bucket. She sprinkled some water on the young mother's face and gently tapped at her cheeks. Slowly, the mother regained consciousness and drank some water from the woman's hand.

We all drank from that bucket, too. We had not eaten lunch, and a minute later our stomachs began making noises.

We did not know what time it was. The guards had collected our watches along with our money and the women's earrings, necklaces, rings, and bracelets before they had imprisoned us in the tunnel. But after what must have been several hours, one of the guards came with eighteen *naan* flatbreads and gave everybody one. They vanished in minutes. Those who finished first looked at the others who were still eating. Some of them had not had any breakfast either.

One of the women asked the time, and the man who had brought the bread said it was 6:00 p.m. We had been in that tunnel since midday, but it felt as if it had been much longer.

Some of the men were yawning and ready to sleep, but there was not a mattress or a blanket. My father asked one of those ragged-looking men for something to sleep on.

"You would be the luckiest man to have it," the warlord said.

He disappeared along the tunnel and came back in half an hour with five mattresses and five blankets for the eighteen of us. The tunnel was filled with the stale smell of sweat.

The young mother was shivering from the cold, damp air. She needed a warm place and good food. Her baby needed to be kept warm in a soft bed. The other women gave her one of the mattresses and two blankets. But she still was shivering under the blanket, and crying and saying things that we could not hear clearly.

We now learned that she had lost her husband that morning, when a rocket struck their house.

"The last time I saw my husband was this morning when he was half-alive and half-dead," she told us after a long silence. She spoke softly, as if she were talking to herself. It was the first time I heard her talking like a normal person. "He said, 'I cannot make it, let me die here by myself.'" Her lips trembled, and tears streaked down her cheeks. She sighed deeply, full of pain, and continued.

"We had eaten our breakfast together. He said we would go to Pakistan, where his parents live, to get visas for England.

"We'd met each other and become engaged when we were studying in the Faculty of Social Law at Kabul University. Then his parents fled Afghanistan when we were in our fourth semester. They had to go; his father was involved in political affairs. My husband was their only child, and they did not want him to come back to Afghanistan. But we were in love, and he suffered from being away from me. Two years ago he returned to marry me."

She was speaking in a whisper. Slowly, by telling us her story, she was making us a part of her family, as if she were our sister, to ease the shame of everything that had happened to her in front of us. "This morning when we were eating breakfast in the dining room, he looked at me and said that he was so lucky to have a wife like me, and he kissed me. I went to the kitchen to get butter and jam from the fridge, then I heard a huge noise. Then I was under the ceiling beams, with the earth and straw from the roof all on top of me. When I wanted to stand up, I could not move. But I was at the corner of the kitchen, and there was less rubble than in the middle. I finally pushed a beam off me. When I stood up, my mouth and nostrils were filled with dust and the smell of gunpowder and smoke. I started calling my Ahmad for help. He did not answer me. The beams from the ceiling were blocking the door. I was stuck in the kitchen with the smashed jam jar still in my hand. I climbed out from the kitchen window to the courtyard.

"The dining room ceiling had totally collapsed. I struggled to move the thick beams, but they were too heavy for me. I looked around the courtyard and found a shovel to dig the earth from the roof that had buried my husband.

"As I was working, the contractions came several times, but I still continued. And then I saw my husband's leg. I recognized his jeans. It was the only part of him that I could see. I nearly fainted, but I said to myself, 'Be brave.'

"After an hour of hard work, I dug my husband out from under the rubble. He smiled at me and said, 'You made it through, I'm very proud of you, just remember that I love you so much that I can't put it in words. I don't think I will live, but tell my parents that I love them so much. Tell them they are the greatest parents in the world.' Then he touched my stomach and said, 'Tell our child I wanted to see him, but God didn't want us to meet in this world. Tell him I am waiting for both of you.'

"Then he put his head on my lap and asked me to pat his hair. I patted his hair and I was crying. He looked at me and said, 'I hate seeing tears in your eyes. Don't cry for me, it was my destiny, and I'm going to a better place.' Then he said, 'Smile, smile, smile!'

"His breathing became very heavy. Then, after a great shake, it stopped. He still had a smile at the corners of his mouth but his eyes were wide open, horror-struck. I closed his eyes and left him there." At last she started to weep. Then she started shaking because of the cold, and the loss of so much blood.

One of the women went to her and held her tightly to try to keep her warm. No one said anything. We were feeling the woman's agony at being here with strangers at a time when she should have been with her family.

I started to shiver.

My father took a blanket for me. I used half of the blanket as a mattress and half of it to cover my body. I fell asleep right away, thinking about Ahmad and the son he would never see.

I woke up a few hours later. My father and some other men were doing push-ups to warm themselves up. Some of them were shivering and their noses were red. When they breathed, little clouds came out of their mouths. My father patted me on my head and told me to sleep; I slept again.

But all too soon somebody was kicking me on my back. At first I thought I was dreaming, but it was real, and it was painful. When I woke up, I saw a big guy standing in front of me and shouting, "Wake up, wake up . . ."

My father was begging him not to hurt me. "He's a little kid," he said.

A minute later, still half-asleep, I found myself with the others at the place where the tunnel ended in a wall of dirt. Everyone had shovels.

We were separated into three groups. Most of the men were set to digging, making the tunnel longer. We were never told where the tunnel led or why it was being dug. We knew we should not ask. The women put the loosened earth into buckets. And four men and I carried the buckets of earth to the entrance of the tunnel and dumped them outside. I wanted to stay outside even though the sun hurt my eyes, but one of the guards was always standing there to make sure we did not escape. Once when one of the men was slow going back into the tunnel, the guard beat him with a heavy stick.

The young mother was holding her baby. When the baby cried, she began breast-feeding him. A few hours later, she was released, because she could not do any work.

We worked for a couple of hours. Then we had a loaf of coarse, dark bread—the Russian kind they made at the yellow silo bakery for poor people—and a glass of water for our breakfast. Breakfast, lunch, and dinner were all the same, a loaf of Russian bread and a glass of water.

That second night, we started talking to one another and trying to get to know one another better. We made some jokes, too, even though everybody's lips were sealed against laughing. Everybody started talking about their lives, kids, wives, husbands. But no one talked about politics, or why we were being held captive, because we were all afraid of one another.

The commander and four of his thugs came with their guns hanging from their shoulders. One of them had a bag on his back that was so heavy that he could hardly carry it. He put the bag in front of us and opened it. The bag was full of handcuffs. The commander started handcuffing the hands and feet of all the men. Then, with a long chain and heavy padlocks, he connected each of them with the man next to him. My father was right in the middle. No one could move. Even a small shift in position could hurt the others.

He handcuffed three of the women together, separately from the men. Only one woman and I were not handcuffed. The other four captors watched passively as he fastened the handcuffs and tugged on them to make sure that the locks held tight.

Then he looked at the woman who was not handcuffed and said, "It is better you don't struggle and yell or curse. It is better you take off your clothes now for me. Soon, one by one, we will be finished. You cannot imagine how fast we release. We are away from our homes and our wives. We are at war, and war without sex is like poison."

She was confused at what she was hearing. "Are you fighting for peace in this country, or to do shameful things?" she asked sharply, as if she were a teacher speaking to a naughty student.

"You're going to be a problem, I can see that," the commander told her.

The commander started tearing the woman's clothes with his knife.

My father moved to stand up and say something, but the handcuffs held him down. Then one of the thugs hit him on the head with the butt of his Kalashnikov. I tried to run to him, but the commander grabbed the back of my collar.

I yelled, "Let me see my father," but instead of letting me go, he slapped me on my head so forcefully that for a moment I saw strange lights, though the tunnel was very dark.

Blood was running from the top of my father's head to his jaw and was dripping from his chin. He was slumped over and unconscious. The men handcuffed to him on either side tried to ease him into a sitting position.

In a few moments, the woman was naked, cursing and spitting at the commander. He climbed on her. I closed my eyes. I was deeply ashamed to be seeing these things. She screamed piteously. When he had finished, he wiped the spit off his face with his sleeve, then stood up.

"Don't use all your energy on me, there are more coming," he said with a laugh. As he spoke, three more thugs came up the tunnel to where we were being held. They were laughing, too.

The other women wept in low voices. They knew that tomorrow night the same thing would happen to one of them. They should have been in their homes with their families. All that seemed so far away. The men closed their eyes, but they could still hear the sound of the woman's cries.

She continued cursing for six of them, her voice growing coarser and coarser. By the seventh man, she went quiet.

They continued long into the night. After the last one had finished, a boy who was about eighteen came with a bucket of water and left it in front of the woman. She was unconscious.

Later, five men whom I had not seen before came with sleepy eyes and guns hanging from their shoulders. One of them splashed the bucket of water on the woman. She took a deep breath and sat up, and then she looked around to find something to cover her body. All she saw were her torn, wet clothes. She covered herself as best she could, then put her head on her knees and wept.

One of the other guys bent down to unlock the men's handcuffs and unlocked the padlocks. The other four were pointing their guns at the men and women, their fingers on their triggers. Once the locks were open, the captives started rubbing their wrists and ankles. I ran to my father, who had regained consciousness by then but was badly hurt.

Suddenly, one of the captives jumped at the guard who was collecting the handcuffs and chain and knocked him onto the ground. The captive was on top, punching his opponent's face with his right hand, trying to get his gun with his left hand. The other four captors pressed their backs against the tunnel wall, pointed their guns at us, and said, "If any of you move, we will kill you all."

One of them took a grenade out of his military waistcoat pocket and said, "This will be enough for all of you. *Do not move!!*"

The captive kept struggling, but the guard under him managed to push his gun into the captive's chest. Suddenly, we heard a loud gunshot. The captive's face went pale; his eyes were wide open with horror, and his brow glistened with sweat. He raised himself up and looked at all of us, then dropped onto the guy under him.

The guard on the ground struggled to get up. The other thugs had to help him. When they turned the victim on his back, there was a tiny hole right at his chest where his heart was. The exit wound was bigger than the entrance. The exit wound is always bigger than the entrance; this is something children in Kabul had come to know.

I looked at my father. He made a motion with his eyes that told me, "Do not say anything." Throughout the time we had been in the tunnel we had hardly talked at all, and never about what was happening to us. I was young, but old enough to understand that it was dangerous to speak.

They half carried, half dragged the body out. One of them stood in front of us, pointing his gun at us. Nobody spoke. Everybody was staring at the bloodstains on the ground.

Now there were sixteen of us.

Days passed. The routine was the same every day. The commander and his men used the women during the night in the presence of all of us, and forced the men to work as slaves in the day. The commander was always there, but the others changed every night. We never saw the same ones twice. Our food was a piece of bread with a glass of water three times a day, though twice we were given rice and lamb. Those who did not work hard were whipped like donkeys.

I lost track of the days. I was very hungry, and feeling weak. I had hardly enough water to drink in all this time, and could barely walk.

By the end of about two weeks, only seven men and two women were left besides us. The rest of the men had been killed by the commander, two I remember for refusing to work, one because he was too weak and sick. One of the women was let go because she cried so loudly and in such pain all day and all night the commander got fed up with her. Another woman was dragged outside after they had used her. We never saw her again.

One day as we were starting to fill the buckets with earth, a tall Hazara guy came to the tunnel to inspect the commander's work. I turned my back, tried to make myself appear very busy in the dim light, and did not look at him.

The commander was trying to be very nice to that tall man, but the tall man did not care and paid no attention to what the commander was saying. The tall man walked the length of the tunnel to see how far we had gone. He looked at his commander and said coldly, "You have done very little."

Instantly, I knew his voice.

"Hey, Berar!" I shouted.

He looked at me and said, "Who are you?"

"This is Qais," I said.

He pointed a torch toward my face.

"Qais *jan*, what are you doing here?" There was surprise in his voice as he spoke to me, using the title "*jan*," a sign of affection and respect.

"I didn't come here by myself. My father and I were brought here. To work like slaves. Berar *jan*, I'm very, very thirsty, but I am not allowed to drink water at work time," I said. "Please, can I have something to drink?"

"Whose order is that?" he asked me, as he knelt in front of me.

"This man's," I said wearily as I pointed at the commander.

"How do you expect people to work for you if you do not give them enough water? You don't buy water, do you?" he said.

"No, sir," the commander said, staring at his feet like a bad child.

"What is 'No, sir'? Get the hell out of my sight! Bring some water, for God's sake," he shouted, and the commander hurried off.

Berar asked me for how long I had been working there. I said for maybe two weeks. Then he asked me what I had been eating. I told him. I also told him about the commander and his men having sex with the women in front of us, and about killing the men.

Berar put his hand on my mouth, closed his eyes, and said, "Stop, stop, it is enough." He was silent for a moment and then he shouted, "Stop working, please!" He stood up, and the men stopped shoveling, wondering what was happening.

"I do not know why this man has been so cruel to all of you. And I do not know what to say to you now. There is a war. You know that. The people who are trying to kill us Hazaras all have guns that the Americans gave them. Maybe you know that, too. All we have is shovels. We need a tunnel to protect ourselves.

"I told him to use new people every day. I told him to get people from the street, and to give them good food, and make them work for one day, and at the end of the day let them go home. How can I apologize to you for all that he has done to you?" he asked. His face looked stricken.

"Please go to your homes, go to your families who are waiting for you," he said softly. We dropped our shovels and buckets and headed silently toward the mouth of the tunnel.

For a second time, we had been rescued by somebody we had known in our old life, from the time before being Hazara and Pashtun meant we were supposed to think of ourselves as enemies. Kabul was a small town then, and people like my grandfather and my father knew everybody, or so it seemed when we walked through the shopping district and many people greeted them by name: Pashtuns, Tajiks, Uzbeks, Hazaras, Turkmen, Jews, Sikhs, and Hindus—everybody.

We came out into the daylight and the air. The men were happy to stand straight again after so many days, but the two women were ashamed of how they looked and kept trying to cover themselves.

"Wait," Berar announced. "There is one thing that must happen before you leave." We froze in fear. Our minds were set on leaving. And now there was something else we had to do.

Berar told us to walk with him to the silo. He also called his commander to join us, along with two other Hazara men we had not yet seen.

The commander, who had been so ruthless, carried a bottle of Coca-Cola in his hand. After a sip he belched.

Inside the yellow silo, we climbed a staircase all the way to the roof. It was about eight stories, but it felt much higher as we climbed one flight of steps after another. We could hardly make the climb, we were all so exhausted. Our fear increased with every step. We did not know what would happen next. I knew that Berar was my friend, but I did not know what he was doing. Even I was afraid.

When we stepped out of the stairwell onto the roof, it was very windy; it could have easily knocked any of us down, because we were so feeble. Everybody held on to somebody else. I held my father's hand. The roof had a railing around the edge, but it did not look sturdy. The weather was very clear, and we could see for a great distance.

Berar was standing in the middle of the roof. He called us to come. We all surrounded him. His commander was standing near to him. Still sipping his Coca-Cola, and still burping. Suddenly, Berar turned around and kicked the commander in the stomach. Berar was very fast, like in the kung-fu movies. The commander fell to the ground and coiled like a snake.

He cried out, "Why?" He was rubbing his stomach. Berar did not answer. Then he nodded at the other two men. One man picked the commander up on his shoulders, and in one fast move carried him over to the edge of the roof and tossed him off.

We were too shocked to know what was going on. We all listened to one long scream, and then a thud. There was fear in everybody's faces. They thought he would toss all of us, one by one. But I did not believe Berar would do that, though he looked a lot taller and broader and stronger than the last time I had seen him.

Berar picked up the half-drunk bottle of Coca-Cola and flung it over the edge of the roof. "Now we are all happy!" he said.

But no one was. Not even Berar, who studied the ground far below, searching for words.

"This man was supposed to have been put to death in Pul-e-Charkhi prison, but he was freed when the Mujahedin overran it," Berar told us. "In a war, every man is needed, so he was sent here. But wicked people like him bring shame to us Hazaras and to the Mujahedin. Some who were released from the prison are now seeking their private revenge in the name of Mujahed. Some of them joined the factions that came from Pakistan. They have taken weapons from all these countries who are using Afghanistan as their playing field. They are everywhere. They are sick, and their only cure is death."

He had turned his face back to us now. "Please, go to your homes. I ask your forgiveness for all the bad things that have happened to you here."

He came close to me, sat on his heels before me, and patted my hair. "Give my best wishes to your grandfather," he said quietly, then he kissed me on my cheek and left. His men followed.

An old man who had been held with his sons walked first toward the staircase, and his sons followed him. Then the two women, then my father and me, and the others after us. In front of the silo gate, we all said very formal and cold goodbyes to one another. We knew we would feel shame if we ever saw one another again. We all went quickly in our different directions.

My father and I headed for Qala-e-Noborja. My father was very weak. He could hardly walk. As we left the silo, he said, "The life of cruel people is short." He said nothing else all the way home.

When my father opened the courtyard door, we heard the women crying. My father asked me what was wrong. He asked me in a way as if he thought I would know, as if I had been at home and not with him for the past two weeks. I just said, "I don't know."

"Do you think someone died?" he asked with an exhausted voice.

"I don't know," I said again.

"But why are they crying? Something must be wrong!" my father said.

"I hope not," I said. Because all I was thinking about was eating something and washing all the mud from me that had turned us the color of dust. My sweater, my jeans had lost all their color. I wanted to sleep for a day, not listen to women's weeping.

We walked into the courtyard. I could hear my mother's crying all the way from the room at the far end where we lived. There were other unfamiliar voices with her, voices raised in sorrow.

Through the thicket of lilac bushes at the center of the courtyard and the fruit trees, I could see my uncles and cousins preparing lunch in one corner of the broad courtyard, with flames licking the big pots, and huge amounts of smoke rising around them.

The courtyard was full of men. Even from across the courtyard I recognized most of them. They were our relatives. I could see other men I knew in one of the ground-floor rooms. A nice voice was reciting from the Holy Koran. All the men were facing away from us, listening to it.

We went to those pots, and my father asked his brother through the curtain of thick smoke, "What is wrong? Who died?" I was standing next to my father and looking into those pots to see what was being cooked. One was full of meatballs. I grabbed one. It was very hot, and I could not hold it in my hand. It dropped on the ground and rolled on the earth. No one noticed. They were all busy.

My uncle touched my father's face. "Am I not dreaming? Are you here?"

"I'm very tired and hungry. Can you give me something to eat?" I said.

My uncle did not answer me. He walked away very slowly, backward, looking at us as he went as if he had not heard me. It was weird seeing him acting like that. He looked frightened. He was still not sure that we were alive and not ghosts. My father followed him.

My cousins circled around me, but none of them talked to me. I thought they wanted to tease me, and I did not have the energy to play now. Wakeel was taller than all of them, with pale skin that looked even whiter than usual. He touched my shoulder, fast, as if I were hot as fire, and said, "Is that you, or your ghost?"

"What?" I narrowed my eyes.

"We thought you and your dad had died. Your mother has been crying for you for two weeks."

This was not making sense to me.

"We thought that you both had been killed. Grandfather invited all of our relatives to hold a funeral. All these people are here for you and your father, because you are dead."

"Please stop saying stupid things. I'm very hungry; I just want something to eat."

"We are not joking, Qais. This is all for you." Jerk was standing next to him, nodding vigorously. "Look, there are your coffins. We were about to do the burial rituals after lunch," he said. The coffins were made of wood, and they were covered with black cloth. One was about six feet long and the other one was four feet.

"What is in it? It is definitely not me in there," I said.

"Things like your reel and a few kites, and some of your best marbles that you kept and never played with, and your school clothes and some of your notebooks and your diary. We put them there. Grandfather asked us to do it," Wakeel said.

"You put in my reel, and my kites, and my marbles and my diary? What the hell are you thinking?" I said. I ran toward the coffins and opened the small one, and I saw all my stuff there. Wakeel wanted to take them out. I shouted at him, "Do not touch anything! Those things are mine!"

"I'm not getting them for myself. I'm taking them out for you," he said.

"No. Leave them there," I said.

Wakeel looked at me strangely. "Do you want us to bury them, then?"

"No, just leave them alone!"

One of my other cousins said, "Maybe he wants to get buried with them." All the rest started laughing.

I opened the long coffin. Inside was my father's favorite carpet, which he used to put on his bed. Now it was nicely spread inside the coffin. His physics books were piled in one corner, and his boxing gloves were next to them. There was also his suit, shoes, socks, and his favorite mug, which had a crack in it.

"If my father sees all these things in this box, he will beat you all like his punching bag," I said. My cousins were always a little bit afraid of my father, and this quieted them.

"We did not do this," Wakeel said. He was sounding very panicked. "Our uncles have put all your father's things here. We were busy doing yours."

One of the other cousins looked offended and said, "We were just trying to give you a good funeral."

I did not usually talk to him, so I did not answer him.

Jerk came up to me, looking very sad. "I'm very sorry for what I did to your kite string." I could not understand what he was talking about, and I did not care. "Those times when they said you were cutting your own kite, I did that. I used a razor to cut halfway through your string, so that it would break when you put the kite in the air."

I suddenly understood, and felt anger rising. That miserable little Jerk. My hunger and exhaustion faded as I felt my fury growing. I pulled my arm back to swing at him, but I was so weak I knocked myself off balance and started falling backward. Jerk reached out to hug me. He was crying now. But I was already too far off balance when he embraced me to keep from falling, and I pulled him down on top of me. I did not have the strength to push him away. I would beat him up later.

"Where were you for these two weeks, anyway?" Wakeel asked earnestly.

"Why are you so dirty?" a girl cousin asked.

"Please don't tell us that you returned from your grave," another said.

Even though Wakeel was my best friend, I did not want to go through telling all that had happened to us. Instead, I looked for my father.

My sisters came out of our rooms, drawn by all the noise. My older sister looked at me strangely, as if she were not sure whether I was actually me. Then, looking frightened, she quickly took my two little sisters' hands and led them back inside.

Then I saw my mother kissing my father and hugging him and crying and muttering something that I could not hear. She seemed to me like a kind of crazy woman I had seen in Indian movies. She and my father were surrounded by all our women relatives.

I heard her ask somebody where I was.

"I'm here, I'm okay." I waved at her from where I was standing. I had thought about her many times when we were in the tunnel, wanting to tell her the things we were enduring. Sometimes I wondered whether I would be like Ahmad, who did not live to see his son in this world, and I would never see her again. Now she was running toward me, shouting.

"Get away from those coffins!" She hugged me and kissed me more than a hundred times. My face was almost wet from her lips and tears. Or maybe they were my tears.

My mother drew my father and me inside and led us to a corner of our room and sat us there. My mother was fluttering around us like a butterfly. She kept drying her eyes and her runny nose with her sleeves. She gave my father three pillows instead of one. She did not know whether to laugh or cry. I had never seen her like that before. She was not herself anymore.

Relatives whom I usually saw only at wedding parties followed us in and crowded along the walls. My youngest aunt whispered into my father's ear, "Ask your wife to sit next to you. She has been crying for two weeks. She'll go crazy if you don't help her control her feelings. She is in a state of shock. Do something."

Numbly, he asked my mother to sit next to him, though usually men and women do not sit together when there are visitors present. She sat next to my father for a few seconds, then jumped up again. "I have to prepare lunch for you two."

"No, no, we're not hungry; I want you to sit next to me," my father exclaimed.

"I think Qais is hungry. You both look very thin," my mother said.

"No, no, he is all right. We had a huge breakfast this morning and we're still fully stuffed. Just come and sit next to me," my father said.

I smiled at her and pretended I was not starving.

My father wanted me to make room for my mother, but she said, "No, no!" and squeezed herself between both of us. She started patting my hair and staring at my father without a word, as if she had not seen him for years.

Kids were peeping through the windows and giggling. No one knew what to say. Maybe no one wanted to say anything, because it was the sweetest moment any of us had had in the time since the fighting had started.

My mother broke the silence. She jumped up from between us and almost frightened me. She kneeled in front of my father with her back toward the others. She cried very loudly, "Is this really you or am I dreaming? Please tell me it is true!"

My father leaned forward on his knees to embrace her. "Yes, this is me. I am here for you. I will never go anywhere. I'm fine, I am fine. It is okay now, it is okay."

I could hear the heavy breaths of my mother and my father as they clung to each other. My father was rubbing her back. My mother was shaking silently. Tears came from her eyes, though they were closed; my father's, too.

The men and women in the room were now laughing in low voices, but at the same time wiping their own eyes. Finally, my mother stood and asked me and my father to come with her to another room nearby that was empty. She seemed suddenly to be aware that everyone was watching the three of us, and she wanted to be alone with us. She turned to the others and said, "We will be back soon." She ordered my uncles to prepare lunch for everyone. Now she seemed to be herself again.

In the empty room she kissed me and my father over and over again. She never minded the dirt on our faces, or maybe she could not see it, or maybe she did not know what to do except to kiss us. She never asked me or my father what had happened to us during the past two weeks. Maybe she did not want to know. She was only happy to have us back.

A few minutes later, we rejoined the others. Everyone was laughing and enjoying one another's company; the funeral had turned into something like a wedding party. We spent the whole day singing and dancing, with my uncles playing flutes and drums, even though there were two coffins in the courtyard ready to be buried. Instead, we used them as benches for the guests. I was worried, though, that if the thin wood on the lid broke, my kites and reel would get smashed. Each time I looked at Jerk, I wanted to smash his face. "I'm not going to let him get away with what he did," I told myself. "He made me look very stupid."

My sisters told me about the new novels they had read and the new movies they had watched. My little brother looked at me and smiled. My cousins told me about their past two weeks' adventures and who won the bets on kite fighting with the neighbors. They showed me their money to make me feel jealous. They had no idea what had happened to me, and until now I have never told them, or anybody.

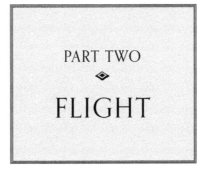

PART TWO

FLIGHT

7

❖

The North

By now we had been living in the Qala-e-Noborja for well over a year while the war in Kabul writhed around us. All this time, the front lines shifted like angry snakes. Today the Panjshiris would control one sector; tomorrow it was in the hands of the Hazaras; and the next day it would be held by Sayyaf, and a couple of days later, Gulbuddin, or Dostum. Rockets streaked over our heads, not caring where they landed.

Almost every evening, there was more talk among my uncles and my father about leaving Kabul. The smuggler who was going to take us to Russia had heard that a funeral had been planned for my father. We had never given him any money. So he took somebody else. He did not know that we had come back from the dead. We never saw him again.

One morning at breakfast while my father was eating some yogurt, he very calmly told my sisters and me, "I have decided that we shall go to Mazar and stay with your mother's sister for a while." Mazar is up north, on the other side of the Hindu Kush mountains. We had gone there many times before the fighting had started. Once we had flown there in an airplane.

I asked whether Wakeel was coming with us. My father said "No." Then I asked if Grandfather was coming. He said "No." I was stunned that we were going away and leaving them. I went to the other room and told Wakeel. He thought I was joking. He came with me to our room and saw my mother packing. He asked my father whether he was coming with us.

"Not this time, Wakeel," he said kindly. "We are not going on a picnic. We are heading to Mazar to spend some time with Qais's aunt. My hope is that while we are there, I can find a way to take everybody out of Afghanistan. Then I will come back and get you guys."

"Shall I come, too?" Wakeel asked, as if he had not heard what my father had just told him. My father always bought him whatever he bought for us and took him wherever he took us, and he could not understand why he was being left behind.

"No, there is just not enough space in the car for all of us," my father said.

"There is plenty of space in the car," Wakeel said insistently. "There were fifteen of us and the baby when we came from our house to this place. Don't you remember?" He looked at me and my sister for confirmation. We were afraid to say anything, because my father was in one of those moods where we could not tell whether he was angry. We nodded, but tried to avoid looking at our father's eyes.

"That was a short distance," my father said. "Now we are going to the other side of Afghanistan, easily ten hours of driving." His voice was getting a little bit hard.

"That is okay," I said, "we can squeeze in the backseat."

"No more discussion," my father said with a loud voice that startled us all. "I said 'No,' and it stays that way. No more discussions."

After Wakeel's father had disappeared, all my uncles had done their best to help him. But he was closest to my father, who had always included him in everything my immediate family had done, as if Wakeel were his own son. I did not understand how he could even think of leaving Wakeel behind.

This was the first time I was going to be really separated from Wakeel. With all the uncertainty that had contorted our lives since the day his father had disappeared, the one thing that each of us could count on was the other.

One day about a year before, I had searched for him everywhere, but I could not find him. I climbed the ladder to the roof of the Qala-e-Noborja to look in the hiding place that we always used when we played hide-and-seek. He was sitting there, alone, staring into space. When I tapped him on the shoulder, he acted startled and looked at me. I asked him what he was thinking about. He said it was nothing. He sounded sad. I asked him whether something was wrong. He said "No."

Wakeel was always cheerful and happy. Is he hiding something from me? I asked myself.

I sat down next to him and said nothing. I started staring at where he had been looking. For a few minutes we remained silent. He glanced at me several times, and I kept staring into space. He waved his hand in front of my eyes, and I pretended that I did not notice. He tapped on my shoulder and asked me what I was looking at. I told him I was imitating him. He smiled.

He said, "You are lucky that you're Qais, and not Wakeel."

"Why?" I asked. "I wish I were Wakeel, who is very good at flying kites, and having lots of friends, and being very popular at school, and climbing trees, and being the oldest child of his mother and the older brother to his sisters so he can order them around to polish his shoes and bring his tea and water. Who in the world doesn't want to be Wakeel?

"Look at me," I went on. "My friends are the little kids. I am no good at flying kites. I'm not as popular as you are in school, and not all of my cousins, aunts, and uncles love me like they do you. I can't order my older sister to do anything for me. She always bosses me around. Who in the world wants to be Qais?"

"I do," Wakeel said.

"Why?" I asked, very surprised.

"Because you have a dad, and I don't," he said, his voice shaking. "Every day when you wake up, your father kisses you on the cheek. Every day you exercise with your father, he lets you beat him, he plays with you, he teases you, he sits on your bedside when you are sick, he wakes up in the middle of the night to check on you when you're having nightmares or you mumble in your dreams, he warns you when you do something bad, he points out your mistakes, he tries to fix them with you, he wants you to climb higher on the ladder of your life, he is with you all the time. You can let yourself fall back, and you know there is your father, who will hold you." The words were coming out in a rush. "Who will hold me when I fall back? When I tumble and break into bits and pieces, there is no one to collect me. I have to collect myself and get back with my life. I want my dad. I want him to hold me when I fall back." He burst into tears and rushed out of the hiding place, tripping as he climbed down.

I did not know what to do. Should I run after him and give him a hug? No, I was younger than he; I cannot do that, I told myself. His dad should give him that kind of a hug.

An hour later, Wakeel had his cheerful glow on his face again and was making jokes that made everyone laugh. But suddenly I understood that for all these years his jokes had been chasing a shadow from his soul.

"Only a dad can fill the space of a dad, not your uncles nor your grandfather, only your own dad," he told me. Then he recited a couplet from his favorite poem by Hafiz: "To make one heart happy can be greater than making a thousand sacred journeys."

Once, when we were sitting in the lowest part of the garden of the Qala-e-Noborja near the pool, Wakeel told me that he was worried what would happen if his father came home; he would not know where to look for us. He would go to Grandfather's house and not find us there.

"I think he is still alive," Wakeel said. "If he had died, he would have sent a sign."

"What kind of sign?"

"I don't know. I will know it when I see it."

An hour later, we were ready to go. We did not have much to take. Our few clothes quickly went into our two suitcases and then into the trunk of the car. My mother gathered up whatever food we had in the house and put it in large sacks. Grandfather and my uncles and aunts and cousins all stood around the car to say goodbye to us as we drove away from Noborja.

Wakeel ran after our car. The car was faster than he was and left a track of dust in the air. I popped my head out of the front seat and waved at him, trying to smile. My sisters were looking back at everyone from the rear window and were waving as well. When we disappeared around the corner near the British Embassy, Wakeel stood in the middle of the street, despair all over his face, shoulders drooped, breathing hard and lost in the dust.

I felt very sad. I was very angry at my father for leaving Wakeel behind, and did not talk to him as we drove out of Kabul and up the steep hill at Khair Khana that leads north. I put on a frowning face, and my sisters did the same. My father made some jokes. And though they were new and funny, I did not laugh and my sisters did not either.

"Look, we could have taken Wakeel, but what would his mother do?" He was looking straight ahead, but we knew he was talking to us. "She has no one else. I will come back for him and the rest of them in two weeks." Then he turned on the car radio to the BBC World Service.

My sisters and I wanted to hear Afghan or Indian songs, but my father only wanted to listen to the news, especially for any information about Mazar. We did not tell him to change the station, since we were determined to maintain our anger with him.

As we left Kabul behind and started driving north across the Shamali Plain, I looked out through my window and saw the remains of Russian military trucks everywhere. Some lay sideways or upside down. Most of them were broken into bits. Almost every field had one, and people farmed around them. A burnt-out tank lay in a river; water was rushing through it and little kids with wet clothes were sitting on it, watching the passing cars. Years of rain had rusted the hulks; the sun and dust had bleached their paint. Some of the kids were pulling on their steering wheels, taking long journeys across their fantasies. A Russian jeep hung halfway down a steep valley wall, as if it were held by some kind of superpower.

I started counting them. I quickly reached one hundred. After a while, counting became boring, and I stopped.

We climbed up the side of the Hindu Kush mountains next to a fast-moving river that twisted back and forth around tiny villages perched high on its banks. Near the top, we reached the Salang Tunnel, which cut through the high peaks. Many of the lights in the tunnel were broken. Some were very yellow and gave a little light. The tunnel was filled with exhaust from other cars and big trucks. We raised the windows. My father drove very slowly to get around the holes in the road.

The hours rolled by faster than our car could go on the badly damaged road. As we drove down the north side of the mountains, we started following another river, this one much wider. On either side, fields were green with growing things even though it was early autumn. But beyond the fields, where the sides of the valley rose up, everything was bare rock. I looked at all these things very carefully, because I knew we were soon going to a different country and I might never see them again.

By midafternoon, we were driving through a beautiful valley on a narrow gravel road, toward a high gorge between two steep mountains. As we passed through the gorge, my sisters and I popped our heads out of the windows to see the birds flying from one hole in the cliffs above to the next. We could hear a fast-moving river as it crashed over the rocks at the bottom of the gorge and echoed between the high walls above.

We passed through the gorge and out onto the flatlands that stretch north to Russia. Suddenly, my father pulled the car over to the side of the road and stepped out. He stood in front of the car and took a deep breath. He looked at the blue sky and gazed at the mountains. A smile appeared on his face, as if something unknown were revealing itself only to him.

"Is something wrong with the engine?" my mother asked, as she stretched her head out the window.

Without turning around my father shouted, "This is Tashkurghan!" Ahead of us we could see many walled gardens and a small town a mile beyond. Crowning a hill between us and the town was a very large mosque with a high dome. My father started walking across a field toward where all the water in the broad river we had been following was rushing through the narrow gorge.

I leaped out of the car and followed him. He kept walking with big strides, looking up the wall of the gorge at the mountains, until he reached the riverbank. He splashed some clear water on his face and did not care that it dripped on his clothes.

"I have been dreaming about this place for months," he said. "I used to camp here with my friends for weeks at a time."

"When was that?" I asked. By now we were friends again, even though I had not forgotten my anger. I had realized that if I stayed openly angry because Wakeel and Grandfather were not with us, everyone would be very miserable. So, I was friendly to him. But I did not tell him my secret thoughts, which were still wrapped in bitterness.

"Oh, it was a long time ago. Before I married your mother," he sighed. "Well, not very long. It just seems like a long time ago. It seems like ages. All of those friends are living in Europe now, and I'm still here."

He reached over and ran his wet hand through my hair. "Come on, let's camp here for a few days." He walked toward the car, and I followed quickly after him.

It sounded great to me. Sometimes we had camped for a night next to Qargha Lake near our home or in a neighbor's garden, but never in a wide-open place like this.

By now, everybody was out of the car. My father took a large sheet of blue plastic out of the trunk. In each corner was printed "UN" in big letters. "We will use this as a tent," he said. He led the way down across some stony places to a flat field near the river, which flowed away from the road once it had escaped the gorge.

My sisters started helping my father and me to set up the plastic over some straight tree branches we found along the road. My mother was quiet, and my father looked at her several times to see whether she liked the idea. She just seemed happy to see us happy again.

A village man on a mule approached, sitting on a load of carrots piled in handwoven bags on the mule's back. As he came closer he asked, "What are you doing here?"

"We're camping," my father said.

"Be careful, this place has wolves. They come out at night," he warned us.

"I'm not afraid of wolves. But thank you for telling us," my father said, and the man rode on. Then my father drove the car down the gentle slope from the road into the field and parked it near our tent.

It was the middle days of autumn, sometimes windy, warm during the day and cool at night.

Each day, we swam in the river after breakfast and fished there in the afternoon. At night we made a fire in front of our tent and listened to my father's jokes and my mother's folktales, which sometimes frightened us. Some nights we just gazed at the sky, sparkling with millions of stars.

After all the bad things I had seen in Kabul, especially in the past couple of months, I felt like these were the best days of my life. I wanted to stay there forever, away from Kabul, away from the war. But then I would think about Grandfather and Wakeel, and wonder what they were doing while we were enjoying ourselves surrounded by such beautiful nature.

After a week, my father was ready to move on to Mazar, to my aunt's house. But we urged him to stay next to that river for one more week.

We continued our swimming and fishing. Sometimes we climbed in the mountains.

One morning after breakfast, the sky was very cloudy, and we stayed in our tent to study our schoolbooks, which we had brought. A gentle wind was blowing through our tent, occasionally turning the pages of my book. The wind was coming from the north. It grew stronger, and the sky got darker. Low clouds were bearing down on us.

My father gathered us in the corner of our tent. I wanted to go out and feel the wind blow against me, but he did not let me. "Stay here," he commanded in his I-am-the-father voice. The wind grew stronger by the minute. Then rain started falling, driven hard by the wind, and then harder and harder, and louder and louder. It was almost screaming, with lightning occasionally shrieking across the sky. We almost never had storms like this in Kabul. It was very exciting for me.

My father clutched my little sisters to his chest, as if the wind might take them away. My mother held on to my little brother so tightly that nothing in the world could separate them. My brother was crying most of the time because his teeth were starting to come in. We called him "the crying machine." We all had nicknames. Mine was "Dizzy," because sometimes for several minutes I would stare at nothing while I was thinking about something. When someone called me, I did not notice. I do not know what that had to do with being dizzy, but that is what they called me.

Now the rain beat our tent in waves. It was so loud that we could not hear one another speak. Lightning cracked again, each time getting much closer. The thunder was so close that it hurt our ears. This was no longer any fun. We were in the middle of nowhere under a makeshift tent.

The rain stopped as quickly as it had started, but the sky grew even darker, almost like a black night, though it was only midmorning.

Suddenly, the ground started shaking like a small earthquake. We heard huge crashing noises above us in the gorge that were louder than the wind. When we looked out from underneath our piece of blue plastic, we saw a massive stone bouncing down the side of the mountain behind us at a furious speed. My father yelled at us to get out of the tent. We all rushed out, not knowing where we were headed, and scattered in three directions.

I had escaped death twice in Kabul in the past year. Now it looked like I would be killed in this place that had seemed like paradise. I thought of Prophet Noah and the storm and the rain for forty days, and how he survived and saved others' lives. But he had no problem with stones roaring off a mountain and shaking the earth.

The stone rolled right through our tent. It smashed the center pole, snapping it like straw, and kept going down to the river. Our food and clothes were crushed into the ground. Not knowing what else to do, we went and sat in the car, still very frightened.

We were stunned. The stone could have rolled so many other places. My older sister said, "Maybe the stone did not like our tent." For the first time ever, I thought she was right.

Half an hour later, the sky was perfectly clear. The sun was a bright orange ball. The wind was fragrant. The birds started singing again. It seemed that nature thought nothing had ever happened, but we had lost our tent and everything we had in it.

We spent the rest of the day in our car. Before dark, my father and I walked around the area to see whether it was safe to spend another night there. He was carrying a heavy stick in his hand, and I was carrying a thin one. We had not seen any wolves or any other wild animals. But the evidence of the storm was all around us. We found a branch of a tree to use as a new center pole. It was not straight.

Night came. Through the many holes the rock had made in our tent, we could see clouds passing quickly in front of a half-moon. We ate smashed bread with squashed mulberries for dinner. The crying machine was quiet now, and his mouth was half-open as he slept next to my mother on the one pillow that only he had.

My father listened to the BBC World Service on the car radio. They were saying something about a fight in Mazar between two factions. When I asked my father what they meant, he told me things about a man named Dostum. I had seen Dostum on television, sitting on a tank with his trousers rolled up to his knees. But I had not paid much attention to who he was.

For seven more days we stayed there, a bit shaken, but not sure what to do next. In the mornings the sun was not so bright as when we first came. We could feel the seasons changing, as the days grew shorter and the nights longer and cooler.

After a week we heard from BBC World Service that Mazar was safe again. The fighting between factions there had ended, at least for now.

My father told my mother at breakfast that after lunch we would leave for Mazar. All this time we had been in Tashkurghan, we had been only one hour away from Mazar, had the pavement not been broken by the fighting. It had rained hard again during the night. We were all a little cold and damp. That made it easier to leave this place that we had come to love. Also, our supply of food was low. Breakfast did not take long to eat. All we had was some apples we had found on trees that had planted themselves near our camp. My father had caught some wild ducks by the river early that morning using long, sharpened sticks, but he had not had time to cook them yet. He had learned to hunt as a young man, when Kabul still had wetlands. He never let me go with him, though, because he said he needed total concentration, and the slightest noise would frighten the birds and we would go off hungry.

After breakfast I helped my father clean our car. My mother and my sisters were collecting our clothes in the tent. My father started to check the engine. There was no need for me to be with him; I let him do it by himself.

The rain had stopped now, and I went to see the river, which was about half a mile from our tent. I said goodbyes to all of the trees, stones, and birds that I had come to love. I felt as if the mountains were saying goodbye to me as well. We had all become good friends, except for the big stone that had rolled onto our tent. I did not go to him, though he was still nearby in the river.

But something was not right with the river. The water was gray and breaking in waves over the stones. Dust floated on its surface. The fish seemed unable to swim, as if they had been struck blind. Some of them were dead and were being carried away on the rising water.

I could not understand why the river was acting this way. I stood on the bank and let the water run over my toes. Very quickly it rose to my ankles, and then to my knees. I was beginning to feel a little afraid of the gray water. I wondered whether it was angry at us for leaving.

I picked up a fish that stared at me and wiggled only weakly. As I was holding it and saying my thanks to the river for all it had given us, the water suddenly climbed up to my thighs. It was very strong and nearly took me away with it. I scrambled up the bank and looked up the gorge between the two mountains. The water was climbing its walls and speeding in my direction.

Nothing could hold back that water. It was much bigger than the river. I could see that it ran wherever it wanted and washed away everything that stood in its way.

Would it reach our tent and our car? Would it take away my family, and I would never see them again? This river would never let such a thing happen to me. He knows me, I told myself.

I quickly climbed to the top of the riverbank and raced toward our tent, shouting at my father, "Get them out of the tent. A flood is coming!"

My heart was beating like that of a frightened deer, but I never stopped running or shouting. My father was in front of the tent, lighting a fire to cook the ducks that he had caught. He stood up, confused. The rain had stopped an hour ago. How could a flood be possible? he appeared to be asking himself.

I fell down several times. My clothes were muddy, but I kept running, gasping for breath and shouting at him to start the car. At last he saw the wall of water where the peaceful river had been. By the time I reached the car, everybody else was already in it.

The water was fifty feet behind me, rushing fast as if it were trying to knock me down. It made a terrifying roar as it pushed large stones and tree branches in front of it. The water was no longer gray, but almost black.

I was the last person to get into the car. As soon as I put my first foot inside, my father hit the accelerator. The tires spun in the muddy ground for a second. Then the car jerked forward and sped up the sloping field to the road as if it, too, were afraid of the oncoming flood.

Everybody except my father looked out the back window and saw the flood wash our tent away. It was like a nasty person using a bucket of water to destroy a kid's sand palace, like the ones we had built in the sand pile at Grandfather's house. The flood took all of our clothes and what remained of our food with it.

Before we could reach the road, the flood overtook us. First, it

covered the tires, then rose halfway to the windows. The engine began to sputter, and the car slowed down. My sisters and brother were
crying.

My father was in a panic and mumbling prayers under his breath.
My mother was saying, "Calm down . . . calm down . . . we will be all
right," but we did not know whom she was talking to. No one was
listening to her anyway.

Now the water was inside the car, almost up to our ankles. My
sisters were holding their feet up as the water came level with the seats.
The engine kept sputtering, but the car finally lurched onto the road.
When we reached a high spot, we opened the doors, and the dusty
water rushed out even faster than it had come in.

We got out and looked back at the field. It was all underwater now.

We had escaped from death once again, only to discover that we
had nowhere to go.

The announcer on the BBC World Service was saying, "A mis-
understanding between two commanders has resulted in a resump-
tion of hostilities in Mazar-e-Sharif this morning. The fighting resumed
shortly after one in the morning, with both sides reporting casualties.
Two children and an old man who were on their way home after
shopping were killed this morning." The announcer mentioned their
names, and asked their families to come to the hospital in Mazar to
collect their bodies.

Now we could not go to Mazar. But we no longer had a tent, or food.
My father drove half a mile toward the town, then parked the car
by the side of the road, where it widened. Everyone was stunned. My
father's face was white, as if there was no blood in it. My mother was
rocking the crying machine in her arms. The rest of us were silent, too
numb to say anything.

The sun began to disappear behind the mountains, and the moon
started to rise. The night air became cooler, and we were all hungry.
My parents had some money, but there was no shop where we could
buy anything.

My father left the car to say his evening prayers on the roadside.

We locked the door behind him. Whenever another vehicle approached us, I was afraid they might stop and kill us to steal our car. I was even afraid of the people who were riding donkeys when they ambled past. They looked frightening to me, even though they were normal people. They had not seen many cars, and they kept staring as they swayed by. I am sure that when they got home they talked about us.

When my father had finished praying, he winked at me from where he was sitting on some gravel. I said to my mother that I wanted to take a leak. She nodded, and I got out of the car. I peed, then I went to my father.

He put his hand on my right shoulder as we were walking away from our car toward several walled gardens at the edge of the town.

"Tonight you have to steal something. Can you do that for your father?" he asked me with his eyes wide open, looking for me to answer him. I stopped walking, but he kept going. I became a little afraid and ran to catch up with him.

"But you told me that stealing is a big sin, when I stole your money from your jacket pocket a few months ago. I told you I had made a mistake, and you said that kind of mistake can happen only once. If I repeat it, it becomes an unforgivable sin. Do you remember that, Father?" I asked, as he walked past one walled garden after another.

"Yes, I do remember. But sometimes you have to do something that is wrong to make things right," he went on in a steady voice. "If you steal some pomegranates, you will save your sisters and brother from hunger. You and I can sleep with empty stomachs for a night, but I'm worried for your mom. She doesn't have enough milk to feed your brother. She has to eat something," he said.

Then he stopped and pointed with his right hand to a large garden nearby and said, "You have to go over there very carefully. Nobody should see you. Be aware of your four sides, and fill this bag with pomegranates." He always carried a large cloth bag in his pocket for when he went to the bazaar, and now he gave it to me. "When you come back with pomegranates, tell your mother that you bought them from somebody who was selling them," he said.

I said "All right" and started walking toward the garden bravely.

But then I thought about it some more, and I felt very sad that my father picked me among all his children to be a thief.

I remembered Grandfather telling me, "Avoid three evils: lying, stealing, and gossiping." Even though Grandfather was not here, his words were there with me, and they were stronger than my father's. I walked back toward our car, but stopped when I saw my father walking slowly toward me.

"What is wrong? Why are you back with nothing?" he asked.

"Everyone will call me a thief!" I said.

"Who is everyone? You're doing this for your father! You know that. For me. I wouldn't call you a thief," he said.

"Why don't you ask one of my sisters? Is it because I have skills in stealing, because I stole your money one time in my life? Everyone called me a thief for weeks after." I felt like I was about to cry.

He sat down on the big round stone where we were standing. All around us were small white stones brought by floods years ago. He asked me to sit next to him.

"I respect your feelings, but you have to try to understand the situation. We cannot buy food for dinner, and we did not eat lunch. We do not have any place to go, and no one will receive us in their houses in this village. It is war, and everyone is afraid of others. The whole village is afraid of us, as we are afraid of them.

"It will take me at least a week to make the villagers my friends so they'll trust me. You go and steal pomegranates from that garden now, and somehow I'll make the owner my friend, and afterward we'll tell him everything about tonight. I'm sure he'll forgive us both. The reason I'm not doing this is because you're smart, and little. If they catch you, they won't kill you. But if they catch me, they'll think of me as someone dangerous. Do you get my point?" he asked.

I thought about all he said. I agreed that he was right about everything.

"All right!" I said. I walked toward the garden. I talked to Grandfather in my heart and told him that I was sorry to be doing the thing that he told me strictly to avoid. I also told him that I was doing this for my father, and he was the one who should be blamed, not me.

When I was next to the wall, I sneaked into the garden very carefully, like I had seen heroes do in movies. Maybe somebody would make a film about my stealing. That made it seem a little funny.

When the wind blew, it moved the leaves of the trees and made them sound like someone's steps. I watched my four sides as I was told. I saw nothing but trees with big pomegranates hanging from thin branches, nearly breaking them. I picked five huge pomegranates that made my bag full and heavy.

It is not enough, I thought. But there was no more space in the bag for even a small one. If I take this to my father, he will fuss about that. "Why did you not pick small ones?" he would ask. But then I thought that I am not paying money for these; nobody should ever complain over something that cost nothing.

First, I tossed the bag over the wall. I was just starting to climb the wall to jump out when I heard dogs barking, very close. I thought the dogs were outside the garden and that they had seen my bag and were fighting over it.

I waited to hear better where the sound was coming from. Suddenly, I saw two big dogs running very fast toward me. They were inside the garden. From the light of the moon shining through the trees, I could see their muscles straining as they ran.

I froze in place. My mind was not signaling me what to do next. I thought for a moment and asked myself, "Should I stand here and let the dogs tear me into pieces for my stealing, for the sin I just committed?" I thought that Grandfather was punishing me. But Grandfather always told me, "Never be afraid of anything; let others be afraid of you." I knew I had to escape even though they were bigger than any other dogs I had ever seen, even bigger than the ones in the garden of Haji Noor Sher in Kabul. Water was running from their mouths as they barked. Their eyes were so red, they looked like they were filled with blood. I tried to be courageous.

They had now reached me and were close enough that I could have petted them, but they were not those kinds of dogs. I felt a wave of fear. The instant they saw that, they snapped at me. Their teeth were long and sharp. But I got my courage back and continued staring in their eyes, stiff like a sculpture. They stepped back. Each of them seemed twice as big as me.

Someone called to them from the other end of the garden, an old man's voice. One of the dogs turned halfway toward the voice, then he came back and barked at me a few more times before running off. The other one bared his sharp teeth, but held back. The old man was still calling and whistling.

Someone started throwing stones into the far side of the garden, making the trees rustle. The dog stopped barking at me and looked at the trees instead. The stones were big. It was definitely not a kid throwing them. The dog ran to find out what was dropping from the sky.

I heard my father's voice whispering urgently from behind the garden wall for me to climb out.

I pulled myself up on the wall and was halfway over when the dog lunged and bit my leg. I could almost feel which of his teeth were tearing into my flesh. My father saw my face and guessed what had happened.

"Don't shout! Be brave!" my father said hoarsely.

He thrust his hand up to me and pulled me toward him. The rough mud-brick wall scraped my stomach. The dog let go and started barking again.

I jumped down from the wall and landed on the leg that had been bitten. I started to shriek in pain. My father put his hand over my mouth.

My leg was bleeding. I could not see how badly I was hurt. My father tore his prayer bandanna that he always carried on his shoulder and tied it tightly around the wound. The dog on the other side of the wall was going crazy.

I wanted to look at the injury, but my father did not let me see it.

"It is nothing; it is just a small scratch. You'll be fine," my father said.

I did not believe him. There was fear in his voice. I never heard my father speak with a shaky voice like that. I kept walking like a cripple with all my weight on my right leg. The skin on my stomach felt like it had been scraped off.

I made it back to the car and climbed into the front seat. My mother was in the backseat, tapping my little brother's back and singing a lullaby to make him sleep.

She did not notice my leg, but she could see the fatigue on my face. She stopped singing and gave my little brother to my older sister, who had snuggled next to her. "Are you all right? You look like hell!"

I said nothing. She looked at my father, who was standing outside. He said nothing. "I'm fine," I told her. "We were just attacked by some dogs, and one of them bit my left leg, and it hurts a little."

"What dogs? We didn't hear any dogs," she said.

"Because your windows were all rolled up," I answered, trying not to let the pain be heard in my voice.

"Let me see it," she said quietly. I turned around to show her. She looked at my wound, shook her head, and started to clean it with a handkerchief. It was still bleeding and dripped into my mother's lap.

She rolled down the window all the way to the bottom and shouted at my father, "Why have you let such a thing happen? Did you just let the dog chew his leg while you watched?"

My father was quiet. My little brother woke up and my mother shouted at my older sister to take the crying machine out of the car.

She asked my father for a bottle of water from the trunk, washed my wound, and put some alcohol on it, which stung. Then she sat next to me in the driver's seat while my father was out walking up and down the road, holding my little brother and breathing the fresh cool air.

"You didn't buy those pomegranates, did you? I know there is no shop anywhere nearby." She was looking into my eyes very intently. "Tell me what happened, and don't make me ask you twice, and don't disappoint me with your lies," she said sternly.

Her eyes were fixed on my mouth until I finished.

"I'm afraid to let you out of my sight till we get home. Don't do anything like this again," she said, then she hugged me.

"Okay!" I said. I wanted to cry. I remembered being in our courtyard, helping Grandfather weeding, eating on one long tablecloth, making jokes with my cousins and aunts and watching TV together.

Those things seemed so far away. I sighed several times to ease the pain.

"What is the matter, Qais?" my mother asked. She was holding my head against her chest and rubbing my back. I could not force words out. There was a faint ringing in my ears, and I wanted a place to hide.

"Is it still hurting?" she said.

"Yes, Mother," I said.

"Or is there something else that you haven't told me yet?" she said.

"No, there is nothing. It just hurts and it is itching, and I'm very tired," I said.

"Okay, then sleep as long as you want." She tapped me on the back as if I were a baby. I fell asleep in her arms. But I knew that I was a thief, and that my sin was unforgivable.

8

❖

The Garden of Hamza's Father

I woke up and was alone in the car. My parents, sisters, and brother were seated out on the ground having breakfast. They had cheese, butter, milk, yogurt, homemade jam, hot *naan*, and fresh tea. I rubbed my eyes to make sure I was not dreaming, but it was real. Everybody's mouth was full. My stomach was floating from hunger. I opened the door to join them. When I put my left foot on the ground, the pain was so sharp I felt as if a hot knife were ripping through me. My father came and helped me. I did not ask where all the food came from. I was just happy to be seeing butter, jam, and milk after two weeks.

"A villager invited us to his house," my mother said.

"A villager? Who is he?" I asked.

"Oh, I think you know him," she said.

"I know him? How?"

"Because last night you heard his voice calling his dogs," she said.

I froze with fear and shame. "The man in the garden where I stole pomegranates?" I asked. My sisters looked at me sharply. They all said in one voice, "You stole pomegranates? You are a thief?" Then they started softly hissing, "Thief, thief, thief."

"Not again!" I said.

"Shut up, girls! He did it for me. I told him to do it. If anyone says the word 'thief,' she will be spanked!" my father said.

"His son knocked on my window this morning," my mother said, "while we were asleep in the car. He already had set this cloth here with all these things. He said that his father thought that we were modern nomads with our car."

We all laughed at "modern nomads."

"Do they know that I stole pomegranates from their garden last night?" I said.

"Yes, his son saw you," she said.

"They will call me a thief," I said. I felt shame rising in me.

"I don't think a host calls his guest a thief," she said.

"He may call you Mr. Thief," my old sister said, and my other sisters hid their faces as they laughed, too. I sighed as I sat down to eat.

After we had finished, a boy my age crossed the road and said hello to us. Then he started collecting the dishes, stacking one plate on top of another. When he stood up, he invited us to go with him.

"My family is waiting for you," he said very warmly.

The boy led us to the garden of the pomegranate trees and opened the gate. The garden was very large. It had two small one-story houses, one built along the northern wall, the second along the southern wall. There was a long tent in the middle made from some simple black cloth that was stretched over some poles and staked to the ground to make a place of shade. An old man appeared from one of the buildings and came toward us. He shook hands with my father. He greeted my mother and gave *salaam*s to us. Then he asked me what was wrong with my leg.

"Your dog was hungry last night, so I let him have a chew on my leg," I said, trying to make a joke to cover my shame.

He laughed and replied, "You should have knocked on my door. I would have given you more than five pomegranates."

My father said to the old man, "It was my fault; I was afraid that no one would welcome us in this village, especially in the night. Since the fighting started, everyone is afraid of everyone else."

"That is true, but now I know you, and we're not strangers anymore. We are a family," the old man said.

The dogs started barking. I jumped, but I could not see them.

The old man continued, "You are welcome to stay in my house for as long as you want. Those rooms over there are for guests." He pointed to those along the south wall of the garden. "You have water, electricity, TV, and radio. I will send you some blankets. There are mattresses and pillows in the rooms already. If you want to eat with us, you're most welcome."

"You are very generous," my mother said. "But we cannot be bothering your family with unexpected guests." She smiled, and the old man smiled, too.

"Yes, you are right! You are unexpected guests, but unexpected guests are gifts from God. Our door is always open to them; they bring the charity of God with them," the old man said. "I'll send you some dishes, and you can cook your own food. Please use any of the herbs, vegetables, and fruits of this garden."

"You are very kind," my father said.

"This garden is not mine, it is God's," the old man replied. "He gave it to me for use by those who need it for as long as they want. In fact, He is the owner of everything, and whatever He gives us, it is with us for only a few days."

His family came to greet us. He had four daughters and three sons. Among them was a woman who was much younger than he, almost the same age as his oldest daughter, and very pretty.

"Is she your wife?" my mother asked.

"Yes, she is my second wife. We married five years ago," the old man said. His wife was very shy. She invited us to her house at the far end of the garden, and we followed her as my father began discussing politics with the old man and his sons. A few minutes later, he joined us and whispered to my mother that our host was a great man.

Later, after we had had our first hot baths since leaving Kabul, we ate a magnificent lunch with them in an area shaded by almond trees. It seemed as if we had known one another for years. The old man told us to call him uncle and call his wife aunty. We talked about our lives. My father told them how he and Grandfather had lost their six thousand carpets, and now he had nothing except his family and a car.

"God gave them to you, and He took them back," the old man said.

"I'm a boxer. I can beat any man. Afghanistan has sent me to Russia and all those Central Asian places for matches. But how do I fight against madness like this?" my father said with a heavy sigh; I could tell he was thinking about his boxing victories in Tajikistan, Uzbekistan, and Turkmenistan.

"The good times and bad times are both the same, like spring and autumn of life. Neither of them last forever." The old man had a gentle smile on his face, but when he talked he was a very serious man. "The problem for our country is where we are located and the neighbors we have. Our stupid politicians let them interfere in our affairs."

After lunch he showed us the guest rooms. When we passed the tent in the middle of the garden, the two big dogs jumped out of it and frightened us. My little sisters hid behind my mother. Strong chains were fastened to thick collars around their necks, but they were jumping with so much force, I was afraid they would break free.

"These dogs are good for security, especially during the night. They will tear anyone apart who tries to get in this property," the old man said.

"Do they have names?" my father asked.

"Yes, the white one is Shir [Lion], and the gray one is Palang [Tiger]. Shir doesn't harm anyone unless someone attacks him or tries to hurt him. He is a fighting dog and has never lost a game. But Palang is very cruel; he likes to wound people."

"Palang bit my leg," I said.

"Don't worry, my son; he'll be your best friend soon," the old man said, then he called one of his sons to bring him the leftovers from lunch. He gave them to me to feed them to the dogs. I threw the leftovers to them. First they tried to leap at me, but soon they were busy eating.

The guest rooms were nicely painted. A beautiful red carpet with big motifs lay in the middle of the largest room, and mattresses stretched along all the walls; they were covered with long, narrow carpets. A small TV with a video player was in the corner.

"Perhaps you'll let my eldest son take your kids out and show them around," the old man suggested. We heard a big engine start with a roar behind us. His son, who was about Wakeel's age, was seated on a large tractor and invited us to get on it with him.

"How is my airplane? It makes a lot of noise, doesn't it?" he said as we climbed up to the platform behind the seat, and he put his foot on the gas.

"Yes, and it has bigger tires than other airplanes," I said.

"Do you like this place?" He shouted into my ear over the big noise of the engine.

"I don't know yet. You have to show me around, then I can tell," I said as we drove out of the garden onto the main road.

The sky was churning with dark and white clouds. The sun was lost among them and seemed ready to drop like a stone. The wind ruffled the surface of the wheat fields.

On both sides of the road as far as I could see, the fields were yellow and ready for harvest. The farmers were working with their scythes, holding a bunch of wheat stalks in one hand and cutting them with a smooth sweep of the other. Others were collecting pomegranates and almonds in sacks that drooped behind them on their backs. Their hands moved deftly through the branches.

I asked the old man's son whether he had ever traveled out of his village.

"No, and I don't want to. I love my village. I can find all that I need here. People respect my father, and me because I'm his oldest son," he said.

He pulled over and told his sister to take my sisters to the riverside, where she could introduce them to the other village girls. This was a branch of the same river along which we had camped, but there was no sign of the flood that had nearly carried us all away only a day earlier.

"All the girls from the village go there every day in the afternoon to fetch water for dinner. The village boys meet at the mosque," the old man's son said.

"Can we go to the river, too?" I asked. "I want to go swimming."

He laughed. "Don't ever try to go to the riverside at this time of day. If you are seen, someone will shoot you. Sometimes the girls take baths there."

"Are the girls carrying guns?" I asked.

"No, no. One of their fathers or brothers will shoot you."

"You have snipers here, like in Kabul?"

"No, but we have hunters, and they are everywhere. If one of them sees any boy or man going to the riverside at this time of the day, he will shoot."

"What about strangers? They don't know this rule," I said.

"You're not a stranger anymore. My father already announced in the mosque this morning that he wanted to host you guys for as long as you want to stay."

"You mean, all the villagers know about what I did last night?" I asked with a renewed sense of shame rolling over me.

"That is why all the villagers agreed to let us help you. They said that you guys had nothing to eat and nowhere to go," the old man's son said.

"They will call me a thief," I said despondently.

"No! They are not so stupid and rude to call their guest a thief." My mother had said the same thing. I was very relieved to hear this.

He showed me his hunting place nearby. He had some wooden ducks in a pool of water he had dug where the land began its rise to become a mountain. A narrow stream of water flowed down from the mountain's springs into the pool. Each time the wind rippled the surface, the wooden ducks bobbed as if they were real.

"When the birds are crossing over our village, they see my wooden ducks and think it is safe to land. When they land here to play or drink water, I catch them. I will teach you how to shoot," he promised.

"Have you ever seen Kabul?" I asked.

"No, I don't want to. It is a horrible place. Every trouble starts from there, and it spreads all over Afghanistan. I wish Kabul did not exist. I belong here. Everything that makes me happy is here."

He started reciting an old poem:

"'There is no room left in my heart for anything but the beautiful faces of my village girls. You have to know, how you will see her face with the light of the sun and the moon reflecting in her eyes. Wait and hope with all your vain fancies and dreams to see her face on a cloudy dark night.'"

He stopped and smiled at me. "I'm talking about my girlfriend. I'll show her to you, but you must promise not to fall in love with her, because she is mine. Okay?"

"Yeah, all right!" I said.

"If her beauty enslaves the heart of any man, I'll tear out that heart," he said with a suddenly serious, almost harsh voice, despite his poetic words. "Be careful, okay?" he said. I nodded my head, but I was a little afraid of him now.

We got off the tractor and walked for ten minutes without talking. He took me to the end of the village, where a very large courtyard with a garden stretched as far as I could see along the base of the low mountains that rise up behind Tashkurghan.

"That is her house," he said. His voice was soft now, and I relaxed. "We really love each other, but nobody knows, except for my mother. Please don't say anything about it to anybody."

"I can keep a secret," I said.

"Now, I'll make you my reason to get into the house to see her," he said. He sounded excited.

"How?" I said.

"I'll knock on the door. She or her brother will open it, and I'll introduce you as my guest. I'll say that you would like to see the garden. If she opens the door, she will know everything, but her parents won't. Your job is to tell them that you are my cousin, and you came from Kabul to visit us, and you would like to see the garden. The rest of the talking is up to me. Do you understand everything?"

"Yes," I said. This was an adventure, and I was enjoying it.

He knocked on the door, and a young girl opened it. She was a real beauty.

She instantly lowered her eyes and hurriedly said *"Salaam."*

"I dreamed about you last night, and now I'm here to kiss you," the old man's son teasingly said.

"Get out of sight! My parents are at home, and my brothers are watering the flowers in the courtyard," she said in a panicky voice.

"Today I'll ask your parents for your hand. I'll ask them to make you my bride and sharer of my life," the old man's son said sweetly, with a smile as gentle as his father's.

"Don't make a fool of yourself. My brothers will beat you to death if they hear this. Go away before someone sees you," she whispered, and looked behind her.

One of her brothers suddenly appeared behind her like a mushroom after the rain.

"Who is it?" he asked.

"Oh, it is me," the son said. "This is my guest, Qais. I mean, my cousin. He came from Kabul with his family. I was showing him around, and he asked me if it was possible to see this garden. I told him it is my father's friend's garden. So, if you don't mind, I want to show him inside."

The brother welcomed us in.

"Sarah, show them around, and make them some pomegranate juice," he said to his sister. "You guys feel at home. I have some work to finish. We'll talk later."

Sarah took us to the garden. I could see almost every kind of fruit tree there is, with ripe fruit hanging from the branches. When we got to the end of the garden, Sarah turned to me and said, "If you don't mind, we want to talk in private for a few minutes. You just walk around, and eat whatever you like. Meet us here in ten minutes. Is that all right with you?"

"Sure, it's not a problem," I said. She gave me a grateful smile.

I walked all around for almost half an hour, until I got tired of being alone. I snuck behind a tree to see what kind of private talks they were having that were lasting so long.

But not a word was being spoken. They were just sitting face-to-face. The old man's son was looking right into the girl's eyes, and she was beaming at him. When he broke the silence, he spoke in a strange, poetic way.

"Do not forsake me," he beseeched her. Maybe he was making a joke. But the girl did not laugh.

"How could I forsake you?" she replied tenderly. "For you are all my life."

"You are mine, for I love you and must die if you forsake me," he said.

"I feel the same for you," she replied.

Do all the men in this village talk like that to their girlfriends? I wondered. Maybe they had seen too many Afghan movies where both lovers die before they get to see each other a second time. I eased out of my hiding place and ate another pomegranate.

An hour later we were ready to leave the garden.

"You can come anytime you want," Sarah said to me. "Next time, introduce me to your sisters. I want to meet them. Hamza will drive you here." It was the first time our eyes met. I felt warm inside, but nobody else saw it. I felt guilty, because I had promised not to fall in love, but what could I do? It was not up to me. It was up to my heart, and the heart cannot be controlled when it comes to love. I knew this from the Indian movies.

"Who is Hamza?" I asked her.

"I am Hamza," the old man's son said.

"Oh, I am sorry. I never asked your name. It is good to know your name," I said.

Sarah looked at both of us as she was standing at the threshold of the garden gate and holding the doorknob. "I thought you two were cousins," she said sharply, and waited for a reply.

"Yes, that is right. He is my cousin, but he didn't know my name. I think he never asked," the old man's son said.

"Hamza, what is going on? Is he your cousin, or someone you don't know? My brother will talk about it in the mosque tonight. If they find out that you lied to them, it will be dangerous for both of us," she said with great worry.

"Oh, relax, relax. It is not a problem. He is my cousin, I mean my guest. He will explain everything to you the next time he and I come. Sometimes cousins forget their cousin's name," Hamza teasingly said.

"Tell me one thing. Is he your cousin or guest?" she asked.

"The truth is, we didn't know each other until this morning. He is my guest."

She looked at him angrily. Someone called her from inside; it was an old woman's voice, probably her mother.

"Do you trust me?" Hamza asked.

"Yes, I trust you," she said with forgiveness edged with concern. The calling became louder, and she shouted back that she was coming.

"This is not a problem for us. You just have to relax. Everybody in the mosque knows him and his family. They are our guests, and they'll be with us for a few weeks at least. And I call him cousin. We are a family now," Hamza said.

"I trust you," she said with a beautiful smile, and closed the door after us as we left.

We spent three weeks in the garden of Hamza's father while we waited to hear that the road to Mazar was safe. The dogs did indeed become my friends. I took them for walks to the mountains and wished that Wakeel were there to go with us. I showed Palang the sign of the wounds that he had given me. He did not know what I was talking about, and he licked them.

Hamza taught me how to hunt. Every other day we went to his beloved's garden. She always had pomegranate juice waiting for me, and while I drank it, they had their private talks. The first day it was for a short while, but after a week it seemed like hours. One day I sneaked behind a tree again. They were not having those stupid movie dialogues that day. It was more interesting than that. I felt guilty, and never watched them again. I walked all around until Hamza called me to go home.

My family was happy, too. My mother sang old Indian songs when she cooked. Everything came from the garden and tasted better than anything we had eaten since we had fled Grandfather's house. In the mornings, my job was to take two straw baskets into the garden and fill them with tomatoes, cucumbers, squash, eggplant, peppers, pomegranates, apples, walnuts, and almonds, and then give them to my mother. Some days I could hardly carry the baskets by the time they were filled, we had so much to choose from.

My older sister became very busy, helping my mother with all the cooking. They spent many hours together talking about things. Other times, she asked my father to climb the mountains and see the view. My father was always happy to take her and our next sister on long walks in the fresh air. He loved the exercise and their company.

When my mother took her nap in the afternoon while my little brother was sleeping, my older sister took my younger sisters to the river to get drinking water with Hamza's sisters. They learned from the village girls how to carry a clay water pot on their heads without holding it with their hands, or at other times how to embroider hats. My older sister told them stories about life in Kabul, and what it was like to go to school. None of Hamza's sisters had ever been to school, though they knew how to read.

Since I had never seen my older sister act so pleasantly before, I decided to be nice to her. But when it came to me, she had not changed. She always found some way of making fun of me. She and I were supposed to eat from one plate. Afghans believe that sharing a plate improves the appetite. She would say things like, "He finishes everything on the plate before I take three bites. And he makes noises while he eats, like a cow." I stopped being nice to her.

Late one afternoon after hunting ducks, Hamza and I climbed up to the highest mountain to look down on the whole village. The sun was setting in the west. There were no clouds, just the gold of the sun and the deep blue of the sky.

"Have you ever talked to nature?" Hamza said.

"Sometimes," I said.

"Do you hear when it talks back to you?"

"What do you mean?" I asked.

"Nobody knows what I mean. Anytime I tell anyone what I can see and hear, they think I'm crazy. But you have to know that everything talks to you if you are very honest with them," Hamza said.

"You mean like mountains, and trees, and rivers, and the wind, and things like that?" I asked.

He nodded. "And to learn how to be honest, you have to start thinking about who the architect of the skies and earth is." Hamza was quiet for a moment. "When you build a building, you have to put pillars and walls to hold up the roof. But the sky has no pillars or walls. Only God can make architecture like that."

"Does God talk to you?" I asked, very surprised.

"No, He talks to us through his creatures," Hamza said.

"How?" I asked.

"The moon floats in a dark blue space, and shames billions of stars by its light. She has things to tell you; in fact she is talking to you," Hamza said, then we looked at the moon, which was just rising behind us. He had a funny way of speaking poetically, even when he was not with Sarah. At first I had found this strange. But after a couple of weeks I was beginning to enjoy it. The moon was perfectly round, and as the last of the daylight faded, it spread its softening glow across the land so we could see the whole village below.

"How did you learn all these things?" I asked.

"Open your eyes and ears, and you can learn anything you want," he said in his sweet voice. "The rose has given its power away to its thorns for its protection. But the nightingales never give their voices to crows. The moth flies around a candle until it burns its wings. But a deer runs away from hunters as far as it can."

"You are a poet," I said.

"No, I have eyes that are open, and I use them well," he said.

The wind started blowing. A few small clouds edged over the horizon, and the moon took control of the sky. We carefully climbed down.

I opened the garden gate. The dogs jumped playfully at me as I was thinking about what Hamza had told me. What he said has stayed with me from then until now. He made me think about things I had never thought much about before, like how God had created the stars, moon, sun, sky, the universe, and all of nature, and for what reason, why we are here, what is our mission in life, and how one can take pleasure from all these things we have been given.

That night, our families ate dinner together. Afterward, when my father and Hamza's went to listen to the BBC World Service, we heard that the fighting in Mazar was coming toward Tashkurghan.

My father made his decision right away. He said to the old man,

"It sounds as if we must leave Tashkurghan tomorrow morning." Hamza's father nodded.

My father had been going to mosque early in the morning with the other village men to say their morning prayers together. After prayers the next day, he shared what he had heard the previous night from the BBC. Then, in the way that Afghan people always do when they must leave the company of those who have welcomed them, he asked their permission to go.

When he came back from the mosque, we were having breakfast. He sat down and took a cup of tea from my mother, then told us, "We cannot now go to Mazar. I don't think it is safe to go back to Kabul. So we will head for Bamyan. We have heard no reports of fighting there, and I believe that we will be safe there. I have received the mullah's and the village men's permission to leave here today. They say that they will leave their homes, too. The war will reach this place in two days, maybe sooner. As soon as we finish eating, we will pack," my father said.

My older sister looked at him and said, "But, Father, Bamyan is in the middle of Afghanistan. We are supposed to be going to another country where there is no war."

My father looked at her and said very kindly, "We will. But not today."

After breakfast we went to the old man's house on the other side of the garden to say goodbye and to thank them. The old man was again listening to the BBC; his sons were playing chess; his wife and daughters were embroidering a tablecloth together. Each daughter had a corner in her hand.

Hamza's father rose and embraced my father. "This is your home, and its doors are always open to you." Then his sons hugged my father and me, and his wife and daughters hugged my mother and sisters.

"Are you staying or leaving?" my father asked.

"I think we are leaving as well," Hamza's father said. "We will go to Pakistan, to my brother's home; he has been living there for ten years. I received his letter yesterday. He is very worried. He wants to send Hamza to America to live with his son."

"What about your garden? Will you leave it just like this?" my father said.

"Yes, I cannot do anything about it. We all know that these holy warriors don't fight to drive out foreign troops from our country. They fight to loot us. This factional fighting is just an excuse to steal from us, and even to steal our wives and daughters."

"Alas, alas," said my father, nodding his head.

His wife wrapped two fried chickens in newspaper and put some fresh beans in a pot, along with two pumpkins, some potatoes, and a few cabbages in bags. My mother did not want to take them, but the woman kept insisting. Finally, my mother accepted the food and thanked them for their hospitality and all their help.

Just as we started to drive off, Hamza's father ran toward our car with a big bag on his shoulders. He stood in front of our car, panting. He winked at me to come out. He gave me the big bag and asked me to lift it. I tried but I could not. It was very heavy.

"Can you eat them all?" he asked me.

"What is it?" I said.

"Pomegranates!" Hamza's father said.

He was smiling, but I felt very small. "No, I can't eat them all," I said with a renewed sense of shame that not even the kindness of the old man could dismiss.

"I'm sure you can, and I know you'll share them with others. Remember me and my dogs when you eat these pomegranates. That is all I want," Hamza's father said. I felt a little bit better when he bent over and kissed me on my forehead.

He helped me put the bag into the trunk and waved us off toward Bamyan.

The town's mullah was standing on the roadside and signaled for us to stop. My father halted in front of him and rolled down his window. After greeting the mullah, he introduced him to us.

The mullah wore a white *shalwar kamiz* and a long green-and-blue-striped *chapan* coat on top of it. He had a black turban, and the rims of his eyes were darkened with kohl, as men do who are religious. His mustache was shaved, but his beard was long, almost to his belly. When he talked, his beard waved, though he was a calm talker.

He gave my father a *tasbeh*, a string of prayer beads, and said, "I can't give you more than this. I should have invited you to my house so we could eat together, but I didn't know that the war would come here and separate us."

"Your *tasbeh* will always remind me of you and God," my father told him. "If God is willing, one day we will see each other again, and we'll talk about these days."

"I'm waiting for that day, if not in this world, maybe in the next one," the mullah said.

"Are you staying or leaving?" my father asked.

"I'm staying here. You know I can escape from my country, but I can't escape from my death. I'm breathing the last days of my life anyway. I'm seventy-five years old. If death comes tomorrow to me, I'm happy to welcome it. There is no difference between today and tomorrow," the mullah said.

"You are a brave man," my father said.

"I wouldn't call it bravery. Death is part of life, and whoever takes it earlier, he or she will be at the head of the caravan for the next world. Either today or tomorrow we will join that caravan, so why not sooner rather than later?" the mullah said.

"Let me tell you something," he added, "a story of Mullah Nasruddin:

"Mullah Nasruddin was awakened in the middle of the night by the cries of two men quarreling in front of his house. Nasruddin waited, but they continued to argue. He was unable to sleep. He wrapped his quilt tightly around his shoulders and rushed outside to separate the men, who had come to blows. But when he tried to reason with them, one of them snatched the quilt off Mullah Nasruddin's shoulders, and then both men ran away. Mullah Nasruddin, very weary and perplexed, went inside.

"'What was the quarrel about?' his wife asked him.

"'It must be about our quilt,' replied the mullah. 'The quilt is gone, the dispute is over.'

"You see what I mean? Our country has become a Mullah Nasruddin story. This war is all about what we have in this country, not about you or me. Once they get what they want, then they won't care about anything else," the mullah said. "Almighty God protect you and your family from all dangers."

They hugged, and my father got back in the car and began driving quickly toward Bamyan before the mullah could tell another story, or anyone else showed up.

9

❖

Inside the Head of Buddha

The Kuchi nomads follow their goats, sheep, and camels through the mountains in search of new pastures. They never settle anywhere for long. Though my grandmother was born a Kuchi and my grandfather had come from herders who spent long seasons in the mountains with their flocks, my family and I did not think of ourselves as nomads. Yet we were enjoying our new life on hillsides, in the gardens of strangers, a few days here and a few days there, never in the same place for long. I knew we were looking for a quiet place to hide from the rockets while we found a way to leave Afghanistan. But despite rockslides, floods, and biting dogs, we had found a way of pushing the everyday threat of war from our minds as we thought about where we were going next, or where we had just been.

Bamyan is at the very center of Afghanistan, high in the mountains. We had to go back across the Hindu Kush to get there, but this time we took an unpaved road through a mountain pass to avoid any fighting along the main road. It took fifteen hours of slow, rough driving over deeply rutted roads to reach the Bamyan Valley. It had been an endless day; our bodies were longing for rest. It was well after dark when we were finally on a better road approaching the town.

The car jerked to a halt, waking those of us who were falling asleep. A blue plastic rope was stretched across the road between two wooden poles. It was called the Bamyan Door. It did not look like a door to me.

A man rushed from a mud house next to one of the wooden poles. He had a Kalashnikov hanging from his shoulder. He asked my father where we were going. My father explained that we were heading to Bamyan City. The man said we were not allowed to go in this late at night, and we must park somewhere along the river and come back tomorrow.

My father did not try to argue; the man had a gun. He drove back in the direction from which we had come for a few hundred yards, and parked the car on a level spot next to the river. My mother gave us some of the food that Hamza's family had shared with us.

It was a beautiful night, but much cooler than in Tashkurghan. In the crisp air, the sky was like a dark piece of silk studded with tiny diamonds. The silence was dense, with only the quiet sound of the river and the twittering of some night birds to challenge it. We squeezed ourselves into the car's seats to stay close together and keep warm as we slept. Though it was crowded, I felt as if I were on a soft bed after the hours of bumpy roads.

We set out a picnic breakfast along the river the next morning and took our time over it. After all, we were nomads now; we moved when we wanted to. When we finished eating and had packed everything back into our car, we headed once more to Bamyan City. The guy who had stopped us the night before at the "door" was sitting in front of the mud house with his friends. They all had Kalashnikovs hanging from their shoulders.

They stopped us again and my father explained that we were refugees from Kabul, looking for a safe place to live for a while. They silently searched our luggage piece by piece, though there was not much, then to our relief lowered the blue plastic rope and let us drive through.

My father slowly drove toward the main Bamyan bazaar. The town was small and filled with the smell of wood fires and horse manure mixed with saffron, pepper, cardamon, and dust.

He pulled into a car *serai*, an enclosed parking area. We walked up and down Bamyan's one main street for a while. It was full of donkeys, goats, and people dressed very poorly. Then we went to a *chai khana*, a teahouse, for lunch. We climbed a bamboo ladder to the second floor, though a few of the rungs were missing. My father went first, with my mother and my baby brother behind him. My little sisters had a hard time climbing up. I had to help them, since I had been appointed to look after them. Another bamboo ladder led up to the third and fourth floors. There were no proper stairs.

The *chai khana* was a large room filled with kebab smoke. A tiny TV was in the corner of the room; I could hardly see it through the smoke. The men were sitting cross-legged on platforms two feet high, their shoes left behind on the floor. The plates in front of them, whether filled with food or only scraps, were alive with flies. Some of the men were eating, some were drinking tea while watching an Indian movie, and some were snoring while hundreds of flies had parties on their hands and feet and around their mouths.

My mother was the only woman there, and my sisters the only girls. The men who had been chewing kebab stopped chewing. Their mouths hung half-open as they stared. The ones who had been drinking tea and watching TV put their glasses on the floor and turned where they sat to get a better view of us. My mother pulled her headscarf forward an inch and pretended she was there alone with my father and her children.

All the men's faces were furrowed like plowed earth. Deep wrinkles cut into the corners of their Asiatic eyes and along their foreheads. They watched us for the most part in silence, and when they did speak they whispered.

All of them were Hazaras. I remembered Grandfather having told me that most of the Hazaras lived in central Afghanistan. He said that when he was still traveling with his uncles, driving their flocks to Bamyan to find high mountain pastures that stayed lush all summer from the last of the melting snow, they had been treated very warmly by the Hazara people there. Though they were not Kuchi nomads like my grandmother's family, who traveled in regular routes around the country, my grandfather's people also were herders, who left their home with their flocks each summer to search for pastures. Often, they had spent summers in the green Bamyan Valley, which was only a week's walk from their village in Maidan.

They traded some of their sheep, goats, or cows with the Hazaras in return for grazing rights and a place to set up their tents for a couple of months. I hoped the Hazaras would treat us well, too, even though we did not have any animals to trade with them, and we were not real nomads anymore but modern nomads in a beat-up old car.

Berar used to tell me good stories about Bamyan, where he was born. When he worked for our family, he used to leave all his money with Grandfather. After several months he would ask for it, and then send it all home to his parents. Grandfather always made jokes with him, telling him to spend some money on women while he was a young man.

Berar used to say, "If you build a house, a lot of people can use it, but a woman can be used only by a husband. A house is more efficient than a wife."

I looked through the smoke in that *chai khana* to see whether he was among those men, but he was not. I was disappointed. Since that morning on the roof of the silo, I had never seen or heard of him again.

We ordered kebab, which is about the only lunch you can get, not just in Bamyan but in restaurants all over Afghanistan. On the wall was a photograph of the two enormous Buddha statues that had been carved into the cliffs at Bamyan almost two thousand years before. They looked very strange to me. They did not have faces.

After we had finished eating, my father suggested that we go see the Buddhas and their caves cut out of the cliffs behind them. They were just a short walk from the *chai khana*. We climbed down the bamboo ladder, with me passing first my hesitant younger sister to my father and then a very happy crying machine who kept smiling and pointing at all the donkeys. There were no cars on the road, so my sisters and I could run ahead of my parents, shrieking as we went, feeling free and lighthearted in a way we had not been for a couple of years.

As we approached the smaller Buddha, though, we all became

very quiet. He towered over us, and I found myself holding my breath. I had seen a photo of him in my schoolbook, but there he looked as flat as the page. Here, I felt that Buddha could walk right out of the mountain. How could a statue be so tall? I asked myself.

I had never seen a statue before, not even a small one. In Islam, statues are *haram*, forbidden, and have been since the time of the second law of the Prophet Musa, or Moses. Only God can make a living creature and breathe life into it, we are taught, and men should not make statues and try to be like God. Nothing had prepared me for the sense of awe that filled me.

Grandfather once told me that he had climbed to the top of the statues with his stepfather. The statues had been carved from the soft stone of the cliffs, their backs merging with the hill. He had told me about all the caves in the cliffs behind the Buddhas, and of all the paintings on their walls. He said that Bamyan had once been a place filled with holy men.

"Buddha lived six hundred years before Prophet Issa [Jesus]. And Prophet Mohammad, peace be upon him, came six hundred and thirty years after Prophet Issa. If you learn about Christianity and Buddhism, you will value Islam even more than you already do."

My father found the opening to the stairs that led to the top of the smaller Buddha. I had never seen stairs like those before. They were cut from the stone right inside the cliff. Each step was at a different height and angle, just as Grandfather had said.

Slowly, we all made our way up. The only light came from occasional holes cut in the rock; we had to feel our way along in some places. My father was carrying my little brother, who was enjoying the adventure as much as the rest of us. By the time we got to the level of Buddha's shoulders, we had all run out of breath, and our faces were red, even my father's. Through a large opening in the rock wall, we had a spectacular view across the valley with its rows of crops and fruit trees everywhere. We edged one another to get a better look, and to smell the sweetly scented air that rose off the fields below.

We climbed a few more steps, and just behind the head of Buddha found ourselves in a cave as big as our living room in Kabul. The walls of the cave were twenty or more feet high; the floor was littered with loose rock. The air was still and cool, and the only sound was the wind blowing through the small openings on the stairs, like the finger holes on a flute.

The cave was connected to other smaller caves beyond it. Just as Grandfather had said, the walls of all the caves were covered with paintings. Even in the dim light, the colors were bright in rich shades of red, white, green, black, blue, and purple. Some showed bare-chested men and nearly naked women in strange poses. Others were of birds and animals of many kinds, like lions, tigers, cats, eagles, and pigeons, and men hunting them with spears or bows and arrows. They were all interlaced with patterns and symbols, some looking like the tracks of the creatures being hunted. Others were more difficult to understand.

I asked my father what those paintings meant. He was looking at the hunting scene and replied, "Do you see the man hunting the lion with his arrows?" I nodded. "The others are proud of him. So, they painted a picture of him on the walls to remember his courage. That is how people passed history along to the people who came after them. This was the way of telling stories before the alphabets were invented."

I pointed to a large wheel with many spokes that looked like a spider. "What does that mean?"

"I don't know. It meant something to somebody. The archaeologists and historians might know." Then he looked at my mother and said, "You know, this cave is a perfect size for us. We can stay here for as long as we are in Bamyan."

My mother looked at my father the way she did when he was telling jokes. But my father said, "I am serious. It is our home now." My mother smiled at him. All the rest of us smiled, too. My father always told good jokes.

"It is impossible," she said flatly when she realized he had actually meant what he had said.

My father did not hear her. "You know, even the king used to buy a ticket to visit this place. Tourists from all around the world used to come here." But tourists had stopped coming years ago, and the local people had no reason to climb up to the caves.

My mother had a lot of looks. We could tell by her look what she was thinking, and her eyes were disbelieving. But when she saw how excited we were by the idea, she looked at my father again. "Do you know how high this place is?"

"Yes, and I have never lived in a place like this before." He walked over to one of the holes in the wall. "Look, you can see the whole world from here," my father said excitedly. "I think this is the mouth of Buddha, and we can look right through it." Buddha actually had no mouth; his whole face was missing. But that did not hinder my father's imagination. The opening was long and low, and it did, in fact, have a great view.

"You're just like a little kid," my mother said.

"So, you tell me what to do," my father responded a bit plaintively. "I don't have money to pay for a hotel, and I have no idea how long we'll have to stay here."

"But what if somebody falls?" my mother said. "What about these babies?" She held up my little brother and gestured with her arm toward my youngest sister. "Do they have wings to fly if they fall out those holes?"

In Kabul, I was always afraid of being killed by a rocket, but if I fall down from Buddha's head, I thought, at least I will die happy.

My father knelt on the ground and asked everybody to come closer. We all stood in a line in front of him, except my mother, who stood behind us holding my little brother, who was gurgling at the paintings on the wall.

"Do you want to live here?" my father asked us, and we all shouted "Yes," almost in one voice.

"But I have rules. If you accept them, we will live here," he said. "Rule number one: Everybody has to be careful climbing up and down the stairs. Rule number two: Everyone is responsible for the one younger than him or her. Rule number three: Those are all the rules." He smiled at us, and we smiled back, then he looked at my mother, and we all looked at her. We could not tell whether she was happy with the idea or not. But we stayed, perhaps because there was no place else to go.

For an hour, my older sister and I kept running up and down the stairs, bringing things up to our mother that our father took out of the car. There were so many stairs, and they were so hard to climb. But I was moving as fast as I could because my father had promised a bigger ice cream to whoever made more trips. She was moving very slowly, and I knew I would win. By the time we had taken everything up, I was soaked with sweat. But I had made almost twice as many trips as she. I told her proudly that I had won. She smiled and said, "You're a complete idiot! There is no ice cream in Bamyan. These people don't know what ice cream is. This is not Kabul, stupid!"

I looked at my father. He had a silly smile on his face. I was furious at him for tricking me.

"I owe you a huge ice cream," he said. "A huge one. You show me the shop around here, and I'll buy it for you." Now he was making fun of me. My sisters laughed at me. I ran to the next cave, ashamed of having been so stupid. But my curiosity soon led me back to my family when I heard my father banging two big nails he found in the car into a spot on the walls of the cave where there were no paintings. Then he strung up a cradle for my little brother across a corner of the cave. Later, he hung a *kilim* at the entrance of the cave to make a door.

My father went to the bazaar to buy some cooking pots, plates, spoons, forks, and other necessities. My mother sent me to get her some water in buckets. I went to a spring not very far from the Buddha. My older sister collected a few bricks and flat stones at its feet. We took the bricks and water to my mother, who built a hearth for cooking in one of the smaller caves next to the large one. That small cave became our kitchen.

My father brought back some lamb along with some tomatoes, onions, carrots, potatoes, radishes, and parsley. My mother built a fire, which she was not used to doing. The smoke made her cry. She was wiping her eyes and nose. Soon her face was covered with black smudges from the smoke. My father teased her, but then helped arrange the wood in the fire and put stones around it so my mother could set a pot on them. She cooked the meat with all the vegetables and made a simple stew that was as good as anything we had ever eaten. We ate it in the large cave, where the men with the bows and arrows watched us.

Soon it was dark, and we had no light. My father had forgotten to buy candles. He always forgot one or two things whenever he went shopping; that is how my father is. If he did not forget something, how could we know he was actually our father?

Through the opening that my father was calling "Buddha's mouth," a ray of moonlight was weaving itself into patterns of white lace on the floor. It was our lightbulb for that night, a huge one, and very far away, but all we needed for our new home.

I was the first one to fall asleep that night, even though my mattress was not long enough, and my quilt could barely cover me from head to toe. It was cool in the cave. A gentle breeze kept blowing through it all night long. I woke up after a while and had to pee. My father told me to use the ledge of the next cave down. It felt very strange peeing from such a high place. I was already finished before I heard it hit the ground. It was amazingly loud.

The next morning I was up earlier than the others. I looked out through an opening in one of the cave walls. The sun was still half-way behind the bare and sharp rocks of the mountains. But already daylight was flooding in, making patches of bright light amid the darkness. Below me, the valley was full of fields and trees. The leaves on some of the trees were still green; others had already turned yellow in the midautumn chill. A gentle breeze was moving the branches, and some of the yellow leaves were falling down into the white-tipped, fast-running water of the river. Dogs were playing along the banks. Piles of wheat that had been harvested on each plot of land made neat piles at regular intervals. Cows were eating straw as women milked them. There was no sign of war. A warm feeling just from being there swept through me.

I decided to see what was in the other caves while my family slept. When I pushed aside the *kilim* door, a burst of cold wind whirled through the opening into the cave. I shivered in my thin cotton *shalwar kamiz*, but I knew that in these caves, and outside in the valley, adventures were waiting to happen. It was time to start.

As the days passed, the memory of war began to fade, like the image of a bad dream. I wanted the rest of our family to be with us. Especially I wanted Wakeel, so we could explore all the other caves and the secrets of the mountains, like a place called the City of Screams, where another war had happened long ago. A man named Genghis Khan had killed many people there. It was hard to believe that anything like that had ever happened in Bamyan; it was so peaceful now.

Grandfather had told me that for centuries people from all parts of the world had come to Bamyan to understand the wisdom of Buddha. I wanted to know more about Buddha, but I could not find anybody who could tell me much. Everybody was Muslim. But I noticed that the local people still felt something special for the Buddha statues. They believed that he was taking care of them.

I discovered that several other families were living in the caves. Most were Hazaras who had fled from Kabul; some came from a neighborhood close to ours. My sisters and I soon had many friends from among their children.

Early one morning as I was climbing down from behind Buddha's head to play with some of the other kids, I saw a group of unusual-looking men in one cave walking in a circle around a fire, completely silent. They were dressed in white and reminded me of Gandhi from the movie we had seen; they wore the same kind of clothing.

One of them looked Hazara; the rest were Asians, but not Afghans. They kept making circles around the fire. I wanted to join them, but then I was afraid that they might push me into the fire. It was not such a big fire, but enough to burn my feet and clothes.

I waited near the door for them to stop. I wanted to ask them what they were doing. But after they had finished, the short ones bowed to the Hazara-looking man, who bowed back to them, and went out without saying anything. They walked right past me without looking at me, as if I were not there. Only he stayed in the cave.

I went in and bowed to him the way I had seen the others do. He bowed back to me as he stood next to the fire. I asked him why they had been circling around the fire.

He said, "Fire has two faces, like woman." He had a strange accent, unlike anything I had heard before, and when he spoke, he left out some of the words. "If you worship it, it gives you its blessings, and if you insult it, it burns you as it burns itself." Since then, I have always thought of fire as a woman with two faces. But I did not really understand what he meant, or who these men were. Were they Muslim? I had never seen such a thing in a mosque. I never saw them again, except for the one who looked like a Hazara, though I later learned he was not. In my explorations I discovered that he lived in a cave nearby. Sometimes I would go to visit him. He did not say very much, but his silence made me feel calm.

I told my mother about him. She said that maybe he was a monk from another country visiting Bamyan.

My little brother was beginning to walk. He wanted to do it all the time. In the caves this was a problem. We all had to watch him so he did not fall out. He never went far from my mother. When my mother had to feed our youngest sister, he became jealous. She had to give him a small lump of sugar to distract him. He loved sugar and would eat as much as anybody gave him. Sometimes when I wanted to take him out of the caves to go walking with me, I put a little sugar in my palm. He ran to me. I gave him some, and he followed me all the way to the river, or to wherever I wanted to go. He held on to my middle finger. For a time when we first arrived in Bamyan, he was my special friend, though a quiet one, but I had to trick him to be with me.

Autumn showed its face by turning everything completely yellow. The days shrank, but we enjoyed the clear weather and went for long walks through the town. Nearly every day we passed the larger Buddha statue, but we never went into his caves. They were filled with other fleeing families like ours, and we did not want to intrude on their privacy. The larger Buddha was very impressive, but he was not our Buddha, so we did not have such strong feelings for him.

Winter came unexpectedly early that year. Soon the bumpy roads disappeared under thick snow. Every morning my father had to shovel aside the snow at the bottom of the steps so I could go get our bread fresh from the baker's clay ovens.

After a few days the entry to the cave was reduced to a narrow lane between two walls of snow. Our cheeks got red as we slid down the slope that led from the bottom of the stairs to the road. In front of Buddha, our breaths became small clouds, and we laughed at the sight of them. We had never seen this much snow in Kabul.

When my father came back from shoveling or shopping, he had to shake the snow from his large felt coat. Under it, he was wearing a jacket with its fur turned inside. Felt and fur coats were what everyone wore in Bamyan. I could not find anyone who did not have one. It was not like Kabul, where it snowed only for a day or two, and then warmed up. Here it snowed for weeks without any end. When it did not snow, it was sunny, freezing, and windy.

My mother was always making tea to keep us warm. On days when it was snowing too hard to go out, my father built a fire in a part of the cave that had no paintings, and we all sat around wrapped in our quilts while my mother told stories about all the Afghan kings and heroes. Amazingly, it seems that they had all spent time in our cave, or at least that is how my mother told it.

One day the snow was too deep for me to go to the bakery. My father went and brought back some extra flatbreads, so we would not have to go out again later. Since there were so many, I asked my mother whether I could bring one to my friend the monk. I never saw him eat, and sometimes I worried about him, since he was an old man and had no family to take care of him. She gave me a piece that had been on a hot stone by the fire and was still warm.

I went down the stairs to his cave and found him sitting near his own fire, though it was too small to make much heat. He wore only his light cotton clothes, with his shoulders wrapped in a white woolen *patu*, the long blanket that for most Afghan men is their only coat in winter. Yet he did not shiver. He was very happy to receive the bread, and offered me some tea that he had made from leaves that he had gathered from the valley.

We sat together for a long time. When he poured the tea into a very small bowl and passed it to me, his hands moved very precisely, very gracefully. It was only tea in the bowl, but the way he offered it made it seem like something far more valuable. I drank it very slowly, to make it last, and looked at his face as I did. He spoke with his eyes more than with his mouth. I felt very happy to be with him, though I do not think I could have explained why if I had been asked.

I asked him to tell me about Buddha. For a long time, he said nothing. He just looked at the bowl of tea he was holding. Slowly, he shifted his gaze to me and spoke very softly.

"The earth will never be without flowers and trees," he said. "For as one dies another comes to take its place, and it has been like this since the creation. Like a rosebud, the world and its affairs are closed up tight, waiting for a warm spring breeze. We must always be like the warm spring breeze, and open the buds of every kind of flower."

The cave felt very warm, despite that small fire.

In the cave where we were living, though, everyone complained about being cold, especially at night. One day my father found someone selling mattresses that were filled with wool and he bought five of them. These were much better than the thin ones we had brought from Kabul. My mother stitched the new mattresses together, then sewed several of our quilts together, as well.

That night we all slept together. My mother and father lay in the middle with my little brother between them. I was next to my father, and my sisters next to my mother. We all clung to each other to stay warm.

Two and a half months had passed since we had come to Bamyan. We worried all the time about everybody, and worried even more because we had no way of getting news. We heard reports of fighting in Mazar and Kabul, so we knew it would not be safe to go there. We settled into our caves, where we had developed our routines. Every day included time with schoolbooks, with my mother teaching us reading and writing, and our father teaching us arithmetic.

My father became very friendly with many of the men in the town. He went with them to their mosque on Fridays, though they were Shi'a and we are Sunni. But a mosque is a mosque and anybody can pray there. People with good hearts can always rise above narrowness.

When they heard that he was a teacher, they asked him whether he would teach their sons physics and chemistry when school opened again in the spring. My father told them that he was happy to help them.

We heard rumors about a terrible battle that had been fought somewhere north of Bamyan near a place called Doshi. We had driven through Doshi on our way to Bamyan. We did not want to believe it. It had been such a peaceful place.

"Mazari's troops attacked Masoud's troops and were defeated badly. Masoud's troops are coming to Bamyan." We heard this from men, women, kids, everyone. The people in Bamyan were afraid of Masoud. He was a Tajik from the Panjshir Valley. His soldiers had treated many Hazaras very cruelly. Mazari was a Hazara commander who had gained the reputation of a cruel warlord. His forces had clashed with Masoud's in other places, such as our old neighborhood in Kabul, but so far there had been no fighting in Bamyan.

Though we are Pashtuns, we had been treated very well in Bamyan by everyone there. Whenever another one of the refugee families in the caves cooked something special, they sent some to share with us. We did the same for them. The shopkeepers in the main bazaar were all Hazaras. When I went to one of their shops to get something we needed, I told them that my father would pay them later that day or the next day. They did not mind.

It felt like our old neighborhood in Kabul, where everyone respected my father. Even now, when the divisive brutality of war was threatening to overtake us again, none of our neighbors ever failed in their hospitality even for a moment.

But there was a feeling in the air, a look of worry that settled into people's eyes. There was only one topic of conversation anytime anyone met. My father and the other men would gather in shops, and in the caves, and in the mosque, sometimes listening to a radio with its poor reception because of the mountains, sometimes speculating about what might or might not happen. If a newcomer came to Bamyan, everyone wanted to know what he knew, and then whatever he had said would be talked about for days after.

People said that Kunduz was peaceful. It was back across the Hindu Kush mountains, almost on Afghanistan's northern border with

Tajikistan. My mother was born there, and we had lots of relatives there. Some of the other refugees had already decided to go there. My parents talked about whether we should try that ourselves.

With all our moves, I began to wonder whether Wakeel and Grandfather would ever find us. The day we had left Haji Noor Sher's house, Wakeel had said that he would go to Mazar by himself and join us there. Had he gone? Was he there looking for me? Had something happened to him? There was no way of knowing. I had no information about him or Grandfather, only a great worry.

I became very sad and went to talk to my friend the monk. He had always answered my questions so wisely. I wanted to ask him why men always want to kill each other.

"Everyone has a purpose," he replied. "Everyone has to be good at something to feel fully connected to this cruel world."

I did not understand. "But they kill thousands of innocents," I said.

"Warriors are born with certain skills. But still, the warrior has a mind, too, and knows the difference between bad and good. Those who kill the innocent are confused. They are men with damaged souls," he said.

"Do you feel connected to this cruel world?" I asked.

"There is a time for being connected to this world," he replied, speaking slowly and choosing his words very carefully, "and a time for not being connected." We sat quietly for a few moments. We both knew that if Masoud's forces reached Bamyan, they might kill him.

"Will you stay here if the warriors come, or will you go somewhere to save your life?" I asked.

"I will do what is best," he said.

"You mean you have a place to hide?" I queried.

"Of course I do," he said.

"Far from here?" I asked. "Is it in Afghanistan?"

"I can't tell you that," he said.

"You will never leave this Buddha, will you?" I said knowingly.

"As a candlewick drowns in its own wax, and a moth flies around it till it dies, I want to drown in Buddha's knowledge and die at his feet. To tell you a hard truth, even the king when he is away from his home is like a beggar."

"It is the last time I'm seeing you," I told him. "We're leaving here for Kunduz tomorrow." I asked his permission to go and stood up. He also stood and laid his right hand on my head.

"Go well, tomorrow and always. Never hesitate to do good things. I'm sure you will be successful in your life," he said. He shook hands with me as a gentle smile spread across his full, wrinkled face.

That night, we made a fire to light our cave as we organized our few belongings. The fire crackled in front of us, and from time to time a spark jumped out, as if trying to escape. I wished we could escape from Afghanistan like the spark from the fire, but there was no way out. All the paths were blocked; all the doors were slammed against us.

Early the next day we packed the car and prepared to leave Bamyan. It was snowing, and all the mountains were covered. It was very beautiful to see, but very cold. The Buddhas did not mind cold or heat. They had been standing there days and nights for centuries.

I bowed in front of our Buddha as I had seen those monks do and said my goodbyes. I felt sorry for leaving the Buddha there alone, especially after we had been made to feel so welcome living somewhere inside of him. But he did not mind, or maybe he did. But I could not see it. A few minutes later we were in the car heading toward Kunduz, all shivering from the cold.

I had always expected I would see our Buddha again. But the storm of ignorance that has been raging in Afghanistan for so many decades smashed him to bits before I could return. I once lived inside his head. Now he lives in mine.

10

❖

Borderlands

After about six hours of driving over the Hindu Kush once more, we made our first stop in a place that was in the middle of nowhere and surrounded on four sides by mountains.

We could not see a track, or a road, or an animal footprint, or anybody to give us directions. We had not used any of the regular roads, since we did not know where the front line and its fighting was. We had followed several old dirt tracks that seemed to lead in the right direction and which we hoped were too small for the factions to use with their trucks full of guns. But now we were lost, and had no earthly idea where to go next.

Also, in these few hours, we had gone from winter to summer. Bamyan is very high in the mountains, and we were now nearly a mile below it. The weather had changed completely. The sun glowed orange, the sky was perfectly clear. We had left the snow behind and could see heat rising from flat stones.

A couple of hours before, we had packed away our fur and felt coats, and now we were in a desert, sweating. The water we had brought from Bamyan was long gone; we had expected to be in Kunduz by now and had not used it as sparingly as we should have. Our throats were dry, and we kept hoping that our route would go past a brook or a stream. But there were none.

My father parked the car under the shade of a mountain rock. Dragonflies hummed all around. He let the car engine cool for a while, then with a small pipe he took some water out of the radiator. It did not look very good, but it was the only thing we had to drink. Everyone wanted the first drink. There was not enough for all of us to have as much as we wanted. He gave us one sip only, not more, and in the end, there was nothing left for him.

We were desperate to find someone who might know the road to Kunduz, but there was no one, only the dragonflies, and we could not speak their language to ask them.

Finally, after an hour, when we were happy just to be out of the car, we saw a man on a mule making his way slowly down the side of the mountain. My father and I ran to him to ask him where, in fact, we were. If we knew that much, perhaps we could find our way.

"This place is called Nahreen," he said from atop his mule. "And this mountain in front of us is called Mongol's Mountain. If you continue driving to the north for four hours, you'll get to a town called Shekamish, which belongs to Takhar Province, then after another four hours you will reach Khan Abad, which belongs to Kunduz Province, and then another two hours will get you to Kunduz City."

The man told us that the roads were not good, but that came as no surprise after what we had driven over. He also warned us not to stop for anyone, "not even for little children, because they are all robbers and killers."

We thanked the man and got everybody back into the car.

Now we had another ten hours of driving ahead of us. We had wanted to get to Kunduz before dark, because of the robbers. My father started driving as if he were in a race. He hit every bump of that very bumpy road with too much speed, and the car jumped off the ground, squashing us against the ceiling. In the wild ride, we forgot our thirst and hunger. As we flew along, my father kept one eye on the road, and the other on the gas gauge. We had not seen a gas pump in hours, not even a village. About an hour after leaving the old man, we saw a little boy with a few gallons of petrol standing along the road. There was no pump station in sight, just the boy. We were afraid to stop, thinking he might himself be a robber. But we had no choice.

My father told us to stay in the car with the doors and windows locked, and be ready to go in an instant if anybody else came along. Even my father did not get out of the car, he just rolled down the window and spoke to the boy. The boy charged my father twice as much as we usually paid, and he was very slow about putting the petrol in the tank. Every set of eyes in that car swept the landscape around us as he did so, looking for the first sign of trouble. But no one came to bother us, and my father gladly gave him the money.

That was the only stop we made. In several other places small kids waved at us to give them a ride to the next town. We sped past as the old man had told us to do. As we did, my sisters and I saw men come out from behind big rocks nearby with their Kalashnikovs hanging from their shoulders. That was how it worked in those places. If you stopped to help a little kid who looked poor and desperate with torn clothes, guys with guns would jump out from hiding places and rob you, and maybe rape the women, too.

It took us two hours longer than the old man had predicted for us to get to Kunduz. We arrived long after dark, exhausted, hungry, and very, very thirsty.

We went straight to the home of my mother's brothers. They were extremely surprised to see us at one in the morning, but woke everyone and welcomed us to their compound. Their wives and daughters quickly set about making a meal for us, and bringing us jugs of water and pots of tea. The men and the boys showed us their houses, which were each surrounded by good-size courtyards that had doors connecting one to the other. Quickly, they arranged spaces for us to sleep, and some of the older boys carried our belongings from the car.

There were so many cousins I had never met before. They looked a lot different from my cousins on my father's side in Kabul, whom I knew well. They had bigger eyes with darker eyebrows and crinkly hair. They were a little shorter, and had narrow shoulders.

As late as it was, my aunts quickly prepared rice with chunks of meat and carrots, and a big plate of salad and roasted aubergine with some apple juice. We ate while my cousins, uncles, and aunts watched us. There were so many of them. They did not all fit in one room. Some of them were peeping in through the window at the back.

They were very talkative, all speaking at the same time, like sparrows. There were no rules like those my grandfather had established for us in our house. He used to say, "When someone talks, you listen until he finishes, then you talk. If someone older than you talks, you don't talk." But no one knew about that in Kunduz. I could not hear who was saying what. I ate and wished Grandfather were there to teach them the rules.

Some of them talked to me in Pashto. I found this very strange. My sisters and cousins and I in Kabul always spoke Dari at home, even though we are Pashtuns and can speak Pashto fluently. Sometimes when we had guests who could not speak Dari, we spoke Pashto among ourselves to put the guests at ease. But here everyone spoke Pashto. Maybe they thought I could not speak Dari, as I was a guest.

A few days later, I found out that they could not speak Dari properly. When they used Dari, it was as if they were translating Pashto expressions into Dari. It sounded funny, and they had a strange accent. My sisters and I found that very entertaining. A few times we caught them laughing at our accent. But it did not take us very long to become good friends. We had discovered twenty new cousins our own ages.

We spent three weeks with them, enjoying living in a house again, though I missed our cave sometimes. We could go out walking in the street. My father finally bought me the ice cream that he had promised me in Bamyan. My cousins went to school, and we helped them do their homework and read their books. Maybe we could live here now, I thought. We will find a way to tell Grandfather and Wakeel where we are. Maybe they were in Mazar-e-Sharif now, waiting for us.

I saw how happy my mother was. With the restrictions on travel imposed by the Russians, and then dangers from the factions, she had not been home to Kunduz for many years. She spent hours every day greeting old friends and distant relatives whom she had not seen in a long time. Her brothers' wives did not allow her to do any housework. They gave her some of their very best clothes and treated her like a queen, bringing her tea and fruit. My father had known several of my mother's brothers when they had been in Kabul studying or working for the government. He went to see their businesses and talked with them all night, with lots of laughing about old times.

But war never stopped chasing us. Now it came to Kunduz. Small groups started fighting to control each neighborhood, exactly as had happened in Kabul. Both day and night, we heard gunfire, especially Kalashnikovs, as well as rockets and bombs. Kunduz is a very small city; gunfire at one end is easily heard at the other. We knew about war, and we guessed that these fights between factions would soon get out of control as they had in Kabul. Then it would be hard for us to leave. We had never planned to be in Kunduz anyway; our real destination was Mazar. So we decided to leave while we could. Some of our cousins did, too, after they heard our stories of how the war had trapped us in our basement in Kabul while many horrible things happened around us.

The grown-ups knew the names of all the commanders and the factions, but to me they were all the same, and I shut them out. They were the guys who were keeping me separated from Grandfather and Wakeel. That was all I needed to know about them.

Now they were about to separate me from my new cousins as well.

One morning we all got up early to say goodbye to two of my Kunduz uncles and their wives and kids, who were leaving to go over the mountain passes to northern Pakistan. It was a difficult journey, with no certainty of what they would find when they reached Pakistan. They would drive as far as they could, but they knew that they would have to leave the road at some point and go over the mountain pass on foot. They took very little with them, mostly food. We gave them some of our warm clothes from Bamyan. They would need them, along with very good shoes.

Some of my uncles decided to stay in Kunduz, hoping for the best. Some others were planning to head to Wakhan, the little finger of Afghanistan that points east, toward China, where it is very cold in all four seasons. They had summer houses there. War rarely reached Wakhan even when there was fighting in all the rest of Afghanistan.

"Let's go there," I said. "We can all go together."

My uncle was sitting on a *toshak* cushion, drinking tea. He put down his cup, leaned forward, and gave me a gentle hug. I knew that meant "no," but I wriggled free from him, though I was very fond of him, because I did not want to hear "no." But we could not go to Wakhan, my mother said, because we were not used to such cold weather.

My father had been looking for smugglers from the day we had arrived in Kunduz. Perhaps, if he had had more time, he would have been able to find one. But with the fighting coming to Kunduz, the border crossing to Tajikistan was being closed more tightly than ever, and even the smugglers would have had problems getting us out. The largest bribes that the smugglers paid to the border guards would not be enough with the war raging so near.

In the end, instead of trying to go north across the mile-wide, swift-flowing Amu Darya River, which separates Afghanistan from Tajikistan, we fled west to Mazar, where my mother had a sister, and which we had been trying to reach since we had left home six months before. We had heard on the BBC that things there had settled down for the time being. We had to travel on a small road that was usually full of bandits. But even they had fled.

My father drove very fast. I held on to the padded armrest on the door. My mother held on to the little ones but did not say anything, because she, too, wanted us to finally get to Mazar.

The fighting did not get fierce in Kunduz right away, but in the end Kunduz was destroyed as thoroughly as Kabul. We lost six of our relatives before it was over.

In Mazar, my mother's sister was very relieved to see us. My mother had sent her a letter from Kabul a week before we left, explaining that we would be coming to Mazar. Then we had been stuck in Tashkurghan and had gone to Bamyan and Kunduz. She had no idea what had happened to us. No one did. She told us that she had written a couple of letters to Kabul, but that she had no idea whether they ever got there. No one had answered her.

Like my mother, she is a very calm person. Once she got over the excitement of seeing us, she quickly found room for us. We had visited her many times in the past and enjoyed her large house near the edge of the city, where the streets end and the open fields stretch a mile southward to a line of blue mountains that rise with no warning.

There was no sign of Wakeel. Why had he not come? I was very worried about him and Grandfather. We had had no news from anyone in Kabul in all these months of travel. I asked my aunt, hoping she had had a letter, or maybe even a phone call. But nothing.

Every day we went to the shrine of Hazrat Ali and prayed for peace in our country and to keep Mazar safe. Hazrat Ali was the cousin and son-in-law of the Prophet Mohammad, peace be upon him. Some people believe that Ali is buried in Mazar. In fact, the very name of the city—Mazar-e-Sharif—means "the very important grave." Other people say that Zoroaster, the great Aryan prophet, is buried there, too. For all these reasons, people go there to pray.

Hazrat Ali is my ancestor, so when I came to the shrine I had a special feeling of visiting an important relative, and being in a place where other relatives had done important things.

My grandfather's grandfather, Mullah Abdul Ghafor, had come to Mazar during the holy month of Ramazan for several years, and had copied the entire Holy Koran in great swirls of calligraphic script as he sat in silence for forty days in a special building next to the shrine called the Chila Khana. His Koran is now in the National Archives in Kabul. It is one of the largest ever copied. When he was getting old, he said goodbye to his sons and walked to Mecca. As he left, he told them to celebrate his death rituals when they saw an unusual white bird at the top of the minaret of the mosque near his home.

Many years later my grandfather—Mullah Abdul Ghafor's grandson—went to Mecca. According to people he met there, Mullah Abdul Ghafor was well remembered as a man of great humility, who for many years had been the cleaner of the area around the Holy Ka'bah, the House of God. The people in Mecca spoke highly of him, though years had passed since his death. In his honor, they treated my grandfather with great respect.

My grandfather told them about the white bird that had come one day to the top of the minaret, and mentioned the year and the season.

The people in Mecca said that that was when Mullah Abdul Ghafor had died.

I thought about my grandfather's grandfather and the white bird, wondering how such miraculous things could happen in this same world where we had had to flee our home to survive.

The shrine became my life. As long as I was there, my parents knew that I was safe. Some days I would study its blue and yellow tiles for hours, looking for patterns. Each one did not mean much by itself. Together, they had a big meaning and looked very beautiful. During these weeks in Mazar, though, I began to feel that my life was only a set of loose tiles and nothing more, and a deep feeling of loneliness settled over me.

I had been sure that when I reached Mazar, Wakeel would be there.

When I tried to talk with my father, he did not want to talk with me. He left the house early in the morning and came back late at night, always in a bad mood. He stopped trying to teach us school lessons.

My mother was busy either doing housework for my aunt, who went to work every day, or visiting cousins and friends. She had relatives in more than one hundred houses in Mazar, and they all wanted to see her.

There was no school. It was winter, and school would not be open until the second day of spring. Even if there had been school, we would have had to spend weeks to get our records transferred from Kabul. Our schools there, though, were closed because of the fighting, and there was no one who could send us anything.

My older sister spent most of her time with two girl cousins who were a few years older than she and a couple of other girls from the neighborhood. They spent hours together, whispering. Whenever I came close to them, they stopped talking and looked at me strangely, and asked with their eyes, "Why are you here?" If I stayed even for a minute, they would start to say things like "Hey, what do you want here? This is for girls only. Go about your own business." I tried my best not to be near her when she did not want me around, which was pretty much all the time. One day, though, I saw her in the neighbors' house when she and the other girls were putting on makeup.

They had lots of cosmetics in front of them. One was shaping her eyebrows with a pencil, another was darkening the area under her eyes, another was putting something on her eyelashes. Each one had a different color of lipstick. I was very excited, because I knew I could get my sister in trouble. But when she came home to eat, her face was scrubbed clean.

At the shrine, I asked the mullahs many questions. They always invited me to say prayers to the throne of God Almighty and told me that prayers are the key to every earthly problem. They also said that destiny shapes human life; whatsoever is written in man's destiny, that is what comes. Our complaints cannot change anything. We must embrace life happily with all its sorrows and joys.

At first, I enjoyed listening to them, but after a while, they just said the same things over and over with different words, and I got tired of it. Nothing they said could stop the war.

I never got tired, though, of being at the shrine of Hazrat Ali. I loved everything about it: the tiles that caught the sunlight and looked like gems, the towers all around it, the white pigeons outside, and especially the place where Hazrat Ali is said to be buried, under a monument full of precious stones and surrounded by a gold railing with the Holy Koran carved on it in great vines of sweeping letters.

Every day after breakfast I went there to see the pilgrims who had come from all over the country, despite the dangers of traveling in wartime. They spoke in many languages and with many accents. I liked to imitate the sounds that they made and let them roll around inside my mouth until I could turn them into words.

Later, I joined the young boys who came each afternoon to the shrine's garden to play a game called *gursai*. I remembered Grandfather's telling me how he had played in there when he was little. It was probably the same game. A boy takes his left foot in his right hand and hops about on his right leg, and using his right shoulder tries to knock down his opponent, who is advancing in the same way from the opposite direction.

I made so many new friends while playing *gursai* that I decided

I was never going to leave Mazar, even if the war came there. I had never had so many friends outside my own family before. I just wanted Wakeel and Grandfather to come soon, and I prayed for that every day. I knew that Wakeel could beat all the other boys at *gursai*.

In many ways, our life had become like a game of *gursai*, as we went hopping from one place to the next, hoping nobody would knock us down.

11

❖

My Teacher

One day when it had snowed overnight and I was not able to go to the shrine, I stayed home. All day long, I could hear thuds coming from next door. The following day it snowed again, and the thuds continued. In fact, I had been hearing this sound from the first day we had arrived in Mazar, but I had not been home enough to pay attention to it. Finally, I asked my aunt about it.

"Those people are carpet weavers," she said. "They moved in a few months ago. They are good people, except for this noise they make."

I had learned how to make a simple carpet knot in school two years before and had made a small carpet, which I had given to the principal of my school. He put it in a green frame in the hallway. Whenever I passed it, I felt very proud to see my name under it, even though it was not very well made. I had long wanted to learn how to weave a complicated pattern in a carpet, but I had never had anyone to teach me.

"Do they make big carpets?" I asked my aunt. "They make so much noise." When I had made my little carpet, I had not made thuds like the ones I was hearing here.

"Go and see for yourself, if you like," my aunt said.

I borrowed my aunt's sandals to walk the short distance from our gate to theirs. The snow stung my feet and went halfway up my legs inside my cotton *shalwar* pants. I began to run and was happy to see their door was open. Nobody invited me, but I ran inside anyway. In the courtyard, the snow had been shoveled away, and a warm sun was drying up the puddles left behind.

The house had big rooms. Each one held a large, flat loom that stretched out only a few inches above the floor, like a Chinese table. In the first room, about seven people were making a big carpet on a very wide loom, men and women together. They sat on the part they had already woven and leaned forward to tie the next row of knots.

They stopped when I came in, some in the middle of tying a knot. I told them I lived in my aunt's house next door. None of them said anything. I was too curious about what they were doing to feel uncomfortable.

At first, they were shy, and no one spoke to me. But when I sat next to them and tied a few knots, they relaxed when they saw that I could tie a knot correctly. They spoke softly in Turkmeni, and I did not know what they were saying. The kids were working with their parents. Everything was very different from my aunt's house, where my cousins and I spent most of our time playing games, and my older sister tried to boss me around, when she was not watching one of the Russian television channels that we did not have in Kabul. Here the kids looked at me quickly when they were speaking. Even though I did not know their language, I knew they were talking about me. Slowly, they tried speaking Dari with me, and we found a way to understand one another.

The women wore lots of jewelry. Their bracelets and bangles made music when they were pounding the weft threads tightly into place with a heavy metal comb. Their earrings hung low each time they bent forward to tie their knots. They wore rubies, pearls, and emeralds, and their clothes had these same bright colors.

I spent time tying some knots at each loom—nobody told me to stop— and I ate lunch with them, too. It would have been impolite to leave at lunchtime. They all sat around one tablecloth; it looked like they were having a party, like the dinners we had eaten in Grandfather's courtyard. At least sixty members of the Turkmen family were crowded into that house.

After lunch I went to the far end of the courtyard where I could hear a single person's combing. I opened the door and I saw a woman seated at a loom that, unlike all the others in the house, rose up in front of her. It was much smaller than the others. Though her loom had space for two people, she was alone. The other weavers in that house used ten to fifteen colors of wool. She used more than fifty. Her wool was a better quality, and her knots were much smaller than the others. She was making small geometric patterns; the others made big traditional patterns that were easy to weave.

She was a woman of unusual beauty, probably in her early twenties, with very dark and expressive eyes. When a Pashtun man sees such a beautiful woman, he becomes a poet. It is what we have been doing for thousands of years. I was far from being a man, but I quickly made a poem in my heart about her. She was paradise, and music, and charm. And she was making a magic carpet.

I said "*Salaam*," and she smiled in reply. I said "*Salaam*" again. And again she did not answer.

I took the extra hook and sat next to her. I made my first knot. She looked at me. She opened my knot and redid it. There was nothing wrong with my knot. Why did she open it, I asked myself. I made a few more knots. She continued to look at me with a silent smile. When I looked at her, she lowered her eyes, then opened my knots once again and redid them. I was a little bit annoyed, but I said nothing. After all, I was a guest. I continued making more knots, and when I finished, she opened them all and redid them.

"What is wrong with my knots? Why are they not acceptable to you?" I asked.

She smiled at me and continued tying her own knots. She was very fast. She could make sixty knots in a minute.

"It is very rude not to answer someone's question," I said in a joking kind of voice to be polite, but I meant what I said.

This time she ignored me and did not even look at me.

"What, do you think I am stupid?" I asked her. The joking voice had gone.

She smiled at me again and began combing. She slipped the teeth of the comb through the threads of the warp, and pounded the knots she had just tied with surprising force for such a delicate hand until they were snug against the row below.

"Say something, please!" I said.

But she never talked to me, and she never accepted my knots. I felt very insulted.

I got up from her loom and went to an old woman whom everyone called Mother, and I told her what had happened. She laughed at me, and I began to dislike her, too. Maybe they are all insulters, I thought.

"No, my son, she doesn't hate you, and she doesn't aim to insult you either." She spoke Dari, but with a strong Turkmeni accent, and I had to listen very carefully to understand what she was saying.

Mother sighed. "She is the sweetest of all among my children."

"But she never talked to me. She didn't even say 'Salaam,'" I said.

"Because she can't hear you," Mother said. "She is deaf. And she is mute. She is pure love, and her thoughts are even more beautiful than she is. She has never had any bad feeling for anyone. She is the happiest creature, I think."

"Is she your child?" I said.

"Yes, my youngest child," she said.

"I didn't see her at lunch," I said.

"She eats when she is hungry, not at regular times like the others. She has her own strange habits. Sometimes she sleeps for twenty-four hours, and sometimes she is awake for twenty-four hours. She never uses the same wool as we do, and she has never woven the same patterns we weave," she said.

"What kind of wool does she use?" I asked.

"Only the wool from the back of the sheep, which is finer and softer than any other. She spins her wool much finer, and she colors it with her own dyes. She makes all the dyes from plants. When we dye wool with such dyes, we often have to use some chemicals to get the right color. Not her. She uses only vegetable dyes," she said.

"Where did she learn all these things?" I asked. Mother shook her head and shrugged.

"It is her special talent. She was born with it," she replied.

"It would be very interesting to watch her make dyes from plants. My grandfather says that the best carpets have vegetable dyes," I told her.

"She doesn't let anyone watch her when she dyes. Not even me. She is very private. We want her happy, so we do not interfere," Mother said.

"Her designs are prettier than yours, and much finer," I said.

"We draw our designs on paper and have two of the boys put them on graphs. Then we work according to the graphs. But sometimes she doesn't sleep for a couple of nights, and all that time she is making a new design in her mind, as if she were drawing it on paper," Mother said.

"What are you asking my mother?" A handsome man who looked about twenty-five came out to the courtyard and knelt before his mother. In his hands was some wet wool. He was the first person I had met in that house who spoke Dari easily.

"We are speaking of your youngest sister," she replied.

"Oh, she is a real mystery," he said. "She is an unanswered question, an unsolved puzzle." He handed the wet wool to his mother and asked her something in Turkmeni. They spoke for a few minutes, then he walked to some pots nearby with fires below them and threw the wool into the pots.

He stoked the fires below the pots until they were blazing and made the dye in the pot boil. Then he took a batch of light-colored wool and dipped it in what looked like black water. It came out dark blue. Then he rinsed some gray wool in reddish water until it was a deep red, like mulberry.

The old woman took her water pipe from the shelf of the cupboard behind her. She packed it with tobacco and lit it. She sucked the smoke, and the water pipe made a bubbling noise.

"Does she read and write, your daughter?" I asked.

"How can she read or write, since she can't hear or talk? You tell me," Mother said.

"Well, because she is special and unusual," I said.

"She is special in many ways, but she doesn't read or write. She writes numbers only. To be frank with you, none of us can read and write; we are all illiterate, but we are the best carpet weavers."

I was always surprised when adults said they were illiterate. Grandfather had taught himself how to read and write both Dari and Pashto, and even Arabic. I wondered why other people could not do that.

"When she finishes her carpet, she writes the price in sand with a stick. First we thought they were very high, but later we discovered that she chose correct prices," Mother said. "When she made her first small carpet, we sold it to one of our dealers. He kept it in his shop for a year, happy to have such an unusual piece. Soon it became famous, and people who saw it in the shop started calling it Suleiman's magic carpet. That dealer became my daughter's special customer. But he does not sell her carpets to anyone. He thinks her carpets are holy," she said.

"No," I said. "I don't believe it."

"It sounds strange, doesn't it? First we didn't believe it either, but his wife told us that he spends at least one hour of every morning in a room where he keeps them. He does not allow anyone else to go into that room," she said, puffing some smoke out of the pipe.

"Can I buy one of your daughter's carpets?" I asked.

"Don't ask me. Go and talk to her yourself. We have never interfered in her business. You should also talk to her customer. He says they are beyond value. That is why he never sells them," she said.

"So that means he has never used them either," I said with amazement.

"Exactly. He says they are not for use. They are made to be worshipped," she said, and breathed out another plume of smoke.

"Do you think he is right?" I said.

"No, not for a minute. It is all delusions," she said. "He says she is another sun in the earth, and his eyes sting when he looks at her. My daughter is only my daughter, not the sun. But I have seen that his eyes hurt when he looks at her. Tears start dropping after two minutes only."

"I wonder if I could work with her to learn a few things?" I said excitedly.

"Take an ablution, then you can work with her. Tie small knots, and don't make mistakes. And don't waste wool. These are her rules, and she will let you work with her for as long as you want. But be careful, she can read your mind, too," she said as she began sucking her water pipe once more.

"I never saw anyone take ablution to make a carpet." I laughed. "I'm not praying or going to the mosque. I just want to tie a few knots with her."

"That is her rule. If you want to work with her, respect her rules," Mother said.

I went to their bathroom. I did the ablutions for my head and my hands, splashing the water above my wrists, almost to my elbows. I skipped those for my feet, since it was so cold. I went to the daughter's loom and sat down next to her. When I picked up the hook, she grabbed it from me and she told me with hand gestures that my ablutions were not completed.

I went back to Mother and angrily asked whether her daughter was spying on me while I was taking my ablutions.

"I told you that she can read your mind," she said, grinning. "She knows more than you think. Be honest and truthful with her."

This time I took a complete ablution. I went back, sat down as before, and this time she let me work with her.

The minute I sat next to her, I felt something unusual, something inexpressible. Although I did not know as much about carpets then as I do now, the carpet on her loom was unlike any other I had ever seen. She had started with the basic geometric patterns that Turkmen people have woven for centuries. Inside each one was a small floral pattern like those that Iranian weavers have perfected. The scrolling vines and flowers just seemed to grow out of the geometrics and wind around them as if they were a trellis. Because she was using more than fifty colors, the flowers almost looked three-dimensional, like a wood carving.

After I tied a few knots I looked at her face, which was so beautiful. She had such transparent eyes that it seemed possible to look straight through them. Sometimes I found myself staring at her. This made her uneasy, and she narrowed her eyes, twisted her head away. It was her way of asking me not to stare at her.

Whenever I tried to tie knots fast like she did, she pressed on my forehead with her index finger, smiled, and shook her head. She was telling me not to try to compete with her. I tried hard to be as fast, but it was impossible. She motioned for me to fill in the areas of a solid color, and showed me which shade to use.

I stopped going to the Hazrat Ali shrine except to pray on Fridays, and I forgot about my *gursai* friends. I had found someone who was quickly becoming as important to me as Grandfather and Wakeel.

Every night I told my family about the carpet weavers next door. My father was not interested. He was listening to the BBC, as always. But my aunt told me many things about them. She explained that a lot of the Turkmen people had come to Afghanistan when the Russians were making problems for them in their own country. And many others had been here from long before.

"They are the ones who brought carpet making to Afghanistan from Central Asia somewhere. That was centuries ago."

"The best carpets made in Afghanistan are made by these people," my mother added, "especially by the women."

I wondered who was cooking for the kids, if they were all making carpets.

"They marry in their early teens, and become mothers of large families before they are thirty," my aunt went on. "They spend most of their lives on their looms, from early childhood until they become grandmothers. They are always competing to see who is the best carpet maker. People tell me that they can tie as many as ten thousand knots a day," my aunt said boastfully, as if she were one of them, "because they have small fingers."

Every night, I had a dream about the young woman. I could hear her speaking very clearly to me then. Sometimes she teased me, and I teased her back. That never actually happened when I was sitting next to her. We were serious about our work. Though she was more than ten years older than I, it would have been unusual for an eleven-year-old boy like myself to be allowed to spend time alone with a young woman like her, at least among Pashtuns. But Turkmen, like the Hazaras, are more practical than strict. These people knew my aunt well. She was highly respected throughout her neighborhood and was always doing kind things, such as bringing medicines to the neighbors when they were sick, though she had no medical training. They expected me to be as decent and polite as she was.

Whenever I needed to ask my teacher something, I just looked at her and she knew I had a question. The first time I asked one, I spoke very loudly. She smiled and let me know that I did not need to shout. She drew her finger across her lips, then pointed at her eyes and then my mouth, indicating that she could read my lips.

She conveyed information to me mostly with her hands, though she could make perhaps a dozen different sounds. In the first days before I understood her gestures, she sometimes got red with frustration when she was trying to tell me something, such as "Go and do your ablutions." When I thought I had understood what she was saying, I would repeat it slowly to her. She would watch my lips. If she shook her head from side to side, I would have to try again.

I discovered that she did not like to be asked several questions at once. So when I did ask her a question, I waited until she was ready to answer it, even if that meant a few hours later, or a few days. Anyway, we could not talk much while we were working, because our hands were busy tying knots. But if she stopped to eat lunch, or when we had finished for the day and she was sending me home after the *muezzin* called the *azan*, then she would respond.

By the second week, I had to repeat what she said less and less often, maybe only once in five times. In the third week, it was almost as if we were talking normally. When I was with her, hours melted away, and then she was telling me that I had to go home so she could say her prayers. It was only when I looked out the window that I realized it was almost dark. Day after day went by this way. My parents were happy I had found a hobby where I could learn new things and enjoy my time, but they never said much about it. They were relieved that I was not wandering in the streets, making friends with boys whose families they did not know.

Strangely, my older sister had nothing to say about it either. But our cousins, who were the same ages as some of the kids in my teacher's family and knew them, often teased me. They whispered into my ears things like "I know you are in love with her," as well as some other vulgar things that made me feel very shy. There were too many of them for me to challenge, so as soon as they started saying those things, I walked out of the room to their loud laughter. I turned red and could not dare to face them for hours.

One thing I wanted to know was how my teacher invented her designs. She explained that she studied many other carpets before she made a design of her own. When I asked whether she took the patterns from other carpets, she firmly shook her head "No."

She then tried to tell me what she had in her mind when she was creating a design. But she could see that I did not understand what she meant. She took the hook she used for pulling the carpet threads through the strings of the loom and started drawing odd shapes in the dust of the courtyard. They looked almost like Chinese letters. I really did not know what they were.

"Are those some kind of patterns?" I asked, pointing first at what she had drawn, and then at a design on a carpet. She shook her head emphatically.

Suddenly I said, "Signs?" I do not know why, or where that word came from. But she smiled and nodded vigorously. She went on to convey to me that if I wanted to design carpets, I must never just copy. I should be creative, and there would be no limit to the designs I could invent.

I never really knew what she meant by "signs," nor could I ever truly understand the connection between the shapes she drew in the dirt and the patterns she wove on the loom.

She taught me how to graph a design on paper. I explained to her I could weave a traditional large, octagonal, dark blue *fil poi* (elephant foot) motif from memory, having included one on my carpet that had hung in my old school, but she insisted that I use a graph until I had woven a pattern many times, especially when weaving a complicated design of my own. I never saw her use a graph herself, but it was a good lesson, and one that in time would help my family and me survive.

As I got better at tying knots, I began trying to compete with the other weavers my age, and the ones younger than I, in a friendly way. Maybe I was just trying to show off. I was faster than a few of them, and desperate for some kind of attention. My father did not even see me anymore. I wanted somebody to notice that I could do something well.

Whenever she saw that I was trying really hard, she looked at me and smiled. Sometimes my fingers got tired, but her smile was more precious to me than my hands. My hunger for it turned me into one of the fastest weavers in her house.

As I watched my teacher's carpet take shape, I sometimes had dreams of Suleiman's magic carpet at night. Suleiman, they said, was given so much power by Allah that not only was he very wise, he also could rule over the beasts, the evil spirits known as *jinns*, and other creatures that we cannot see. And he could order his carpet to lift from the earth and carry him anywhere he wanted to go. I wanted to go high in the sky and fly to beautiful places. But mostly I wanted to go up to the best kites, cut them, and bring them to our courtyard, so Wakeel and I could fly them.

On Fridays, she did not work and her family always had guests. Once I went, but she was very busy with other girls, laughing often. I felt jealous that they were with her and I could not be, and I ran out. The next Friday, she saw me and introduced me to them. I felt pleased that she had allowed me to meet them. But once I had done that, I felt shy to be with the women and excused myself and ran back to my aunt's house. Anyway, my aunt always made a big lunch on Fridays.

On the other days, though, I was happy to eat with my teacher's family. They ate at exactly 12:30 p.m., while in my aunt's house there was no fixed time, which I never liked.

Everybody had a job. The boys prepared the eating cloth in the middle of the floor of a large room that had no loom. They spread the bread around the cloth along with plates, spoons, napkins. The girls brought the bowls of food from the kitchen.

We sat around one large cloth. Mother and the other adults all sat at one end. The boys sat along the sides, three or four eating from one bowl or a large plate. The girls sat from the middle to the bottom, doing the same. Everyone seemed to talk at once. I did not understand a word, only that they were really loud and talked very fast. When Mother spoke, though, they all listened.

When we finished eating, the boys and girls collected everything together and took them to the kitchen, where Mother washed the dishes as she hummed or sang Turkmeni songs softly. Then she came back to her place, loaded her water pipe, and smoked for a time before we all went back to work.

A couple of times, they invited me to stay with them for dinner. I ran to my aunt's house, told my mother that I would eat next door, and ran back. They cooked over the fire in the courtyard. Even in the cold winter while there were mountains of snow all over the courtyard, the girls gathered around the fire, cooking, chatting, and enjoying one another's company, dressed in their colorful clothes. The boys had a circle of their own around another large pot, mostly showing the power of their arms to one another. The grown-ups drank tea around the large woodstoves inside, laughing and shouting for more tea. And the younger ones ran one pot after another to them.

When it was time to eat, they all gathered around one cloth, as at lunch. Everybody took a piece from a large homemade *naan* while waiting for the food to arrive. First came small bowls of soup, made of seasoned vegetables along with chickpeas, beans, corn, and smashed wheat. Then there were large round plates of delicious *qabli pelau*. My mother is a good cook, but I will never forget that *qabli pelau*. Then bowls of meat cooked with potatoes. Then an enormous salad. Then a large bowl of yogurt. And finally jugs of water with glasses. As soon as the grown-ups took their first bites, the others followed their lead.

For the first few minutes nobody talked. All you could hear was the sound of spoons against the plates, and noisy sounds of chewing, as if they had not eaten for years. As the plates became half-empty, joking and laughing rose above the noise of eating.

Once, when my teacher ate with the rest of the family, I watched as she "talked" as much as the other girls with her limited sounds, signs, hand gestures. They were quick in understanding her. She even must have told jokes, because from time to time they all laughed at something she had conveyed to them. I enjoyed watching her laugh, which made her more and more beautiful to me.

The grown-ups leaned back on their huge pillows and asked for more tea and sweets, while the girls collected the plates. The boys folded the tablecloth. Then one of them brought a pitcher of water and a large bowl for everyone to wash their hands, followed by another boy carrying small towels.

After the girls washed the dishes in the courtyard near the fire, they collected some charcoal in a pot and covered it with ash. They brought the pot inside, set a small table over it, and covered it all with a large quilt. Then they tucked themselves around the table and pulled the quilt all the way up to their necks, leaning back on the pillows behind them. Warm, they gossiped and giggled as they ate sweets, especially the sesame-filled meringue known as *conjit* that is famous in Mazar.

The grown-ups soon left for their beds. The boys sat around the woodstove and were warned strictly to not make more fire, so they would have enough wood left to last the rest of the winter. As soon as the grown-ups started snoring in their rooms, the boys sneaked in more wood. They drank tea and played cards, winning small amounts of money from one another, sometimes shouting at one not to cheat, and the girls hushed them.

A TV was on for as long as there was electricity, but nobody watched it. As soon as the electricity went off, the girls brought lanterns and lit them.

This continued until midnight, when they finally went to bed so they wouldn't fall asleep on the loom, tying one knot after another and, as they said, "making a wall with knots of thin wool." From the sounds we heard through the wall of my aunt's house, they seemed to have feasts like this every night.

After a few months in Mazar, my father heard on the BBC that the leaders of the various factions were holding an assembly for peace. They said they would go to Mecca and take an oath together that they would not fight with one another anymore. My father said it was time for us to go to Kabul, to go home. We were all very happy, especially me. I wanted to tell Grandfather and Wakeel and my other cousins about all we had done and seen.

Early the next morning I told my carpet teacher about our leaving. I delayed telling her until the last minute because I thought that my father might change his mind. When I went to see her, the car was already waiting outside for me. She looked at me for a few seconds. Quite unexpectedly, her eyes filled with tears.

We could communicate now as if we could speak with our voices. She told me to use my mind skillfully, and I would be a brilliant carpet weaver and have a successful carpet business one day.

I kissed her hands in the custom of showing respect for a teacher, and she blessed the top of my head with a kiss. Then I said goodbye to her family, and she escorted me to the courtyard gate, where we said our goodbyes. I started missing her even as we were waving to each other.

I remembered one of Grandfather's sayings, "Love makes the old feel young, and it makes the young feel like a child. If you separate the lover from his beloved, they both feel destroyed."

I felt a little bit destroyed, but the destructions were inside me, and only I could feel them, nobody else. This was a time for rebuilding.

The fighting was over, and we would help Grandfather rebuild our house. We did not need to go to another country. We would fly kites again from the roof. We would all sit around one cloth for dinner. And Wakeel and I would never have to be separated again. It was a time for joy.

But at that moment, as I settled into the front seat and we headed toward Kabul, I felt a deep sense of emptiness that increased as mile after mile separated me from my teacher.

12

❖

Caravan

Once again we were on the road, but for the last time. The sky was clear; the sun was bright. Winter had ended and quietly turned to spring while we had been distracted by our life in Mazar. Everything was turning green. The peach, almond, and apricot trees had clouds of pink blossoms filled with humming bees. The sparrows' *chuk-chuk* calls were everywhere.

We said little as the car moved away from Mazar. We were all lost in our own thoughts.

I was already thinking of when I might come back and see my carpet teacher again. Perhaps she would teach me how to dye the wool the way she did. Then I thought of my school, my classmates, my cousins, and all the things that I would tell them about, what I had seen and been through. And I wondered what they had been doing.

My father was probably thinking how he would start his life again with all his carpets gone and his gym in ruins. I had heard my mother tell her sister in Mazar that she missed going to her job. Maybe she was thinking about the bank, and whether she would find her job waiting for her when we got back. She had never quit. But like most people in Kabul, she had just stopped going when it became too dangerous to move around the city. That was nearly a year ago now.

No one talked, not even my littlest sister, whom we called "the chatterbox." And the crying machine was silent, too. The truth is, it had been a long time since he had been a crying machine, but somehow the name stuck to him even though he had a nice row of teeth now. That morning he was looking out the window and smiling at everything he saw.

Mazar was soon behind us. The road had bumps now. Holes were everywhere from the rockets, but the earth was damp from the spring rains, and in some places we could see grass where there was only desert the rest of the year.

Two hours later, we passed through Tashkurghan. The road goes around the village, on the side of the hill. We all looked down as we passed to see if we could spot the garden where I had stolen the pomegranates. We wondered what had happened to that kind family in the months since we had seen them, but we were too much in a hurry to return to our own home to stop and visit theirs.

For another hour or more we moved across the low, sandy hills of Samangan Province toward the Hindu Kush. Suddenly my father was shouting, "Hold on! Everybody hold on!"

My mother grabbed the little ones. "What's wrong?"

"The brakes are not working. Something's broken."

He kept pumping the brake pedal, but the car kept moving at high speed.

"Relax, relax," my mother said. "Let the car slow down on its own."

A few minutes later the road leveled out, and the car began to slow down. My father eased it over to the side of the road, where it stopped. He let out a sigh of relief and jumped out and checked under the hood.

"The brake fluid box is empty," my father said. "We can't go anywhere without brakes, but they won't work unless we find some brake fluid."

My mother looked around at the empty land and asked in her usual practical way, "Where will you find brake fluid?"

"We should wait for a car to pass by, and I'll borrow some. Just enough to take us to the next town," my father said.

We waited on the roadside for two hours, but no car passed, only a group of Kuchi nomads who stirred up a huge cloud of dust as they drove their cattle across the unpaved road and moved on up the

hillside to pasture their herds. Every time we saw nomads, they reminded me of Grandfather. I have always thought that being a nomad
is the best way to live, constantly moving from place to place, away
from city troubles.

My father took his teacup from the dashboard and told us that he
would be back in a few minutes, and then headed toward the Kuchis.
We watched him as he went farther and farther off until he stood in
front of a herd boy who was sitting on a big rock, blowing his flute.
We watched as the herd boy got up from the rock, milked one of his
sheep, and filled my father's cup. My father came back with a cup of
milk in his hand and a funny smile on his face.

"What are you going to do with a cup of milk? It is not enough for
all of us," my mother said.

"But it is enough for our car to quench its thirst. This time, our car
will drink milk," my father said.

He poured the cup of milk into the brake fluid box, then he started
the car. He drove a short distance and braked.

"Our problem is solved," he shouted excitedly from his window.
He put the car in reverse and backed up very fast to where we were
standing, then hit the brakes. The car threw up a plume of dust.

We all climbed back in the car and headed for the town of Samangan up ahead, where we would get lunch. We went to a local restaurant in the heart of town with beautiful views on all sides. We ate
kebabs and drank tea, then headed back to the car to continue our
journey toward Kabul. I was still thinking about my carpet teacher,
and the unexpected combinations of many bright colors that she used
in her carpets, instead of only the deep reds and dark blues that most
other Turkmen carpet weavers used.

My father tried to start the car, but it sounded broken. He checked
the engine but could find no problem. He did not know very much about
cars, anyway. Maybe the car did not like the taste of milk, I thought.

I asked the owner of the restaurant whether there was a mechanic
shop around. He told me that there was one a quarter mile to the south.

My mother and my sisters went back inside the restaurant while
my father and I pushed the car all the way to the mechanic shop. It was
a small, shabby place with old tires and used spare parts all around.

There were more than fifty cars and trucks in a long line waiting to be fixed.

A guy whose face was completely blackened with oil shouted at us. "Hey, hey, hey, stop, stop! Where the hell are you putting that car?"

"Our car is broken," my father said.

"Are you blind? Can't you see these other cars and trucks?" the mechanic said.

"No, I'm not blind, I can see them, but what is that supposed to mean?" my father asked.

"It means your car will be fixed after I finish fixing these cars," the mechanic said.

"You must be joking," my father said.

"I don't make jokes with my work, and I don't have time for talking. Either park your car at the end of the line over there, and come back in two months, or get your car out of my sight," the mechanic said. My father shifted from one foot to the other, as he did when he was about to enter a boxing ring. He looked directly at the mechanic and spoke softly and urgently.

"I'm with my wife and kids. We have been on the road for almost eight months. You have no idea what we have been through. Now we're finally able to go home to Kabul. Please fix my car. It worked perfectly well until an hour ago. We don't have any house here, and we don't have relatives to stay with. I don't have enough money to pay for a hotel for two months," my father said.

"Look, I don't know you. My job is to fix people's cars. It doesn't matter whose car I'm fixing. But I have to fix these cars first, then it is your turn. Some of them have been here for months. If I spend all day today fixing your Russian Volga, tomorrow my other customers will kick my ass," the mechanic said.

"So, I have to wait for two months for my car to be fixed?" my father said.

"Exactly," the mechanic said.

"It is not possible," my father said. His voice was tight in a way I had rarely heard it.

"Look, I understand your problem, but you should understand my problem, too. Most of these cars belong to warlords. If I don't fix their cars by exact dates, they'll put their guns up my ass and shoot. I have a wife and kids, too, and they need me."

"Is there any other mechanic around?" my father said.

"There were five in this town, but the bastards ran away because of this fucking civil war," the mechanic said.

"If you're the only mechanic in this town, you must be making a lot of money then," my father said, trying to tell a joke and make the mechanic his friend.

"Oh, fuck the kind of money that comes with threats from war-lords," the mechanic said.

"Oh, this is very sad," my father sighed.

"Yeah, it is really fucking sad," the mechanic said. "Excuse my language, young man." He pointed to me. I did not answer, and just smiled at him. I found it very entertaining the way he talked. I had not heard many people in Kabul talking that way.

"Can you just take a look at my car, and see if it is anything that I can fix?" my father asked.

"Yeah, let's see," the mechanic said, relenting a little.

The mechanic opened the hood, climbed up on top of the grille, and squatted over the engine block. He spent ten minutes probing the engine, checking dipsticks, pulling on belts.

"It needs a few days' work," he said as he climbed down. "So, in this case it has to wait its turn, and that's going to be two months, at least."

"What is the problem?" my father asked, very surprised.

"You used bad gasoline that was full of sand. Now the sand is all through the engine. I will have to open even the smallest parts to clean them," the mechanic said.

My father sighed deeply, and with the mechanic's help we pushed the car to the end of the line. As my father and I walked unhappily back to the restaurant, his face was once again drowned in worries; a cloud of sorrows surrounded him.

We rented a room above the restaurant and spent the night there. My father could not sleep at all. Every ten minutes I heard him sighing until I fell asleep. I woke up early in the morning and saw big brown bags under his eyes. He looked very tired as he gazed at the mountains through the window.

As we were eating breakfast my father said, "I have enough money to feed us for a week, and after that God knows what is next."

"Let God take care of things. He can see us. He will help us, as always," my mother said.

"Maybe you're right, I should not worry so much," my father said with a heavy sigh. But he remained deeply anxious.

After breakfast my father went to the mechanic's shop to see whether he could find a solution. My mother and my sisters stayed in the second-floor room. But I wanted to get away from the smoke that filled the room from the restaurant below, where they cooked kebab from early in the morning until late at night. The restaurant always had customers.

I took one of my younger sisters and walked up the slope behind the restaurant. We sat on a large rock surrounded by mountain grass near the road. We had a sweeping view of the rounded hills that stretched for several miles until they became mountains in the distance. Everything was green in those early days of spring. I counted more than twenty shades of green and wondered how to capture them in a carpet.

I could hear the songs of a donkey driver from the bazaar and the flute of a herd boy from the hillsides. The whole land seemed ready to burst into song. I saw the girls from the town going down to a stream to fill their pitchers with water. They wore their best clothes. Young men stole glances at the girls as they walked past with their pitchers on their heads.

When the villagers passed us, they saw that we were strangers. They made *salaam*s to me, and some of them shook our hands. They all invited us to their houses. They all seemed very hospitable and sincere. No one seemed to be in a hurry, and their deep peace created an air of timelessness. They had a world of their own, calm, serene, and indifferent to what was going on anywhere else.

The next day I went again to the same spot. I found the herd boy there with his sheep and goats pasturing around him. He looked about my age. He was sitting on the big, round rock where we had been sitting the day before, blowing his flute. I said *"Salaam,"* and sat next to him. He said *"Salaam alaikum,"* somewhat formally, and hurriedly hid his flute under his shirt.

"I heard the sound of your flute yesterday. I tried to find you. You play very beautifully, like the masters on the radio," I said.

"You liked it?" he shyly asked. He lowered his eyes.

"Oh, yes. I love the sound of a flute, especially when I am hearing someone who plays as well as you," I said.

He spoke to me in Pashto, and I replied in Dari, but we could understand each other.

He took his flute out from under his shirt and started playing again. His hands were shaking a little. He played a few traditional Afghan songs.

"I only know these four or five songs. If you know better songs, play them for me. I want to hear them from you," he said.

"No thanks, I can't play," I said. "My father plays well, but I never learned."

"It is very easy to play," he said. "Sing me any song, then I can play it for you," he said.

I sang an Indian song. We laughed, and then he played it. We did that several times until we got tired of it.

As we sat there, he started making letters in the sand with his shepherd stick. After a few moments, I could read "Omar Khan."

"Who is Omar Khan?" I asked.

"It is my name," he said. "Can you read and write?"

"Of course I can," I said, surprised by his question.

"I know how to write my name only," Omar Khan said. "Can you teach me how to read and write?"

"Yeah, it is not a big deal. I'll teach you how to read and write, and you teach me how to play the flute," I said.

"Done!" he said as we shook hands.

I wrote five Dari letters in the sand. I pronounced them and he repeated them after me. Then he wrote them again, several times. By then it was midday, and I had to go to the restaurant to eat lunch with my family. As I said goodbye, he asked me to come back after my lunch. I did, and he was there waiting for me, with his sheep and goats quietly grazing around him. I taught him five more Dari letters. By the end of the day he had learned them all.

The next day we met again, and I asked him about his life. He told me that he was a Kuchi boy. I told him that my grandmother was a Kuchi long ago, and that my grandfather had been a shepherd when he was young, had lived with my grandmother's Kuchi family for a year after he married her, and had traveled with them all over Afghanistan.

A broad smile appeared on his face. He looked at me for a few seconds without saying anything, and then he said, "We are cousins!"

He jumped up from his stone, grabbed my wrist, and pulled me after him. "Let me introduce you to your other cousins over there," he said, pointing toward several long black tents hung with colorful bands down by the river. The tents were surrounded by children, goats, sheep, and camels, along with some donkeys and horses. The children and the baby goats were running in and out between the legs of the camels as if they were pillars carved from stone.

As soon as I walked into the Kuchi camp, I was overwhelmed by the strong smell of animals, which were all over the place. Girls my age and older, dressed in bright red, blue, and green, rushed inside their black and gray tents as soon as they saw me. I knew I was not supposed to look at them, but I could not help looking at the long woven bands strung across the tents.

Then I saw the men, all staring at me. They were tall and muscular, with dark eyes, thick eyebrows, and long hair. They were dressed in khaki-colored *shalwar kamiz*. All wore turbans or hats. Some had long daggers hanging from their waists that looked like swords. There were several men near a tent cutting large chunks from a cow they had just slaughtered. Their clothes were bloody. They stopped when they saw me. Boys my age came out of their tents as Omar Khan and I walked farther into the camp.

About a hundred pairs of eyes were staring at me. I began to feel a little nervous and somewhat shy. Old women slowly emerged from their tents and added their curious eyes to my discomfort. Apart from them, I did not see any other women anywhere, as they all remained inside their tents. I was only eleven, but because we had not had very much to eat for many months, I was very thin, which made me look taller. The women could see that I was a stranger, and they must have thought I was a man.

All around me, I was surrounded by Kuchis. Nobody spoke. The only sounds were kids crying inside some of the tents, and some sheep that were baaing and cows that were mooing. The baby goats kept jumping and running after one another, paying no attention to the people as they played with the chickens and the cats.

I looked at Omar Khan. Unlike the others, he had a big smile on his face and was completely at ease. He introduced me to his father, Amir Khan. His father looked at me sternly for a long moment, then gave me a big, welcoming hug. As he wrapped his arms around me, I could see over his shoulder that all the faces in the camp were growing big smiles. Now I did not feel like a stranger anymore. I felt like I was at home. Their smiles had the warmth of my grandfather's smile. The men all looked like they were my uncles.

After hugging Amir Khan, I had to do the same with all the other men and boys my age and older. Then I kissed the old women's hands as a sign of respect. They kissed me on the head in return, and rubbed their right hands on my head in blessing.

I was filled with excitement and wished I had known these people all my life. I had very unexpectedly entered the world of my grandmother, whom I had never known but had always wondered about. I wanted to tell Grandfather everything that was happening.

Omar Khan's father asked me to introduce him to my father, and I took him to the restaurant. My father talked to him in Pashto in the Kuchi manner, which is very loud, like you are shouting at each other instead of speaking. The boy's father was very happy to hear my father talk as he did. He asked my father about his ancestors and figured out that my father's great-grandfathers and the man's great-grandfathers truly were distant cousins. That meant we were all part of the same family.

My father and the man hugged each other warmly. Then the man kissed me and my sisters and told us to call him uncle, and he called my mother "sister." Straightaway, he invited us to his tent. He would not let us stay in that restaurant for one more minute. He helped us collect our stuff. An hour later we were in a Kuchi tent, drinking green tea, with more than a hundred men, women, and kids watching us.

Their tents were dark inside. They were made from black goat hair that had been pounded into long, wide strips of felt and stretched across a wooden framework that could be taken down easily, folded, and carried on the backs of camels. A single tent could shelter a very big family. During the day it furnished shade; at night its sides could be lowered to give protection from the cold and wind. From a distance, an encampment of Kuchi tents stretched long, black, and low across the dry land.

Their life was measured in their herds of camels, sheep, and goats, and in the passage of the seasons and the years as they moved their herds from one grazing place to the next, from one end of Afghanistan to the other.

Omar Khan introduced my older sister and me to more than forty kids. They wore ragged, dirty clothes. They looked like they had not washed for months. He told the other kids that we were their cousins. I wondered how many more cousins I had whom I did not know. Finding so many cousins from my mother's family in Kunduz had been a big surprise. Now here were all these Kuchi cousins from my father's family who looked at us with wide eyes, but said nothing.

Omar Khan's father, Amir Khan, set up a new tent and put all our belongings inside. Like on many of the other tents, colorful, long woven bands were hung on the outside of ours. Then he invited my father and me to another big tent, where we found all the Kuchi men. My father said "*Salaam*" and embraced them all. I imitated him. They tied a turban on my father's head and gave him handmade slippers. Amir Khan put an embroidered hat on my head and called me Qais Khan. And a few hours later we ate with the Kuchi men, while my mother and sisters ate with the Kuchi women in another tent.

We ate Kuchi bread-cake, spiced rice, kebab, and thick Kuchi-style yogurt. I could see that my new uncles and cousins were very fond of meat. Amir Khan said a Pashto proverb as his mouth was full of kebab: "Even burnt meat is better than vegetables." And the rest laughed. After dinner we drank green tea and ate dried melon until midnight. In every sentence they used a proverb. Some of them started their sentences with a verse or two from a famous poet.

At midnight we went to our tent, which we found full of Kuchi women surrounding my mother and sisters. My mother was telling them about our travels since we had fled Kabul.

A few minutes later, they all left us to sleep. My mother blew out the lantern that they had given to us, which is called a "hurricane," though we have never had a hurricane storm in Afghanistan. Some foreigners had brought us that word along with the lanterns. My mother and father slept in one corner with my little brother. My sisters slept in another corner, and I slept in a corner of my own. Before long, though, my whole body began itching, like I was having some kind of reaction to a drug. My father whispered to my mother that something was biting him. My sisters and I shouted that something was biting us, too.

I lit the hurricane lamp and looked at my legs. An army of tiny grayish insects were all over me, jumping and hopping like they were playing *gursai*. I hurriedly shook them off. My mother told me to take off my clothes outside of the tent and shake them there. I went outside, tearing off my clothes. A minute later I was naked and shaking my clothes as hard as I could.

I heard someone giggling. I looked all around me, but I did not see anyone. All the tents were dark and quiet, and the sky was very starry with no moon. I heard the giggling again as I continued shaking my clothes. This time it was more than one person's voice. I looked to my right, and I saw nobody. Then I looked to my left, and saw a group of kids hiding behind a tent and laughing. I narrowed my eyes to see whether they were really there and took a step toward them; I saw more than twenty kids, including Omar Khan, staring at my naked body. I ran quickly inside our tent without stopping to put on my clothes before I entered.

"What the hell are you doing?" my father shouted.

I saw that my mother and my sisters were staring at me. I was deeply embarrassed and quickly ran outside as I heard my sisters laughing. Then the Kuchi kids started giggling and looking at me again.

I walked toward them, still naked, and stood before them with my clothes slung over my shoulder. I was angry now, and I did not care who looked at me, although it is very shameful to be naked in front of another person.

"What the hell are you laughing at?" I demanded.

They became quiet for a second, then ran off laughing very loudly. I put on my clothes. The itching had stopped for the moment, and I went back to our tent, wondering how to face my father, mother, and sisters. I thought about the day that Wakeel and I had seen Haji Noor Sher after his bath and made fun of him. Maybe I was being punished for laughing then.

"What is wrong with you?" my father said.

"When I was shaking out my clothes, a lot of kids were looking at me. I panicked, and without thinking I ran inside," I said.

"All right, go to your bed and sleep. Be careful next time," my father said.

My sisters were still giggling. I looked back at them fiercely, daring them to tease me in the morning, and they started to laugh openly. My father shouted at them to shut up, and this made them laugh even louder.

I lay on my bed, angry and bitten, but before long I was asleep. I was glad that Grandfather was not there to see me. He would have made jokes about that night for the rest of my life.

I woke up later than usual. There was no one else in our tent. I found Omar Khan outside giving orders to the other kids. When the kids saw me, they grinned. I greeted them and asked Omar Khan about my family. First, he laughed a little about the night before. Then he told me that my family was in the stream, bathing.

I asked him about the insects that had been biting me.

"Those are fleas from the sheep and goats and camels," he said. "You will soon get used to them."

Get used to them? I thought. How does someone get used to fleas?

I went to the stream nearby. My father was in the water in his underwear. He was splashing around as if he were in a warm bathtub. He told me to jump in. I took off all my clothes except my underpants and jumped in. It was freezing, and I yelped. My father laughed as I ran out of the water, where the wind made me even colder. I started shivering. My feet were muddy and there was no towel to dry myself.

I looked for my father to ask him for his towel, but he was no longer in the stream. Suddenly, he was behind me, pushing me into the water. It felt even colder than before. My father was standing above me and laughing as I shivered.

"You are a Kuchi now," he said. "So you have to learn how to live like a Kuchi." I slammed my open palm across the top of the water and drove a wave of freezing river water into his face. He laughed and dove for me, while I wriggled out of his way. When I landed a fist against his left shoulder, his eyes lit up.

"Okay, now we are going to be boxers!" he exclaimed as he started fending off every punch I aimed at him. Sometimes I stumbled backward when one of his blocks hit me squarely. He was laughing. I was laughing. He was my father again, but this time he was not letting me beat him. After I began tiring, he grabbed me to pull me out of the water, and it turned into a big hug like I had not had from him in months.

An hour later we were back in our tent having our breakfast. We had tea, milk, butter, yogurt, and bread. After breakfast Omar Khan took me to an empty tent. There, to my amazement, was a blackboard and a piece of chalk. When I asked him where he had found these things, he just laughed. He left me there and ran outside and whistled three times. A moment later he came back in with more than twenty other boys. Each had a notebook and a pencil. Once again Omar Khan introduced me to his cousins—my cousins, too—and told them that from today I would be their teacher. Omar Khan ordered everyone to sit in a line on the dusty ground. Then he asked me to write the Dari letters on the blackboard.

Everything happened so fast that I had no chance to think about it. I did what he asked. The boys became very quiet and started copying what I had written on the blackboard.

"Teacher, what do these signs mean?" asked a boy who was older than I.

I felt a strange shyness, because he called me "Teacher." My father was a teacher. No one had ever called me a teacher before. I cleared my throat with a fake cough, then I said, "These are Dari letters. All together, they make the alphabet. If you learn them, you can read and write."

I pronounced each letter. They repeated them after me. Then I checked everyone's notebook for mistakes. I remembered my teacher had done the same to me and my classmates. But that was in a real class where we sat on chairs and wore clean clothes.

Their handwriting was straggling, but not large. Most of them wrote very tiny to save space in their notebooks for the next lessons, since they were not given money often to buy books and pens.

A few hours later our class ended. I thought that if Grandfather were here, he would have been very proud of me. I ran to our tent to tell my mother that I was now a teacher. My mother was sitting outside of the tent, milking a cow. I was shocked. I had never seen my mother milking a cow before. She had been born into a wealthy family who had servants to do this kind of work. I asked when she had learned to do that. She smiled and said, "About twenty minutes ago!"

She looked sideways at me with her cheek against the side of the cow and asked me, "Am I doing this right?"

"No, you are squirting the milk onto the ground, not in the pot," I said.

She looked down and started laughing. The cow kicked the pot, and the milk spilled onto the ground, where the thirsty earth drank it quickly. The cow walked away as if she did not like to hear us laughing. Maybe she thought she had been insulted.

A Kuchi woman who was very beautiful was sitting next to my mother, rocking a large clay pot. It had a small opening at the top and I could not see inside it. Something in the pot was sloshing loudly. I asked the woman what she was doing.

"It is whey, for lunch, and it is good for putting you to sleep," she said. "The rest we will eat tonight," she added, nodding at the pot.

As I was talking to my mother, I heard a crowd of girls pronouncing *"Alef, bey, pey, tey, sey, jem, hey, khey, dal, zal, rey, zey . . ."* These were the first letters of the Dari alphabet. The sound was coming from inside our tent. I entered and saw my older sister in front of a blackboard with ten Dari letters already written on it. She pronounced the letters, and the Kuchi girls repeated them after her. My sister had become a teacher, too.

From then on, all the Kuchi kids called my sister and me "Teacher," even though most of them were older than we were.

A week later, my class and my sister's class held a reading and writing competition. It was just simple words using the letters everybody knew. My class won, and two days after, we had another. This time, my class lost. Every day, the Kuchi kids were getting better and better. They were very fast learners and drew the letters in the dirt whenever they had a free second during the day. They had their own competitions, one on one, and soon they were writing words we had not yet taught them, though full of spelling errors.

My father thought it was very funny to have so many new teachers in the family. Every night he asked us what we had done, but he never tried to tell us how to do it. Meanwhile, his beard grew. He always wore a turban now. My mother started wearing Kuchi clothes and jewelry. Sometimes I could not pick her out of a group of women, milking the sheep and the goats as well as the cows, and shearing the sheep's wool. My father learned how to wash wool in the river and slaughter animals and cut them into pieces for cooking or for sale to the villagers.

My older sister and I taught the kids, our cousins, for three hours early every morning. Afterward, I went with Omar Khan and other boys to take the flocks to the pastures for grazing on the hillsides. My older sister went to the stream with the other girls to fill their pitchers. She also learned how to make Kuchi embroideries. She already knew how to hold a pot of water on her head without holding it with her hands. She had learned that in Tashkurghan. The Kuchi girls were very surprised to see her doing it like they did.

When my father went with the men, and my mother was with the women, and my older sister had gone off to get water with the Kuchi girls, it was my job to take care of my younger sisters and my brother. One of my sisters was happy with her own company. She would be next to me for hours, but I would hardly know she was there. She did not say much, did not complain about anything, and never cried to have something.

The next sister, though, cried for hours when she did not get what she wanted. She was afraid of no one, neither my mother nor my father. She would just cry stubbornly until somebody solved her problem. Then she became friendly and did not leave that person's side.

My brother would be very quiet until he wanted to eat something sweet. Then he would live up to his nickname. Both of my parents loved him, because he had such soft cheeks. He never went far from my mother.

On the first Friday that we were with the Kuchis, Omar Khan said we should go to the river and catch some fish.

"Do you have fishhooks?" I asked.

"We don't need fishhooks," he said.

"Do you use a net?" I asked.

"No," he said.

"Then how do you catch the fish?" I asked.

"With a generator," he said.

I did not know what he was talking about.

"It is a Kuchi trick. I will show it to you, but you have to help me carry this generator to the river," he said.

The generator was heavy. It was a struggle to get it to the river. Meanwhile, the other Kuchi boys were pasturing the herds on the hillside.

We put the generator on a flat rock about twenty meters from the river. Omar Khan connected one end of a wire to the generator and put the other end on a tree branch near the river. A few minutes later, all the uncles came. They carried many big stones to the middle of the river. Two hours later the river was dammed.

Everyone got out of the water. One of the uncles turned on the generator. Another one dropped the end of the wire into the river. The generator made some sputtering noises and stopped. I did not know what was going on until I looked at the river and saw that it was filled with fish floating on the surface. They had all been electrocuted. While some of the kids pulled the wire out of the water, Omar Khan and several of his uncles jumped into the pool and started throwing the fish to the riverside. The rest of us began collecting them. Half an hour later, we had four large bags of fish on the back of a horse and carried them to the tents for a Friday fish party.

The next Friday we did not have gasoline for the generator, but Omar Khan asked me to go to catch fish with him anyway.

"How will you catch any fish today?" I asked.

"Today I will show you another Kuchi trick," he said.

We all hid behind a big boulder that was way back from the river. One of the uncles took a grenade from his pocket. He pulled out the fuse and threw the grenade into the river.

Seconds later, the water splashed all over the riverbank with bits of sand, gravel, and fishes flying into the air. Even where we were hiding, little pieces of fish found us and stuck to my face and in my hair, which was long then. I smelled like fish for hours after. The river turned gray as hundreds came to the surface. We waited there for a few minutes to let the silt in the water settle down. Then Omar Khan and his uncles jumped in to throw the fish onto the riverbank. This time it was five big bags we put on the back of the horse. A few hours later we had another fish feast.

On the third Friday, there was yet another trick.

The grenade had completely destroyed our dam from the week before, so it took us about three hours to block the stream. Then the uncles came leading a horse that was carrying a large bag of caustic soda, and another bag full of empty bottles. The uncles and Omar Khan filled the glass bottles with the caustic soda, and then we crouched behind that same big rock and threw those bottles into the river. When the caustic soda in each bottle touched the water, it exploded like a bomb, though not as forcefully as the grenade. Again, we went back to the tents with five bags of fish.

Everybody had to clean his or her own fish and cook them. The Kuchis used only powdered laundry detergent to wash their hands, and it smelled worse than the fish. I saw Omar Khan rubbing his hands with lemon and orange to kill the fish smell. This was another Kuchi trick, of course.

———

We spent more than a month camped with the Kuchis in Samangan. The spring rains had ended, and the pastures on the hillsides were starting to brown. There was not enough grass left for the herds. On the Friday night of the fourth week, Amir Khan said that by Monday they would move to Mazar, and then farther west to Andkhoi, where they could find fresh grasses for their flocks.

Our car had not been fixed yet, and we still had to wait another month. But my father did not have enough money to feed us and rent a room for a month. My father decided that we should go with the Kuchis as far as Mazar. There my mother, my sisters, and I would stay with my aunt, while my father would return to Samangan to get the car fixed. He would rejoin us as soon as it was repaired, then we would go to Kabul together.

On the Sunday night of our fifth week, the Kuchis collected their stuff. Early the next morning we started our move back toward Mazar. Though we wanted to be heading home to Kabul, we were excited to be traveling with the caravan.

The caravan moved slowly, with huge, shaggy camels lumbering down the rocky slopes followed by sheep, goats, and fierce-eyed watchdogs. The men, tall, lean, and severe looking, walked proudly back and forth among their herds and cattle. They carried rifles on their shoulders. Sometimes, the silence suddenly was broken by harsh words from the leading camel driver, who spoke in a jargon known only to those of his profession and to his camels.

At both the head and the rear of the caravan, the women walked openly, contemptuous of veils, as they swung along blithely near their camels. They were as beautiful and ethereal as old romantic paintings. Some of them were black-eyed and tan-skinned with raven hair. Others were fair and blue-eyed with golden or red hair. The sun and wind had given them red cheeks and lips that contrasted sharply with their dresses of somber black.

The littlest kids, two or three years old, were strapped between the two humps of the Bactrian camels. As the camels joggled along, the kids slept in a sitting posture. Every now and then a child would whimper, but would soon be lulled to sleep by the padding camel feet and the tinkles of bells that hung on the camels' long necks. Older kids would walk alongside the one-humped camels, but when they got tired, they climbed up on the striding camels' backs like monkeys. There they settled themselves in front of the hump for a nap.

Occasionally, a newly born camel walked up from the rear and nuzzled its mother, its woolly body in strange contrast to its long, unsteady, thin legs.

The Kuchis carried all of their possessions with them. They lived very simply, but not poorly, and had many richly colored carpets of their own working, with big traditional geometric patterns; from what I had learned from my teacher in Mazar, I could see they had used many vegetable dyes, and they were as soft as velvet. These carpets were bundled together with the tents and cooking utensils and slung on either side of the camels.

From a distance the camels looked like they were bobbing up and down like large rag dolls.

The nomadic life was accustoming us to hardship, making us strong and teaching us courage. We walked for six hours, until we stopped for lunch. Then we walked again until dusk approached. It was very trying, but I could now understand why Grandfather was so much in love with the way the Kuchis lived; as he had said, "It is carefree, and secure, and finds the best in every season in a way that can never be monotonous, like Kabul life."

I walked in front of the herds with my father and the other Kuchi men. They spoke Pashto very loudly, as if they were all deaf. I asked my father why they were speaking so loud. He said, "This is how Kuchi people talk."

Then I spent some time with my boy cousins who were lost in the dust among the sheep and goats. They each carried a stick in their hands. Then I went to see my sisters. Their colorful skirts and embroidered jackets were covered with a thick layer of dust, which turned them the dull colors of the men's clothes. When the Kuchi girls saw me, they stopped talking and glared at me to let me know that I was not welcome there. I was their cousin, but Kuchis have strict rules about men being with women and boys being with girls, which I was still learning. After I left them, they started talking to one another again.

My mother was always in the back, coughing and sneezing from the chalk-like, powdery dust. She could not walk as fast as the others. She did not have proper shoes, only sandals. The dry air and the dust made her heels crack. Sometimes she rode on one of the one-hump camels. Everybody stared at her as if she were doing something wrong, since usually only little kids and old people did that. Her white skin was becoming tanned by the sun, but the dust made her look as if she had put her head into a bran flour bag.

When the sun dropped behind the mountains, we stopped wherever we were: one day on the skirt of a mountain, one day in a desert, and one day in a green valley near a village. In less than an hour, a few Kuchi men could set up a few tents, while the women began to prepare dinner. Some breast-fed their babies as they cooked. A few hours later darkness covered us, except for where the starry sky with a half-moon dropped light toward us.

We had three huge fires every night, one for the men, one for the women, and another for the kids. Every now and then the fire cracked and a spark broke free. Youngsters were busy boiling water for tea, while the men reclined against huge pillows to drink it. They were as fond of drinking tea as my aunts and uncles, draining several cups, one after another, in minutes.

These were sociable people who enjoyed every meal like it was a feast. The Kuchi women often cooked *shorba* for lunch, a meat soup filled with carrots, potatoes, turnips, spices, and lots of dry or fresh hot pepper. When townspeople came to the encampment to buy animals, skins, or fleeces, the cook just added another few cups of water to the pot, boiled it, and there was enough to serve the guests. To eat it, we tore our *naan* into small pieces and put the pieces in a large bowl. Whichever woman was in charge of cooking that day would then pour the *shorba* over the bread chunks. Five to ten people would then eat from that one bowl. If I did not eat in a hurry, I might eat only one or two bites before the bowl was empty. Then I had to fill myself with bread and yogurt, whey, or *quroot*, dried yogurt that is hard and sour and always carried by the Kuchis.

At night, the Kuchi women would sometimes make kebab, or rice with lamb. They did not clean the rice before cooking it. Each time I took a bite, sand crunched in my teeth or I would find myself chewing a stone. Several times my father joked, "The sand and pebbles are cooked very well, but why is there so much rice mixed in?" The men laughed and boasted, "Kuchis' stomachs can digest even iron."

I was grateful for the food that the Kuchis were giving us, but I did not like eating so much meat. I often cut an onion into small chunks, mixed it with yogurt, and ate it with bread, while the others stretched out their hands to eat their soaked *naan* from one large bowl.

After dinner two men played drums, the deep-sounding *dol*, and other men formed a circle and danced the *attan*. Slowly at first, they raised one foot and spun around, then faster and faster as the *dol* drove them into a spinning fury. One by one, some of the men dropped out when the beats came too quickly and they got too tired. On the last pounding beat, everybody cheered the couple of men still dancing.

The whole night was spent enjoying one another's company, singing and dancing. Sometimes they hooked up a string of bulbs to the generator and made the desert night come alive with electric light. The women continued cooking until very late.

Finally, we drifted into the tents and slept. The flocks dozed outside, and the fierce-eyed watchdogs stayed vigilant.

Three weeks later, late on a Monday afternoon, we got to Mazar. We left the open country, and our line of camels swayed into the town along the main road. When we reached the shrine of Hazrat Ali, the caravan stopped briefly so the men could go pray. After the prayers, my father told Amir Khan that we could not continue walking with them any longer, and that we had to leave them there.

Amir Khan became very unhappy upon hearing this, but he forced a smile. He and the others had known we would leave them in Mazar, but none of us had wanted to think about it or talk about it.

"We will always carry this great memory of being with you and your kind family," my father said as he was hugging Amir Khan goodbye. "And we will be always thankful for your hospitality and sincerity."

"We also will remember you and your family as one of our good memories," Amir Khan said. "Don't forget to visit us in Jalalabad in the wintertime. Please bring your father."

Jalalabad stays warm all year. That is where the Kuchis had their permanent homes.

Then my father hugged the other Kuchi men one by one and said his goodbyes. I imitated him again, like the first time we had met them. This time, though, we knew all their names. We knew who were the best dancers, who told the best stories, who were the best kebab cooks, and who were poets.

My mother and sisters kissed the Kuchi women. My father and I waved farewell to them from a proper distance.

Then I went to my boy cousins. I hugged Omar Khan first, then the others. Omar Khan held out a handmade envelope to me and asked me not to open it until the next day. I promised I would. Then all the other boys handed me their own envelopes and said their shy good-byes. They tried to disappear from sight quickly. They were not good at goodbyes at all. My hands were full of their envelopes.

I noticed that my older sister was surrounded by a group of Kuchi girls handing her Kuchi jewelry and kissing her farewell. They hugged her very tenderly, then one by one they disappeared inside the dust of the herd.

We stood on the roadside in front of the shrine and its blue-tiled towers, and watched them as they went farther and farther away until they disappeared from our sight. The farther they went, the closer I felt to them.

My father said wistfully, "They will just go on walking and walking over the same routes that our ancestors have followed for centuries. I wish Dad were here."

We did not say anything. I put the handmade envelopes into my pockets as we got into a taxi. But the taxi did not feel right, somehow. I wanted to run after my cousins. I wanted to shout at them to take me with them.

A few minutes later, we were in my aunt's house. She was very happy to see us again, but very surprised. We had had no way of letting her know what had happened to us, or that we would be coming back to her house. Happy as she was, she did not let us go into her rooms, because we were so dusty and dirty and full of fleas. She brought us tea in the courtyard. After we drank a cup, she sent us one by one to the bathroom for a shower, while she found us clean clothes and sent what we had been wearing to be washed in very hot water with strong soap. Then she let us in.

After I had bathed, I ran next door to surprise my carpet teacher. I knocked on the door several times, but nobody opened it. Then I pushed the door and entered the courtyard. All the rooms were empty. No one was there. Frightened, I ran back to our house to ask my aunt about what had happened to them. She told me that they had left for Tajikistan a few weeks before. Tajikistan! I was stunned with disappointment. How would I find my teacher in Tajikistan?

My aunt went to her bedroom and came back with a small package. "She left this for you," she said.

Even before I unwrapped the plain white cotton, I knew what it was. I looked at it very carefully. It was my teacher's rug hook. I could see her beauty in that hook, and it reminded me of her smile and her eyes filling with tears when she said goodbye.

I kissed the hook. It smelled of her perfume. I cried without knowing why I was crying. My aunt kissed me on my forehead, hugged my head, and said, "She loved you, too, but it was her decision to go to Tajikistan. She convinced her family to leave Afghanistan, and her family always listens to her. They believe that she is always right about her decisions."

"She is not an ordinary person," I murmured, then asked my aunt many questions about why my teacher would have wanted her family to move. But neither my aunt nor anyone in her family knew the answers.

I wrapped the hook in a pure silk handkerchief that I had bought from the Mazar bazaar when we had been there a few months before, and I put it in my suitcase with other special things that I had found in all the different places we had gone.

That night I went to sleep very early, and I saw my carpet teacher in my dreams. I also saw Omar Khan and my monk friend in Bamyan, and Hamza and my other friends in Tashkurghan. Wakeel was there, too. We were all together.

I woke up early in the morning, and everyone else was still asleep. I started reading the letters that I had been given by my Kuchi cousins. I began with Omar Khan's letter. He was the one who was dearest to me, and the one I most understood. I had learned a lot from his love of life.

Dear my best friend and kind cousin,

I will always remember you in the cage of my heart, for you gave me the sight to see my path. Until I met you, I always thought I was living in darkness, and from the moment I met you, I found my light.

You lit a candle in me. Its light can show me my path, and this light will always remind me of you.

Sincerely, Omar Khan

I read this letter several times. Omar Khan, I could see, was a poet as well as a herd boy. What he meant by "light" was being able to read and write.

I opened the second letter and it was from Aaron Khan. Aaron Khan was dark and skinny, with bulging eyes like a crab. He spoke in a hurried voice, half swallowing his words, and glancing furtively about as though he was planning to run off and hide. When he was excited his very eyeballs seemed to tremble.

Knowledge is the candle of life, and you gave me a candle that I can use for the rest of my life. I don't know how to say my appreciation for the precious gift that you gave me, but I believe someday I will meet you and give you a gift that is worth giving. If not in this world, in the next world, as we all believe this world is a bridge to the next.

Best regards, Aaron Khan

The third letter was from Solomon Khan. He was quiet and had his father's combination of sad eyes and winning smile, even though his teeth were very ugly; they protruded from his mouth and grew in a double row in his upper jaw. This kept him busy, as his fingers were constantly in his mouth, trying to loosen and yank out the teeth in the back row. He meekly permitted those who wished to put their fingers in his mouth to feel his teeth. I could find little in common with him that we could talk about. He was always sitting off by himself in some dark corner of a tent, or spending his evenings at the hillside.

Still, it was pleasant to sit close beside him there on a big rock and say nothing for a whole hour, watching the crows wheel around the domes of the tents when they stood out in relief against the red glow of the sunset. The birds soared and plunged, then suddenly spread a black net across the fading sky and disappeared, leaving a vast emptiness behind them. When we watched something like this, we had no desire to speak, for our hearts were full from the joy of seeing it.

Dear my cousin,

Knowledge is that precious wealth that nothing can compare to it. You gave me that wealth and I gave you nothing but silences. I know that you understood the secret behind the silences. That was all I could give you for the time being. I hope we meet another time and exchange more.

Best wishes, Solomon Khan

One by one, I read them all. The letters had many writing mistakes, many misspelled words, large and straggling, but I could read and understand them. With practice our cousins would get better, my older sister and I agreed. That is how we had learned Dari. What moved me was how creative their writing was, and how full of images. And when I finished reading them, I read them all again, over and over.

The next day, I went to the Hazrat Ali shrine and met my friends with whom I had played *gursai*. They all were amazed by my story of living with the Kuchis. While I was in the shrine, I prayed to ask God to keep my carpet teacher safe wherever she was. My father spent a week with us in Mazar, and then he decided to go to Samangan to get our car, which should have been fixed by now. He would come back to Mazar and drive us all to Kabul. For the most part, the ceasefire seemed to be holding, according to the reports my father heard on the BBC. There had been no serious fighting during the weeks we had been with the Kuchis. My parents felt it was safe to go home. After nearly a year of wandering, they wanted to be settled again.

There was no more talk, at least for now, of going to another country. I was disappointed; I had thought that perhaps I could look for my teacher. But I was also desperately missing Wakeel. He had not come to Mazar as he had promised he would. But I understood how hard it was to travel.

We waited for my father for three days, but he did not come. On the fourth day, my aunt introduced us to her neighbor who was a helicopter pilot.

He told us that he had a flight to Kabul the next day. If we wanted to go, he would take us. That sounded like a good idea to me, but we wanted to wait for my father, so we could all go together.

My mother, my aunt, and her husband talked about it late into the night, while I listened from my bed.

My aunt said, "If you wait for him to come back to go to Kabul together, maybe on the way the car will break down again. It may take days to fix. Then the poor man has to drag you all with him to somewhere, and you know he has no money left. But if the car does break, he will find a way to fix it, or just leave it behind, and make his own way to Kabul."

Finally, around midnight my mother agreed, though reluctantly. Before she could change her mind, my aunt immediately went to her neighbor who had offered to fly us. She took me with her, while my mother started gathering what few belongings we had, and knocked on the neighbor's door, waking him up. My aunt apologized and told him that tomorrow he should pick us up before going to the airport. He smiled sleepily, nodded, and closed the door.

The next morning, my mother, sisters, brother, and I climbed into the helicopter without my father. The cockpit was full of pomegranates in big bags. We ate them as we looked down through little windows to the Hindu Kush mountains that we had already crossed three times, so slowly, in fear and in hope. In only fifty minutes we were at the Kabul airport. We took a taxi, and a half hour later we were at Noborja. Nobody knew we were coming. We had not known ourselves.

As we walked through the outer gate into the garden and then past the heavy wooden door with the clanking chain into the courtyard, a couple of my cousins saw us and then their mothers, and then my uncles. They started shouting and running toward us. We got only as far as the tall acacia tree before we were totally surrounded by them.

Then I saw Wakeel. He came out of one of the rooms on the upper floor to see what was happening. For a moment or two, he stood very still, watching us as we were being hugged and kissed by many of our relatives, while still others were running out of their rooms as they got the news. Then he bolted toward the stairs and sped down them like a kite dropping for a kill, and raced across the courtyard to us.

I was so happy to see Wakeel again. In the months since I had seen him, he had lost some weight and looked skinny and a little taller, but his face glowed with happiness. I could sense that he was feeling waves of relief, like a dry land after the rain. But he could not find words for his emotions.

He hugged my sisters and my mother, but when he reached me, he tagged me on the shoulder and said, "Hey, where the hell were you?" Everybody was watching both of us.

"That is all you can say?" I asked disappointedly as emotions were racing inside me.

He could not hold his tears anymore, and I was not ashamed to let mine go. He hugged me as I shook silently with sobs and squeezed me tighter in his arms. Finally, he got back enough breath to say, "I was so worried that something had happened to you guys. You said you would be gone for one month. But it was almost a year." He wiped his eyes.

I could not answer him. My throat was still blocked. I wanted to see my grandfather. He was inside the house and had not come out. Wakeel took me to the upstairs room where he was seated with two of his friends. When I saw him through the door, I ran to him and kissed him on the face over and over, and hugged him for several minutes without saying anything. I did not want to look in his face, because my eyes were full of tears, and I did not want him to see them. My heart was pounding, and I was trying very hard not to cry out loud. Grandfather did not say anything, but simply held me in his large arms.

After a while, Grandfather said, "Hey, Gorbachev, how did you get here?"

I pulled myself away from him enough to look him in the face. I kissed his hands formally and managed to say, "We all came in a helicopter. The others are downstairs." I felt like I was choking when I spoke, and I could not say more.

Grandfather's eyes were now as full of tears as mine. "Give me another hug," he said, maybe because he did not want me to see this.

Trying to make a joke, he said, "You didn't say hello to my friends. Did you forget all your good manners?" I unwrapped my arms from around his neck and said *"Salaam"* to them, but it came out with a squeak. One of them was drying his tears with the end of his turban.

At that moment, my mother and the others walked in. For the first time ever I was glad everyone was there with us. Usually, I wanted to be the one talking to Grandfather for hours without any interruption. But that day I could not. My mother kissed Grandfather's hands as he kissed her head. Then my grandfather asked about my father.

She sat near him and told him everything, as my aunts brought us tea and my mother gave everybody presents, which were only round Mazar flatbread and candies that we had taken to the shrine to be blessed. After an hour, as the grown-ups kept talking, I walked out of the room and found Wakeel in the corridor all by himself, weeping. That made me start again. Then we were both laughing. This was one day when nobody was feeling any shame about crying. We would have broken the noses of anybody who had said anything.

Before the day ended, everything was like it always had been. We both had a lot of stories to tell each other. He had five good kites for me. One had my name on it. He had made that for me himself. He told me that he had flown that one and cut lots of other kites with it. He said that the neighborhood kids were afraid of that kite.

That is how he made me famous in Kart-e-Parwan. Every kid in the town thought that I was the one flying that kite and cutting them all. But it was Wakeel. It had been very mysterious for the kids in our neighborhood that they never saw me outside, but saw my kite every afternoon high in the sky as it proudly roared around, cutting other kites that tried to rise a little higher than mine.

The next day when I walked outside to buy some bread for breakfast, all the kids were looking at me from the corners of their eyes and whispering to one another, "There he is, there he is. 'Qais, the Cruel Cutter.'" I pretended that I did not hear them. I walked past them, holding my head up like a tyrant.

I gave Wakeel some rocks that I had collected from the Buddha in Bamyan. I had to explain everything about Buddha, and why I thought those rocks were precious. He thought I was joking when I gave them to him, but after I told him about the Buddha, and living in a cave behind his head, and meeting the monk, he did not want to take those stones. He thought they were part of my adventure memories and I should keep them. I told him that he was the *padshah*, the king, of all my memories and that he should have them.

Five days later, my father arrived home with our car, which was now running well. Once again we were all together. We all tried to lead a good life. The war seemed to have ended in Kabul. But we were not living in our own house, which lay in ruins on the other side of the mountain. We were still refugees in Haji Noor Sher's Fort of Nine Towers, which had only one tower left.

While we were away, Grandfather had the idea to scatter his sons, so that if the war started again, we would not all be stuck in one place and could look to one another for help in another part of the city. My uncles had been wanting to leave for some time, but they were waiting for my father to come back before they did. Now, one by one, they left the old fort.

One took his wife and children and moved in with his father-in-law in the Taimaskan blocks in the northwest corner of Kabul. Another uncle shared a house with his brother-in-law in Parwan-e-Seh, not very far from Kart-e-Parwan. Another went to live in Khair Khana with a friend.

A week after we returned, Grandfather himself moved to Makroyan to live with his eldest daughter, who was now a widow. The ceasefire had been going on for more than a month by then, and people were beginning to be hopeful that it would be permanent.

Makroyan was a neighborhood of five- and six-story apartment blocks built by the Russians back when they had come as friends. It was now controlled by one of the factions whose soldiers were raping many young girls there, along with looting people's houses and sometimes killing people. My father's sister had lived there for many years but had become afraid of being alone.

Her husband had been executed during the short-lived Communist presidency of Hafiz'allah Amin, whom no one remembers now. But he had held power long enough to kill many of the best-educated Afghans. One day, my aunt heard her husband's name announced on the radio as being among those who had been purged. No reason was ever given.

Though she subsequently had many suitors, she never remarried and lived with her daughter and her brother, my youngest uncle. He was only a little older than Wakeel, so we thought of him more as our cousin. Grandfather wanted to be with his eldest daughter as long as things remained bad in Makroyan.

Wherever Grandfather lived, that is where Wakeel's mother wanted to be. Grandfather told her to remain at the Qala-e-Noborja with the rest of us, even though he especially loved her cooking. But she insisted on going to Makroyan with him. And so did my unmarried aunts. They wanted to be with their oldest sister, who was like a second mother to them.

Now, for the first time in Kabul, we were living without Grandfather and without Wakeel. Since the fighting had started, nothing had made sense. I could never have imagined that we would ever have left my grandfather's house. And now after so many months away, living without Wakeel or Grandfather made the least sense of all.

The big mud fort felt very empty. At night when the wind hit the large trees and lilac bushes in the courtyard, it made a lonely and even sometimes frightening sound. The dogs outside howled in the rutted road. The Qala-e-Noborja no longer felt like the magical place it had been the day we first arrived.

I thought about my friends in Tashkurghan, and about the Kuchis, and the monk in Bamyan, and my teacher in Mazar, and the kids at the shrine. And most of all, I thought about Wakeel. I had waited so long to be with him again, and now he was on the other side of the city.

Because he was older, he was allowed to come from Makroyan to the Qala-e-Noborja on Fridays by himself. Over the next couple of months the ceasefire held, and he came almost every Friday around midmorning. For an hour, he would sit with my parents and talk with them. Then he and I would fly kites for the rest of the day. He always had to be home before dark, though, which meant he missed the best kite winds at dusk.

Sometimes he spent the night with us, but most of the time he returned home since he was the youngest boy among all the family now in Makroyan, and it was his job to run to the bazaar anytime his mother or one of the aunts needed vegetables or herbs, or had *naan* dough ready to be taken to the bakery.

I wanted to tell all my adventures to Grandfather. But he was not there. Makroyan was on the other side of Kabul. It was only a couple of miles away, but it felt like the far side of the world.

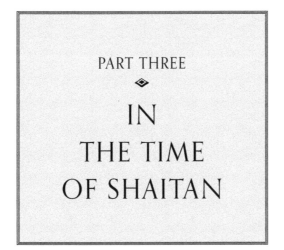

PART THREE

IN
THE TIME
OF SHAITAN

13

❖

The Gold

Now we began the time of pretending. The signs of war were all around us, but we pretended that we did not see them. All but one of my uncles and their families had moved to different parts of the city, but we pretended that we would not be apart for long. We missed sitting around one tablecloth, but we pretended that eating by ourselves was the same as eating all together.

Once or twice everyone came back to the Qala-e-Noborja on a Friday. The grown-ups sat and talked inside, while my cousins and I played in the garden as before, or flew kites. We pretended that we were still living in one courtyard like in the old days. But the grown-ups did not make jokes as they always had. And they never talked about rebuilding Grandfather's house.

When they all left at dusk, we pretended that we would see each other again the next day. Instead, we met after a month or two, because as the weeks passed and the ceasefires came and went, it was still not safe to move around the city.

The war started again in full force five months after we had arrived back in Kabul, even though the leaders of all the factions had gone to Mecca and had sworn that they would never fight again. We pretended that their broken oaths were normal, though every Afghan knows that to break an oath is a serious offense, especially one made in Mecca in the House of God.

The war between the oath breakers locked us all in one room for days and weeks. Sometimes we could not even go to the kitchen across the courtyard, afraid that a sniper might hit us, or a rocket might land as we ran to get some rice, which was often the only food we had left as the days passed and our meat and vegetables were all eaten. We slept night after night with empty stomachs, but we pretended we were practicing for Ramazan.

Once, after several days of eating nothing, I had no choice but to go to the kitchen to get flour so my mother could at least cook us some bread on the woodstove we used for heating the room where we spent our days and nights. My father took me aside and apologized with tears in his eyes for asking me to go, but he explained that if he were killed, there was no one to look out for the rest of the family. I understood. But it took me hours to gather the courage to run the twenty steps there. I ran in zigzags to the kitchen, pretending I was playing hide-and-seek with the snipers on the mountain. They often shot anything they saw that moved. It was their game. But they did not see me. I won the game that day.

Rockets fell by the hundreds. First they made a whistling noise in the air, and then a huge blast that shook the earth when they landed. Bits of rocket and anything they hit rained all around. We pretended that it was fun. We made a whistling noise along with the rockets when we heard them; sometimes we ran out of breath before they landed, and sometimes we did not. When they struck, we made an explosion noise with our mouths and shook our bodies, and pretended we were the earth. Some nights it was hard to sleep because so many rockets were exploding over the city. We pretended it was fireworks on holidays like Great Eid, which honors Ibrahim's willingness to sacrifice his son Ishmael, or Naw Ruz, our new year on the first day of spring.

Sitting every day in one room nearly drove me and the others crazy, but we pretended it would end soon. For days and weeks we did not see the sky, so we pretended that our ceiling was our sky. We read the same books over and over, until we could almost recite them. Sometimes when the stress became too much, I went to another room where I had hung my punching bag from the ceiling. I punched that bag for hours until sweat was running all over me. I pretended that I was getting myself prepared for a match.

A lot of people did go crazy. They walked out of their houses and were hunted down by snipers, who shot them just for the joy of shooting.

As one strange event followed another, we understood—even if we did not say it—that we were living in the time of Shaitan, the devil. Pretending that we were leading normal lives was the only thing that allowed us to survive.

I did not know how to start this new life. Every day I woke up and breathed in and out, and waited for the times to change. I learned that waiting is a skill that must be mastered.

I told myself that my past was finished, and that I had to do something new now. But every day in the cage of my heart, I felt the weight of the memories of the time before.

Many times, I thought about the mother of my carpet teacher, who had told me many old stories that always included a wise lesson. I thought about the bright sky, and snow around us as she spoke in her quiet, mysterious voice. Her face was always close to mine, her wide eyes gazing into mine. Sometimes it felt like she was pouring strength into my heart. She sang rather than spoke. The longer the story went on, the more musical she became. It was an inexpressible joy to listen to her.

I had never known my grandmother. She had died before I was a year old. Sometimes when I was with my teacher's mother, I wished she could be married to my grandfather. When I was with her, it was like she was holding me when I was falling backward.

Grandfather came back to visit and spent several days with us. I would sit next to him while he was reading. It was not important to me that he did not say anything. I was just happy to be there, and, though I was now getting too old for it, I liked to put my head on his lap, to look up and watch him eat an apple and listen to the crunch as he bit it. Sometimes, he would read aloud a poem by Rumi or Hafiz and he would ask me what it meant. I would try very hard to say something wise, to please him. He would smile and tell me, "You learned a lot on your travels."

I told him about our time with the Kuchis. He loved to hear how they ate and made jokes in front of the bonfire until late at night. He asked so many questions about the way they made music, danced, slaughtered their animals, bargained with the people in the towns where they passed and extended their hospitality. As I told him, I relived it all for myself.

He told me that his wife, my grandmother, would always have a strange feeling when she saw a Kuchi caravan passing through Kabul. A part of her wanted to run out of the house when she saw a line of camels plodding through the streets and follow along with everybody else.

One day when my grandfather was reading his favorite book, *Afghanistan in the Path of History* by Mir Ghulam Mohammad Ghobar, my father came in. He had a tray with tea, but only two cups. When he saw me, he told me to go out, but my grandfather put his arm around my shoulder.

My father said, "At least go get a cup for yourself."

When I came back, my father was talking about some man in Hayratan, a town that was on the border with the Soviet Union, which we always just called Russia, about an hour's drive from Mazar-e-Sharif. I listened, though I did not understand what he was talking about at first. Slowly, however, I understood that all those days in Mazar when he had left the house so early and had come home so tired, he had been going back and forth to Hayratan, trying to arrange to have our family smuggled across the border.

Suddenly, I felt stupid for having been so unhappy with my father in those days. I had not known what he was trying to do.

He had been doing the same thing when we were in Kunduz. He had gone north to the border many times, but had never been successful. Being smuggled is expensive. We had had enough money when the fighting had first started. But as time passed, we had had to use most of it just to live on. Now there was very little left.

I looked at my father as he was telling these things to his father, and I felt a kind of respect for him in a way that I never had before. I had blamed him for not having enough money to get us out of the country, for not taking us someplace where nobody could tell us what to do or how to be. Many times I had wanted to ask him why all his friends were living in America or Europe, but we were still in Afghanistan. I had never dared to say that. But I had been resentful. Now I felt ashamed.

I understood as I never had before what a tough man my father was. I thought of how he had carried us from one place to another to save our lives, like a cat carrying its kittens in its mouth.

My father now had to start his life again. Once, he and Grandfather had been important carpet sellers. Now he had no carpets to sell, and no money to buy new ones. He borrowed some money from a friend and bought one carpet from a shop in Chicken Street, a small one. Then he sold it to another dealer for a tiny bit of profit. That was the start of his new business.

Every day, he carried a carpet on his shoulder all over Kabul to sell it for a few afghanis more than he paid for it. Slowly, slowly one carpet became two, and two became four, and four became eight, until one day after five months he had eighty carpets and owned them all. As he sold them, he built up a small cash reserve to pay smugglers. To get to Russia, though, he would need to sell hundreds of carpets.

He never stopped worrying.

Perhaps on that night, now more than two years before, I had sensed what my father and my uncles were doing when I discovered them silently digging holes in the garden. Or perhaps I just pieced together the bits of talk I had overheard whenever there was any mention of smugglers. Someone would mutter something about "the gold" that would pay for them. And "the garden."

My mother and my uncles' wives all had had boxes and boxes of gold jewelry. My father was very much in love with my mother. When they got married, he spent everything he had to buy her gold. Every year at Eid, he would buy her so many new gold bangles that they stretched from her wrists to her elbows.

Whenever my father bought gold for my mother, his brothers had to do the same for their wives, too. Everyone wanted to show off. One uncle's wife wore gold anklets; another had a thick belt, all gold; my mother had a crown of gold. I had seen her wear it only once, at a wedding, and then just for a couple of hours, because too many people were staring at her and wanted to touch it.

At night, when we had gone back to our rooms after a big party, my mother would comment on all the other women's gold. She enjoyed pointing out that her bangles and necklaces were always thicker and heavier than theirs. Probably my uncle's wives were saying similar things about their gold, too. Afghans are competitive about everything.

One afternoon when I was alone with my father, and he was talking about trying to get smuggled to Turkey, I asked him whether he thought all the gold that he and his brothers had buried in Grandfather's garden had been found by thieves. He looked at me with his head tilted slightly to one side, trying to decide how much I really knew.

"It is a big garden," was all he said. I could tell he believed there must still be some gold there.

Now I understood that this was why we had gone before and been captured and sent down into the tunnel. I also understood why he was now insisting on going back, even though we all knew the house had been destroyed.

My mother tried hard to stop him. They argued about it for weeks, but my father is stubborn, possibly the most stubborn man that I know. The ceasefires were irregular and ended unpredictably. But on the days when the guns had gone quiet, my father became profoundly impatient. I could see his thoughts of our old courtyard on his face.

One Friday as we were finishing breakfast, my father asked me to get ready to accompany him. He spoke in a distant tone. I looked at my mother. She was staring at her plate.

I had not forgotten what had happened the last time we had gone there. I knew it would be dangerous. But I was willing to take any chance that could end the pretending and the waiting. Maybe there was still some gold in the garden. Maybe we would find it. Maybe we could pay smugglers and actually escape this time.

We went to the crossroads at the Polytechnic. The flashing yellow traffic light was still over the main crossroad. It had not been shot out yet. We took that as a good sign.

The neighborhood was not at all as I remembered, even from our previous visit. Roofs had fallen in; wild house cats were sneering from broken windows. Ration cans and Russian helmets were scattered everywhere.

When we got to our house, my father pushed open the splintered remains of the thick wooden door. Inside, we walked across the garden to our rooms, staying on the stone path, just to be safe. Once when we had been in Mazar and we were speaking about our house, I had asked my father why somebody would put mines in our garden. He said that maybe they had, but maybe they had not.

"Maybe the man who told my father about those mines was only trying to keep you out of there," my father said. "Did you ever actually see the garden that day?"

"No," I replied.

There were several large holes in a few places that probably had been made by exploding rockets. But most of the garden looked as if it had not been disturbed. I tried to remember where the cucumber plants had been. But after two years, I could not be sure.

All of a sudden I remembered the folk tale of how Mullah Nasruddin had dug a hole on top of the mountain and had hidden his money there. He came back two years later and started digging along the bottom of the mountain, looking for it. After a while, when he could not find anything there, he started to weep. Somebody who was passing by asked, "Why are you crying, Mullah?"

"Two years ago I dug a hole here and hid my money, and now it is not here anymore," Mullah Nasruddin said.

"Are you sure you hid it there?" the man asked.

"Yes, I am very sure, because two years ago the cloud was right here in the sky, and it gave me shade while I was digging. And now you see the cloud is here today, too, but not my money," Mullah Nasruddin said.

I went inside the room where I used to sleep to look for my bed. The room was roofless and empty. It was like no one had ever lived there.

Suddenly, from outside I heard a heavy thud. I looked out and saw five guys in our courtyard, jumping up on the roof of Grandfather's room across the garden from our rooms. They had bundles of thick rope in their hands. They were surprised to see me. One of them wore dusty and torn clothes. He had narrow blue eyes, a brown bushy beard, broad shoulders, and short legs. My father was in another room. He came out and stood next to me. The man came closer and asked my father, "Who are you?"

"I am the owner of this house," my father said sharply.

"But it is ours now," the guy said with a bitter smile. "It is the wheel of life. One day you have everything, and one day I have everything. You enjoyed being in these rooms, and now we are taking the beams to make rooms of our own." He placed an empty clay pot he was holding on the ground. Maybe he had been planning to steal it.

Two of the men had climbed up a bamboo ladder to the roof while we were talking. They tied their ropes into the end of one of the roof beams that lay across the tops of the house's brick walls. One of the others tied the other end of the ropes to a truck that was parked on the road outside. We heard the truck start, and its wheels spin. Black smoke rose over the walls as one of the roof beams was pulled free from its spot and went crashing over the wall into the street.

My father could no longer hold himself back. He was furious. "You bastards! What the hell are you doing?" he shouted at the guys on the roof, who were tying more ropes to other beams.

"Hey, big man, mind your own business," the short guy said.

"Fuck you! It is my fucking business. This is my house," my father shouted. It was the first time I heard words like those from my father.

The short guy climbed down the bamboo ladder. He came over to my father, walking like a lion preparing for a fight. His head hardly reached my father's chest, but he looked very brave, very sure of himself. He tugged hard on my father's beard. With his other hand he tried to grab my father's hair. But my father stopped him with one push and a punch in the nose. The guy's nose broke, and blood spattered all over his clothes.

The two on the roof, who had by then climbed down the bamboo ladder, saw his face was covered with blood. One of them jumped at my father from the back and tried to choke him with a rope.

My father reached over his head and twisted the guy's neck. It made a cracking sound like when you break a dry stick. The guy shrieked. He let go of my father and collapsed onto the ground.

Another guy lunged from the front with a knife. But my father punched him full in the face before the blade could get near. The guy dropped his knife. It fell on the ground. He held his face within his two hands as crimson dripped through the cracks of his fingers.

Two others were holding shovels and looked ready to attack my father. But they looked at their friends and hesitated. One was very pale.

My father ran toward them. They dropped their shovels and sped toward the courtyard wall, climbed it like monkeys, and jumped outside into the street.

My father climbed the wall. "You fucking cowards! Run, you sons of bitches," he shouted.

Two of those in the courtyard were lying on the ground, holding their noses. By now blood was all over their clothes. The other one was still clutching his neck as he walked toward the courtyard gate, groaning.

My father kicked the two guys on the ground. "Leave my house, or I will break every bone you have," my father shouted.

He stood there, breathing heavily, looking around. He asked me whether I was okay.

"You were great!" I said admiringly.

"Oh, come on, I've done sixteen years of boxing. This kind of fighting is like sipping tea," he said with a satisfied smile.

He picked up the intruders' shovels and hid them under some leaves.

"We might need these when we come back," he said.

We went all over our courtyard and checked each room. There was nothing that we could take home with us. Everything had been stolen. There were holes in the walls and floor of each room. The thieves probably thought we had buried something beneath them.

My father and I walked all around. He saw that the earth had not been disturbed where the cucumbers had grown. I thought he would start digging, but he turned and said, "We better go home now before they come back with some more guys." I had been thinking the same. "I will come here tomorrow with my brothers."

My father stepped outside the courtyard with me behind him. Two feet in front of us a strange spray of sparks rose up from the sidewalk accompanied a popping sound. I instantly knew it was bullets. My father ran to the other side of the street and yelled at me, "Move it!" As we ran, a line of bullets followed us, hitting the pavement inches from our feet. We crouched along a shabby wall opposite our courtyard. The shooting stopped.

By now, we had learned that ceasefires did not mean too much. The snipers on the mountain were Panjshiris. But the flat land around our old neighborhood was controlled by the Hazaras. A ceasefire meant that they were supposed to stop launching the rockets at each other that had come from the Americans to be used by the Mujahedin against the Russians. But the Russians were defeated and long gone. However, that did not stop the snipers from shooting people for fun. Sometimes, even in the middle of a ceasefire, there would be a small fight with rockets fired between two factions, and then everything would go quiet again quickly.

My heart was racing, and my clothes clung to my back with cold sweat. I had no time to think about how I had allowed myself, once again, to be drawn into the very heart of the madness of this war. My eyes were fixed on the next building that would provide some cover. We ran to it, then around a corner wall. Under an overhanging roof, we found four middle-aged men sheltering there who had also come to visit their houses. They were trembling like leaves.

We sat there for a few minutes and had no idea where to go. A guy with a rifle crept slowly toward us. He was a sniper, too, trying to shoot the sniper on the mountain.

He pointed his rifle upward and took aim. High on the mountain, we saw a flash of light, and a second later a bullet hit the leg of our sniper. His clothes erupted in bursts of bright red, and his face showed a terrible pain as he cried out.

We all ran from that hiding place to the opposite building, and again a line of bullets rained down next to our feet. I could feel chips of the pavement hitting my legs, but no bullets hit us. We sat there pressed tight against the wall and stared at our sniper. There was nothing we could do to help him. He stood up and ran toward us to take shelter. When he got to the middle of the road, dragging his leg, three bullets hit him in his back. His body hurtled forward, jerking with each hit. His face showed an agony beyond describing.

He turned around, faced the mountain, and fired three times, with spurts of blood jerking out of the back of his hand. Crimson bursts spattered across his broad chest as more bullets hit him.

A friend of his appeared from another corner of the road, but the sniper on the mountain was very quick and hit the sniper's friend, too. The force of the bullets knocked him backward. He died right away.

Our sniper had collapsed into a sitting position. He was still in the middle of the road. He gazed at his feet, saw his torn flesh, blinked with a glazed and mystified look. Then he raised his rifle toward the mountain.

"You bastard! You must die, too," he shouted, and it echoed. We looked where he was pointing. We saw a flash of light like before. Maybe the sniper on the mountain had already squeezed the trigger. The blast thudded into the throat of our sniper. He grunted loudly. His eyes rolled into his head. He never had a chance to pull his trigger. His head slumped onto his arm.

My father stood up, and a bullet hit the wall next to his head. He quickly scrunched down.

"Probably we should just wait here a while," my father proposed. "Maybe they will get bored and forget about us." The other men agreed. We sat quietly without saying anything and let an hour pass.

We were beginning to think about moving again when a large dog ambled toward us. He went to lift his leg against the wall on the other side of the street. As he did, a sniper sprayed him with bullets. The dog was flung into the air, howling. The sniper had let us know he had not forgotten us.

We sat there until night fell.

"We have to creep all the way out of this area," my father finally said.

The other four nodded their heads as a sign of agreement, and then slowly we inched ourselves along the wall all the way to the end of that street and the next one until we got to a roundabout. There we saw trucks with black smoke boiling up from under them, and people running up and down the road.

Hesitantly, we stood up and walked normally. Here on the main road, with so many people, the snipers would probably not shoot at us. This was how war in Kabul was fought. Nothing made sense.

We said goodbye, and we all went our separate ways. Nobody mentioned our sniper who had been killed. But we all knew he had saved us.

My father and I sat on that roundabout and waited for a taxi. I stared at the park across the road where I used to race bicycles with my cousins and play hide-and-seek with my classmates after school. Now the park was dry and dirty. Bullet casings were everywhere. Our neighborhood is cursed, I thought, as a taxi slowed to a halt in front of us.

We climbed into the backseat and headed toward Kart-e-Parwan. It took almost an hour to get there. Neither of us said anything all the way home. And I did not mind.

14

❖

Wakeel

My father opened the door of our room. My mother had just finished her evening prayers. She folded the prayer rug and put it on a shelf. She turned around to go out and prepare dinner. Then she saw us standing on the threshold of the door. She looked like she had cried a lot in the hours since she had expected us to reach home.

My father hugged her. "It's okay, it is okay. We're fine. You see, nothing happened to us. We are the cats with seven lives," my father whispered as he rubbed her back. My mother opened her arms for me, and the three of us stood clinging to one another as if the world and whatever it might bring would never be allowed to separate us.

I needed to bathe, but I wanted to find Wakeel first. My mother said that he had waited for us, but when we did not show up and it was getting dark, he went back to Makroyan to be with our grandfather.

Ever since his father had disappeared, Wakeel always felt very lonely if Grandfather or I was not nearby. He always had friends. Everyone enjoyed being with him. But he needed to know that either Grandfather or I was somewhere close.

"He said he wanted to get a real bath in a tub," my mother explained. There were no bathtubs at Noborja. We washed by pouring small amounts of water over us from the buckets I carried from the

ancient water channel known as the *karuz* at the bottom of the garden. Sometimes we heated it first in one of Haji Noor Sher's large
Russian samovars. "He said he will come back tomorrow."

I wanted to go to Makroyan, too, for a real bath in a tub, and even
more to talk to Wakeel, to tell him what I had seen. I felt like I was
carrying a terrible weight in my soul. I knew he could help take it
from me. He would listen very carefully to everything I told him and
ask questions that only good listeners ask.

But I was too exhausted to go anywhere. I would wait and see
him the next day. I knew his habits, though, and as I lay half dozing
on my bed I could picture in my mind everything he was doing.

After his bath, he put on the blue *shalwar kamiz* that he recently had
had made. He had outgrown all his clothes in recent months and was
getting taller. He stood before the hall mirror after and combed his
hair carefully. He carried his other freshly washed clothes to the
balcony and hung them on the line. From there he could see some
young guys he knew sitting around a fire they had made in the small
park between the buildings. They each had a glass of tea in their hands
and were talking and laughing.

Wakeel hollered at his friends, and they invited him to come down
for tea. He hesitated for a second, trying to decide whether to join
them. He turned on the switch to see whether there was electricity to
watch TV, but there was not.

He said his evening prayers, and then stood before the hall mirror
again and looked at himself. He liked his hairstyle very much. He
had found a new barber in Makroyan who could cut hair very styl-
ishly. He was almost twenty now and had begun to think about
such things.

He went down the stairs and met his friends where they were sitting around their bonfire. He shook hands with all of them and made a
few jokes as he always did. They asked him to sit, but he kept standing.

"Did you come from a city of standing people?" one of his friends
asked him.

"No, from the city of people who just took a bath and don't want their clothes to get smoky," Wakeel joked back.

Everybody laughed.

"Do you want tea?" another friend asked.

"No, thanks!" Wakeel said, smiling. He was already thinking that he should go back into the apartment. The autumn breezes felt cooler down here than they had on the balcony, and he had recovered from the flu only a few days earlier.

He gazed at the clear sky where the half-moon had started to shine, and daylight was fading to dusk. The sparrows' *chuk-chuk* calls were the only sound. They were flying from one branch to the next, from one tree to another, to find their nests and prepare for the night. Wakeel looked around him and took a deep, happy breath.

He was the first to hear the whine of the rocket.

"Get down! Everybody! Down on the ground! Cover your heads. Cover up!" His shout was lost in the explosion of a rocket that landed a few feet behind him. A moment later, another one hit nearby, and then a third.

Then it was so quiet, it was as if the whole world had stopped. The air was laced with the smell of burning cordite, and a cloud of dust rose swiftly to hang above the place where the rockets had landed.

Afterward his friends told us how Wakeel had been the only one standing when the rockets hit. In warning his friends, he did not cover himself in the few seconds that he had. Now he wavered and could not stand anymore. His slender body dropped to the ground. His eyes were wide open, still staring at the sky, at the half-moon. His friends rushed toward him.

Wakeel lay on his side. Springs of crimson spread over his freshly ironed blue clothes. Rocket shrapnel had made dozens of holes in his back. Labored sounds escaped his heaving chest. His mouth quivered. One of his friends sat on the ground and cradled Wakeel's head on his lap and begged him to talk, even as he cried out for help.

Wakeel whispered something and went silent. He had seen so much death. He understood what was happening. Perhaps he had a last wish that he needed to tell someone. Every breath was a fight for him now.

My youngest uncle, who was barely older than Wakeel, appeared from somewhere and rushed toward him, his nephew, his best friend. My uncle sank to the ground and knelt over Wakeel's bloodied body. Wakeel was still gazing at the half-moon. My uncle lifted him onto his shoulder and ran to the road. For the longest time, he could not find a taxi, and even when he did, he knew Wakeel had already said his goodbyes to this world.

Still, he took him to a hospital. He had lost Wakeel's father, his own brother, fifteen years before. He could not accept that he was losing his last connection with his beloved oldest brother.

"He is dead," the doctor said.

It was around eight o'clock. We already had had our dinner. I was ready to sleep, hoping that the image of the sniper's body would not stay lodged in my mind and keep me awake. My father was watching the news on television, which reported that rockets had landed in Makroyan, despite the ceasefire. They were Gulbuddin's rockets. Ceasefires meant nothing to him.

I heard a loud knocking on the large gate that opened to the street. My father sent me to see who was there. I had nearly been asleep. Resentfully, I went out of the courtyard and across the open space where Haji Noor Sher had always parked his large Chevrolet with the canvas roof that was a twin to the one owned by the king.

I opened the gate and found my uncle with his face and clothes drenched with blood. We looked at each other, but he said nothing. It was several moments before I realized that the blood-soaked body on his shoulder was Wakeel, and then only as my uncle was already walking past me. He carried Wakeel's lifeless body to the courtyard.

I wanted to follow him, but my legs were shaking. There was no strength in them to carry me. I held tight to the handle on the gate, then tried to walk again, but I felt that my stomach was falling down. Somehow I managed to close the gate. My uncle disappeared through the archway that led into the courtyard. No! I could not let him take Wakeel from me. No! Suddenly, I was running after them. No!

My uncle laid Wakeel on the ground in front of our windows beneath the tall acacia tree.

My father came out and saw his beloved nephew wrapped in blood. He was shaking his head from side to side, not willing to believe what he was seeing.

He took a deep breath and screamed at heaven, "Oh God, why are you doing this to us?" His voice echoed throughout the courtyard.

Immediately, all of our neighbors in the courtyard were at their windows. A minute later they had surrounded the body, staring at Wakeel, whom they all loved so much.

My only uncle who was still living in the old fort came running out of his rooms holding a book. When he saw Wakeel on the grass, he dropped the book and started slamming the palms of his hands against his head, moaning, and calling out the name of God. His wife tried to make him stop, but he could not.

Wakeel was remarkably long. I had never thought of him that way. His toes were strangely widespread, and his hands were quietly crossed on his chest. I looked at him and looked at him and looked at him. Why was he lying like that? What was I seeing? Nothing was real. A light breeze stirred the carpet of yellow leaves from the acacia tree that had woven itself on the grass. A few of them brushed across Wakeel's immobile face.

A loud cry burst from me, and I wept. I wept for Wakeel. I wept for me. I wept for everything that had happened since the Holy Warriors had destroyed our country and our lives. I do not know how long I cried, but after a while I found myself folded in my mother's arms. She was crying, too.

A few hours later, Wakeel's mother arrived from her brother's house. She had been at her nephew's engagement party. She knelt beside Wakeel and kept muttering things in a deep, hoarse voice. Her eyes were larger than I had ever seen them.

She spent the entire night on the ground next to her son, crying and laughing, like a crazy woman, and sometimes muttering things that we could not hear. I lay in my bed, letting the tears roll silently down my face.

More than at any time in my life, I wanted to be with my grandfather. But it was too dangerous to cross Kabul at night.

Early in the morning, Grandfather and my uncles arrived to take Wakeel for burial. I wanted to help carry him, but though I was thirteen years old, I was too short. I walked next to my father as he and my uncles carried Wakeel out of the courtyard on their shoulders. They carried him on a bamboo litter, still wearing his bloody clothes. His body had not been washed, since he was a martyr.

His mother ran after us, trying to stop us from taking her only son away, but her feet would not let her. She stumbled and collapsed on the ground. She stood again briefly, but then fell down again and rolled onto her back. The other women came and tried to help her. Her hair streamed over the ground, her unseeing eyes gazing into some other world, her teeth clenched. She cried out loud. Slowly they helped her get up.

The other women knew they should try to hold her back, but they let her go, though there is no place for a woman at a Muslim burial. She stood yet again to run after us, but again she fell down, and for a time she went unconscious.

We finished the rituals and put the body in the grave. We had not been able to go to our family cemetery since it was near Grandfather's house on the other side of the Koh-e-Aliabad, and we had no way of knowing whether the snipers on the mountain would respect us as we carried Wakeel's body. So we left him with strangers in a small, old cemetery called Nawabad that was protected from the snipers by the spur of a low, steep hill.

A butterfly appeared over the loose earth of the grave and fluttered around for a few moments before settling on it. The undersides of its wings were powdery white. When it opened them, the tops were such a dark red that it looked like an open wound.

It was lifted by a breeze and borne away. I watched it go. It grew smaller and smaller. I knew it was Wakeel's soul leaving his body, and us, and I knew he was trying to tell me that he was all right. He had always believed in signs. I wanted to be flying away with him, too. I wept again, but a strange, warm feeling filled me that brought a sense of peace of a kind that I had never known before and never have since. The butterfly disappeared from sight as it drifted across the top of the steep cemetery hill.

All around me, Grandfather, my father and my uncles, and all my other male relatives stood frozen in grief. Jerk stood next to his father, looking down and not trying to hide his tears. Though he had been the target of Wakeel's relentless jests, he loved Wakeel, as we all did. Jerk had no one to protect him anymore, or to tease him, or to help him fly kites, or to make him run faster when we played football, or to help him with his homework.

Shortly after we finished the prayers, Wakeel's mother arrived with the other women. She was crying as if she herself were dying. She lowered herself to the ground and knelt next to the grave, arranging and rearranging the stones on the loose earth. We all started weeping with her, but there was nothing we could do for her. I was very grateful that Wakeel had shown me his soul in that butterfly, and that Grandfather was there with me, too.

Though we had finished what we had come to do, we knew we could not leave until Wakeel's mother was ready to come with us. After half an hour or so, she rose and quietly started walking away. The other women, who had been waiting at a distance, quickly surrounded her and let her lean on them as they picked their way down the cemetery's rocky slope.

We walked slowly all the way home. I walked next to Grandfather, but he was so upset that he hardly noticed me. I tried to talk to him, so he would not feel so sad. He did not seem to listen. Then he spoke.

"I have always thought that people's sorrows come from three reasons," Grandfather said. "They always want everything immediately, without effort. They want more than they need. And they are not happy with what they have. But now I realize that the greatest sorrow of the world is to lose a gift from God."

I did not understand.

"Wakeel was the gift of God to us, but we hardly noticed its worth. So, God took it back," Grandfather said.

I told him about the butterfly. He crouched down on one knee, then opened his arms and embraced me. "You always find something that makes me feel better."

His face was level with mine, and for the first time I could see that even his eyes were red and wet. "Do you know what happens to people when they die?" Grandfather asked with a sad smile.

"Yes, of course I do. That is the first lesson the mullah taught me and the other boys on our first day at the mosque," I replied.

"Right. When we die, we believe we go to heaven, or we rest forever, or we turn into angels, or we go to paradise. That's probably all true. But let me tell you something: I believe that when we die at least a small part of our soul enters the one whom we loved the most, and makes that person wiser."

Grandfather had said things like this to me many times. I always understood the words, but sometimes it took me weeks to know what real meaning lay behind them, and what lesson lay in them for me.

Grandfather spent a week with us, then he said he must go to be with Wakeel's mother. I understood. I loved Wakeel's mother and could not imagine how lost she was feeling. She was like a second mother to us. That is why we called her Abbo, which in Pashto means "mother." When we were little, she often looked after us when my mother was at the bank and my father at his school and for some reason they could not come home to prepare our lunch. Abbo fed us, washed us, put us in bed for our naps, woke us up, and took us to the other side of the courtyard to play with her children and our other cousins.

Abbo was always a good storyteller. She knows many stories, funny and sad ones, but now she tells her son's story more than any other. Every time she tells it, her eyes get red, tears roll out of them, and her voice shakes, but she continues until she finishes. Even though it is painful to hear, no one can leave in the middle, because she always tells it as if she had just heard all the details a short while before. She always says the same words, as though reciting something from a holy book. Once I left the room when she started telling a distant relative what had happened. But though I did not want to hear it, I found I could not stay outside and leave her alone with Wakeel. I went back in and sat next to her.

She had asked hard questions of all of Wakeel's friends and others who had been there that evening. She knows every detail as if she had seen them with her own eyes. I cannot imagine how painful that has been for her. It is even painful to listen to her, but we listen to her because we love her.

When Grandfather left to go back to Makroyan, I felt more alone than I ever had before. I had so many things to ask him.

Some days I sat under the acacia tree in the courtyard where Wakeel's body had lain. I was waiting for the butterfly. But it never came back.

15

❖

Inferno

A rocket landed in the room upstairs where my father stored his carpets. It was late on a Friday afternoon in the middle of the summer, when everything was dry and the weather was windy and dusty.

When it hit, my father was drinking tea with the next-door neighbors and trying to buy their carpets, along with an old silver vessel from the twelfth-century Ghaznawi dynasty. It had two hundred pounds of rice in it. The neighbor was moving to Pakistan, and from there to Canada to stay with relatives who had made arrangements through the United Nations.

My father wanted to buy their carpets, because they were at least a hundred years old and still in good condition. He could sell them for twice what he paid. He also wanted to buy the old silver vessel, because he knew that the guys who took those old pieces to Pakistan paid good money. He was trying to buy their rice as well since it came from Kunduz, and was a bit cheaper than the market price for imported rice.

I was just coming back into the courtyard, carrying water in buckets from the tap at the mosque below the garden. In those days, all the neighborhood water pumps installed around Kabul by the municipal government had dried because of a drought, and most of the pipes had been destroyed. Now we had to go long distances to find a working well. The mosque had one in its garden. I had just made my fourth trip. I was tired and was trying to catch my breath.

The noise of the rocket exploding was so loud that in actual fact I heard nothing. I could only feel a heavy and deep wave that shook the entire fort. Smoke mixed with dust started pouring out first one, and then another of the three large windows that faced the courtyard. I was stunned and confused. What should I do with such smoke? How could I turn it off? I was afraid to get close to that room. But I did not want all of my father's carpets to burn while I watched and did nothing. But I could not think of anything. I was very dizzy, and completely deaf.

I saw the mouth of my neighbor's son was opening and closing, but I could not hear a word he was saying. He began touching my entire body, starting from my legs and going up and up. He was look-ing to see whether I was injured. He nodded at me that I was all right, and we turned and looked upstairs.

My father had rushed back from the neighbors' house when he had heard the explosion. He met me just inside the gate of the court-yard, where I still held my buckets full of water.

I read horror and fear on his face. He asked me something. I could not hear him, but I instinctively knew he was asking whether my mother and the rest of the family were okay.

My mother and sisters had been watching a Bollywood movie downstairs, directly under the room that was hit. When the rocket exploded, it shook the whole fort, and the dust puffed out of the ceil-ing and cracks in the old mud walls.

Now my mother came running out into the courtyard with my sisters. She was almost dragging my little brother, even though he could walk now. In her arms, she had my newest little sister, who was only a few months old. From head to toe they were all covered with dust. They looked lost and confused and were probably deaf like me.

My father could see that they were not injured, and so he looked up at the storeroom, where all his hard work and our hope of ever fleeing Afghanistan were turning into smoke.

He grabbed my two heavy buckets full of water as if there were nothing in them and rushed up the outside stairs to the terrace in front of the burning room. I followed him. He jumped inside the room through the one window clear of smoke, holding one bucket. Then he gestured to me for the other.

Now he was inside. Lost in the thick, black smoke, he threw the water from the first bucket, unsure of where it was going. Where it hit, the smoke turned to fire, as if he had poured gasoline on it. He threw the second bucket, but he was suddenly surrounded by fire; he was in the heart of it. I could see he was shouting for help.

I shouted at him to run out through the fire before it got stronger and even more uncontrollable. I heard myself in my head louder than I actually sounded, and it was painful. Perhaps he heard me, or perhaps it was just his instincts. He leaped through the fire and jumped out the window. His shoes and trousers were in flames. The fire quickly rose to his chest and back.

Someone screamed at him to roll on the ground, probably my mother. The fire on his back appeared to go out when he rolled on it. But when he rolled onto his chest, the flames on his back flared up again. He kept rolling back and forth. My mother brought a bucket of water from our bathroom inside the house and poured it on him. Smoke mixed with steam rose over my father as he kept rolling back and forth on the earthen, now muddy, terrace.

He stood up, surrounded by steam with smoke rising up all around him. We could hardly see his face. His clothes were badly singed, but somehow he was unharmed.

He grabbed another bucket of water that my sister brought from the house and rushed toward the windows. By now the fire was pouring out all three of the big windows. There was no doubt now that my father's carpets were fueling that fire.

My mother raced after him, yelling, and held his shoulder to stop him from going into the blaze again with his small bucket of water. It was like spitting on such a fire.

My father shouted back at her as she tried to drag him away by one arm, but he shook her off and stood there as every second the fire grew bigger. I watched it all like a silent movie, as I could still hear nothing. The roof beams by then were burning, and one of them collapsed onto his carpets. Slowly, his head fell down on his chest in despair. He put the bucket full of water by his feet.

One hour later, when the fire had already consumed the thick beams of the ceiling and what was left of the carpets, the firefighters arrived. None of their equipment fit through that one very small door into the courtyard and the angled passageway within. The fort with its high walls was like a large open box, and the firefighters had no ladders long enough to climb over and get inside it.

Our neighbors brought their narrow bamboo ladders, and eventually three firefighters climbed up the walls from the garden side and started pouring water into the heart of the fire. The blaze sent shadows of the dark and bitter-smelling smoke of burning wool over the whole neighborhood. The sky choked on it.

More neighbors arrived. But when they heard the muffled, defiant roar of the fire, they knew there was nothing they could do.

There was now thick, white smoke in place of the orange flames, and the black smoke lessened. The firefighters were finally able to go into the room and check for hot spots. The fire still smoldered in crevices in the walls.

After a couple of hours, it appeared to have died down. But the firefighters did not let us go in. The mud bricks in the walls had a lot of straw in them, with wooden posts and beams buried within. It could all flare up and start burning again at any time.

The courtyard was still full of our neighborhood people. Slowly, one by one they left, as night came, shaking their heads sadly, and talking about how big the fire had become in such a short time.

My father and I walked inside the burned-out room. The ceiling had fallen in, and everything was hot and steaming. He started looking for his carpets under the tons of mud that had been the earthen roof. He was breathing very hard.

He tried to dig the hot earth with his hands. It singed his fingers, and he shouted at me to bring him a shovel instead of staring at him like a nutcase. I was now beginning to hear again, but with a loud ringing in my ears.

I brought him a shovel. He shoveled for half an hour without stop. He was soaked in sweat. His burned clothes clung to his back, and I could see every muscle straining. With each minute, his shoveling got faster and faster. Finally, he reached the floor and found nothing except a layer of ashes where his carpets had been.

"Oh God, why have you done this to me? Do I deserve this?" he cried out. It scared me. Such heavy grief from the depth of his soul.

A strong wind started to blow. Some of the half-burned wood caught fire again. My father cried for water. I brought him two buckets from the storage tank in our bathroom, and he poured them where the fire had blazed up. A minute later another crevice in the wall caught fire. We threw water there as well. Then another place flared up, and another, until seven o'clock the next morning. My father and I did not sleep that night, or eat either.

He did not want my mother and sisters sleeping in the rooms beneath the one that had burned, and so he made a shelter in the corner of the courtyard for them. All night, they kept waking up, hungry and cold, dreaming that there was another fire they had to put out.

The next night, my sisters were still afraid to move back into those rooms downstairs, though by then they were safe. Everything smelled of smoke, however, and was covered with dust.

We all slept in the shelter my father had made the previous night. We made a fire in front of it for light. It reminded me of those nights with the Kuchis when we ate and laughed and told stories with the sounds of the animals nearby in the darkness.

But we were not with the Kuchis anymore. Fire had a different meaning to us now. I was lying between my father and mother, and the sound of their breathing assured me of their sleep, though with my mother you could never tell. Sometimes she would wake in the middle of the night and stare into space with tears on her cheeks.

That night I had seen her crying again. I reached out and touched her on the shoulder and asked whether she was all right. She quickly turned her back without replying. She never sobbed or wailed or sniffed like an ordinary person. She cried when nobody could see or hear her, letting the tears empty out of her in a stream of silent sorrow.

The next day we moved back into the downstairs rooms, even though they still smelled smoky. My father was deeply depressed. He did not help us carry our things back in. He sat under the acacia tree where Wakeel's body had lain, his head on his knees, sitting like that for hours. It was as if he were dead himself. My mother asked him to have lunch with us, but he did not eat or drink anything. His lips were dry, and brown bags had formed under his eyes.

Finally, around one o'clock in the morning he came in and lay next to my mother. He was cold and shivering. My mother covered him with her blanket and hugged him until he stopped shaking. The next day, he did not talk to anyone. He just sat next to the window, staring outside at one spot, not knowing what he was looking at. When my sisters and I talked, we whispered. When we walked, we tiptoed. And when we ate, we tried not to make any sound with our spoons and forks.

After a week, he began to ask for a few things, like a glass of water, or a cup of tea. My mother began to cook everything salty or oily, knowing that my father did not like this. He started fussing about the salt and oil. My mother shouted back at him not to complain. He left the room and went out. My mother smiled at us and said, "He'll come back happy like before." We did not know what she was talking about.

Three hours later my father came back with bags of fruit and a few kilos of beef. He had a sad smile on his face, like his own father's. That night my mother cooked us good food, and my father began to make jokes. The noise of forks and spoons started again. We did not have to whisper or tiptoe anymore.

The factions had started fighting yet again, and again trapped us in one room like mice in a hole.

The rockets were raining all over Kabul City nonstop. Gulbuddin was firing his American rockets at the Panjshiris who lived in the area around our Fort of Nine Towers. Dostum, the Uzbek commander, was also sending his rockets against the Panjshiris, both to our area and to Makroyan. The Hazaras were sending rockets against the Panjshiris, who were also sending rockets to the Hazaras. Sayyaf fired rockets from the high mountains west of Kabul aimed at the Panjshiris and the Hazaras. Sometimes three thousand rockets fell on Kabul in one day. When the rockets stopped for a few minutes, it was unnaturally silent. But, in fact, there was never truly silence. The house was always talking to itself, the clicking of the clock in the next room, the periodic judder and whir of the refrigerator when we had electricity. From the bathroom the drip, drip, drip of water from the nozzle into a big pot full of water. Every now and then out on the road, there was the whoosh of a passing car or the rumble of a truck.

We listened for the sound of the releasing of the rocket, then its landing that shook the ground like an earthquake. In two months, twenty-nine rockets landed in that fort and its garden. The last of the nine towers still stood at the corner of the old fort, but it no longer made me feel safe. For more than a hundred years, the towers had protected the people inside. Not anymore. Not in this time of Shaitan.

One reason why Grandfather and the rest of the family had all moved to the solidly built blocks of Makroyan was that they thought it would be safer there. But they were as trapped in Makroyan as we were at the Qala-e-Noborja in Kart-e-Parwan. For weeks we had no idea what was happening to them. Were they still alive, dead, wounded? We had no phones; no one was in the street to carry a message. My father stopped listening to the BBC and the other news channels, because they made us even more anxious, telling us about the casualties and announcing the names of the injured in hospitals and the lack of blood for transfusions, or medicine, or doctors.

For whole days and weeks we sat at the corner of the room, murmuring our prayers and waiting for a rocket to kill us all together. One night when the noise of the exploding rockets was too loud to let me sleep, I climbed up on the roof of the old fort and sat near the one remaining tower. I watched one rocket after another fall on the flat-land neighborhoods in front of me. Each time when a rocket whistled overhead, I was momentarily surprised that it had not killed me. But a part of me no longer cared. I simply presumed that one of them would soon land next to me, and that I would not live to see the morning.

Sometimes my father, mother, sisters, and I wrote letters to my grandfather, aunts, uncles, and cousins. When there was ceasefire for a day or two, we sent those letters that we had written days or weeks ago with anybody in the neighborhood we could find who had to go to Makroyan for some reason. In the same day we might receive a bunch of letters from all of them, if one of my uncles could make the trip. Then the war would set in again, and we would not hear from each other for weeks.

Those were the worst days of my life. Yet there was something sweet about them. Whenever I wrote letters, I was very careful to use the right words in the right places. I expected the same careful attention to detail from those who answered my letters. In those days when most people were worried about staying alive, I was focused on how to write a beautiful letter and express my feelings accurately about everything, and in precise chronological order. I was only just finding my way into my teenage years, but with life so fragile, the schooling I might have had, or the sports I might have played, or the work I might have done meant nothing.

After two months of constant war all over Kabul, once again we had a ceasefire for a few weeks. Grandfather came to our house and spent those days with us. I was so happy to sit next to him, and to put my head on his lap and listen to his breathing when he was reading or eating or talking to others.

The night before he returned to Makroyan, he talked with my father and mother late into the night, long after the rest of us went to sleep. After he left, I went to sit under the acacia tree feeling a deep loneliness. A short while later, my father came and sat down next to me.

"We made a decision last night while you were asleep." My father paused, and then continued with a deep sigh. "Now while we are having this ceasefire, you and I are going to Pakistan. We'll rent a house there, and then come back for the others. We'll stay there until Kabul gets peaceful again."

"Isn't it going to be hard to live in a strange country?" I asked.

"We will all die if we stay here. At least we will survive in Pakistan. I'm sure you'll get used to it soon. You'll find good friends, and you will go to school again, I promise you," my father said. He had a kindly half smile. That made me feel like this was really going to happen.

I asked when we would go.

"Tomorrow," he said. He put his arm around me and let me fall against his strong chest.

16

❖

The Dog

The next day around five o'clock in the morning, we said good-bye to my mother, brother, and sisters. By six o'clock, I was on the seat next to my father in an old minibus full of people. Some of the people were sitting on the floor on bags of clothes.

I had a glass of black tea in my hands and was slowly sipping it to wake me up. I enjoyed looking at the mountains and thinking about nature after the months trapped inside the fort. Now Kabul was behind us, and we were heading toward the Khyber Pass. I had heard about the Khyber Pass from my history teacher in school, as I had about the Buddhas in Bamyan, but I had never seen it. I was excited that soon I would be passing through it.

The minibus was quiet, except for the sound of the engine, and the occasional coughing or sneezing of some of the passengers. Some were having a nap. Some were looking out the windows as we twisted our way down the sides of mountains where Kabul was nestled. Sometimes the driver had to slow down because of large holes in the road. Mostly, though, he drove fast despite the steepness of the mountains.

As we were approaching the small town of Sarobi, I was pouring more tea from my thermos. The driver hit the brakes, and my tea spilled all over my clothes. I felt the warmth of it spreading across my lap. The other passengers shouted at the driver to be careful. The driver turned around in his seat and put his index finger on his lips. The bus doors opened, and a man followed by two bodyguards stepped inside our bus.

They eyed us coldly. There was nothing even close to a welcoming smile and no Afghan hospitality in their eyes. We were all quiet as they scanned us, one by one.

The old man who was sitting in the seat in front of us turned around and whispered to my father that the man's name was Commander Zardad.

Commander Zardad had badly pitted cheeks and the thickest black eyebrows I had ever seen over big, dark, sunken eyes, so black that they demanded full attention. He weighed only about one hundred fifty pounds, all of it bunched tightly into a black leather jacket and *shalwar kamiz*. He selected several men and women from our minibus, including my father, and led them off the bus, then told the driver to continue his journey to Pakistan. The panicked driver started the engine. I jumped off before he could drive away.

Zardad looked me in the eye and said, "You are not invited."

"You have my father, and I want to stay with him," I said.

"Then you must come," he said, and slapped me on my shoulder gently like an old friend.

We walked for ten minutes up the side of the steep mountain to get to his camp. He had more than two hundred men, all armed and resting under the shade of their tents. Some of them were drinking tea, some of them were asleep, and some of them were just staring at us.

We were led into a large tent that was open on one side and told to sit down. None of us did. We stood there frozen. Inside the tent, several corpses were laid out on the ground. They were naked and looked like they had been badly bitten all over.

One was a girl who looked to be in her early twenties. She was petite with yellow hair that streamed all around her head. She had a pretty face and a slender body with long legs. Her shoulders were narrow, hardly more than a dozen inches across. Her breasts were small, but they looked almost like they had been shredded.

There were bite marks up and down her arms and legs, especially around her thighs.

A dead man next to her looked like a statue that had been cut from white stone, as if all his blood had been drained. Like the girl, he seemed more like an American or a European than an Afghan. He was very muscular. But he, too, had been bitten all over. His throat had been slashed, and so had his wrists and thighs and ankles. I could see no bruises on his hands; he had not been able to land any punches on his attackers. There was a cold, desperate horror frozen on his face. His mouth and eyes were wide open.

Some other bodies that lay near them were covered with white sheets that had bloodstains all over them.

"You see these people?" Zardad said. "They avoided giving me their money, and in the end they lost their lives as well as their money. If you guys love your lives, give me your money, and you are free to go."

My father took out all his money from his pockets and gave it to Commander Zardad.

"Where is your house?" Zardad asked.

"In Kabul," my father replied without emotion.

"Why are you going to Pakistan?"

"To see if we can live there," my father said.

"You don't have a wife and more kids?" Zardad asked.

"Yes," my father said.

"Why are they not with you?"

"I couldn't take them with me to Pakistan now. I have no house for them there. After I find a place, I will go back for them," my father explained matter-of-factly.

"You must be a rich man. Let's make a deal. I let your son go home and bring more money, then you're free to go. Does it sound good?" Zardad asked, his big eyebrows raised up.

"We don't have much money. Just enough for us to live on for a while. If I give it all to you, how will I feed my kids?" my father asked.

"Don't answer me with a question," Zardad shot back.

My father lowered his head and said nothing.

Zardad shouted out, "Dog!" I looked around, expecting to see one of his men come with the kind of dog that was used for fighting.

I looked at the corpses with their bite marks and became very frightened. Why did Zardad want a dog?

A man entered the tent. He had big teeth, like long, yellow fangs. He laughed when he saw us.

Zardad rasped an order. "Tie him."

Two of his men grabbed my father from behind while another one pulled off his *kamiz* shirt, then his *shalwar* trousers. They tied his hands and feet with chains to a large frame made from thick wooden beams. They pulled his wrists upward to the top corners of the frame. His feet were spread apart and chained to the bottom. He looked like one of the carpets I had seen him stretch so many times.

When my father could not move anymore and all eyes were fixed on him, Zardad ordered the man he called Dog to start. Dog opened his mouth wide and sank his teeth into one of my father's biceps.

My father cried out in pain and shouted that he did not have any money. This time Zardad ordered the man to hang by his teeth from my father's other arm. He closed his jaws on my father again and raised his feet from the ground as he had been told. My father was screaming now, and turning redder and redder.

I watched in disbelief. I had seen so many things since the fighting had begun, and so much cruelty, but I had never imagined anything as unspeakably strange as this.

The fanged man continued biting my father all over: his arms, shoulders, thighs, chest, underarms, neck, and buttocks. My father continued shouting while Zardad sat casually on a chair, twenty feet away, watching him and sipping his tea. He showed no emotion despite my father's piercing yells.

I could hardly even breathe. I understood that I was watching my father die, and my mind raced as I thought, "How can I take the responsibility for my family? I'm only thirteen years old."

And then the shouting grew quieter, as my father began to lose strength. His eyes closed. His body hung limply in the chains. His wounds were bleeding badly.

Zardad finally ordered two other men to release him. They undid the chains, and my father collapsed on the ground. They grabbed him by his wrists and dragged him thirty feet across the gravel, scraping the skin off his back as they went. He lay there, not moving, just moaning.

Then the two guys came and grabbed me. They pulled off my clothes except for my undershorts and a thin chain around my neck with a picture of Mecca hanging from it. They fastened the chains that they had used on my father around my wrists and ankles. Strangely, as they pulled the chains tight, cutting into my skin, I felt a sense of relief. I had cheated death so many times since the war had started. Today it would all end.

The man with the fangs slowly walked toward me. His mouth was outlined with my father's blood, but his skin was deathly pale, as if he had no blood of his own in his veins. When he walked, he seemed like he hardly had enough energy to propel himself.

When he bit me the first time, it was like a saw or a sharp piece of metal was sinking into my arms. The pain was so powerful that the light started instantly going from my eyes, and everything around me got darker and darker. I shouted louder than I ever have.

"Don't touch him," my father shouted hoarsely. He tried to stand. Two men ran over and held him back. Dried blood covered his whole body, except for his face. "Come and do it to me!"

"No, your son has fresher blood and tender skin," the man whispered so softly that I hardly heard him. "You've got old blood. This is more fun with your son." Then he bit me on my left leg. This time it was worse than before. Then on my shoulder, and on my back. I could do nothing but howl.

One of Zardad's soldiers stepped forward. "Please stop for a while, sir. Give them a break." The soldier spoke in Pashto.

"I'm not taking orders from you. You're taking orders from me," Zardad snapped back. Until now he had spoken only in Dari. He did not even look at the soldier. He was still staring at me.

"Yes, sir, I know it, but I just want to have a couple of hours of sleep and these bastards keep screaming and waking me up," the soldier said.

"Hey, I'm having a good time. Don't fuck with me," Zardad said.

My father forced himself up from the ground. "What kind of a Pashtun are you?" he spat hoarsely at Zardad, speaking in Pashto.

"Are you Pashtun?" Zardad asked in amazement.

"Of course I am," my father said, his voice hardly louder than a whisper.

"Why the fuck didn't you tell me?" Zardad said. He got up from the chair where he had been watching and walked toward my father, studying him more closely. He stood over my father for a moment, then ordered his men to untie me and give us our clothes back. "I don't torture my Pashtuns," Zardad said airily as he walked back to his chair.

My father and I put on our clothes as best we could. Every time I moved, the places where the fanged man had bitten me ached like something was still tearing my skin. I was so stiff with fear, I hardly knew what I was doing. Blood ran out of the wounds and soaked my clothes. All the while, the man with the fangs was looking at me fiercely, angry that he had lost his prey and could do nothing about it.

"What about the others?" my father asked. He could not stand up straight. "Release them, too."

"You're free to go," Zardad said, like he was giving an order.

"You're not torturing these people for their money, are you? You're torturing them because you enjoy doing it," my father said.

"If you say one more word, I will forget you're a Pashtun. Understood? Go, and don't ever look back," Zardad shouted.

My father did not say anything. We left there and walked in small, painful steps along the steep path back down to the road. Ten minutes later we were in a highway taxi coming along the main road from Jalalabad to Kabul, headed toward our home.

"What is all this?" my mother asked, looking at the blood on our clothes. Her eyes were wide, her mouth open, and her face pale.

"We were bitten by a dog," my father said as he was hugging her. Then he fainted, and his body slumped onto hers.

My mother cried to me to help her with my father. We half carried and half dragged him to his bed. I told my mother what had happened to us but kept it short, because I wanted to lie down as well.

She ran outside and came back with our neighbor who was a nightshift doctor.

A few minutes later, the doctor injected him with something that made him totally numb. The doctor started to wash the wounds, first with alcohol to disinfect them, and then with a few things he mixed all together. He rubbed the wounds gently, then covered them with rolls of bandages.

When the doctor had finished my father's wounds, I showed him mine. My shoulders and arms had begun to itch and then ache. The puncture wounds of the bites were still bleeding a little, especially those on my right arm, which were the deepest. He did for me the same things that he had done for my father. He was amazed how I had endured the pain so far. But pain was our way of life now.

I woke up early the next morning and was still in bad shape. There was a blotchy redness and intense heat around each bite wound. Each one throbbed. I noticed a nasty drainage from the bites on my left leg. All the wounds were swollen to nearly twice the size they had been the night before. When I moved, I felt like something was tearing my skin.

It took us two weeks to recover. My mother would not let my father even speak of going to Pakistan again. She said that what had happened to us was a bad sign. She said that if we lived in Pakistan, it would be worse than Kabul.

"You are superstitious," my father said.

"Yes," my mother said bluntly. She was pacing the bedroom like the leopard that had been in the garden. My father watched her for a few minutes, and then told her he would like some tea.

She stopped, looked at him, and raised her finger like she was pointing to me or my sisters. "I am not going to Pakistan," she said very firmly. "I'm going to stay in Kabul. And if I die, so be it. But I'm going to die on my own piece of earth, not in some strange country."

My father knew argument would not change her mind. She walked silently from the room to get him his tea.

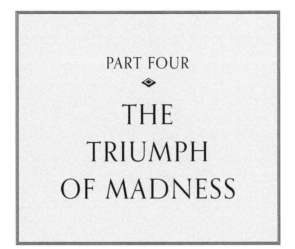

PART FOUR

THE
TRIUMPH
OF MADNESS

17

❖

A New Kind of Justice

We entered a time of waiting. The fighting would end, we said, if we waited. Our lives would come back to us, if we waited. Or we would find a way out, if we waited. If our gold was still in Grandfather's garden, then it would wait there for now, just as we would wait at Noborja.

The fighting in Kabul eased, and a school near Noborja reopened. After so much thirst to go back to school, I was now disappointed by it. The school was shabby, not like the well-maintained building that the educated families in our old neighborhood had supported. There, all the teachers had known my name and my family. I was treated well and was excited by every new thing I was taught.

In this new school, many of the students came from rural areas north of Kabul, like Shamali, Parwan, and Panjshir. They spoke Dari with accents from those places that sounded strange to me. Some of their families had come to Kabul with the Mujahedin. Some of them liked to fight more than to study. In Dari we say, "If you sit with good people, you will become a good person. If you sit with bad people, you will become a bad person." The students were not really bad people, but I picked up a lot of bad habits from them.

I went every day, though, mostly because there was nothing else to do. I had missed more than two full years of school, but so had most of my classmates. We were all behind, even though some of them, like me, had been educated at home by their parents. Living in a war had also taught us many things.

Somehow I had ended up in the eighth grade. Perhaps that was because I was thirteen and looked like I should be there. I went for four hours every afternoon. The kids in the first six grades came in the morning, including my younger sisters. My older sister went to a girls' high school not far away. For as long as the ceasefires held, we could go every day.

Most of the teachers were as discouraged about life in Afghanistan as the students. The teachers tried hard to convince us that what they were teaching was important for us to learn. Maybe it was.

Sometimes in our classes we talked about the various factions, and which one was good and which one was bad. In the end, we agreed that none of them were good. Rockets still fell on Kabul sometimes, though we were never sure which faction sent them. Meanwhile, we were hearing about a new faction called the Taliban that was taking control of the cities in the south and was slowly moving into the east. Many people said they would make a circle around Kabul and drive all the other factions away. We did not know much about them. We were sick of commanders and factions.

We were more worried by our principal, who had eyes that were red like fireballs. Every day he slapped students who had been fighting until they started to cry in front of all the other students. He was a stupid man who told us to fix a faucet that was dripping precious water by jamming a stick up inside it. We did that, and we got very wet when the water squirted all over us. Then he slapped us for getting ourselves wet.

Nobody slapped him, though, when somebody discovered a dead cat in the cistern. It had been there for at least a week, and we had been drinking the water.

The one class that I did enjoy was taught by our Dari language and literature teacher. She was pretty and always cheerful. She helped me understand for the first time that there is more to a story than its plot. She told us that images created by words can have hidden meanings. I started rereading all the books that we had at home, like a detective, looking for hidden meanings that other people who were not as smart as I was could not see.

The textbooks that the school gave us had very little literature in them. Some poetry, some short stories with hard and fancy words, and some history about famous poets and writers. So, our teacher assigned us other books to read, mostly novels. A lot of the boys hated reading, and they sulked. But there were a few of us who found that every book that our teacher asked us to read was better than the one before.

Our teacher recommended novels she thought would help us understand things that are not taught in school textbooks. Mostly they were novels by Iranian authors such as Amir Ashiri, Parwiz Qazi Sayed, Aroniqi Karmani, and Jawad Fazil. She also suggested a few Western authors as well, such as Maxim Gorky, Fyodor Dostoyevsky, Leo Tolstoy, Anton Chekhov, Jack London, and Thomas Mann. *Crime and Punishment* was too much about hardship, misery, and pain. I read the first few pages, but then put the book back in its place in my cabinet and told myself that I would read it when I was no longer living in Afghanistan.

She spoke to us softly in a low voice, but in a way that everyone could hear her. When she came into the classroom, everybody stopped talking immediately, and nobody teased anyone during her lesson as we did during other classes.

One day she told us that she had received her degree in Russia, and she would have liked to have been a professor at Kabul University. But she had three sons, the oldest four years younger than we were, and she had to be home most of the time. I do not think she taught for money, because her husband had a good business in an electronics shop he owned. I think she taught because she loved literature. I was only beginning to understand what literature was, and I was excited to learn from somebody who loved it as much as she did.

As the months sifted into years, I began to notice hair on my body where it had never grown before. At first I was frightened that all the tension of the war was turning me into a monkey. I remembered the pictures in my schoolbook from all those years ago. Could it be possible that war turned humans back into monkeys?

Then, new kinds of dreams, especially about women, left me excited and self-conscious. Whenever I looked at a picture of a pretty girl in a magazine, I felt something strange.

It was not like in the old days, when a young Afghan guy could take a girl on a date. Since the Mujahedin had come, a young man had to get married to have a girlfriend. I did not want to get married at that early age.

Instead, I spent hours and hours in the gym lifting weights and training as a boxer. My arms were getting thick, and my chest began to look like a man's. Sometimes when I stood before a mirror without my shirt, I saw a body full of muscles, like those statues in the books about Plato and Socrates.

One day I pretended I was the statue of Apollo. I was posing like that with my left arm raised for a couple of minutes without knowing that my father was at the door watching me. He made fun of me for several weeks afterward. He would look at me, then hold up his left arm. I did not like him making fun of me, but at least I got to hear him laugh.

My father told jokes when we ate, but he was not happy, except when he put on his boxing gloves and was showing me how to fake a right jab, or come back with a left hook. He would not allow anyone to mention carpets, or smugglers, or Grandfather's house.

A day came when I felt like I had been living at Noborja longer than in our own home. But it had been only four years.

On a Thursday night in September 1996, we heard lots of cars running up and down the roads. There was no shooting, and no rockets. But all the roads all over Kabul were unusually busy all night.

The next morning, like other Fridays, I planned to eat my breakfast late with my family, and then, if no factions were firing at us from the mountain, go watch our neighbors playing football for an hour in the road in front of the fort. Afterward, I would come home and listen to the radio drama before we ate a big lunch with my grandfather or any of my uncles who had been able to come. While they sat and drank tea for the rest of the afternoon, I would go to the garden and sit in the shade of the grapevines to listen to sparrows make *chuk-chuk* calls and read one of my Iranian novels.

But on that Friday as I approached the gate, I could not hear any football noises from outside. Only silence.

Our front gate of corrugated steel had been shot full of holes like a colander when a rocket had landed in front of it five years before. The rocket also killed a little boy who had been feeding his donkey from a pile of trash nearby. We never had money to replace the gate and used it the way it was.

I looked through one of the holes outside to see why no one was kicking a football where the dirt road widened between the gate and the wall of the old British Embassy to make a broad playing area. But there were no footballers. Instead, I saw men who were strangers. I had never before seen such people, not even in my dreams, or in movies, or in any novel or history books.

They looked like Afghans, but were dressed strangely in long black and white turbans and very long *kamiz* that hung down over their *shalwar* trousers way below their knees. They were carrying whips.

All of them had outlined their eyes in kohl. Their beards were untrimmed and long. None had proper shoes. Instead, they wore slippers, and their feet were dusty. Most of them had snuff in their mouths. A few of them spat brown saliva into the dust in front of them, and then cleaned their mouths with the ends of their turbans.

None of them spoke. They looked lost, like men who had come from a forest or caves and had never seen buildings before.

I thought at first they might be vampires. I knew that vampires did not exist, except in stories to scare kids. But what else could I be seeing?

I could not see even one of my neighbors around. Not one. A fear rushed through me. Perhaps they had all left the town the night before without telling us. Or maybe these vampires had eaten them and were now staring at each house to see whether anyone was still inside to prey on.

"It is not possible," I reassured myself, while not being sure of anything.

Ever since the conflict between the factions had started, it usually took months for one to overcome another and take control of a neighborhood. Now this new faction seemed to have taken over the whole town with no fighting and no casualties. I had to know what was going on.

I opened the door as quietly as I could and stepped outside. Three of them heard the squeak of the gate and ran toward me. Their faces were fierce. They raised their whips.

One of them came close and asked me whether I knew where Ahmad Shah Masoud was. They were all speaking Pashto with the Kandahari accent, which has more ups and downs than the Pashto we speak in Kabul. Maybe they were part of this new Taliban faction that we had been hearing about.

"I don't know," I said fearfully in Pashto. They softened when they heard me speak their language.

"Do you know Fahim?" the same guy asked me.

"Everybody knows him," I said. Marshal Fahim was a Tajik and one of Masoud's close allies.

Another one of them pushed the two others back and grabbed me by my collar. His hands smelled like shit.

"Are you Fahim's son?" he yelled.

"No!" I shouted back.

"Where is his house?" he asked me as he held my collar tightly. I pointed toward the Bagh-e-Bala, a tree-covered slope that rises up steeply half a mile west of Noborja, where there used to be a garden built by the Moguls.

He was still holding me and said, "Show us his house."

I took them to Fahim's street, and from the far end pointed out to them where his house stood. The guy who had held my collar let me go.

I raced home and told my family what had happened. But they thought I was making it all up, except for my mother. I could tell by the way she listened to me that she believed me.

As he always did on Fridays when guests might come, my father had shaved very carefully that morning, and was wearing his best trousers and a neatly pressed, white short-sleeve shirt. He decided to go out to see what I was talking about.

My mother did not want him to leave the house until we heard some more news. But my father, always practical, said, "There's no fighting going on. If there is a new faction in town, I want to make them my friends."

My father came back in half an hour looking angry. There were stains of fingerprints on his face and the mark of a whip on the back of his white shirt.

"What happened to you?" my mother asked, her voice high with worry.

He did not answer. He walked across the room, sat on the floor in the corner, and put his head on his knees and his arms around his legs.

My three little sisters stopped jumping on my parents' *toshak* and throwing pillows at one another. My mother sat in front of my father and raised his head up. "What is wrong?"

"They whipped me," my father said.

"Why?" my mother asked in amazement.

"Because I had shaved my beard. They called me an infidel and a Communist," my father said, incredulously. "They said that the beard is the symbol of Islam."

"Islam is about what is in your heart, not what is on your face," my mother stated.

"I told them that if the beard is a symbol of Islam, then a goat must be a Muslim since it is born with one," my father said, looking slightly dazed as he spoke. "Then they whipped me."

"What kind of people are they?" my mother asked with disgust.

My father put his head back on his knees, and my mother kissed his head. She beckoned for us to leave the room with her and let him alone.

My mother covered her head with a scarf and went to find out for herself what she could about this new faction.

She came back after fifteen minutes. Her eyes were full of fury, and she was limping.

"Some guy with a big black turban and torn clothes and a long beard whipped me on my legs," my mother exclaimed.

"Why?" my father asked, angered and bewildered. He jumped up from where he was sitting, prepared for a fight.

"Because I was not wearing a *burqa*," my mother said. We could all see that she was suffering from the lashes.

"What the hell is going on today? Where did these weird people come from?" my father asked.

All of my sisters had come to see what was going on. "I don't want any of you to step outside of this house today," my mother said to them firmly.

"Who are these people?" my oldest sister asked my father.

"I don't know." He gazed at the ceiling and murmured, "I never had a chance to ask them."

My mother asked my older sister for a bandage and alcohol to disinfect the whip wounds on her legs. One of my little sisters turned on the radio to hear the Friday drama. Instead, we heard a strange kind of singing. We thought it must be a part of the drama, but it continued for hours. From that day, we did not hear the radio drama again for five years.

All the songs were in Pashto with no instruments, no soft background music. We heard the same type of songs from outside, from cars going from one street to the next with loudspeakers at high volume. They were songs, but they were without music.

None of our relatives would be coming for lunch that day, I was sure. And I had no appetite. I went earlier than usual to the garden to sit under the grapevine and to read and to put these new guys out of my mind. As I was settling into my usual place, I saw something shining on the ground next to the garden wall. I left my book on the ground and went to see what was there. A Kalashnikov with several boxes of bullets next to it lay in the tall grass by the wall. Nearby was a plastic bag with thirteen grenades in it.

I did not touch any of them. I was afraid that they might be wired to a mine somewhere. I called our old *chowkidar* to come see them.

The doorkeeper shuffled toward me, leaning on his stick. The end of his dirty turban hung in front of his face. It was covered with stains from the tobacco juice he was always spitting. He looked at the weapons and spat.

"They must belong to Masoud's people," our doorkeeper said. "Masoud escaped from Kabul last night. Zalmai's wife told me."

"But why are these weapons here?" I asked.

"Those who couldn't escape with Masoud had to get rid of their weapons. This new faction is saying that if they find any weapons in anybody's house, they will put them in prison," the doorkeeper said.

He knocked at a grenade with his stick. I jumped back.

"We have to hide them somewhere," he said. He opened his turban and spread it on the ground. With no fear, he gathered the Kalashnikov, the bullets, and the grenades into his turban, then he slung them onto his hunched back. He carried them across the garden to the far side where there was a pit toilet. Carefully, he dropped them one by one down the hole. Then he pressed them with a shovel until they all disappeared under the filth.

I walked all over the garden to see whether there were any more weapons. I found more grenades and some mines that looked like a yellow butterfly, two RPGs, hundreds of bullets, and six guns.

I hid one of those guns under my trousers for myself. It was the kind I had seen many times in James Bond movies. Now that I was fourteen, I understood that I had the responsibilities of a man. A gun felt like a good thing to have. We put the rest in the toilet and pressed them down until they all sank under the mess in the pit.

I continued to walk all around the garden to see whether I had missed any other weapons. While I was pushing aside some bushes, someone from the street threw two bags of grenades over the wall into the garden.

"Who the hell is that? Is our garden your trash ditch?" I shouted. I climbed the wall to see who it was.

He was a tall man with broad shoulders, running like a scared dog, trying to disappear from sight.

I shouted at him several times and cursed him for being a coward, but he did not look back as he disappeared around the corner.

I opened the bags. Each bag had twenty grenades in it. I took them to the toilet and dropped them one by one until they had all sunk out of sight.

For a week, more and more weapons came over our wall. We

collected an armory of guns, grenades, RPGs, bullets, butterfly mines, and things we had never seen before. For a week we kept putting them all in that pit toilet.

By the end of that week, there was no longer enough filth to cover all the weapons. We sent everyone in the fort to use the weapon-toilet to help cover what was in there.

One day, as I was relieving myself, I looked down through the hole to see the barrel of a Kalashnikov pointed up at my bottom. It was too late to stop.

At the beginning, some of our neighbors were afraid to use the weapon-toilet. They thought that they might cause explosions. But my father was a very good convincer.

He said that there was a rumor that if the Taliban—now we knew that was who they were—found anyone with weapons in his house, they would put the suspect in prison and whip him to death.

We all heard, "Once you are in their prison, it is almost impossible to get out, unless you bribe them with a huge amount of money." I do not know how people knew these things. The Taliban had been in Kabul only a week.

We still did not know much about them. Most of what we had heard came from the BBC. They told us how the Taliban had taken control of Jalalabad, the last city in Afghanistan before the Khyber Pass leads into Pakistan. From there, the Taliban were moving toward Kabul. Other Taliban fighters had taken control of the main road to Kabul that comes from Kandahar and the west. And still more Taliban controlled a smaller road through Logar Province to the south. The only road from Kabul that was still open was the one that went to the north.

The Mujahedin government had become weaker and weaker as the years of civil war had gone on. They could not fight back, because they were so busy fighting each other. When they heard that the Taliban had captured Sarobi, a town halfway between Jalalabad and Kabul and close to where Zardad had his camp, they panicked. They knew that thousands of Taliban would be in Kabul by the next day, showing no mercy.

So the Mujahedin factions raced out of Kabul in the middle of the night on the last road that was open. They hauled truckloads of guns and ammunition to their bases in the Panjshir Valley and across the Hindu Kush mountains in the north, so the Taliban would not get them. But that did not matter. The Taliban had been given all the weapons they needed by Pakistan.

When the first group of Taliban had arrived in Kabul, they had expected a fierce fight. Instead, they found that the Mujahedin factions were gone and the streets were empty. They were confused to find themselves in such a silent city, but they did not take long to let us know that they were now our rulers.

Every day we heard new decrees from Mullah Omar, the head of the Taliban, from Radio Sadai Shariat (The Voice of Islamic Law), received from the office of Amer bel Maruf wa Nai As Munkar (Department for the Promotion of Virtue and the Prevention of Vice).

One day: "Every man in Afghanistan should grow a beard."

The next day: "Every woman over twelve should wear a *burqa*."

The next day: "Kite flying is forbidden."

The next day: "No one should be seen to keep pigeons or fighting birds in his house. Pigeons are for shrines and mosques."

The next day: "No one anywhere in Afghanistan should watch TV. If anyone is ever found to be watching movies, he will be punished in public and imprisoned for six months."

The next day: "Every man should go to the mosque five times a day for prayers."

We could say nothing. Everyone knew, however, that sooner or later a new faction would take over and things would change. This was Afghanistan, after all. This was how things worked.

At the end of the broadcast Maulvi Nazami, the head of Radio Sadai Shariat, said, "We say the right things so that we can be loved."

A few weeks after the Taliban arrived, I saw one of them hanging out the back of a van with a loudspeaker in his right hand. He was shouting, "We, the Students of God, are bringing justice to this city and the other cities all over Afghanistan. If anyone has any interest in our justice, come to Kabul Stadium and witness our justice. Today at two o'clock."

I had been on my way to school and told some of my classmates whom I met about the strange announcement I had heard. I said that I wanted to go to the stadium to see what the Taliban meant by justice.

Some of my classmates said that they wanted to go, too. Afghans are always hungry to learn anything new. So instead of going to our classes, we headed across Kabul, hanging out the doors of an over-crowded bus.

The stadium was filled with men and schoolboys as full of curiosity as we were. A pickup truck drove into the middle of the field. That was surprising. Grass is hard to grow in Kabul, and no sensible person would drive a truck, even a lightweight one, onto a playing field. There was a loudspeaker on the back of the truck. Two Taliban wearing black *shalwar kamiz*, long hair, and white turbans stood on the truck. Even from the seats we could see the black rings of kohl around their eyes.

"We call ourselves Taliban, which means the Students of God. We never do wrong," one of the men on the back of the truck said into a microphone. "We never do wrong even by mistake. Everything we do is right, so we can be loved. Everything we say is right, so we can be cherished." As he spoke, he kept rotating so he could address every part of the stadium.

A moment later, two other Taliban brought a man onto the field with chains around his wrists, feet, and neck. The Talib with the microphone said the man was a thief who had stolen a pair of shoes from a shop.

The Talib's voice got higher and louder, which made the loudspeaker screech. "This guy has stolen a pair of shoes from a Kabul shop. He deserves amputation. Our justice for thieves is amputation. If we don't have justice toward thieves, they will take control like Genghis Khan, or English people, who are the biggest thieves of our time. Then it will be impossible to control them."

They stood the thief in the middle of the football field and opened his handcuffs. Two Taliban held his right arm down on a table. A doctor injected the man's right arm with anesthetic, then took a saw and cut off the man's hand while he watched. One of the Taliban took the hand and waved it around to the crowd. The hand was still bleeding, and the pale fingers seemed to our horrified eyes to be moving very slowly. The thief went numb and collapsed. Two other Taliban took him by the arms and dragged him off the football field.

The spectators were shocked. A stunned silence filled the entire stadium. I had been to the stadium many times with my father, but this was the first time I had experienced such total quiet there, though it was packed with thousands of men.

My classmates and I did not want to stay any longer. We stood up to leave. Some other people stood up to leave, too. But Taliban came from all directions, beat us with whips, and ordered us to sit and see the execution.

They brought another man with cuffs on his hands and chains on his feet.

The eerie silence was broken by the Taliban announcer: "This man killed his neighbor four years ago, then he escaped to Iran. When he came back, we arrested him. Now someone from the victim's family will shoot the killer in the head, and you will be witnesses."

Then a Talib handed the victim's relative a gun and asked him to shoot. The relative fired the gun and shot the murderer through the head. The bullet hit his forehead and came through the back of his head. His body shook for a few moments on the ground.

At the end, the announcer said, "We will conduct two more acts of justice on Friday. Now you can go, and you will come back next Friday. No tickets needed."

I ran out of the stadium, determined never to go back there ever again. But in the weeks that followed, a new principal who was a Talib was appointed to our school. He ordered us to go several more times, to see more of the Taliban justice. We saw women whom the Taliban said were prostitutes stoned to death. We saw men who were accused of being homosexuals killed by having a mud brick wall toppled on them. Since the Taliban left Kabul, I have never gone there again.

At the front gate of the stadium, a few Taliban gave every pass-erby a paper with a big headline in large black type at the top:

JUSTICE
REPRESENTS EQUALITY

Imprison the violators. Amputate the thefts, execute the murder, topple wall on homosexuals, and stoning to death the prostitutes!

We imprison the violators to be a lesson to them for futures that no one denies our Islamic virtue.

Amputation is needed for thieves to stop more thefts in the future. Execution is needed for murderers to stop more murderers. Stoning to death is needed for prostitutes to stop more adultery and prostitutions.

Adultery and prostitutions carry AIDS with them. Killing prostitutes are every Afghan's duty.

There are three types of punishment for homosexuals.

1. Take these people to top of the highest building and hurl them to death.
2. Dig a pit near a wall somewhere and put these people in it then topple the wall on them. If one does not die, then he is not a sinner and not a homosexual. The wall should be toppled on blamer.
3. Homosexual hair should be shaved and he should be taken around on top of a donkey upside down with a blackened face displaying to society.

Be aware! We bring in action the second punishment.

We beat the sinners with whips for the minor offences. If they die under the whipping, it means they were the sinner of sinners and he or she died clean.

Whoever had written the announcement was somebody who did not know correct grammar. When we turned the paper over, we saw a headline about the Taliban's rights for women. Below it was a long list of things that women could and could not do. My friends and I read it. I turned to my friends and said, "Wow, women are in cages." The list was long. Some of the rules were strange.

WHAT ARE THE TALIBAN RIGHTS FOR WOMEN?

The parents should not keep their daughters inside their house. They should get them married as soon as they are ready. This is the advice from us, and since we are the Students of God, we know better than others.

Poor and widow women should be assisted financially by their blood relatives. Widows should be remarried by her father-in-law's family.

Women should not step outside of their residences. In case of emergency, they can go out but they should not wear fashionable clothes to attract the attention of other men, because she belongs to only one man (Husband) or soon she will be property of a man (Husband). If any woman is seen outside with fashionable, tight, and charming clothes, she will be chased to her house, and her brother, father, or husband will be punished and imprisoned. Woman should only be attractive to her husband inside her house. Women have the responsibility of a teacher for their children and a helper to her husband.

Women's makeup is forbidden unless they do it for their husbands inside the confines of her house, but men can use kohl outside of the house and inside.

Women do not have as much brains as men, therefore they cannot think wisely as man. So, we refuse to allow them to become involve in politics.

Whoever is holding this paper; he or she should give it to other women or read it to them, so they know our rules and observed them.

Sincerely! The Taliban rules.

I took that paper home and showed it to my mother and sisters. They showed it to our neighbors. Soon everybody had read it or had a photocopy of it.

At first, people made fun of the incorrect grammar and bad spelling. But soon, women understood that these things were serious.

When the Mujahedin factions had arrived and had issued their version of Islamic laws, women were forced to cover up, but they could still go anywhere and do anything they wanted, if the fighting allowed. Now that the Taliban were in control, females mostly disappeared from Kabul's streets.

The men faced their own strict set of rules, as well. One of the strictest was having to go to the mosque five times a day rather than praying wherever they found themselves. The mullah there had an attendance sheet. He called out our names to find out who was present and who was not. He would put a cross before the name of an absent man and report him to the Department for the Promotion of Virtue and the Prevention of Vice. The next day a Talib might come and imprison that man for a week or so.

For the first few weeks, every day someone was imprisoned for being absent. But as the months passed, the decree was not enforced so strictly, unless one of the mullahs disliked someone.

In our neighborhood, there was a man we used to call Malem-e-chaq, the chubby teacher. He had six sons and was extremely rich. He even had a swimming pool in his garden. The mullah did not like him at all, though I do not know why. Malem-e-chaq was a good man. Yet, the mullah kept a strict account of when he came to the mosque, so the poor man had to be there five times a day, except when he went to other countries for his import-export business. But before he left on a trip, he had to tell the mullah where he was going, and how long he would be away. So did his sons, who had shops to run in other parts of Kabul. A few times my father did the same thing when he had to go somewhere.

Before prayers, the mullah talked about Islam and religion for ten or fifteen minutes and asked people in the mosque basic questions about Islam. In these new days, the mullahs in charge were either all Taliban or had become Taliban, or acted like them, except for one old mullah who had seen his entire family—wives, sons, daughters, brothers, and his mother—wiped out by a Russian bombing raid. He was then a farmer. One day he had stayed a bit longer in the fields after the others had gone to the house to eat. A Russian plane roared overhead. Bombs exploded and threw him to the ground. When the dirt that was swept up into the sky by the blasts had settled, there was no sign that there had ever been a house, or that he had ever had a family. The Taliban were told these things about him and left him alone.

One evening before prayers, our mullah asked the first line of people in the mosque, "If you fill two buckets, one with alcohol and another one with water, and take them both to a thirsty donkey, which one will the donkey drink?"

A guy from the first line said, "Of course the water."

"Since the donkey avoids drinking alcohol, then you have to hate it yourselves and not even touch it," our mullah said.

A guy raised his hand from the second line and asked, "If there are a few drops of alcohol in a glass of water, is it still as bad as pure alcohol?"

"If I piss a few drops in your glass of water, will you drink your water?" our mullah said.

"Of course not," the guy answered.

"The alcohol is a million times worse than my piss," our mullah said.

In my family, now only I could go to school to study, and my sisters had to stay at home. The women teachers in my school also were told to stay at home. I missed my literature teacher's lessons, but I never stopped looking for hidden meanings in my books.

The school year ended for the winter a few weeks after the Taliban arrived. When we got the results sheet for our exams, I had the highest grade for Dari literature. I wanted to tell my teacher, but I did not know where to find her. I never saw her again.

When the schools reopened for the new school year on the second day of spring, it was time for me to start high school. I had wanted to go to the school where my father taught, Habibia. It was the best school in Afghanistan. But it was about five miles from the Qala-e-Noborja, and my parents were afraid to have me travel so far with so much uncertainty.

Instead, I went to a school nearby. It was named for a king who was dead. Our king who was alive was in Italy and had not come back to save us. We had stopped waiting for him.

For all my life, except when we were fleeing or the fighting was too heavy, I had seen my father go to his school. I had watched him prepare for his classes the night before. I had seen him thumb through his well-worn books with the eagerness of somebody discovering something new. I had heard his enthusiasm when he spoke about his students. I thought high school must be an important and exciting place. But the Taliban took from me all the joy I had expected to feel.

The boys were told to wear *shalwar kamiz*, a long one according to Taliban standards—tunic below the knees, trousers above the ankle, with a black turban and slippers instead of proper shoes. We were prohibited from wearing shoes in school, because we were told that shoes get stinky easily. The Taliban did not like to wash.

Most of the teachers had taught at that school for years wearing suits and ties, but now they all wore turbans and *shalwar kamiz*, except for the academic dean, who wore a suit and a necktie every day for nearly a year before he, too, found a *shalwar kamiz*. A Talib was appointed as the principal of the school and told the teachers to stress religion in all our subjects. We were taught that the history of humankind began with religion, and we were born with religion, and we had to die with religion. Religion was involved in the sciences, history, philosophy, psychology, arts, everything. If we know our religion, the Taliban principal said, we will know ourselves.

At the beginning, it was interesting to learn about Islam, because in the time of the Communists, we had no religious studies at all. All we were taught was how to respect Communism. They told us that it was our duty to invite others to be Communist to enlarge the wheel of Communism, because only Communism could help mankind.

My formal schooling seemed to have had two subjects only: Communism and Islam. Perhaps it was not surprising, then, that I was happiest at school when I was wrestling with my classmates in the classroom, breaking their noses in boxing competitions or flexing our arm muscles for one another to show our strength. We talked a lot about sex and played card games with cards that had sex pictures on them, which we passed around in school.

My head was always shaved now; I looked like a bald man. I could no longer wear my choice of clothes. I could not watch movies. I could not fly kites. In short, I could no longer be myself.

We heard that some Taliban were now living in what was left of our old house. Our former neighbor told us. He had gone to visit his own house nearby. He was asked by the Taliban in our place who the owner of the house was. He told them that we were not in Afghanistan. The Taliban instructed him to inform them if he heard that we had come back to Kabul. They told him that they would get money from us and split it with him. The next day he came to the Qala-e-Noborja and told us all this.

With the Taliban living there, there was even less reason for anybody to talk about the gold in Grandfather's garden.

We heard rumors that if the Taliban knew that you had a lot of money, they would put you in prison until you gave it all to them. So, in my family everyone became silent about the gold, and we were told never to talk about it to anyone.

On the streets I noticed that people were now wearing dirty clothes. Even people whom I knew had money wore clothes that were dirty, trying to look poor. One of our neighbors was imprisoned. A few months later we heard that his brother had come from Pakistan and given the Taliban a lot of money, and then they both left quickly for Iran.

Sometimes we heard talk about a rich Arab named bin Laden. We were not sure who he was. One of our neighbors said he was living nearby in the big house that had been owned by the man everyone called the Pimp of the King. We went by that place many times, but we never saw him. And we were careful not to look directly. There were always many Taliban at the gate. They used the place for big meetings, and their black Land Cruisers were always going in and out.

Grandfather came from Makroyan twice in a month and stayed with us for a night or two. Now that I was in high school, he talked to me like I was a grown-up man. He talked about things that made me feel shy at first. Sometimes he would ask me questions about these strange feelings I had when I thought about pretty girls. Sometimes he would ask me philosophical questions about Socrates, Plato, and Aristotle. Sometimes we would talk about Judaism, Buddhism, Islam, and Communism.

I think he wanted to see how much I grasped from life, how much I had learned from school, from the books he had given me to read, and from the things he had told me.

Since he knew I was very interested in Socrates and liked to read Plato, he asked me questions exactly the way Socrates asked them of Callicles, Chaerephon, Gorgias, and Polus when they met in Callicles's home. It was very much as if I had found myself with Socrates, whom I revere, and he was present in the body of Grandfather, whom I loved more than anyone in the world. It was a pleasure beyond description, to be with two such people at the same time.

These conversations lasted for hours; we hardly noticed how time passed.

I did not feel that I had to go out or entertain myself when he was with us. But when he was not there, I felt imprisoned sitting at home, with little to distract me but reading or doing push-ups. And any time I did go out, it was uncomfortably quiet. The streets should have been filled with kids playing, and vendors pushing carts, and donkeys. Instead, all I saw were Taliban, everywhere. They always acted so strangely.

People looked nervous all the time, too. They were not afraid of rockets anymore. Now we had peace in Kabul, and we did not see blood and corpses and body parts on the streets anymore. But it was an unhappy peace, a frightened peace. We did not know what was going to happen next.

We waited.

18

❖

The Prison

In the second year of the Taliban, I got fed up with their rules, and began breaking a few of them: growing my hair out, sometimes not wearing my hat or turban, and dressing in jeans and T-shirt—but only in our neighborhood. I did not go beyond half a kilometer from our house.

One day before going to school, I bathed and did not have enough time to wait until my hair got dry. I slung my unwound turban on my shoulder, took my books, and walked toward school, letting the sun dry my hair as I went. The weather was balmy, and it felt good to be without a turban for once.

All of a sudden, a black Land Cruiser filled with Taliban popped up from nowhere and stopped in front of me. A black pickup truck with more Taliban followed. One of the Talibs stepped out of the car and started beating me on my back with a heavy whip. I did not know what my crime was, and he did not give me a chance to ask him. Everything happened very fast.

After beating me for almost five minutes, he pushed me toward their vehicles. I asked them what this was all about. But none of them answered or even talked to me. They kept whipping me.

I stopped asking questions and punched one of them in his face. He fell on the ground like something heavy that someone had dropped.

All those hours in the gym practicing boxing had taught me some things.

Now there were ten of them, jumping out of the Land Cruiser and the truck, running toward me. They began beating me again with three heavy whips, and kicking me as I lay coiled on the ground. Every time a whip or a foot landed on my head, I saw stars in the daylight. I forgot about being so strong and looking like the statue of Apollo.

Finally, they carried me to their pickup and dropped me into the back. As they handcuffed me to the side rail, I lost consciousness. Sometime later, I found myself in a barber shop, sitting on a chair in front of a mirror. I hardly recognized myself. My face was covered with wounds and marked with dried blood. My hands and feet were still handcuffed, and all of my body ached like I had a severe fever.

The barber shaved my hair, then the Taliban drove me to the Shahr-e-Naw prison in central Kabul, right across from Zajanton hospital, where I had been born. They still had not told me what I had done, and they did not let me contact my family.

In the prison, they put me in a dark room, alone. For the first few days, usually early in the morning, someone came and tied my hands to chains that were hanging from the ceiling and beat me with a whip. Each minute passed like hours. Whenever I demanded to know why I was in prison, he remained silent. When I insisted on an answer, he said that he was told to say nothing.

The beatings left me with a dislocated shoulder and lots of whip welts all over my body, especially my back and chest. For those first few days the pain was intense, and the heat was stifling. There were no doctors to treat my shoulder. Flies swarmed around the cuts on my face, hands, and feet and drove me crazy; after a while I did not have the energy to brush them off.

They slid me a piece of hard bread and a glass of water under the door. A bucket in the corner of the room was for me to use as a toilet. It took all my strength to crawl to it.

From time to time, I could hear jeeps coming and going in the yard outside. Each time, the guards made noise unlocking the padlock on the slatted gate to the street. Every time the gate swung open, I squinted out the tiny window to see the Talib commander lounging in the driver's seat of one of the jeeps, and leering at all the little windows like mine where about twenty other prisoners were being held.

Later, when he came to my cell, he thwacked his whip against his boot tops while he accused me of blasphemy against Islam and beating a Student of God. He was the only one to wear boots.

When I asked him what my blasphemy was, he beat me. After that, I decided that silence was my only course. It reminded me of my Kuchi cousins, who had taught me how to use silence to step back from the world around me and let the answers to my problems form in my mind.

The only company I had was the Holy Koran, which they left for me and the other prisoners on a shelf in each cell. At the mosque, the other boys and I had already read it several times in Arabic. We had been taught how to make the sounds of the Arabic words, because we used their alphabet for our language, Dari. But we had never been taught what the words meant, except for sometimes when my grandfather translated some of the verses for me. So, we had no way of understanding what we were reading, even though we held competitions to see who could finish memorizing his verses first.

This copy of the Holy Koran had a translation in Dari under each line. It was like I was reading the Koran for the first time. I could finally understand what these Arabic words that I had recited for years actually meant. I discovered what a treasure trove of tales the Koran is, filled with good advice, a real guidebook to the human experience.

At night in my cell, after I had put down the Holy Koran, I played those tales and their wisdom over and over in my head like movies. And I thought for hours about their meaning and what lessons lay in them for my own life.

For example, Sura 29 begins: "Do people think that when they say: 'We are believers,' they will be left alone and not be tested? We tested those who have gone before them. God surely knows which of them are truthful, and He surely knows which are liars. Or do the evildoers think they will escape Our reach? How poorly they judge."

I read this in less than a minute, but I thought about it for hours, searching for the deeper meanings, in the same way that our Dari language and literature teacher had taught us to look for what we could not see even in books that were not the Holy Koran.

I thought about the Taliban. They said they were believers, but a lot of what they were doing was not in the Holy Koran. The Koran says that "God surely knows which of them are truthful, and He surely knows which are liars." Did the Taliban and the other factions and all the other evildoers think that they would escape God's reach? "How poorly they judge."

But what about me? I began to think about the evil things I had done, like when I had broken our neighbor's window and then denied it, or had rung people's doorbells and run away, or made fun of the weak boys in our neighborhood, or called people names behind their backs, or beaten up guys in school for no reason but to show that I could. These are all *haram* in Islam, forbidden. But I had done them all. Before I could think about what the Taliban were doing, I felt I must first repent for all these things I had done. I promised to myself never to do them again.

I read the whole of the Holy Koran as fast as I could. Then, after a couple of days, I decided to read this Dari translation again, to understand it better, and to savor the stories. Reading also kept my mind from the physical pain I was experiencing.

But the lessons I was drawing from the Holy Koran slowly worked through my mind and made the emotional pain inside me even worse.

I lay on the cement floor, staring at the ceiling with the Holy Koran open next to me. Tears rolled out of my eyes as I recalled one wrong thing after another that I had done. I kept thinking about my parents, sisters, and brother, and how I had been so mischievous toward my parents, and how I had bossed my sisters and made them do things for me, because I was a boy, such as ordering them to polish my shoes or iron my clothes, then criticizing them for not doing it the way I wanted, or complaining when the food they cooked was a little salty or oily. I had used my position for the wrong reason. And I easily could have done those things for myself.

I thought about my mother and how worried she would be, not

knowing where I was. I began to think about how much pain I had caused her. Carrying me for nine months. Feeding me, washing me, clothing me, taking care of me day and night. And what did I give back to her? Always pain and worries. The same with my father. He had worked day and night to make life possible for us, sometimes under the worst conditions, and what did I do for him besides give him anxiety? What was he feeling now? And as the older brother to my sisters, what had I done for them? Slapped them when my parents were not home, knowing they had no one to whom to complain? Called them names? Why?

For hours I would ask myself what made life worth living. Is there only pain that you give to others, or pain they give to you? Why do we misuse our power? I in my way, and the Taliban in their ways. What good does this bring to humanity? I'm no better than the Taliban, I thought. Maybe I deserve this treatment. But what about my parents? How can I send them a message that I am in the right place, being punished for all the wrong things I have done, and they must not worry?

"Maybe I should kill myself," I thought several times, especially when the ache in my shoulder felt like a piece of hot steel being pushed into my bone. But I did not want to give my parents even more pain. They would blame themselves. I could not do it, though there were many times in that stinking cell when I had stopped caring about this world, this life, or my feelings, desires, and wishes.

After a week, the Taliban took me out of that small, dark room and put me in a larger one with other prisoners. We had to pray five times a day and study religious subjects in the prison mosque. After prayers, we had to carry heavy stones from one room to the next, and then carry them back.

During the night, we did not have enough blankets to keep ourselves warm. Sometimes I woke up in the middle of the night, shivering, and did push-ups. I remembered that my father had done the same thing in that tunnel four years before. Some people ran around the room to keep the blood in their veins circulating. We could not exercise for more than about ten minutes at a time, though, because we did not have enough energy.

I did push-ups with the right arm only, which is very painful to do. For a few seconds it made the pain in my left shoulder go away. I learned then how to cheat my brain; a temporary pain in one part of the body makes you forget the permanent pain in another part of your body, at least for a few moments. I felt I was triumphing over the Taliban by overcoming my pain. I could do four push-ups at the most. Sometimes I laughed, though only for a second as sweat clustered over my forehead. Laughter in the depth of pain is an uplifting feeling, though a short-lived one. I suddenly understood what Socrates meant by "Pleasure can also come from pain." Suddenly, something I had never understood made sense. I felt as if my head were illuminated with millions of lightbulbs.

Over the next ten days, I lost twenty pounds. I could hardly move my body or talk.

One day, after I had been in the prison for nearly two weeks, I saw a piece of broken mirror on the ground, about the size of a hand. When I looked in it, I saw a face that was not mine. I laughed at myself, but that exposed my teeth. Even in the times when we had had very little to eat, I had never seen myself so toothy and skinny. I still had a few muscles left on my arms and chest, but only very tight ones.

At the end of two weeks two of the jailers asked me some basic questions about Islam. I answered them all. They took me into a room that was cleaner than the rest and asked me some more simple questions about Islam, like how to take ablutions, whose answers I had known since I was a child. Then they told me to recite the verses from the Holy Koran that are used every time we pray. I kept waiting for something more difficult.

The older jailer, who was in his forties, kept nodding his head as I responded. His sandy-colored beard moved up and down in time to the rhythm of the prayers that I was reciting. For every answer I gave, he smiled and said "Very good, son!" in a calm voice, as he rubbed his left hand on the large belly beneath his gray *shalwar kamiz*.

The other man was skinny and half his age. He looked at me, as we say, "as if I were his family's enemy." His dark brown eyes, tan skin, and black *shalwar kamiz* contrasted sharply with his white turban. He asked harder questions in a loud voice and acted disappointed when I answered them correctly. I wanted to ask him some questions, as well. I was sure he would not know the answers. But I did not.

Finally, they told me I could go home. Some of the prisoners who could not answer the questions stayed for two more weeks.

"Why did you imprison me?" I asked the older jailer as I was leaving the room. But it was the younger one who answered.

"Because you were not wearing a turban, and your hair was too long."

"But it was not more than three inches," I replied.

"You must keep your head shaved at all times, and wear a turban or a hat. We keep the violators at our prison, so they understand how serious their crimes are. It is our job," the jailer said forcefully. "We are here to help you."

When I came out of the prison, the sun's glare blinded me for a few seconds. Slowly, slowly I opened my eyes and everything began to look normal.

I did not have any money to get a taxi to go home. I could hardly walk, because of my lack of energy, but I had no alternative. I knew my family would have been looking all over Kabul for me for the past two weeks I was in the prison. That forced me on. Somehow I managed to walk the two miles from the prison all the way home, stopping several times to rest. I was worried that people might somehow know that I had been a prisoner. Maybe they would ask me how I had hurt my shoulder, which still ached. But there was almost no one in the street to see me.

When I arrived home, I found my mother on a prayer rug facing toward Mecca and praying in a loud voice, "Oh God, keep my son in your peace. Save him from any dangers of the world. Wherever he is, give him the message that his mother is always waiting for him and tell him to come home . . ."

"Your prayer is accepted," I said softly from behind her.

She turned around with an amazed look on her face. Unusual for her in the daytime, tears sparkled on her cheeks. A smile spread across her face, which revealed the wrinkles that now owned the corners of her eyes.

Later that day, my father brought his friend who was a champion wrestler to the room where I was trying to rest. He told me to stand up, and when I did, he grabbed my arm and forced my shoulder back into place. I screamed like somebody had thrown me into boiling water. By the time I finished howling, I realized that the pain in my shoulder was mostly gone.

The ache in my soul, however, was not so easily fixed. It is still there, as fresh as if these things had happened yesterday.

19

❖

A Precious Jewel

I was beginning to feel that I should take care of my family. My despair in prison had forced me to think about my life in a new way. I did not feel like a kid anymore. I was almost seventeen years old. "At seventeen, a Pashtun son should be a shoulder to his father." This is what Grandfather used to tell me. In Afghanistan, even a sixteen-year-old is considered a grown man. But I did not know how to help.

My father had become so discouraged after the fire destroyed all his carpets that he quit the carpet business completely. He had kept his teaching job at Habibia High School during the fighting, though neither he nor any of the other teachers or the students could actually go there for about two years. Once things quieted, he was again riding his bicycle the five miles around the mountain every day to the school to teach his physics classes. Teachers, though, were paid very little. To keep us going, he also began buying and selling flour and cooking oil that came from Pakistan.

He worked very hard. For a while he disappeared from our life. We woke up in the morning and he would not be there. We went to sleep late at night and he would not have returned. When we did see him on Fridays, he seemed to be in agony. After breakfast, he would ask my youngest sister to walk on his back and his legs to ease the pain in them. The rest of his Fridays were spent sleeping; we whispered when we talked and we tiptoed. He was too busy to pay attention to what we were doing. It was not like the old days, when he had made a schedule for me every day to do things in an organized way.

I felt that I was getting to be like a stray dog. I was trying to find a sense of peace for myself, trying to find someone who could guide me in the right direction, to the right path. I went to several mosques to listen for the invisible voice, but the mosques did not feel the same as before. It felt like I was being forced to say prayers the way the Taliban wanted. Talibanism: it was not the Islam that I knew from what I had read in the Koran or from what Grandfather had taught me.

I went to Grandfather to get his advice, but he was too busy thinking about how to get our house back, and he was very afraid, not knowing what to do. I had never seen Grandfather like that. He had always made me feel safe, but now I did not know how to make him feel safe. He told me not to be dependent on anyone else. The time had come when I should make up my own mind and be my own guide, he said. I was not so sure.

I started thinking about my carpet teacher, seeking her advice. I went to quiet places, trying to hear her.

Under the Taliban, the country grew increasingly poor, dismal, and isolated. The Taliban's chief concern above all others was that men must respect the hours of prayers and women must be separated from the rest of society.

I frequently cursed my country for allowing ourselves to be ruled by our neighbors, by the English, by the factions, and now by these Talibs. Most Afghans had nothing but contempt for the Taliban, whom we considered illiterate peasant extremists. They had originated from the poorest and most backward parts of the country, where literacy hardly was known.

While the Taliban ruled, no one smiled. It was as if the Taliban had stolen our smiles. Or maybe the people just forgot how, except when they went to the jewelry shops to buy gold for their daughters' weddings. Afghans were still determined to give their daughters gold when they married, even if they could have no music at the wedding.

A jeweler friend, who was a few years older than I, had a shop near the Qala-e-Noborja in the Kart-e-Parwan neighborhood. We had met playing volleyball in a nearby park, and I spent a lot of time in his shop; it was one of the few places where I could hear laughter. His customers would spend an hour or more bargaining to get the cheapest price, and they made lots of funny jokes while they did so.

My friend knew how to make his customers feel happy. That way they would spend more money and buy things they did not need.

One day I was sitting next to one of his assistants, who was polishing an old necklace with hot water and sawdust. He dipped the necklace in boiling water for a minute, then he rubbed it hard with a toothbrush and put it in sawdust. Half an hour later, he took it out and polished it with a kind of soft brush until the gold gleamed like it was brand-new. I was getting interested in becoming a jeweler. This, I decided, was how I was going to help my family.

That day nobody came to buy anything. My friend was bored. He kept yawning and gazing at the busy road, frowning at the frowning faces of the people who were walking past the shop. He was deep in his thoughts. The only sound was the whooshing of the Taliban cars, running up and down the road recklessly.

A woman with a dirty *burqa* entered the shop and raised her hand to my friend. She was a beggar and was asking for money. Her hand was dirty like her *burqa*, and her brown skirt was full of tiny little burned holes. I thought she was some kind of drug addict.

My friend was still staring outside with his elbows on top of his desk and hands under his chin. The woman gently pulled on my friend's sleeve as a way of asking him to give her a few small afghanis. My friend looked at the woman, took a few afghanis out of his pocket, and gave them to her. She got the money and stuffed it into her pocket, then she raised her left hand. Her left hand was clean with long nails and they were polished red. She had a beautiful hand.

On her palm was written, "I am available, and my price is 10,000 afs." This was about fifty dollars.

"Can I see your face?" my friend excitedly asked.

She looked outside to make sure there were no Taliban nearby, then she pulled up her *burqa* for a second and covered her face again quickly.

"Let's go to the back room," he said to her.

My friend had a small storage room at the end of his shop.

They were there for almost fifteen minutes. My friend came out with sweat on his forehead and a look of contentment. He told me to go in, that it was my turn. He would pay for me if I did not have money.

I did not know what to say. I had never had sex before. My mind was screaming at me to go and experience these feelings that were filling my dreams. But my heart was whispering to me not to do it.

I remembered the woman whom I had seen stoned to death in the stadium, because her husband complained to the Department for the Promotion of Virtue and the Prevention of Vice that his neighbor had had relations with her. Indeed, the Department for the Promotion of Virtue and the Prevention of Vice had stoned the woman and the neighbor both.

I thought that if the Taliban captured me, they would stone me to death in public. That would be not only a severe death, but very shameful to my family.

"What are you waiting for? Go in! She is waiting for you," my friend said as his assistants snickered quietly. "She's fantastic." I looked at him, and then at his assistants. They were not more than eight or ten years old. Their coolness assured me they had seen my friend with other women before.

"Do you want to go in, or should I dismiss her?" my friend asked with an annoyed tone.

I did not know what to say. Then without knowing what I was doing, I walked toward the back room.

She appeared to be in her midtwenties. She wore a red bra and panties. She stood straight and relaxed, like the letter *alef,* with her back against the wall. Her skin was soft, and faintly glossy.

I did not know what to say or what to do. She smiled at me and asked, "Do you have any experience?"

I did not answer her. In fact, I did not know what to say. I was frozen there. My eyes stared at her, and my mouth was paralyzed. It was the first time in my life that I had seen a beautiful woman nearly naked, waiting for me to have her, and she was right in front of me, asking me a question that I was unable to answer.

"I said, do you have any experience?" she asked again, and her tone was a little more serious.

"No," I said.

"It is okay. I'll help you," she said.

"How?" I asked, as I stood there staring at her perfect legs. I felt like I was in an oven, and sweat began to form on my forehead and on my back. My heart was beating fast and seemed to be in my throat.

She slid down and slowly crept toward me on her knees on the bare concrete floor. Now I could see her breasts. I trembled. She grabbed the bottom of my *shalwar kamiz* and tried to pull me toward her.

I stepped back, suddenly afraid to touch her, or to let her touch me. I felt like I was a deer being attacked by a lioness. At the same time, I was trying to look brave, and not to show my fear. Deep inside me, I wanted to let her do whatever she wanted to me. I ached to learn the feeling of being with a woman, and to feel her body against mine.

"It is okay. You don't have to do anything. I know it is your first time. But trust me, it'll feel great," she said.

I stepped back a few more steps. Now my back was on the cold wall. She was standing again, very close to me. Her breasts were touching my chest. I could feel her warmth, smell her perfume. We both stared into each other's eyes as if we were trying to find something there. Her breath brushed my face. My heart started to beat faster, even faster than before. My legs began to shake. It was as if she were sending electric current into me, and my body was too weak to receive it. I could feel that I was getting redder every second, as all the blood came to my face.

"We don't have to do this if you don't want to. Maybe you should do it with someone your age," she whispered kindly. She understood my shyness.

She stepped back and turned toward her clothes. Now her back was turned to me. She put on her trousers first, then her shirt and skirt. I wanted to hug her from the back and kiss her entire body, and hold her in my arms. But I did not have the courage. I was filled with confusion.

Now she put her *burqa* on her head, and, with the veil still up so I could see her brown, almond-shaped eyes, she turned around and walked toward me. She stood before me, but not as close as before, and said with great sadness, "I'm not doing this for the joy of it. I'm doing this because I have to. Selling myself is the only possible way I have to earn any money." Her eyes began to fill.

"Can we talk for a minute?" I asked her. I did not want her to leave.

"Talk about what? About my blackened life?" she asked as a tear rolled down her cheek, then dripped onto the concrete floor.

I did not know what to say. I did not want her to cry. "Why don't you marry someone who would look after you? You are a pretty woman; you can make a good wife," I said. I did not know why I was saying this. I just wanted to make her feel good.

She sat on a chair in the corner. I was still standing. She motioned to me to get another chair and sit.

"Who is going to marry me?" she asked.

I did not know what to say.

She took a deep breath in and lowered her head. She was looking at her hands as she kept intertwining and releasing her fingers. "I was not born a prostitute, I was not born in a prostitute's family either. I was born in a well-educated family, in a family of well-respected people." She spoke very clearly, using good grammar and a high form of Dari that is not usually heard on the street.

"My father was a general in the Ministry of Interior Affairs; he was a man of honor, a man of respect, a man of pride. He was educated in Russia, and he was very serious about our educations. My mother was a teacher, like me. My brother was studying in the Medical Faculty, and my sister was studying social law at the University of Kabul."

I was listening carefully to what she was saying, but still very conscious that she was a woman whom I might touch.

"I taught chemistry in the same school with my mother, who taught literature. I had graduated from the Pharmacy Faculty. I'm the oldest child of my parents. I was married six years ago, and I have two children." The words were tumbling out.

"My husband had gone to my parents' house to tell them the news of my newly born son. A rocket landed in my parents' house and killed them all. In the end, there was nothing left for a burial. They were all turned into pieces and bits and mixed with the earth.

"I was living in a rental house with my two kids when the Taliban came. They closed the girls' school, and did not let any women work outside of their houses, as you know. I had no money to pay my rent. So, I was kicked out of that house by the landlord. Now I'm living under a tent in Parwan-e-Seh.

"I don't have any relatives from either side of my family in Kabul. They have all fled to foreign countries. I don't have their addresses to ask them for help. After the Taliban closed my school, I started begging for a few months. But I never collected enough money to buy five *naan*. Most of the time, I went hungry. I put my kids to sleep with empty stomachs."

I was becoming absorbed in her story, and forgetting about what had brought us together.

"About a year and a half ago I met another beggar, and she told me to sell myself. She said that there are a lot of customers for a body like mine. She also told me that prostitution is an art, not a black or shameful act. I cursed her and walked away from her. I continued my begging for another month, but I still couldn't collect enough money, and my kids began to get skinny and sick. My daughter is the older one, and she is four years old; my son is three.

"One day while I was begging along the Kabul River in the jewelry shops there, a jeweler showed me a bundle of money. He said if I came to the back room, he would give me all of it. I told him that he was disgusting, and he laughed at me as I walked away.

"I thought about my kids, who were suffering from malaria. I went back to that shop and I went straight to the back room. He came and used me. I didn't know what was happening to me. I was there like a body without a soul, like a doll. I was used by a couple of his friends, too. An hour later, I had the bundle of money, and I took my kids to a doctor.

"That night I cried the whole night without knowing why I was crying. I had not cried that much for my parents, my brother, my sister, or my husband when they died. The next day I didn't go out. Whomever I looked at, I thought they knew the truth about me. I couldn't even look at my own kids. I hated myself, and I wanted to kill myself. But I couldn't do it. 'Who would give my children the love of a mother?' I thought." She wiped her tears with her sleeves and looked at me.

"Why am I telling you all these things? You don't know me, and I don't know you," she said, and started to sob softly with her head down.

"You have to tell them to someone, to feel light, to feel free. You can't carry them all within you. You have to share them with someone," I said. I was surprised at the words that were coming from my mouth. How did I know to say these things? I was using all the proper forms and grammar, as she was, though almost no one ever spoke that way anymore.

"You're just a damn kid. You haven't seen the cruel face of life," she said, standing and covering her face with her *burqa*. She ran out of the shop without taking her money. My friend shouted at her to come back later for it.

I grabbed the bundle of money from the desk and caught up with her, walking slowly next to her. She did not see me because of the *burqa*, but I could hear that she was still crying quietly. The street was nearly empty. It was in the hot days of July. A few dogs were resting in the shade of walls, and little boys were carrying pots of yogurt with herbs toward their houses. She noticed me after a few moments; she stopped in the middle of the street and pulled up her *burqa* to look at me as I was standing in front of her. The hot sun was cooking my back. The little boys stared at her, because they had not seen any woman's face on the street for two years, since the Taliban had come.

"Why do you care for me? Do you know me?" she asked me. Her voice shook. Her beautiful eyes were full of tears waiting to come out.

"No, I don't know you, but I'm a human like you, and we should share the sorrows and the joys together," I said.

"And how will you share my sorrows with me? It is not just me who needs someone to share her pain with. There are thousands of people like me who are even more desperate."

I did not know what to say. She grabbed the money from me, pulled her veil down, and walked away without looking back, the dust blowing after her and settling on her blue *burqa*.

20

❖

The Length of a Hair

My mother gave me some money and a list of what she and my sisters needed: trousers, skirts, shawls, scarves, and other small things.

After the arrival of the Taliban, they hardly went out. They did not like wearing the *burqa*. They could not see through those little holes. In fact, if they left the house, it was only to go to the wedding parties or funerals of close relatives. For those occasions, I hailed them a taxi, or I called a relative with a car who collected them from our gate and dropped them at another gate. While they were in the car, their heads were completely covered with shawls, even their faces, and they could not see which road they were on.

I hated shopping for them, but what could I do? I was the only one available; with my father always working, they had no one else. We left the crying machine with a neighbor. My little brother had, in fact, become a joking machine. Everything he said was funny, and he made everyone laugh. He was the sweetest kid and knew how to keep us entertained.

I took my shopping bag and headed to the main bazaar in mid-afternoon. On my way there, I was stopped by a Talib in front of the high-rising Ministry of Communication. He wore the usual long, white turban and long, black *shalwar kamiz*. But he had a pair of scissors in his hand instead of a gun or a whip.

He asked me to take off my shirt. I thought he was joking. Nobody in my life had ever asked me to take off my shirt in the middle of the road.

"What do you want to do with my shirt?" I asked him in Pashto.

"I have nothing to do with your shirt. I want to see your armpits," he said.

"Why?! Look, look, there is nothing in my armpits. No hashish, no opium. I'm an athlete. I don't use drugs. You see I have muscles," I said as I raised my arms and flexed them.

"I need to see how long the hairs of your armpits are. They shouldn't be longer than one inch," he said insistently, and commanded me to take off my shirt.

"What does the hair of my armpits have to do with you?" I wanted to ask. But I had been to the Taliban prison once and did not want to go back again. I pulled off my *kamiz* in the middle of the road. The passersby on either side of the road watched me from the corners of their eyes, but they kept moving and kept their silence.

The Talib pulled out a hair from my left armpit and measured it. It was a tiny bit longer than one inch. He frowned and told me that I was in big trouble. I pleaded with him to measure a different one. He pulled out another hair from my right armpit and measured it. That one was just less than one inch.

"Some of the hairs are long, and some of them are short. When was the last time you shaved under your arms?" he asked.

"Two, three weeks ago," I answered as I was putting my shirt back on.

"Give me an exact date," he shouted, frowning.

"I don't remember," I said. In fact, I had never shaved my armpits at all.

"I want to see your penis and testicles," he said matter-of-factly as he stared between my legs.

"What? Why?" I asked. Panic was replacing my anger.

"Because I said so," he calmly replied.

"You know they look the same as yours," I said very seriously to mask my fear. I did not want to take off my trousers in the middle of the road for a stupid and illiterate villager who called himself a Talib.

"This is your last chance. If you don't show me your penis and testicles, you'll be in prison in ten minutes, and I'll see them there," he warned.

"Oh God! What the hell is wrong with this man? Please God, help me!" I screamed inside myself.

"Why don't you show me yours first," I challenged, playing for time until I could think more calmly what to do.

"Do you have an interest in my penis? It is quite big, and there is a lot of semen in my testicles," he said with a totally different tone. "My boy loves it, but he is not as white as you." He suddenly smiled a warmly engaging smile, even though he was a Taliban, and they hated any sign of happiness.

Now I understood why he had stopped me. We had heard rumors that the Taliban who had been fighting on the front lines against the Mujahedin would go to the prison during the night so they could relax by raping young boys who had been imprisoned for no crime.

This man wanted to use me every night with his frontline friends until they got bored with me and found someone new, or younger, or with whiter skin. I had seen some of those frontline Taliban, as we called them, a few days before in the park near the Qala-e-Noborja. They had long, dirty hair and untrimmed beards. They were full of lice since they did not wash for months, despite what the Holy Koran told them about cleanliness. The worst ones were from the tribal lands between Pakistan and Afghanistan, or from Chechnya or some of the Arabic countries such as Yemen and Syria. They had no interest in Afghanistan. They just wanted to kill people.

I could not let such a thing happen to me, to my life. I would bring shame to myself and to my family, even if it was done by force.

I did not know what to say, but I knew that I had to get away from this man any way I could. I opened my trousers and, very self-consciously, lowered them to my knees. Passersby stared at me. I glared back at them.

The Talib sat on his knees and pulled out two hairs, one which he called "the hair of your penis forehead" and another one from my testicles. Then he asked me to tie up my trousers. He measured them both with a ruler. I was looking closely at his hands, which were trembling. Both hairs were curly; I could not even guess how long they were. The one from "the forehead of my penis" was nearly two inches, and the one from my testicles was one and a half inches.

"Boy, you are in big trouble. I will have to sentence you to one month in prison," he said, a devilish sneer growing as the corners of his eyes narrowed.

He gripped my right arm tightly and pulled me toward his car, which was parked at the roadside. Another Talib, who was lounging in the driver's seat, stood up and opened the door. They pushed me into the back. Then my captor went off and stopped another young man who was hardly more than a boy.

As I sat in the backseat, the Talib in the driver's seat was holding the steering wheel and listening to one of those Taliban songs without music. The singer was mixing verses of Persian love poems with some random Urdu words. Only the singer himself knew what he was singing about.

We both watched as the Talib examined the armpits of the boy he had stopped. The boy was younger than I, and paler, and very handsome. They loved white-skinned boys.

I was determined to escape.

Not far from me, in front of the Ministry of Communications, I saw a group of builders who had been working nearby, constructing the largest mosque in Kabul. They had finished their work for the day and were heading home. As they came alongside our car, I opened my door, jumped out and shouted very loudly, "Bomb! Bomb! Bomb! Bomb! Bomb! Bomb under the Taliban car!"

There were more than thirty builders. Instantly, they panicked and scattered like a flock of frightened pigeons. People on the sidewalks also started running to get away from that Taliban car. The Talib who had been in the driver's seat was equally frightened. He raced toward the new mosque with some of the builders.

I ran in the opposite direction, toward a bakery. When I entered, the baker asked me what was happening outside. He could see the panicked people through his window. It was real chaos. Nobody knew what was going to happen next. Everywhere, people were yelling "Bomb! Bomb! Bomb!" They were all trying to hide. I saw a few middle-aged men who had stuck their heads under a pushcart with the rest of their bodies hanging out.

"They think there is a bomb," I answered, breathing hard. "But there is no bomb. I shouted, 'Bomb! Bomb!,' so I could jump from that Talib's car. They arrested me for nothing. So, they could use me in the prison," I told him.

The baker looked at me in bewilderment, then terror.

"Get out of here! Get out of my shop!" he shouted at me.

"If I were your son, would you let them take me to prison and use me for days and nights? Are you a stonehearted man?"

"You can see I'm a Hazara. You know that they hate us. If they find you in my shop, they'll kill me," he said. I tried to stay where I was, standing inside the shop. But he was a strong man with big arms and broad shoulders and was a head taller than I, and he pushed me out the door.

Now I was outside on the street again. The people were still running up and down. I did not know where to go or where to run. I felt very desperate and lonely. Suddenly, I felt myself being pulled back inside the shop. It was the baker. He practically picked me up and carried me all the way to a room at the back of his shop. He was gripping my left arm very tightly. I tried to speak, but in my terror I could not think of anything to say.

The back room was huge, almost twice as big as his shop. It was full of very large sacks filled with wheat flour, corn flour, and sugar. The baker brought me to a corner where there was a mountain of flour sacks. They were put one on top of another, all the way to the ceiling. He told me to climb over those sacks and jump in behind them.

I did what I was told. There was hardly enough space between the sacks and the wall to squeeze myself in. My nose filled with flour. I sneezed several times, one after another. The baker shouted at me to shut up. I tried my best to hold my sneezes back, but it was very hard.

My nostrils kept itching, and I had to sneeze. The man shouted again with his thick voice.

I stayed there for four hours until it was completely dark and there was no sign of any Taliban outside. By then, people were hurriedly walking toward their homes, as they always did. The pushcart men were pushing their carts slowly, as they always did.

The baker called for me to come out from my hiding place. A boy who was younger than I brought me a pot of water to wash my face. I was powdered white with flour.

Some moments later, I was standing near the window and peering outside, still afraid that if I stepped out, the Talib would grab my wrist.

"I'm not letting you go out by yourself. That is even more dangerous for me. I'll take you to your house. I have a car. If someone asks you anything, tell them you're my son," the man said.

I looked at him, not knowing how to express how grateful I felt. All I could say in a shaking voice was, "You are a hero."

Half an hour later, I was sitting in the backseat of the baker's car along with his son as he drove toward the Qala-e-Noborja. He dropped me in front of the main gate. I insisted they come inside and eat dinner with my family. He said that he had to go, otherwise his wife would get frightened if he came home late.

I watched as he drove away down the dirt road, then stepped through the gate. A feeling of weakness was now replacing my fear.

When I went into our house, everybody was angry at me for being so late. I told them what had happened. I do not know whether my father and mother believed me. But my sisters did not believe me, and they were unhappy that I had not brought them the clothes they had asked for. If what I said were true, they taunted, then I would have been imprisoned for a month at least. I was probably at a friend's house, or playing volleyball in the park, or using the parallel bars, because I was addicted to parallel bars in those days, and won every bet I made when I swung on them.

But that night, I shaved my armpits and also between my legs in case any more Taliban wanted to see them.

21

❖

The Secret of the Pigeons

T he next day, I never even left our rooms to go into the courtyard. I tried to sleep, but I could not sleep in daylight. I thought
about the baker. I had never asked him his name.

I arranged some pillows in one corner near a window where I
liked to read, and sat down with a copy of the Bible that had been
translated into Dari. My mother's brother had brought it to me from
Pakistan, where he had to go sometimes. He had a job in the Ministry of Interior Affairs drafting official papers, because he had very
clear handwriting. He had held a similar position under some previous governments, and had simply kept his old job. In the third year of
the Taliban, he came to live with us at the Qala-e-Noborja. Though
he worked for the Taliban, he was not one of them, and he hated their
decrees. But he kept that to himself. He needed to use his skills to
support his family, who was in Pakistan.

Every morning a car came to pick him up at the fort and dropped
him off at the end of the day. That gave us some protection from the
Taliban assigned to control our neighborhood.

He brought other books, too, by Maxim Gorky, Aristotle, and one
called *Plato Selections*. It was his way of defying the regime. All such
books had been banned by the Taliban. Philosophers such as Socrates, Plato, and Aristotle were infidels as well as foreigners. So,

their books should not be read in the Taliban's Afghanistan. Further-
more, since they were written before Islam, they were full of non-
Islamic thoughts.

That, of course, made me more curious to read them.

At noon prayers on Fridays, the mullahs in the mosque would say
that the Holy Koran was the only true book that was sent by God.
But I wanted to read other books that other people believed were sent
by God. I had heard that these books had helped solve the problems
of millions of people for hundreds of generations before me.

I had already read this Dari translation of the Bible once when
my uncle first brought it. I found that it was filled with poetic stories
about the prophets who came before the Prophet Mohammad, peace
be upon him.

Having recently read the Holy Koran in Dari in prison and now
understanding it for the first time, I wanted to understand the Bible
better, so I could compare it to the Holy Koran. The mullahs, however, said that the Bible had ceased to be the word of God a long time
ago, because it had been rewritten and translated many times by different people. The Holy Koran, they said, has never been rewritten,
nor will anybody ever rewrite it, nor can anyone rewrite it. Whoever
rewrites the book of God is an infidel. He is in battle with God, like
Shaitan.

Suddenly, I heard an unfamiliar voice calling my father's name:
"Basir, Basir, Basir . . ." I looked through the window to see who was
out there. My father was taking a nap, as most of my family did after
lunch in the July heat. There were more than twenty Taliban in the
middle of the courtyard, looking all around. One of them was tall
and thin, dirty as the others with a long beard and a big, black turban. He kept shouting, "Basir, Basir, Abdul Basir!"

I hurriedly woke my father.

"Who let them in?" my father asked as he was rubbing his eyes.

"I don't know," I replied. I heard anxiety in my voice.

"Did they knock on the door?" My father was rising from the *toshak*
where he had been lying.

"I didn't hear any knocking. I didn't open the door for them," I answered, my voice now shaking. "Are they looking for me? Did they come to arrest me?"

"I don't know. Let me go and talk to them. You stay here, and don't come out," he replied.

I woke my mother, my sisters, and my mother's brother. When my uncle heard the word "Taliban," he hurriedly went out to talk with them.

We stood back from our windows and looked at the Taliban through the little holes in the curtains. My father was surrounded by them, just inside the passageway into the courtyard. He was talking with the tall, thin one. My uncle showed them his ID card from the Ministry of Interior Affairs. A few of them kissed my uncle's hand as a sign of respect and honor.

They moved toward our rooms at the other end of the courtyard, looking searchingly at the niches high in the wall where my pigeons nested and laid their eggs.

"They're looking at your pigeons," my mother said. "Didn't I tell you a hundred times to take them to a shrine or a mosque somewhere? But you are so stubborn like your father, you never listen to me."

The pigeons had been living in the Qala-e-Noborja long before we moved there, in holes made for them in the mud-brick walls above our rooms.

I had always wanted to keep pigeons, as many Afghans do, even when we were still living in Grandfather's house. My father would not let me, though, saying, "You'll waste all your time on pigeons and not spend it on your lessons. When you have finished nine grades, I'll let you keep some." But I did not have to wait that long.

When we were living in Grandfather's house, one of our next-door neighbors had some pigeons. I used to go to his roof and watch him cutting the extra feathers from their wings and putting rings around their legs. They were of many breeds and colors, and each breed had its own name. I loved it when he held seeds in his hands and they came and sat on his hands, his arms, his shoulders, and his head.

I helped my neighbor keep two large pots filled with water for the pigeons to wash themselves, and two other large pots filled with sand for them to rub the insects out of their feathers.

When we moved to the Qala-e-Noborja, Haji Noor Sher already had many pigeons there. After a while, the pigeons knew me. As soon as I walked into the courtyard, many of them flew to me. Even when I just stood at our windows, they all came.

Most of the time I did not have enough money to buy them seeds. So, I cut hard pieces of stale *naan* into smaller bits for them. I purposely did not eat all my rice, so I could give some to my pigeons. Sometimes even my parents did the same.

The only one who did not like them was my older sister, because it was her job to keep our section of the courtyard swept. She complained that the pigeons left their droppings everywhere, but she liked when they chortled to one another in the early morning. She said the noise helped her sleep better.

"Will they kill my pigeons?" I asked my mother plaintively.

"No, no, I won't let that happen," my mother said, and she pulled me toward her and kissed the top of my head.

"I don't think they'll listen to you. They hate women. Why would they listen to you?"

"But I'll still try," my mother said.

"Are they here because I escaped yesterday and created panic?" I asked my mother.

"I don't know," my mother said.

My older sister was looking at me with one of her evil looks. Everyone said she was pretty; and she was. But she saved certain looks only for me, and this one was not so pretty. "If they arrest you, and send you to prison for a few weeks, then I'll believe that you were not lying yesterday," she said.

"You just shut up!" I hissed at her, and she giggled.

From out in the courtyard, we could hear the tall, thin Talib talking to my father. Most people spoke to my father with respect, because he was a *malem*, a teacher. But the Talib spoke very insultingly.

"You keep pigeons, too?" the tall, thin Talib asked. "Don't you know about Decree Number Nine that was issued by the Department for the Promotion of Virtue and the Prevention of Vice about pigeons and fighting birds? It was released almost two years ago."

My father's face went pale. He did not know what to say. My uncle hurriedly interjected, "Nobody is keeping these pigeons. They're wild pigeons. They came here by themselves."

"Yes, that is right," I heard my father confirm.

"Let me read Decree Number Nine about pigeons and fighting birds for you once again," the Talib said as he took a paper from his pocket.

"'Prevent keeping pigeons and fighting birds! This habit should stop. After ten days this matter should be monitored, and the monitors should go house to house to find the fighting birds. The pigeons and any other fighting birds should be killed by the monitors, and the bird fighters should be punished and imprisoned.'"

The Talib folded his paper. "Now I want to know who the bird fighter in this house is. He needs to be punished and imprisoned."

I was seized with fear. I loved my pigeons. And I knew that if they took me to prison, the Talib who had tried to arrest me the day before would recognize me, and I would have no hope of coming home soon, or of not being shamed.

My mother put a shawl over her head and covered her face. She went to the doorway. She stood behind the curtain that was spread across the door and said in Pashto so the Talib could understand her, "I'm feeding those pigeons."

"Who is that?" the tall, thin Talib said.

"I'm the wife of that man who is standing next to you, and I'm feeding these pigeons. I have one question to ask you: Do you think it is a bad thing, or a sin, to feed a hungry, living being?" my mother asked him.

"No, not at all. In fact, it is a good thing," the tall, thin Talib said. He was suddenly almost polite. It was impossible to know why, except perhaps her Pashto was of a very high form and revealed her as a woman whose sense of dignity demanded respect from others, even Taliban.

"As you say, I am doing a good thing. Then, you don't have to punish and imprison me, do you?" my mother said.

"No, no, not at all. The pigeons will stay here, and there will be no punishment and imprisonment for the keeper," the tall, thin Talib said.

My mother came back into the room with a triumphant smile on her face. We all looked at her with adulation. I kissed her hands. Then I walked outside and greeted all those Taliban as the laws of hospitality demanded, and stood next to my uncle.

The Talib asked my father for an ax and a ladder. My father brought them without asking why.

The Talib ordered one of his men to climb the ladder to one of those holes where my pigeons were nesting. He gave him that ax and asked him to chop a hole near the top of the dried mud wall.

"I think we agreed that we should not hurt the pigeons, right?" my father asked.

"Yes, that is right. But we are here to look for a weapon in this house. I was informed that there is a rifle with a bag of bullets in that pigeonhole," the Talib said.

"We have been living in this house for almost seven years, and I haven't seen any kind of weapon," my father said.

"You don't mind if we dig that hole?"

"No, I don't mind, but if you don't find anything, then you have to fix the mess," my father said confidently.

"Agreed," the tall, thin Talib said.

His man took out a pigeon with her week-old babies and put them carefully in another hole. The other pigeons in that hole started to fight with her; they did not want her there. She did not know where to go. She was worried about her babies and kept struggling and fighting with the other pigeons to protect her little ones. A minute later, the father pigeon flew down and walked near the babies to defend them, but the fighting never stopped.

The Talib kept chopping away. We were all watching him as he made a big mess of the wall. A few minutes later he pulled a rifle from deep inside the pigeonhole. With it was a bag of bullets, just as the tall, thin Talib had predicted. My father's face went ashen.

"You choose a very good place for hiding your weapons. But don't you know that we have better spies?" the tall, thin Talib said.

"It is not my weapon. I have no idea who put it there," my father said. His voice trembled.

"Every criminal says the same thing, but after some beatings they confess. So, now, tell me where the other boxes of weapons are." He paused as he was looking into my father's eyes. "Or I will beat you until you confess."

"I don't know what you are talking about. There are not any weapons in this place."

"Is that right? But you said that there is no rifle in that pigeon's hole, yet there was. We are going to search all these rooms. If we don't find them, then you have to show them to us, or you will die under interrogation," he said viciously. He pressed the button of his walkie-talkie and said, "Send us fifty more Taliban to surround the court-yard and the garden. Don't let anyone out of this place."

Thanks to my uncle's work in the Ministry of Interior Affairs, he had a walkie-talkie, too. He could have asked for help, but if any more weapons were found, he would be implicated as well. He stayed silent. He grabbed my left arm and half dragged, half carried me just inside the doorway to our rooms and ordered me to destroy all those books that he had brought me from Pakistan.

"I'm not going to destroy any of my books. They're not looking for books. They are looking for weapons," I said.

"You idiot, just do what I tell you. If they see the Bible or any of those philosophy books, they will hang us all," my uncle said with a rasp.

"Why?" I asked, confused.

"They will think we all have converted to Christianity or Communism or paganism," my uncle said.

"But that is stupid," I told him. "It is nonsense!"

"What is not stupid and nonsense about them?" he replied. He went back outside to find ways to delay the Taliban from coming into the house.

Now I was afraid. I ran toward our rooms. I put all of my books in front of me. I kissed them one by one. I loved Socrates's dialogues. I still did not want to tear them. But I had to.

I took the Old Testament first. I had only ten more pages left before I finished it for the second time. But there was no chance for that now. I tore out the first page, then the second and third. Then I started tearing bunches of pages at a time, as the sound of the coarse voices of the Taliban outside gave me extra strength and speed. A few minutes later, there was a pile of pages in front of me. Then I took the *Plato Selections* and tore out all of its pages. My mother and sisters helped me to tear apart the other books.

A short while later, my uncle came back in. We could hear the Taliban still at work in the courtyard, breaking down the pigeon roost. He said we must burn all the torn pages. My mother started a fire in a back room we never used that had no windows and no way for the Taliban to see any smoke. They probably would not have come into the house anyway, knowing that there were women inside.

I separated the pieces of the Old Testament and *Plato Selections* and burnt them separately in a metal bucket. I am not even sure why I did that.

My uncle told my mother to bring all our photo albums. He said we had to burn all our family pictures, like my parents' wedding pictures and the pictures that they took on their honeymoon to the Central Asian countries.

In most of those pictures, my mother and father wore Western clothes. If the Taliban saw such photos, they would imprison my parents, or maybe even kill them. These things happened often, and were announced from the backs of their pickups as the Taliban drove from one street to the next, shouting over loudspeakers.

My uncle and my mother started tearing up all those pictures. Tears streamed down from my mother's eyes, and this time she made no effort to hide them.

They put all the torn photographs in the fire with the torn books. The flames rose up, and a few minutes later every image of our family had turned to ashes.

There were pictures of my grandfather receiving a medal from his bank, and standing in front of our old house when it was new, and dedicating the school he had built. There was another one of him with the king, Zahir Shah. One showed him with all of his fourteen children. Several showed him dressed as a pilgrim from the time he had walked most of the way from Afghanistan to Mecca. In moments, his whole life as we had known it from those photos became ashes.

Everybody was coughing from the smoke, which had nowhere to go. I took a deep breath, determined to hold the smoke in my lungs even if I could not keep the books. I put the bucket full of ashes into a *bokhari* stove that we were storing in the back room.

"What about videocassettes and the video player?" my older sister asked my uncle.

"Break them all. Hurry up, quick, quick," my uncle said.

We had more than fifty Indian and American films on video. We had watched them all more than twenty times each. My favorite was the one called *Conan the Destroyer*. I had seen it at least fifty times, even though I did not know a word of what they were saying, because it was in English. Still, I loved to watch it again and again.

I grabbed that cassette and looked at the picture of Arnold Schwarzenegger on the cover. He wore underwear with boots and was holding a sword. Every muscle of his body stood out. I wished he could have been here with us now with his sword to beat all those Taliban. But he was not.

I said goodbye to Arnold Schwarzenegger and tore the cover first. I did not know how to break the cassette. I did not want to put it on the floor and break it with my feet as my uncle was doing to other cassettes. Instead, I took a decorative sword that was hanging above the door to the courtyard. It had been given to my father by the Indian government as an award for winning a boxing competition.

I put the cassette on the floor and held the sword over my head. I looked at my arms and chest. They were not as big and full of muscles as Arnold Schwarzenegger's. Though I had spent a lot of time in the gym, we never had enough to eat. But I decided that he would not mind if his cassette got broken by a person like me and with a sword used only for decoration, not with a real sword like the one he had used in the movie.

My uncle broke the video player into small pieces. He dropped the jagged bits down a hole in the floor where the toilet was supposed to go when we got running water. We threw the broken cassettes after it and burned their covers.

In the hour or so that it took for the Taliban to make sure that no pigeon would ever live in our courtyard again, every one of those so-called infidel books, videocassettes, and photographs had disappeared from our house. And that was a good thing.

As soon as the Taliban had finished tearing up the pigeon roost, they started searching through every room around that courtyard. Even though they did not find any more weapons, they wanted to take my father and me for interrogating. My uncle talked on his walkie-talkie to some people in the Ministry of Interior Affairs who told the Taliban in the courtyard not to bring us in after all. That outraged the head Talib. He was determined to find a picture or a book or anything to use as evidence against us, but nothing remained for him to find.

They did find a picture of a cow that my little sister had drawn in her drawing book with unusual colors. One of the Taliban tore it from my sister's drawing book, held it against my father's face, and said, "I can put you in prison for months for this drawing, but I will stay calm, because I am known as being kind."

"I can see you are a kind man with a soft heart. Your eyes tell me that," my father said, even though the Talib had eyes that were hooded like a cobra.

The tall, thin Talib raised his brows, then winked at the other Taliban to follow him, and they headed toward the door. My father asked them to drink tea with us. The tall, thin Talib declined, saying he was fasting. And they left.

The pigeons stayed for a couple of days, trying to make sense of this madness that was affecting them. But in ones and twos, they flew away to some other roost where they could build a nest and have a life of simple expectations.

Every time I looked at the ruins of where they had lived, I felt that far more than pigeons had been taken from me. Before the last of them left, I buried the ashes of my beloved books under a mulberry tree in the garden.

The next day my father used the public pay telephone, which we called the PCO, and which was very expensive, to reach his friend Haji Noor

Sher, who had never returned to Kabul since the night of his last party and remained in India with his family. There were two PCOs in our Kart-e-Parwan neighborhood. My father and I went to the closer one on the Bagh-e-Bala road. It was very busy, though, and we would have had to wait a couple of hours to make a call. We went to the other one in Baharistan, but the line there was even longer. So, we went home and got my father's bicycle and went to a larger PCO in Da Afghanan, a ten-minute ride from the Qala-e-Noborja if the streets are not too crowded with cars. My father pedaled while I sat on the back.

Noor Sher wanted to know about everything that was happening in Kabul. My father asked him about that rifle. At first he did not know what my father was talking about. He had completely forgotten about it. After a while he said, "That was my father's rifle, and when he died, it disappeared. How did it end up with the pigeons?"

"The pigeons must have taken it there," my father said, trying to make a joke.

"It could be true. Things like that happen from time to time," Haji Noor Sher replied, missing the joke, perhaps because of a poor connection. He asked my father to please go to the Taliban and get the rifle back. But my father never did. Even now, we still do not know how that rifle got there.

My father talked for longer than he could afford with the money in his pocket, and when he finished, the PCO owner told him the cost. I searched my pockets and gave my father all the money I had. It was still not enough, only half. My father gave the man his watch, which he had worn for many years and liked very much. It was a good Russian watch and worth more than the money my father owed the man. But the man agreed that if my father brought the rest of the money we owed, he would give back the watch. For two weeks my father was unable to make enough money to pay the man and get his watch back. When he finally did go to pay after three weeks, the PCO had moved from that place and the watch had gone with it. My father never saw it again.

Before long, we bought another video player on the black market. You could find anything you wanted during the Taliban time if you knew where to look in the back streets of the bazaar. Even porn videos, if that was what you wanted. Owning one was a form of rebellion and a source of personal pride. I found another cassette of *Conan the Destroyer*. One by one, I located copies of Socrates and the other books.

But my parents' photographs of their wedding and honeymoon now lived only in our hearts. They had become ashes, and would remain ashes forever.

22

❖

University of Taliban

At the end of the second year of the Taliban, I graduated from high school. On the day when the classes ended, my classmates and I wanted to have a big celebration. But a celebration without music, which was not allowed by the Taliban, is like a funeral. I had already had one of those.

Most of my classmates were boxers like myself. Since there was nothing else to do, six of us decided to go to the gym, put on our gloves, and have some fun sparring. The gym was in an old building not far from the school. It was nothing more than a room with a few weights, a punching bag, and an area the size of a boxing ring marked out on the floor. We had no ropes. We did not even have proper boxing trunks; when we practiced we just wore our underwear. And, of course, there were no showers. But we did not know about those things and were interested only in seeing who could be the best boxer.

We started punching one another. Not one on one, but everybody on everybody, all at the same time. We punched one another from eleven o'clock till five in the afternoon, until we could not lift a hand even to defend ourselves. Our heads were dizzy and our faces were swollen and badly bruised.

When I came home, nobody recognized me at first. They thought somebody had beaten me up. "We celebrated our graduation!" I explained.

"I'm so glad you graduated only once, not twice," my mother said.

I went straight to my bed and slept until the next morning. It was Friday, and my father was home. When I woke up later than usual, around eight o'clock, I tried to open my eyes, but I could not. I felt my way to the bathroom. I stood before the bathroom mirror and forced open my left eye with my finger. When I saw myself, I was really scared.

Every feature was twice as big as normal. I did not know what to do. I thought I must have had some kind of reaction, maybe from the bite of some insect or a large scorpion. I called my mother. She came and stood at the threshold of the bathroom door. I turned around, and she screamed as if she were being attacked by a wild animal. She began crying and murmuring, "What did you do to yourself? What happened to my son? It wasn't like this yesterday."

Everybody heard my mother's shouts, and they all rushed to the bathroom. My father stood at the door next to my mother. I looked at him with my left eye, which I was holding open with my fingers.

He said, "Who is he?"

"He is Qais, your son," my mother wailed.

I tried to speak but it was painful to open my mouth.

"Hey, watermelon head, what happened to you?" he asked. There was no sympathy in his voice. "Shame on you for letting somebody beat you up like this," my father said.

"Nobody beat me up. I boxed with five of my classmates, and I couldn't defend myself against them all. But I made sure I hit them as hard as they hit me," I said, not knowing whether to laugh or be angry.

"Five? Are you crazy? Are you talking about your friends who have had professional training?" The best I could do was to nod my head.

"Oh my God, he is crazy! He is mad! He is brainless! He is fighting his ass with an ox horn. This is complete stupidity. I haven't heard of such a thing in the history of boxing," my father said. He was looking first in one direction, and then another, but never losing sight of me. He was boxing with his words.

"Now I have become a part of boxing history," I said with a smile that stung all across my face.

My father came closer and slapped me. I shouted very loudly. It really hurt. Even opening my mouth to shout was painful.

"You ninny," my father said, and left, and then my mother and sisters left and I was alone again. I began laughing at myself, though it hurt.

I did not go out for a full week. My parents did not bring me a doctor either. They said it was my punishment. I did not mind. It is hard to explain, but that pain was in its own way a relief from the frustration of not being free to challenge the Taliban. My friends and I are Afghans. We had been trained never to allow anyone to do to us what the Taliban were doing. Our genetic code screamed for revenge. Suffering helped us forget that, at least for a while.

Every morning I washed my face with warm water and salt. It stung like hell, but it was the only way to keep my wounds disinfected. A week later when I was starting to feel better, I went to my classmates' homes. Each one looked at me shyly; some of them were in even worse condition than I.

Three weeks after school graduation, we had recovered enough to sit for the CONCOR examination required for admission to the University of Kabul. It is a very competitive exam. Far more students want to study at the university than there are places.

Most of my classmates had studied mathematics, biology, and chemistry in special private courses to get high scores so they could be admitted to the engineering or medical faculty. None of them had studied religious subjects, at least not the way the Taliban taught them.

I did not go to any of those special courses and was nervous going into the test. I still do not know how I had passed twelve years of school. I was extremely bad in mathematics. My classmates always solved the problems on my math exams for me, because they were afraid that I would break their noses if they did not.

We had four hours to answer the CONCOR's 210 questions. I

finished them all in just under two hours. There were almost no mathematics questions, and nothing on physics or biology. They were all about Talibanism.

I gave the answer sheet to the teacher. He looked at it for a moment, then looked at me and asked in disbelief, "How do you know so much about these things? All your answers are correct."

"I took a special course," I told him with a wise-looking smile. I decided it was better not to mention the prison where I had studied.

I was admitted to the Kabul University, Journalism Faculty. This was where I had most wanted to study, though with my high score on the CONCOR, I could have done medicine if I had wanted.

On the first day of classes, I ironed a white *shalwar kamiz* very carefully and wore my new Afghan-made leather sandals. The Taliban did not allow students to wear shoes, but only to make the point that they were in charge. They said shoes stink. But they never said that about themselves, though they did not wash for weeks and always smelled of dried sweat. After a few weeks, when we saw them wearing shoes, we did, too.

I also put kohl on my eyes with a small stick, like a toothpick. I looked at myself in the mirror. Each year at Great Eid, Muslims slaughter a sheep, goat, cow, or camel when we remember the Prophet Ibrahim's willingness to sacrifice his son Ishmael when God asked him to. My family always slaughtered a sheep. And before slaughtering it, we put some salt in its mouth and kohl around its eyes. I thought, "Somebody is going to slaughter me now."

I took my new notebooks and some old journalism books we had been assigned, tied them on the back of my bicycle, and excitedly headed around the twin-peaked mountain toward the university. It was not far from our old house.

I had wanted to go to university since I was in the third grade. My father had promised to buy me a car on my first day there. Now, here I was with a used bicycle that I had bought on the black market. In the three months since I had been admitted, I had dreamed of sitting behind a microphone with a pressed suit and tie and asking difficult questions of presidents, ministers, and high-ranking officials.

Not far from the looming yellow silo where my father and I had been forced to dig the tunnel, one of my tires had a puncture. As a result, I was five minutes late for my first class.

The class was full of students of different ages from all over Afghanistan. There were about three hundred of them. Most were older than I, with long, unkempt beards, long *shalwar kamiz*, big turbans, and dusty sandals. They all smelled like chicken sheds. "These are the classmates with whom I will have to spend four years," I thought.

The professor was standing before the blackboard, dressed like the students and equally dirty as they. His clothes were full of wrinkles, as if he had worn them for days and slept in them, too. I felt shy for having worn clean clothes that were carefully pressed.

I sat in the third row next to a man about thirty years old who had thick eyebrows, sunken eyes, a bony face, and a slender body. I soon learned that he could not speak Dari. He could not read or write either. I had no idea how he had ended up in the Faculty of Journalism.

But a few days later we found out that ten more people like him were in our class. They had come from the front line after two years of fighting the Northern Alliance, factions that had once fought one another and had now joined forces to drive out the Taliban. They had not passed any exams. They were introduced by the Ministry of Higher Education as "special students."

The professor banged his fist on the desk in front of the blackboard, demanding quiet. We all stopped talking and looked at him. He took his snuffbox from his pocket and put some snuff under his tongue. For a full minute he looked at all of us, then he spat the snuff into the corner of the room. It was the color of chicken shit. He wiped his lips with his turban and spat again. He opened a thick book, read a few lines, and began lecturing about the Taliban version of Islam. He was pacing from one corner of the room to another, and we all wrote down what he was saying in our new notebooks.

The special student next to me was looking unblinkingly at the professor. After one hour of lecturing, the professor asked a few questions about what he had said. The special student next to me raised his hand at every question. He answered nearly all of them.

"How do you know so much?" I asked him after the professor had left and we were having a fifteen-minute break before the next subject.

"I was born in a Muslim family and brought up Muslim, then learned a lot more with my fellow Taliban before I joined them," he said.

"I was also born in a Muslim family, but I don't know as much as you do," I said.

"Then you are half Muslim, and half something else," he said.

"What could that other half be?" I asked curiously.

"I don't know. I guess Communist, or Jewish, or Buddhist, or something else that I would hate to be," he said disgustedly as he walked away.

I wanted to make some friends, and it seemed that was not going to happen with this special student who could not read or write but knew all the answers for our Talib professor.

Fifteen minutes later, a real professor came and lectured us on the use of microphones in studios. He sounded like he had had real journalism training. Though he was dressed in the style of a Talib, his clothes were clean and his appearance tidy. While other students were busily writing what he was saying in their notebooks, the special student next to me stared blankly at him.

Suddenly, we heard loud beeps, and everybody looked at the special student next to me. It was his walkie-talkie. He pressed the bottom and talked loudly in Pashto, then he went out without asking the professor's permission. Twenty minutes later he came back and sat next to me, again without asking permission. The professor stopped lecturing.

"Who let you in?" the professor asked the special student.

"Who is supposed to not let me in?" the special student asked.

"I have the right to say who can stay in my class, and who cannot," the professor said.

"In my village, that is not how it works," the special student said.

From his accent we could guess that he was from somewhere in the south, where most people are very poor.

"This is not your village; this is Kabul University. No one in the ten years that I have been teaching here has ever entered my class without my permission," the professor said.

"It shouldn't matter if it is Kabul University or my village. It is the same land under the same sky," the special student said, and the rest of the class laughed.

"Then why are you here and not in your village?" the professor asked. "It is the same land and the same sky there."

"It is up to me to decide where to be. It is none of your business where I should be, or not. If you go to my village, nobody would ask you why you're there. They may even feed you, and treat you like a guest, like a friend of God," the special student said.

"You are my student, not my guest," the professor said.

"In my village, we go to the madrassa to learn the Holy Koran, and the mullah says that the mosque is the home of God and anyone can go there. Now I'm here to learn something. To me there is no difference between the madrassa and the university," the special student said. "We gain knowledge in both places."

His walkie-talkie beeped several more times, and he ran outside and talked into it. When he came back, he sat next to me again. This time the professor ignored him.

After ninety minutes, the next professor came. He was a Talib. He taught us more about the way Taliban thought Islam should be.

Later, I asked one of the real journalism professors why we had been taught journalism in only one class in the whole day.

"I cannot give you an answer to this question. We do what we are told," he said.

I came home. My mother wanted me to do some clothes shopping for her and my sisters. I told her that shopping for her and my sisters had brought me bad luck the last time. "I am not going to do any clothes shopping for anyone anymore," I said. Besides, I was feeling very discouraged by my first day of university.

She put on her *burqa* and asked me to accompany her, since women were not allowed to walk out without a male relative. Two of my sisters quickly joined us. They had just been invited to a wedding party that night and needed some things to wear. Wedding parties in Afghanistan usually are announced only a day or two in advance, and sometimes on the same day.

In the two and a half years since the Taliban had come, it was the first time that my mother and sisters had gone out to the bazaar. I had bought those *burqas* a long time ago in case some emergency forced them to go out, but they had never once worn them, preferring to stay inside the walls of Noborja. The *burqas* were brand-new, and bright blue, the color favored in Kabul.

We walked all the way to the main road to take a taxi. My sisters were complaining that they could not see through the small netted peepholes of their *burqas*. But there was nothing that I could do for them except try to keep them from walking into other people or falling into holes in the pavement. We took a taxi to Mandawee, the main bazaar in Kabul.

There you can find anything. It is always crowded. Before the Taliban came to Kabul, it was full of all kinds of people: men, women, children, poor, rich, young, and old from all over Afghanistan. Now there were mostly men with turbans and long *shalwar kamiz*. They all looked like they were Taliban, but they were only normal people who just dressed like Taliban. It was safer that way. Occasionally, I could see some women with bright blue *burqas*.

My mother and sisters went into a shop that sold women's underwear. I never liked buying those kinds of things for them. One of my sisters tripped going up the steps into the shop when her *burqa* got caught under her foot. My other sister walked into her, and they both fell sideways onto a pile of underclothes. It was hard for them to get up, because they could not see what they were doing.

The shop was dark. There was no electricity, and only a faint light filtered through the overhanging roofs of the bazaar. A few other women were in the shop already. My mother could not see what was for sale. She pulled up the front of her *burqa*. My sisters did the same. Three other women who were already there did the same as well, once they saw my mother do it.

When the other women heard my mother talking Pashto to my sisters, they started speaking to her in Pashto as well. They were from southern Afghanistan, talking in a way that was loud and a little bit coarse.

The shopkeeper respectfully asked my mother and the others to cover their faces. He seemed a very nice and educated man. But women were not allowed to show their faces to an unknown man. If the Taliban saw that, they would beat the women on their ankles with the cables or whips they always carried with them and slap the shopkeeper.

One of the other women, who was older, said, "Don't worry. My son is a Talib. He will protect us." We all thought she was joking. My mother, sisters, and the other women smiled.

Not even five minutes later, a Talib came along the narrow street of the bazaar, looking into all the shops. When he saw my mother and the others with their *burqa* fronts raised, he marched into the dark shop and started whipping the women's ankles with a thick cable. The women yelled and tried to jump out of the way.

The Talib was shouting in Pashto, "Cover your faces, you silly women," as he swung the whip.

My mother and sisters followed his orders. The others did the same, except for the older one who had spoken to my mother.

Instead, she picked up a teacup from the shopkeeper's table and threw it at the Talib. The cup hit the ground and smashed into pieces. She picked another cup and threw it at him. This one hit him in the chest. The Talib was stunned. So was I, as I wondered whether any woman had ever hit a Talib or thrown anything at one before.

Then the old woman picked up a teapot and threw that at the Talib, too. The tea had been made only a few minutes earlier. It was very hot. The pot shattered, and the fresh-boiled tea scalded him. He began shrieking and holding his clothes out from his skin to lessen the pain.

The shopkeeper quickly started collecting all the other cups from the table. He could see that the older woman was looking for something else to throw. He was afraid all his cups would be smashed. In a harsh voice the woman barked at the Talib, "Go home and behave yourself. Have I brought you up for such a day to whip me on the ankles with a cable? You son of a dog!" she yelled, making a bad reference to his father.

"Mother! What are you doing here?" the Talib asked as he was still holding his sopping *kamiz* away from his chest. He gazed at her with wide eyes.

The shopkeeper, who was fearfully holding the tray of cups, slowly put them back on the table.

She picked up another cup and threw it at her son. The cup hit him on his right arm as he turned around to avoid it, then fell on the ground in pieces.

"Don't you see what I'm doing?" the woman said. She picked up an extralarge red bra and showed it to her son. She was a solidly built village woman. "I'm buying this. Could you buy this for me if I sent you?" she said.

"Put it away, Mother," the Talib said. He was shy and covered his eyes with his right hand.

She reached for another cup, but the shopkeeper had picked up the tray again before she could get one. Instead, she grabbed a package of bras and threw it at her son. It was heavy and landed at her son's feet.

"Get out of here," the woman said. "I'll teach you tonight how to behave."

The Talib turned around to walk out. The shopkeeper said, "Excuse me. Excuse me." The Talib turned around to see what the shopkeeper wanted.

"Your mother has broken three cups and a teapot," the shopkeeper said. "Somebody has to pay for them."

"How much?" the Talib said, annoyed.

The shopkeeper told him the price, and the Talib paid without any bargaining. He did not even look at his mother or the other women. All the women's *burqas* were pulled up again as he walked out. He did not tell them to cover their faces.

The old woman apologized for the inconvenience that was caused by her son. The other women told her that she was a brave woman, and she was very happy to hear that.

My mother quickly became very good friends with her. For the rest of that day, my mother followed her around to all the other shops so nobody could beat her or my sisters if they needed to pull up their *burqas* while they were buying things.

After shopping for several hours, we had lunch in a restaurant and invited the old woman to join us as our guest, which she was happy to do. She had many funny stories, and we laughed like we were having a picnic with an old friend.

My mother gave her our home address and asked her to come and visit us sometime. She said she would, but she never did.

23

❖

Grandfather

We all came home from our shopping trip very happy. When we got there, we found Grandfather sipping tea in our sitting room. I ran to him and kissed his hands, and he kissed my forehead and congratulated me for starting university. I was so happy having my grandfather next to me, sipping tea and patting my head like in the old days.

He had brought some gifts for me to celebrate my first day. He gave me three expensive notebooks and his collection of the *Complete Psychological Works of Sigmund Freud*. I have no idea how he had saved those books all those years, or where he had been keeping them. Perhaps years ago he had lent them to a friend who lived where the fighting or the Taliban had never reached. I was too happy when I saw them to ask. "Now is the right time for you to have them, Gorbachev," he said.

"*Tashekur, Baba,*" I replied, as I gave him a long, heartfelt hug, upsetting his tea onto the carpet. I was thankful not just for the books, but to have him with us. It pushed my disappointment with the university to the back of my mind.

It was only forty minutes by bike to Makroyan, where he lived with my aunt, but I was not allowed to go. My father was afraid to let me go anywhere alone. Whenever I walked out of the courtyard, somebody called after me, either my mother or my father, asking me where I was going. Nobody was worried about my sisters, because it was not possible for them to go anywhere; but after all the things that had happened to me, they were always worried about me.

Grandfather was slowly becoming an old man. It was hard for him to walk all the way from Makroyan the way he once had, and he found the bus tiring. Sometimes he wanted to visit us, but he had no money for a taxi. He was too proud to ask anybody for any. We did not have a phone to call him. Afghanistan did not have much of a phone system anymore. It had all been destroyed in the fighting between the factions. Now, whenever he came to visit us, one of my uncles would accompany him, as had happened that day.

One of my sisters brought me a cup, and I poured more tea for Grandfather and some for myself. It felt like the old days, but I could read a deep sadness in Grandfather's eyes, though he tried to hide it.

I knew he did not want to ruin my first day of university. He did not know that I was already bitterly disappointed, and I did not want to spoil his happiness for me by showing it.

I was looking for a right and quiet moment to ask him what was troubling him, but nobody wanted to leave us alone. It had been a month since we had last seen him, and everybody had been missing him.

Night fell and covered everything with its black coat. My grandfather went out to the courtyard and sat on one of the low, wooden platforms scattered around where my father had once washed carpets. He was gazing at the star-filled, moonless sky. He did not notice me at first when I came out and sat next to him. He was lost in his thoughts. I sat there for a long time before I spoke.

"You are hiding something from me," I said finally. "What is it inside that keeps burning you? Why don't you take it out and share it with me?" I asked.

He looked into my eyes for a full minute. I could feel his discomfort through his eyes, which got watery. Then he looked at the stars again.

"I have kept that fire for a month inside me. If I take that fire out, its flames will burn everyone," he said with his head pointed toward the sky. "It will make you sadder than others," he said. He got up and walked back into the house.

We ate dinner together. My father made some of his jokes, and everyone laughed. I kept looking at Grandfather. His mouth made the gesture of a smile, but not his eyes.

After dinner as we were drinking tea, Grandfather said, "I have unpleasant news for everyone." We all looked at him. He was quiet for a moment and then said, "I have been receiving a letter every morning since a month ago. In the letter someone is threatening me and my sons with death if I don't sell my house to him. He is working with the government, and he is a powerful Talib."

We were all very quiet. Nobody knew how to break the silence as we tried to understand what might happen to our home, the place where we expected to return. Finally my father said, "How do you receive these letters?"

"Somebody is sliding them under the door around three in the morning. When I wake up for morning prayers, I find them. Each one is the same, the same writing, the same words. It has come every day for a month," Grandfather calmly said.

"Have you told anyone else yet?" my father asked.

"No, not yet," Grandfather said.

"While you are here tonight, will he slip another letter under the door?" I asked, deeply concerned about my aunt alone in the apartment in Makroyan without Grandfather with her.

"No. Two days ago I wrote him a letter, and left it for him under the door before morning prayers. I asked him to show me his face. Yesterday I met him. He is a dangerous man. He likes our house, what is left of it, and he wants to buy the land and rebuild. He will choose a price for it. He said he would tell me the price tomorrow," Grandfather said.

"We are definitely not going to sell him the house," my father said. "Let him dream about it. I'm sure he can do nothing."

"He can do anything he wants. He is not afraid of anyone. He would destroy whatever comes into his path. He may kill one of us if I say 'No,'" Grandfather said.

I noticed that the face of my uncle who had come with Grandfather had gone pale.

"May I go with you and see him tomorrow?" my father asked forcefully.

"No, he doesn't want to see any of you. He said that if I tell any of my sons, he will kill me. But I'm telling you, and you'll all keep your father's secret," he said as he looked into everybody's eyes. We did not know what to say.

"Do you want to sell him the house, then?" my father asked, more quietly.

"I want to talk to him and solve this problem peacefully, but if he gets serious and stubborn, then I don't know. He is one of those Taliban from the border. They capture a village and torture people and club them to death, then afterward ask the young boys to do the same to their parents. They tell the young boys that this will make a man of them.

"I don't want the same thing to happen to my sons, my grandsons, and my granddaughters. I don't want to see my daughters-in-law in widows' clothes. I don't want to ruin my family. Money is the dirt on our hands; it comes and goes. We may have some money again, and we will buy a better house," Grandfather said. He said all this with a calm voice.

No one talked after him and there were several minutes of silence. He asked for a blanket, which he wrapped around himself, then went back out into the courtyard and lay down; he fell asleep on the platform where we had been sitting earlier, even though the night had turned cool.

The rest of us sat inside; no one said anything for a long time. Finally, my uncle spoke.

"I went to the old house about six weeks ago. I had to know if any of my wife's gold was still there. I mean, how long are we going to go on living like this?" His voice was filled with frustration.

Nobody answered him. My uncle had gone to the house without telling any of his brothers or his father. Grandfather did not want anyone to go there.

"The garden was full of sacks of potatoes. It looked like they are using it for storage. They saw me and chased me all the way to Makroyan," he said sorrowfully.

Somehow they figured out that he was part of the family who owned the place. This was how they found Grandfather. The Taliban could have just taken the house, but even they knew they could never claim to own it without the papers.

Early in the morning, Grandfather left our house without telling us where he was going. While we had our breakfast my father said, "If Dad sells the house, the gold is gone with it. But I don't know how to stop him. If I did, we might face bad consequences. I don't want to be blamed for the rest of my life by the others."

"So, are we just going to lose all our gold?" my mother said. "We'll never get to another country." The gold was the only wealth we had left. The belief that we would one day get it back had made it possible for us to think that somehow someday we could leave Afghanistan and have something like a normal life.

"What do you want me to do, then?" my father said. "It is not just your gold; others have theirs, too."

"Can you not just go and get the gold, before Father sells the house?" my mother asked. My mother always called my grandfather "Father."

"You heard what my brother said last night. The whole courtyard is full of potato sacks. Thousands of them. We would have to shift all those first. Then, if they see us taking it from the ground, they'll think we have a lot more somewhere else. Then we'll be in worse trouble. They may kidnap us, and ask us for money we don't have. How will I be able to convince these illiterate Taliban thieves of that?"

My mother did not say anything.

All I could think about was having seen Grandfather's spirit so broken.

A few days later, we heard that Grandfather had sold the house for less than half of what it was worth. A few days after he received the money for it, he was threatened by the buyer and forced to give half of it back. Grandfather did what he was told.

From the time he sold the house, he became a quiet man, a man who spoke only two or three words a day.

He bought a new house. It was on our side of Kabul, only a thirty-minute walk from Noborja, about halfway to his old house. It had two floors and a nice courtyard, but it was tiny compared to what we had had before. Two of my uncles lived downstairs with their families. Grandfather lived on the second floor and stayed in his rooms for months without leaving the house. He never talked to anyone. He read and read and read. That was all.

Sometimes I visited him, but he hardly noticed me. We said *"Salaam"* to each other, and a few minutes later he said *"Salaam"* again, and a few minutes later he said *"Salaam"* again. He never said anything more. He just kept reading for hours, occasionally gazing at the blue sky.

Other times, he talked about whatever book he had open. But the two thick volumes of his favorite book, *Afghanistan in the Path of History* by Mir Ghulam Mohammad Ghobar, were always on his top shelf. They were never opened now, and were covered with dust.

After a while, he even stopped reading, and he became gloomier. Dark circles appeared under his eyes, and he neglected his appearance, going about the whole day in a wrinkled *shalwar kamiz* with an unbuttoned collar without combing his hair. It hurt me to see him so uncaring about all the things he had told me were important.

One day in late winter, Grandfather woke up before dawn to take ablution for morning prayers. He still did not like his new house, especially his bathroom with its floor covered with blue tiles. They were very slippery. He liked white marble from our mountains, as he had had in his bathroom in his old house. He always said that Afghan marble is the best in the world. "The rest of the world will notice it one day, and it'll have great value. It will be exported everywhere," he would tell us.

That day, he took ablution as always with cold water and was shivering from the cold. As he hurried to get to his bedroom to get under his blanket, he slipped. His head hit the edge of the sink. He went unconscious and lay there for several hours.

When he came to, the sun was already flooding into the bathroom through a small window. He had missed his morning prayers. He did not remember what had happened to him and did not know why he was lying on the bathroom floor. He wanted to stand up and go to his room, but he could not. He called for my uncle who lived downstairs with his kids, but his voice was not loud enough to wake anybody up.

My uncle came upstairs around seven o'clock as always to ask his father about his breakfast. Sometimes Grandfather wanted his eggs boiled, and sometimes fried. Some days he wanted milk with sugar, and some days he wanted green tea with honey. But this morning my uncle could not find him in his room reading a book, as Grandfather usually did.

My uncle opened the bathroom door and saw Grandfather lying on the ground with blood pooled under his head. He carried Grandfather to his room and asked him what had happened. But Grandfather could barely talk. His face was blue from cold. My uncle covered him with blankets and lit a blazing fire in his tin *bokhari* heating stove. The room was warm after a few minutes, but Grandfather could not feel anything, neither cold nor heat. He fell asleep.

My uncle quickly came to Noborja to tell us about Grandfather. He and my father and I went to several private clinics to look for a doctor. But it was too early, and the clinics were still closed. It was not like the old days, when we could call an ambulance any time of the day or night.

Nobody wanted to take his sick relatives to public hospitals, either. They were filthy. A person would get sicker there instead of getting cured. Besides, the hospitals did not accept patients unless they had been injured on the front line, or had stepped on a land mine, or had been wounded by a rocket.

We waited for more than an hour in front of a private clinic. Finally, the doctor arrived. He was a close friend of my uncle. We took him to Grandfather's house. By now all my other uncles and their wives and my cousins had arrived there, as well as my mother and my sisters and my little brother. There were too many people for that small house.

The doctor examined Grandfather and said, "Some blood vessels burst inside his brain. He needs to have an operation within twenty-four hours. Nobody can do this operation in Afghanistan. We don't have the surgical tools for it. You'll have to take him to India."

"Is there no alternative?" my father asked.

"No. I'm afraid not," the doctor said.

"That will take three or four days!" my uncle protested. "His passport is expired. We have to renew it first. Then we have to apply for Indian visas. God knows if they'll give them to us."

"The best I can do is to take him to my clinic, but I cannot promise anything. Without an operation, he will lose his ability to speak in twelve hours or sooner. If he talks, his words will be loose, and he won't be able to pronounce them properly. In twenty-four hours, he will start losing his memory. In thirty hours he will not recognize anyone. And after that, he will go into a coma. God knows how long he will stay alive after that," the doctor said with a sigh.

Grandfather was listening to all that the doctor was saying. "Will I be able to walk before I start losing my memory?" Grandfather said.

"No, I'm sorry," the doctor said. "Your brain will not help you control your body. You won't be able to lift your arms, or your feet, and you won't feel anything unless we get you operated on."

"So, I will die like this?" Grandfather said as if he were hearing a joke.

"Not if we get you to the operating table on time," the doctor said.

"Otherwise, yes," Grandfather said.

The doctor nodded his head as he was looking at his hands.

There was a moment of silence, a bitter silence. Nobody knew how to break it. My father asked my uncle to find Grandfather's passport.

Grandfather said, "Let's have a good *qabli* for lunch, and celebrate the last hours of my life, and enjoy eating and talking while I can. You don't go anywhere for lunch, Doctor. You stay with us."

The doctor nodded.

Grandfather tried to sound cheerful. We all had cold smiles on our faces to make Grandfather feel good, but inside we had flames of sorrow burning us, and we did not know how to cool them.

"I know I can't bring a real smile to your lips," Grandfather said, "but maybe my joke will. Mullah Nasruddin said, 'When my wife died, half of the world died for me. When I die, the whole world will die with me.'"

Everybody laughed.

"You see, I can still do it," Grandfather said with a trace of pride.

My aunts started wiping tears and blowing their noses.

"Hey, hey, I don't want to see you crying and wiping your noses for me," Grandfather said cheerfully.

We all smiled with tears in our eyes.

My uncle left the room to start working on Grandfather's passport renewal. My father went to find out about whether an Indian visa would be possible. My aunts started cooking the rice and the meat for the *qabli pelau* and shredding the carrots they would mix with it. The doctor wrote a prescription, which he handed to me, and I ran off to the pharmacy. The room was full of my cousins, and Grandfather told them to sit in a circle around him and joked with them.

I came back with the medicine in a plastic bag. In the short time that I had been gone, Grandfather's face had become noticeably paler. But he tried to sound happy and full of energy.

Several hours later we had lunch around one long tablecloth in Grandfather's room. My father had to feed Grandfather, like a little baby, as he was lying on his *toshak* in the corner near the woodstove. Grandfather made some jokes about old people, and we laughed, quietly.

After lunch, the doctor injected him with some painkillers since his head was hurting, and he fell asleep. We did not let the doctor go. Late in the afternoon my uncle returned with a new passport for Grandfather. Early that evening Grandfather woke up. His saliva started coming out of the corners of his mouth without his noticing it, and he was saying things that did not make sense.

My uncles tried to talk to him, but he could not focus on what they said to him. My aunts wept, but he did not object anymore.

"I should take him to my clinic," the doctor said. "It is happening faster than I thought. He may need oxygen very soon."

My uncle stayed with him in the clinic that night; the next day we busied ourselves trying to get visas. The next night I stayed with him. I sat all night long on a chair in front of his bed, looking at him as he was breathing softly. Occasionally, he opened his eyes, looked at me, and then closed them again.

Early in the morning he opened his eyes. This time he did not close them. He wanted to say something. I lifted the oxygen mask so he could speak. He called my name, and I said "Yes." He called my name again, and again I said "Yes." His voice gave out, but his lips still moved a little. And then they stopped. His eyes remained open, seeing the invisible.

We brought the body to his new house. I did not cry at all. I could not tell whether it was nighttime or daytime. They seemed to me the same. I was not feeling hungry or thirsty. I did not know whether I was walking or sitting. Everything seemed like it had stopped.

Meanwhile the little house was filling up with people from all over Kabul who had somehow heard the news.

My father took charge of organizing cars to take us all to Grand-father's village. Though he had left the village many years ago, Grandfather had always kept in touch with many of our relatives there, and had helped many of them without telling anybody.

That same day, we carried him to his village, about thirty miles from Kabul. Even before we arrived, Grandfather's friends and relatives had heard the news. The high-walled house where he had grown up was full of people.

Once we reached there, the news quickly spread all over the village, and thousands of people came. No one there had ever seen so many people at a funeral before. Our family had lived in that village for several generations. The village people used to call my grand-father "President" from the time he was working at the National

Bank of Afghanistan. My grandfather had brought my grandmother there for the first five years of their marriage to live with his mother, and would visit her once every three months while he was working in Kabul. He had fixed up many of the rooms in the old house and had made its walls higher and stronger, but they offered no protection during a war fought with rockets.

One of my uncles, whose wife is from that area, had wanted to go to the village instead of staying in the Qala-e-Noborja. He decided to go with his wife's brother to see whether it was safe. On the way there, they were robbed by one faction who took all their money. On the way back, they took a different route to avoid the robbers and were beaten badly by another faction, because they had no money left to be stolen. We heard worse stories about those roads from other, distant relatives. So, we never tried to take refuge there. Yet the village was a beautiful place, filled with the apple orchards that Grandfather had planted.

When the time came to take Grandfather from the house to the place for his burial about a mile away, my father and his brothers tried to carry his coffin, but everybody there wanted to help carry it. So, they passed Grandfather's coffin over their heads to the next person in front of them.

When they put the body in the grave, and I saw the earth taking Grandfather away from me forever, I could no longer hold back the feelings I had been carrying inside me. I broke down and cried loudly. I could not stop, though I remembered Grandfather's long-ago admonition: "Brave boys don't cry." But I was not brave anymore. I knew that my bravery had been buried with Grandfather.

Many people rubbed my back and hugged me. But it had no effect on me. I would stop only when I was asleep.

We stayed in his village for three days to be with the people there who wanted to say their condolences. Every day, several hundred people came. Sometimes, we had to keep all his close friends and relatives for lunch. After the three days we went home.

Several nights later, I saw Grandfather in my dreams, very happy in a field of roses. I called him, but he did not seem to hear me. I called him several more times, but he never answered. The next morning I stopped crying.

I went through all of Grandfather's papers and books. I gave some of his books to my cousins, but I kept all his papers. He had written the story of his life in those papers. On the first page he wrote, "The richer you get, the more you lose your respect, love, and closeness to poor people around you. Don't forget that once you were one of them, and that your ancestors were among them."

24

❖

One Knot at a Time

After going to Kabul University for only three months, I stopped. I did not have enough money to fix my tire punctures every day, or to pay for the bus. We had spent all our savings on Grandfather's funeral, feeding people in his village. This is how it works in Afghanistan. People come to your house offering their condolences and expecting a lunch or dinner.

My father made barely enough money to feed us poorly three times a day. We could not afford milk, butter, or jam for breakfast anymore. We ate bread and tea with a little sugar. Sometimes we boiled the same tea leaves for several days until there was no color or taste left in them. For lunch, we ate beans and cheap Afghan rice. Most of the time, we ate the leftovers from lunch for dinner, and from dinner for lunch. My uncles and aunts were in the same situation.

I stayed at home for a few days after I stopped going to the university. I did not know what to do with my life. Most of the young men were going to Pakistan or Iran for work. When they came back after several months or years, they brought money and gifts and told about eating good food while they were away. But some of them had also been kicked out of those countries with no money in their pockets. Their money was left behind with their employers. Some of the honest employers sent their money, many did not.

Several times I made plans to go to one of those countries. But my father never gave me permission to go. He was still buying and selling flour and oil. Sometimes we did not see him for weeks. We knew that he had been home only from the rumples we saw in his bed in the morning. Sometimes, I think he was so discouraged, he did not want us to see him.

Once when I tried to talk to him about buying carpets again, he just shook his head. "Carpets are a cursed business," he said, and he would not say anything else.

I was looking for advice, for someone who could guide me in the right direction. Grandfather was not there to help me anymore. Every now and then I saw him in my dreams, always wearing white clothes and a big smile, but he never talked to me. He never told me what to do to help my family. But I was still so happy to see him, to feel that he was in some way still with me. Sometimes I saw him with Wakeel. Wakeel always had his kite and reel with him, and looked as if he had just won a kite battle.

One day when I felt completely desperate, I went running for a couple of hours without stopping. As long as I was running, watching carefully where I placed each step on the broken pavements and roadways, my mind stopped thinking about the poverty that we were suffering, or about my father, who was working so hard and was losing weight from lack of food, or the loss of Grandfather and Wakeel.

I ran so hard that sweat was pouring from all over my body in a way that it rarely does in the dry air of Kabul. Finally, breathing deeply, I sat under a tree on the slope of the Bagh-e-Bala, the very formal High Garden built by the Moguls four hundred years ago at the top of a steep hill just west of the Qala-e-Noborja. I was exhausted. But as soon as I leaned back against the tree to rest, the distraction that the running had brought went away. Once again, all I could think about was our problems. From the Bagh-e-Bala, I could look down and see Noborja with its one last tower. I closed my eyes.

My carpet teacher came into my mind. I had not thought about her for a long time, and when I had, it had always seemed as if she were very far away from me. Now I felt that she was close to me, sitting right next to me. I opened my eyes and looked around. There was no one, only the trees and sparrows making their *chuk-chuk* noises.

I closed my eyes again and thought about the last time I had seen her, when she had said goodbye. "Use your mind skillfully, for you could be a brilliant weaver and seller of carpets one day." She said this with her hand gestures.

As I sat there against the tree, her message rang through my mind very loudly, as if she were saying it forcefully into my ears. I opened my eyes again and looked around to see whether anyone else had heard. But there was no one around. I was alone, but I was not alone. A feeling of peace came over me, and I felt very relaxed and fresh, except the muscles of my legs, which began to cramp and hurt when I got up to walk home.

At home, I looked at the carpet that we had in our sitting room. I thought, I can make a carpet, too. I had learned that from my teacher.

A sudden idea sang in my mind: why not draw a design for a carpet? I took a piece of paper and roughly sketched a design that had been circling in my mind for several months. A few hours later, it had begun to really look like a carpet.

That night I stayed awake until my father came at midnight. He asked me why I was not asleep. I asked him for some money to buy graph paper for drawing my carpet design properly. He did not like the idea. He asked me what I would do with the design. I said that I would be able to sell it and make some money.

"Maybe that is my career," I told him.

"Stay away from carpets," he said with a sad voice. "They will only disappoint you."

The next morning when I woke up, I found the money that I needed next to my bed.

I went to one of the stationery shops in the Shahr-e-Naw business district and bought some sheets of graph paper. As soon as I got home, I started working on my design for a carpet about six feet long and four feet wide. Every day I could see mistakes from the day before, and I had to correct them. Also, the longer I worked, the more ideas kept streaming through my imagination, and I wanted to include many of them. It took me four months to finish it.

When I was finally satisfied with it, I took my design to several carpet factories to sell it, but none of them were interested. Some of them did not even look at it. They said that they received their designs from buyers overseas and worked only according to their customers' orders.

As the weeks passed, I became very discouraged. I nearly tore the design into little pieces. But then I thought about how much of my father's money had been spent on the paper and the pencils, though we hardly had enough to eat, never mind the time I had wasted on it.

"I am not going to university anymore. If I go, I will not learn anything new," I told myself. "I am getting like a stray dog. I should not be like a dog. I eat and shit, that is all I do. I must be like a human, and do something. But what?" I asked myself. "I don't know," I answered myself, despairingly.

"You have to make your own carpet with your design," a voice inside me exclaimed.

"What if nobody likes that carpet?" I asked the voice inside me.

"You don't know that yet," the voice replied.

"Yes, I don't know that yet. Nobody knows what will happen tomorrow," I said back. It was several days later when I suddenly realized that the voice I had heard was like that of my teacher when she had spoken to me in my dreams.

I told my father that I was going to make my own carpet. At first he thought I was joking. But I insisted until he understood that I was serious. He gave me some money to buy wood for a loom. I went to a wood market and bought three long beams. I took them to a carpenter who was my father's friend and asked him to make me a carpet loom.

A week later the loom was ready. I did not have money to pay the carpenter, and I did not want to ask my father for more money. I told the carpenter that I had forgotten to bring the money, and he said that it was all right, that I could bring it the next day. I said I would. But that particular tomorrow never came, or at least not the next day. After four weeks he came to our house for his money. I told him that

I spent the money on something else, and that my father did not know that. I promised him that I would give him his money within a month. I begged him to please not tell my father about it. In fact, I had already told my father about it. He was not happy that I had not been truthful to the carpenter.

The loom had been in my house for two weeks before I had wool, a comb, or any of the other materials I needed, or the money to buy them. I still had the hook that my teacher had given me, but that was too precious to use.

I asked my neighbors to lend me some money, but they said they were in the same situation as we were. I asked my friends and they said the same thing.

I went to the street where the wool shops are located and asked the owner of one of them to give me six kilos of different-colored wool. The shopkeeper weighed the wool, put it in plastic bags, and told me the price. I searched all my pockets, but there was no money in any of them. The wool seller thought somebody had robbed me on the bus. I said, "No. I must have left my money at home." I told him that, if he did not mind, I would bring it the next day. He said that was okay.

I told him, "I am the owner of a carpet factory, and this carpet is an experiment. If it works, and my customers like the new design, I will buy tons of wool from you." He said that he would provide all that I needed. I said that I would buy it only from him, because he was a good man. This is what we say in Afghanistan when we are doing business. And, because we are desperate and poor, we believe it.

My mother gave me all her tiny savings to buy the hooks, comb, and the other tools. The next day I started my work. I had never set up a loom before and did not know how to wrap the yarn around the top and bottom of the loom to create the warp on which I would tie knots. No one in my family had ever made a carpet; we had only sold them. I looked at the book that had pictures of Turkmen people making carpets. I read the book several times. But it was still hard for me to understand. I only knew how to make knots. Not even my carpet teacher had taught me how to set the warp on the loom.

After many days of seeing my warp suddenly sag where it should have been tight, I gave up. I had no idea how I would pay the carpenter and wool seller.

I went back to that same tree in Bagh-e-Bala and sat under it. I closed my eyes, but did not see or hear anything. I sat there for several hours, but nothing happened. Darkness came. I became very hungry. But I did not want to leave without an answer to what I should do. I was pleading in my heart for my carpet teacher to tell me what to do.

Finally, I had to leave. I walked home slowly. By the time I got there, everybody was asleep, except my father, who was not home yet. I went to my bed but just lay there. I was staring at the ceiling. Some hours later, I heard my father come in and fall into his bed. I do not remember ever falling asleep. But that night I dreamed of my carpet teacher. She said, "A carpet cannot be woven in one day. It causes pain, and demands patience. If you let the pain poison you, you will never get to the fringes."

I woke up the next morning. I decided that the time had truly come to follow Grandfather's advice to make patience my companion. It took me two more days to find the right way to do the warping, and then to weave my weft yarn back and forth through the warp threads, as my people have been doing for thousands of years. I had created a few inches of the flat-woven *kilim* needed to anchor the beginning of a carpet. Uncertainty filled my every move. Finally, I had reached the place where the knots started and my design began.

Once I started tying the knots, my mother and sisters sometimes came upstairs to see how far I had gone. Two of my sisters wanted to learn, too. But I did not have time to teach them. Anyway, who was I to be a teacher? Every day I was teaching myself new things. I worked from early in the morning until my father came home at midnight.

My father really did believe that the carpet business had become cursed for us. He would say that we were carpet sellers, not carpet makers. But I listened only to what the voice inside me told me to do. I did not say "Yes" or "No" to any of my father's comments. I pretended that I was deaf like my teacher, and I kept my silence like she did.

Jerk's father was the worst. He always made fun of me. Maybe he was the one who taught his son how to be a jerk. He would say, "Soon your back will be bent like an old man's. You'll look like a cripple, shuffling around. You'll lose your fingers, and eat with your palms. You'll lose the sight in your eyes, and you'll wear thick glasses. Wool will grow inside your nostrils." I did not mind; I kept working.

It took me three months to finish my first carpet. I took it to a carpet shop on Chicken Street, which got its name from the Jewish shopkeepers who had sold chicken there for decades from the time the street was first laid out. After most of them had moved to Israel, carpet sellers took over nearly all the shops, but everyone still called it Chicken Street. The shopkeeper, whom my family had known for many years, looked at my carpet and laughed. I asked him whether something was funny. He said my design was hilarious. He also said that he did not want to buy it.

I insisted that he keep it in his shop. If by any chance anyone saw it and liked it, he should sell it to him. He agreed, only because Grandfather had been his friend.

"But only for a week," he cautioned. I promised him that I would come back at the end of the next week and take it back.

Three days later, early in the morning, I heard a steady knocking on our gate. I was afraid it might be the carpenter or the wool seller. I still had no money to pay them. The carpenter had come several times and asked me and my father for his money. We kept saying "Next day," "Next day," but he complained that the "Next day" never came. I had told the wool seller that I was too busy with my factory to come to his shop and pay him. He believed me. But that had been weeks before. Now, perhaps he was here demanding payment.

I opened the door. There was the Chicken Street shopkeeper. I thought he had brought my carpet back, and I was ready to argue that he had promised to keep it for a full week. But I did not have a chance. He extended his hand, which was holding American money. He gave it to me and asked me whether it was enough.

———————

It was two hundred dollars. I thought he was making fun of me again. I gave him back his money and almost said a bad word to match the hard look in my eyes.

He asked me how much more I wanted. I told him to stop mocking me, but he told me that he had found an Afghan who was selling carpets in Germany and who was very excited about my design. He had asked for one hundred more like it. Could I make them? He extended his hand with the money again, but this time he gave me three hundred. I took it and counted it as if I were concerned that it was all there. But, really, all I wanted to do was to touch it and to feel it moving through my fingers. I felt him watching me, and suddenly I realized I was being very rude. I quickly invited him to come into our house, and I asked my mother to please make us some tea.

Inside, I was thanking God and my carpet teacher. I so much wanted her to be there to hear what the shopkeeper had just said. My eyes filled for a moment, and I told the voice inside me that it seemed what she had said those years ago was really beginning to happen.

When he noticed my wet eyes, the shopkeeper asked me whether anything was wrong. I wiped them with the back of my sleeve and said I would make more carpets if he gave me money to buy more wool and looms. He gave me a thousand dollars. I had never once touched an American dollar. The edge of the paper was so stiff and so sharp, so different from our small and tired afghanis. I looked at it and told him, "I could kill sparrows with this sharp edge." In those days, you could buy a good car for a thousand dollars. You could even buy a visa to Italy for that. Here I was holding it in my hand. But I did not want to go to Italy by myself. I wanted all my family to go with me. So, I spent every penny of it on wool and looms and started making more carpets.

I went to the carpenter and gave him his money. He grabbed the money from my hand without saying a word and looked at me sideways. I asked him whether he could make me a few more looms.

"I will never make a loom for you in my life ever again," he spat with disgust.

"What if I give you the money for them in advance?"

"You don't have money even to buy yourself a *naan*," he said derisively. "How can you give me the money for a few looms in advance?"

I gave him the money for five looms, and told him that I would collect the looms in a week. He looked at me, a little startled, and even though he had my money in his hand, he remained a little unconvinced. I walked out of his shop without listening to what he had to say.

"All right! Don't worry! They will be ready next week! Thank you!" he shouted behind me.

I lifted up my right hand without turning around and made the sign of bye-bye. Money was making me arrogant.

I went to the wool shop and apologized for keeping him waiting for so long for his money. He said not to worry, that all carpet factories were like that, and he was used to it. He did not know that I had lied to him about my factory. But my lie had turned to truth. I bought a couple of hundred kilos of wool.

"I can provide you any kind of wool you need," he said. "I will deliver it to your factory."

My factory. I liked the sound of that. I was beginning to believe it myself. I had not really thought about it yet, but if I was going to be able to make all the carpets that the man in Germany wanted, I would need a factory.

"Okay," I said as I left. "Thank you." My factory, I thought.

That night my father came home very late as always. Everybody was asleep, but I was waiting for him.

"It is midnight. Go to bed," he said. Then he asked me for a glass of water.

When he finished drinking it, I gave him the three hundred dollars. He looked at the money and asked me whether they were forgeries, or some kind of joke.

"No. They are the result of my seven months' hard work," I said very proudly.

He studied them all very carefully, then smiled in a way he had not done for months and said, "Wonderful! Now you are making more money than I do." Then he opened his arms and gave me a big, long hug.

I told him about the shopkeeper, about the thousand dollars, the five looms, the several hundred kilos of wool, and my plans for opening a carpet factory. He looked at me in amazement. But I knew he was pleased.

I taught two of my younger sisters and my brother how to make knots. My brother was still very young, but he had become a very helpful member of our family. He and my sisters and I took turns working on our one loom.

My younger sisters had been spending time with our neighbor's girls in the garden every afternoon. Since they were banned by the Taliban from going to school, all they did was chat or read Iranian novels. When my sisters failed to appear in the garden after lunch for several days, the other girls became worried. At first, my sisters were very secretive about making carpets. They thought they were doing something special, and they did not want anyone to know. But they could not keep secrets from their friends. After about a week, they finally told the other girls about it.

The neighbor's girls came to me and asked me to hire them for no salary. They just wanted to learn how to make carpets. We were Pashtuns. They were Hazaras. Weaving carpets was something that Turkmen did. But we all worked at it together.

Within a few days, most of the other girls in our neighborhood were coming to our house to ask me to teach them how to make carpets. Somehow they had heard about what we were doing. They had all been at home doing nothing and were very bored.

My first reaction was to be worried. If the girls had heard about what I was doing, maybe the Taliban would as well. But I needed weavers, and all the girls were willing to learn.

In a couple of months, my one loom had turned into a carpet factory. My father and I had rebuilt the walls of the storeroom where his car-

pets had been destroyed by the rocket. We made all the bricks ourselves, filling more than a hundred molds every day with mud that
had been mixed with straw, then letting them dry enough to empty
the molds and fill them again. We did not have the money to buy
cooked bricks, and besides, the whole of the Qala-e-Noborja had
been built this way from sun-dried mud bricks. For privacy I blocked
the large windows facing the street with bricks, but kept a little space
at the top to let some air come through.

I had twenty-five looms and about forty girls, including my sisters, making carpets. As soon as I could get new looms made, new
girls would start. From early in the morning until four o'clock, all
those girls tied knots except for one hour when they stopped to have
lunch.

From four o'clock until six o'clock, we had classes. My father
taught them basic mathematics, my mother showed them how to do
accounting, and my older sister taught Dari grammar and literature.
Though she had no interest in making carpets and never learned how,
my older sister was a very good teacher, as she had been when we had
taught our Kuchi cousins. I was very happy that she was teaching my
weavers, though I never told her that. Even though we were now at
peace, I never knew when, like with the rest of Afghanistan, the
fighting would start again.

Hanging over us every minute was the fear that the Taliban might
find out what we were doing. It was against the Taliban laws for the
girls to be working outside their homes, or to be getting an education.
Had the Taliban known, terrible things would have happened to all
of us. In the end, we could even have been killed, but that would
have been easier for us than what they would do to us first. Even
though it was dangerous, my parents and older sister stood with me
at every step.

My rule was that the girls should be present at the factory by
eight o'clock. But they were not allowed to enter through the same
door at one time. The spies of the Taliban would have noticed that.
Instead, they had to come a few at a time from six o'clock in the morning until eight o'clock.

Two of them came in the main gate of the fort. Three of them came in from another door at the bottom of the garden. Four of them came in from a different door at the far corner of the garden that was hidden from the street. The neighbor's girls climbed over the walls between their house and our courtyard on a ladder. At eight o'clock, all the girls were present at the factory. The ones who came earlier did their homework until starting time.

Once my factory started to be successful, so many girls were coming every morning to work for me that Jerk decided to become friendly. He begged me to accept him as one of my students and teach him how to make carpets. I agreed, though a little bit reluctantly. But I did not have any friends, and in those times when he chose to be intelligent, I enjoyed his company. He had a good sense of humor. He was still a jerk sometimes. But that was not his fault; he was just being himself.

He was a fast learner. He learned everything about making a carpet in two months. All his life he had been very competitive with me, but somehow he never learned how to get ahead. He always remained one step behind. Maybe he had been smart all along, though, letting me take the risk first, then doing it better by imitating and improving on what I did.

Soon he bought his own looms and wool and started his own factory on the other side of the courtyard in the rooms his family used. He taught all his brothers how to make carpets and organized a factory like mine. He began hiring all the boys of our neighborhood, paying them more than I paid the girls, feeding them better food and making lots of jokes with them.

Soon I started hiring boys, too, especially some younger ones whose big sisters would have been looking after them, except they were now working for me. But after a while, some of my boy weavers joined his factory for better food, more wages, and funnier jokes. Then all of them went.

Jerk started making fun of me to my face, pointing out that all my boy weavers had come to work for him.

I soon found some older ones who could work faster, but I wanted back some of the first crew, because I had trained them well. For a while, I did not know what to do. Then I had an idea. With the help of a friend who was deeply committed to education, I rented a building with five rooms near the old fort. We bought some chairs and blackboards. We hired a few Dari and English teachers. At the end of each day, I sent all my boy weavers, many of whom had never once been to school, to a course for two hours to learn to read and write Dari and English.

Soon, all the rest of my boy weavers came back to me. Before long, most of Jerk's own weavers wanted to work for me as well. After a month, there was no room on any of my looms and I had to buy more looms so I could hire them.

Jerk was really annoyed. When he saw me, he spat on the ground with disgust. But he could not afford to be disgusted forever. A few months later, he came to me and begged for his weavers, because he could not manage to run a factory with the few who remained.

I told him to stop being a jerk, and he promised he would. But a jerk is a jerk. Even if he lives on the moon, he will still be a jerk.

I sent his weavers back, though they did not want to work for him. But I had promised. I told the boys to come to the course afterward for free lessons, as if they were still working for me. And they did.

A year after I had started the factory, I graduated the first group of girls. They started making their own carpets in their own homes, hiring their relatives and neighbors. Some of them asked me for looms and wool. I had to lend them some since they could not afford to buy them. A few months later, though, after they had sold the carpets they had made, they returned my looms and paid me for the wool. Some of them made carpets for me in their own houses. I paid them for their work. I started paying regular salaries to all the students in my factory. Sometimes I gave them bonuses for very good work.

Soon my neighborhood turned into a carpet-making area. We were making the best carpets in Kabul. Some of the girls had great ideas about colors and were bringing in new patterns. I gave them complete freedom to make what they wanted.

After I had shown that I could make and sell carpets, my father started taking me seriously. He listened to what I had to say. When he saw that we might have some money again, he revived the idea of leaving Afghanistan. I told him that I would make enough money to take everybody out. I told him that we were Kuchis and wanderers by nature, that I would take care of the money, and that he should look for smugglers. He was doubtful at first, but after long discussions in which I wrote out all the numbers on paper of my costs, my production, and my profits, he finally agreed. He was a physics teacher, and he understood numbers.

He started listening to the BBC World Service again to find out what was happening in different parts of Afghanistan, so he could decide which route to take to get us out of the country safely. We made lots of plans. Then we would go over our plans and see what was missing.

The final plan was to go to Iran first, then to Turkey and, eventually, to Italy. Once we were there, we would try to get one of my uncles and his family out. We would work hard and make more money, and then invite another uncle. Slowly, slowly we would get everybody out. None of us had ever been to Italy, and had only a vague idea of where it was. But we were determined to go there.

While my father was looking for smugglers, I went back to university. Though the university taught me only what I had already learned in the Taliban's prison, nevertheless it would provide me with a degree after graduation. That could help me get a job somewhere, and the Taliban's prison could not.

With the money that came from carpets I had sold, I bought a new bicycle. I could even have afforded a motorbike or a car, but I did not want to flash my money around. Most of my classmates were poor, and I wanted to look like I was the same as they.

"When there is danger, conform to the crowd," Grandfather used to tell me. So I conformed. Grandfather was gone, but I carried his good words and advice in my heart.

For the next two years, I studied hard and worked hard. The credits I needed for my degree slowly accumulated, as did the profits from my carpet factory. The strange peace brought by the Taliban made it safe for foreign buyers to return to Kabul, and my sales increased. A woman might be beaten for leaving her home alone, but in other ways the Taliban regime provided a sense of security. Many things worked. The banks. The mail delivery. Offices. Safe transportation all over the country. My father began going out to the villages again to look for older rugs, and to find customers for them among the foreign rug buyers who had started to come back to the Taliban's strange but stable Kabul.

We never lost our desire to leave, though. My mother quietly but insistently reminded us to focus all our energies on getting out. Ironically, the Taliban were making it possible for us to do so.

Then, as so often happens with Afghanistan, events on the other side of the world changed everything for us.

25

❖

A Change in the Air

In the summer of 2001, we started hearing from the BBC World Service that Ahmad Shah Masoud was planning to challenge the Taliban. Masoud was a very intelligent man who had attacked the Russians relentlessly for many years and had prevented them from ever capturing the Panjshir Valley, which controlled the main pass across the Hindu Kush mountains.

After the Russians were driven out, Masoud had served as defense minister of Afghanistan at a time when the fighting between many factions to control Kabul caused thousands of deaths and terrible destruction. He was the leader of one of those factions who were driven out of power by the Taliban.

Everyone was terrified that if he tried to retake Kabul, the mindless war would start all over again, and all our gains of the past few years of stability under the Taliban would be lost. The Taliban were cruel and ignorant, but they had brought order to Afghanistan. We lived in constant fear that the brutal fighting among the factions would start up again. Even the Taliban's strangest laws were easier to survive than the chaos of the commanders.

Masoud had been born in the Panjshir Valley, an hour's drive north of Kabul. Neither the Russians nor the Taliban had been able to capture him. Now he was serving as the military leader of the Panjshiris who bitterly opposed the Taliban. If he attacked Kabul, all the roads would be closed, and we would not be able to get out. Everyone would be hiding in their houses. The streets would fill with bodies, and the gutters would fill with innocent blood. Again.

Only a few weeks before, my father had finally found a smuggler who seemed to be the right one for us. He came to our house several times. We all met him and felt we could trust him. He seemed to be an honest man, not one of those smugglers who take your money and leave you in the middle of nowhere. We had met him through my uncle's friend, whom we had known for many years and trusted.

The plan was that after we arrived in Turkey, my uncle would give his friend in Kabul the money he wanted for getting us there. Then he would hook us up with another smuggler who would take us to Italy.

We were all very relieved that soon we would be making a peaceful life in another country, the rest of our relatives following soon after. We never thought for one minute about the dangers and the hardships that we would face. Nothing frightened us except staying in Afghanistan, despite the calm brought by the Taliban.

The smuggler gave my father a date when we would leave. We had about six weeks to prepare. My mother had already started packing. We could not take much, so she was very carefully choosing the things we could carry. My father was sorting out our belongings. He made several piles. Each pile was intended for a different uncle.

My sisters were going through their clothes, deciding what to take and what to leave behind. They all knew that they could get better clothes in any of those countries where we were planning to go, but they were very sentimental and kept some of their favorites from childhood even though they did not fit. The whole house was a mess, with piles of clothes everywhere in all the rooms.

I was going through all my looms upstairs in my factory. Some of my looms had carpets on them that could be finished before the date we were scheduled to leave. Some of them had carpets that were half-made, and others that were only just started. I put the best weavers to work on finishing the ones that were nearly done and placed one of my better students in charge of the rest of my factory. It was her responsibility to finish all the carpets after we left. She would then contact my uncle, who would take them to my buyer on Chicken Street. These carpets were part of the money we would be paying the smugglers once we arrived in Italy.

After we had gone and the carpets were finished, this same girl would distribute all the looms among my other students, so they could start making their own carpets in their houses. These looms were to be their salaries and bonus for this month. They were very happy about that. But I still had to dye the wool and silk for them for at least one month, since they did not know how to do it. I had been showing a few of my students how to dye wool and silk, but dyeing is very unpredictable since the strength of the dye, the quality of the wool, and the heat of the fire under the dye pot can be slightly different from batch to batch. Learning how to get the same shades of each color in every batch takes time, and they were still making the kinds of mistakes that I had made when I had been teaching myself these things.

It was around seven o'clock in the evening. We were about to have an early supper after a long and tiring day. My mother was cooking kebab on a grill in the courtyard. Every meal now was like a celebration, because we would be leaving on October 15, only a month and five days away. It was also our way of not feeling sad about having to leave our own country, where our family had lived for thousands of years, and where I had lived the first nineteen years of my life.

My mother gave everyone a stick of kebab. It was lamb, very juicy and delicious. My father said, "Let's listen to the news." My mother did not want to hear anything from "the devil box." That is what she called the radio, because it always broadcast evil news. She said it only ruined our time together.

My father chuckled and said, "It is all right. We're leaving this country very soon. Let me hear it while we're here." Then he turned on the radio to the BBC World Service. My mother did not want to argue, because she knew that it would not change anything. Instead, she fussed over the food.

Suddenly, we heard news that made us stop eating.

"Ahmad Shah Masoud was wounded in a suicide attack today at his stronghold near the Tajikistan border. The attackers were two Arabs who had posed as journalists. While they were interviewing Masoud, a bomb in a belt worn by one of them exploded.

"That man was killed instantly. The other was captured and shot while trying to escape. Masoud was rushed to the Indian military hospital at Farkhor, Tajikistan."

We were completely stunned. We did not know what to think. Should we eat and continue our celebration? Should we start mourning? What did this mean? We did not have suicide bombers in Afghanistan.

In the morning we heard that Masoud had died during the night in the hospital while they were trying to save him. All around us, our many Panjshiri neighbors wept loudly.

I had not told any of my classmates that I was leaving. I did not want to make them feel bad that I was going and they were staying behind. I was planning to send them gifts and sweet letters from Italy.

We had all become good friends in the past three years, despite my time away from the university. We even had made those Taliban who had come from the front line our friends. We had taught them how to read and write. We also taught them how to use parallel bars in the gymnasium, how to play basketball, and how to dance. Sometimes we even secretly listened to Indian music with them in our breaks between classes. A few of them quit being Taliban. They were not bad people after all. They were just guys like us who wanted to have a chance at life. They wanted to marry Kabuli girls and to continue living in Kabul.

We told them that they would have to share all the housework with their wives. At first they thought we were making fun of them. Then they realized that we were serious. But they did not want to go back to their lives in the village. In the end, they accepted that they should work equally as hard as women in their homes.

The day after Masoud's death, my classmates and I talked about his assassination. Some expressed deep concern at losing yet one more of our Afghan leaders. Others, who remembered all the rockets that he had thrown at Kabul during the civil war, were happy about his death.

Some of our classmates chided the others as if we were already journalists, saying, "Our job is not to take sides. Our job is to tell the truth and get all the facts." We listened to the BBC World Service as a model of how to present news accurately and as soon as it happens. We carried small radios in our pockets and listened to them during our breaks between classes, usually with small earphones.

One of my classmates was listening to the news while we were talking about Masoud. Suddenly, he shouted, "Quiet! Quiet! Something terrible has happened in New York."

He pulled the plug for the earphone out of the radio, and we listened to the news that a plane had hit one of the towers of the World Trade Center in New York. We had seen the World Trade Center in many movies, especially one with a giant monkey who had climbed it like it was a ladder. We could picture its two towers clearly in our minds. Then, as we stood in the late afternoon sun under the trees on the university campus, we heard with disbelief from that tiny radio that a second plane had hit the other tower. Now the horrors that had filled our lives for so many years were happening even in America. We felt as if something had been taken away from us. "What hope can we have for Afghanistan, if this is what is happening in America?" we asked each other.

The death of Masoud was instantly overshadowed. We completely forgot about him. The BBC World Service said something like:

"The timing of the Masoud assassination, coming just two days before these attacks on the United States, is now considered significant by observers who believe that Osama bin Laden ordered the assassination to help his Taliban protectors and ensure that he would have their cooperation in Afghanistan. The assassins are also reported to have indicated support for bin Laden in their questions of Masoud."

Osama bin Laden. Was that not the name of the Arab they said was living near us in the house of the Pimp of the King?

Some of my classmates said that soon America would attack Afghanistan. The Americans would be like the Russians. They would drop bombs everywhere, destroying every village and city.

I was not so sure. I thought America was too far away to attack Afghanistan. It was on another continent. Why would they come to Afghanistan? If they wanted Osama bin Laden, they would send their intelligence services to arrest him. But they would not attack the whole of Afghanistan for just one person.

"Even if they do," I told myself, "we will be gone. We will be in Turkey, or maybe even Italy by then. But an attack is not likely."

We kept listening to the BBC every day after that, almost every hour. They kept saying that America would attack Afghanistan. One month passed. Nothing happened.

The roads were still open. As each day brought us closer to our departure, we became increasingly hopeful that we would really get away this time, and equally worried that something would happen to stop us.

One week to the day before we left, some of my uncles, aunts, and cousins were at our house. It was late on a Sunday evening, and we had had a long dinner together. They had come to say goodbye and collect the things that my father had separated out for them.

It was a cool evening, so we ate in one of the rooms of the Fort of Nine Towers, instead of in the courtyard. It was good to be together like a family, eating around one cloth. We knew it probably would not happen again in Afghanistan. My cousins were asking me whether I would send them nice presents. I promised to send lots of gifts as soon as we arrived.

In the middle of somebody's joke, we heard an extremely loud noise, like a bomb exploding. The whole ground shook. Some of our windows shattered, but no one was hurt. For many years now, we had lined all our windows with a sheet of plastic to keep the breaking glass from falling on us. We all rushed out into the courtyard and climbed the stairs to the terrace and then a bamboo ladder up to the roof to see what had happened.

We saw a large cloud of black smoke that looked like a giant mushroom rising from one peak of the small mountain between the Qala-e-Noborja and my grandfather's old house, which was topped by TV antennas. Everyone now called it TV Mountain instead of the name it had had for centuries, the Koh-e-Asmai.

We had not heard any planes. We thought that maybe one of the Taliban weapons on TV Mountain had caught fire. But then there was another bomb, which exploded in another Taliban area very close to our old fort. Again, the whole ground shook. We all held on to each other. My father and his brothers ran along the top of the roof toward the last remaining tower to get a better view. Then we heard an airplane that was very high, "way out in the sky, very close to heaven," as my older sister said.

It was too high to be hit by any guns on the ground. Soon there were more of these planes. As we watched, they began to bomb the Taliban camps, and Taliban air defenses, and Taliban training sites. Then they focused on places where the Taliban commanders were and where they had their communications equipment, and their military bases.

"These are not blind bombers," my mother said. "They're not like the Russians or the warlords who just drop their bombs anywhere. Look how carefully they are hitting targets."

We still did not know who these bombers were.

We all tuned our pocket radios to the BBC World Service. By now, everyone had climbed up the ladder to the roof. The BBC World Service was saying something like:

"American and British forces have begun an aerial bombing campaign in Afghanistan, targeting Taliban forces and al-Qaeda. Strikes have been reported in the capital, Kabul, where electricity supplies have been severed at the airport, and in the military nerve center of Kandahar, the home of the Taliban's supreme leader, Mullah Omar, and also in the city of Jalalabad, which has many Taliban training camps."

We saw a large bomb explode out near the airport, where the

Taliban had a big camp. We looked at each other in amazement, but said nothing so that we would not miss a word of the BBC news.

We were all suddenly distracted, though, by my mother, who was shaking her hands in the air and shouting at my father.

"No way! No way!" She was shrieking.

"What's wrong?" my older sister asked, sounding uncharacteristically frightened.

"He says he doesn't want to leave! Your stubborn father doesn't want to leave Afghanistan! Everything is all ready to go, and he says we are not going!" she railed.

I could not believe what I was hearing. So many strange things were happening this night. I had just given away my best kite to my cousin, even though I knew he would lose it the first time he tried to fight with it.

"He is behaving like a camel again," my mother said with despair in her voice. "Once he makes up his mind, nobody can change it," she said as she climbed down the ladder to the terrace below. My aunts went with her.

"What is going on, Dad?" I asked.

"Come here, son. Come here, everybody," he said. Unlike my mother, he was calm and in control. We all sat in front of him in a semicircle. The American warplanes continued firing their rockets at their targets. We saw a flash each time a rocket was released from an invisible plane, and a second flash when it hit its target with a big explosion that shook the ground.

"Afghans have fought each other for millennia," my father said as he was looking at each one of us in the eyes. He had become our teacher, and we were his students. "We have a long tradition of raiding and plundering each other. But two things unite us: love for Allah, and hatred for our invaders and enemies. We are not leaving Afghanistan until we find out if these Americans are our real friends, or enemies in the mask of friends."

"So, this is it? We're not leaving after all?!" my older sister asked. She sounded disappointed and irritated.

"Who cares who invades us?" one of my cousins asked. "I'm sure they'll be better than the Taliban or the factions."

"No, my son," my father said as he reached to him and drew him closer. "Our land is our mother. We don't let strangers invade our land. It's our duty to protect her."

"Our duty is to leave this mess you call a country!" my mother shouted insistently from the terrace below. We all turned our heads around to see her. She was standing in the dark, invisible, except when the rockets hit a target and their flash illuminated her for a second. "Our duty is to save our lives." She strode to the bottom of the ladder that led up to where we sat with my father. She looked my father straight in the eye.

"Before the Mujahedin came to power, we thought of them as life-savers. But they turned out to be the life takers of the innocent. The Taliban are the same. These ones will be no different. They all have the same goal, but come with different names. Don't you get it? Don't you see the pattern? Don't you see where it started, and where it's going?" All the anger of all the years since we had been driven out of Grandfather's house raged in her voice.

"You might be correct," my father replied quietly. "But I'm not leaving until I find out who these people are."

We turned our heads around to see what my mother might say in response, but she was gone. She knew my father better than he knew himself. She knew what answer he would have. She had gone even before he opened his mouth.

The day we were supposed to leave came and went. My father said nothing about it. My mother said nothing to him. I sat in my room, deeply disappointed. I wanted to talk to Grandfather more than at any time since he had died. But he was not there for me.

In the evening, I went and sat under the acacia tree in the court-yard. It had become my habit to sit there when I was feeling badly. In a strange way, I felt close to Wakeel there where he had last been with us. Would I, too, have to die to be able to leave this place?

The bombing continued night and day. This war was totally different from the one with the Russians. Russian warplanes had come in low, destroying whole villages at a time. American warplanes flew high above their targets, unleashing only small numbers of bombs at one time.

Calls were growing from the mosques for prayers as the bombs rained down nightly and neatly on the Taliban and other religious fanatics from Pakistan, Chechnya, Punjab, and Saudi Arabia who had joined the Taliban.

Winter was approaching and the weather was turning cold. Daily life went on. We were so used to war. There was so little left to be disrupted in Afghanistan.

With all the bombing, no one left home except to try to find whatever food was available. It was hard to get news about what was really happening in Kabul. But we had started to notice changes. As the weeks passed, the Taliban, with their long *shalwar kamiz*, black and white turbans, and black-rimmed eyes, began to disappear. They did not go all in one night, the way the Mujahedin had done when the Taliban had taken over Kabul. It was more gradual than that.

From the first day the Taliban had arrived, we had learned quickly never to look them in the eyes, and always to put our heads down and stare at the ground when they passed. Now it was just the opposite. There were fewer and fewer Taliban to be seen, maybe only two or three in our neighborhood. When they saw someone approaching, it was they who looked at the ground and walked past in a hurry, heading to one of the compounds they had seized.

Other things amazed us. A Talib had always sat on a chair in the middle of the intersection near the large mosque not far from the Qala-e-Noborja. Whenever the *muezzin* began his call for prayers, the Talib would take off his turban and place it on the chair as a sign that he had gone to take his ablutions. Sometimes he would even leave his whip. Instantly, everything in the streets nearby—in fact, in the whole city— would come to a standstill. Drivers would stop their cars in the road and head for the mosques. Shopkeepers would rush out from behind their artfully arranged piles of pomegranates and grapes without even thinking about locking their doors. They knew that no one would steal anything. Under Taliban justice, a thief would have his hand cut off.

The day came, though, when there were no turban, no whip, and no Talib on the chair in the intersection. No one knew what to make of it, but just to be safe everyone still followed the Taliban rules.

The American bombings continued week after week, some nights more, some nights less. The planes had no lights; we could hear them for only a few seconds before their bombs hit the ground.

Two or three times since the bombing had started, my mother, her brother, and I climbed the ladder to the roof, wrapped ourselves in blankets against the autumn chill, and watched the flashes of light where the bombs exploded. A few seconds later, we would feel their impact roll right through us as the whole city shook. We would pass the time by making bets on which Taliban base the bombers would hit next. Sometimes my uncle won, sometimes my mother won, and sometimes I won.

We had heard that some of the planes dropping the bombs were being flown by women. That astonished us. How could women do such things? we asked. America must be a great country, everyone said, that they could send their women to defeat the Taliban. We had not seen any of their men yet. No soldiers were on the ground, only planes in the sky.

One night, after the mullah had finished the last call to prayers, we went to the roof. The bombing had been going on for more than a month by then. As we sat down near the one last remaining tower, we started hearing music. Real music, not the Taliban's tuneless singing. It was coming from the house of our neighbor Malem-e-chaq, who lived across the street below the garden. We looked at one another with puzzled smiles. Malem-e-chaq had been brutalized by the Taliban several times because he was rich. Now his sons had placed very large speakers in their windows and music was pouring into the street.

"Have the Taliban finally gone?" my uncle asked, his voice and eyes full of expectation. We could not answer.

We had been hearing stories for the past four days that people in the apartment blocks in Makroyan had been playing music during the night from their darkened windows on the upper floors, but we had not really believed them. Maybe the stories were true after all.

Soon after, we heard more music from another house along the street. Then from another. Then another. Then from our next-door neighbors whose daughters had climbed the ladder to come work in my factory. And then from our own courtyard, where someone had hooked up a cassette player to a car battery, as we had no electricity that night.

Everyone was pulling their speakers out of hiding and placing them in their windows. They were playing music as loudly they could. Any kind of music. Ahmad Zahir. Hangama and Ahmad Wali. Ustad Sarban. Lata Mangehkar. Mohammad Rafi. Jagjit Singh. Ustad Rahim Bakhsh. Ustad Beltoon. Ustad Doray Logari . . . It was over-powering, and it was spreading.

Below us in our courtyard, and in the streets, and in our neigh-bors' courtyards, people were coming out of their houses, cheering, shouting, and just laughing in a way they had not dared to do for all these years. Now, with each note of music ringing through the dark-ness, a message came through that we could hardly believe: The Tali-ban are gone. The Taliban are gone!

All my sisters, my cousins, and our neighbors in the old fort rushed into the courtyard to find out what was going on. They went from one to the next asking questions for which no one had any answers.

I saw my father standing near the acacia tree watching them. From all that he had said since the bombing raids had started, I knew he was waiting to see what would happen next. Had these Americans come to help or to invade? He needed more than music to know that Afghanistan had been returned to us. He looked around for a few minutes, then quietly went back inside.

Malem-e-chaq's sons started playing a recording of the traditional *attan* drumbeat. It cut through all the other music. By the light of a motorcycle that had stopped in the middle of the street behind the garden, we could see two dozen men and boys streaming toward the blasting rhythm. Some wore tight jeans or brightly colored T-shirts they had kept hidden since the Taliban had taken over. Others who had come out wearing *shalwar kamiz* quickly turned around and disappeared into their houses; a few minutes later they were back on the street dressed in Western-style clothes. One young man was in a suit and a necktie. Not even one had on a turban.

A couple of them raised their hands above their heads and gave a clap to signal that the *attan* had begun.

The shapeless mob quickly formed a circle to dance the first steps of the first *attan* I had seen in five years. It hardly lasted ten seconds, though, before all the men started laughing too hard to continue. They stood there shouting and hugging one another, amazed to find themselves dancing, even though that is how Afghans have been expressing their joy for hundreds of generations—until the Taliban. The beat continued booming down the street, and before long, the circle had reformed. Some began to make the measured, graceful steps— ever so slowly at first—while others cheered them on.

Tears had filled my mother's eyes at the sound of the *attan*. She made no effort to hide them, and was smiling too much to care.

As the drumming grew more insistent, she rose up, untied her scarf, and opened the knot of her hair. She leaned back slightly and in the darkness shook her head from side to side. A breeze blew through her hair and lifted it a little. A bomb exploded not far from us, probably at the house of the Pimp of the King, where many Taliban had been living. In the bluish flash of the bomb's light, I caught sight of my mother's face. It was the first time in years that I had seen her with no scarf, just like in the old days. She looked so pretty.

I got up and stood next to her as we watched the men in the street below fling themselves into the accelerating pace of the *attan*, whipping their bare heads around as they spun. A part of me wanted to join them. I was nineteen years old and had never danced; I had always wanted to, even though I worried that I would look like a sheep if I tried. Another part of me, though, was like my father: I could not celebrate until I knew more about these people dropping bombs on my country.

My uncle stood up. He spread his arms wide like an eagle, as if he were going to start his own *attan* right there on the roof of that Fort of Nine Towers. But he only looked up at the sky in wonder.

As another explosion punctuated the pounding rhythm of the *attan*, I put my arm around my mother and thought about all she and my father had done to keep our family safe. I was taller than her now. I had reached the age when it was an Afghan son's duty to take care of his parents. How could I ever do as much for them as they had done for us?

My mother reached around and hugged me as she rested her head on my shoulder. She sighed deeply. I pulled her closer as I thought about all the uncertainty of the coming days.

The men in the street had now been joined by a guy beating a deep-throated *dol* hanging around his neck. In sharp contrast to the others, he was wearing traditional Afghan clothes and a sparkling golden cap. The onlookers went into a frenzy as he strode inside the circle of dancers, beating in time with the drums from the speakers, adding to their urgency.

The *attan* reached the point when the drumming becomes so fast that the dancers generally start to drop out one by one, exhausted. But the faster the drums beat, the more furiously the men threw themselves into it, whirling first in one direction, then the other. On this night, no one was going to quit. In fact, others joined them.

I cheered for those men, though I knew they could not hear me. I shouted at them never to stop.

And they danced. They danced. They danced.

Epilogue: A Journey Still

M y mother was right. The foreigners were more interested in their own politics than in our country. They chased the Taliban away, for a while. But they brought back the same factions who had claimed to be Mujahedin and who had destroyed our country.

Many of the foreigners who came here claiming to help us left very rich. We are waiting to see what they will build, besides their military bases.

For many years we were hoping that they might help us construct water systems so we do not have to carry water in buckets from public pumps, or sewer systems so we can get rid of the stink and diseases of the open ditches we now have. We finally got electricity, but it comes from other countries, even though we could make our own if we had some help rebuilding our hydroelectric dams.

When I see how much money has been wasted by the foreigners, I think of my grandfather. One day, as he was settling himself with a pot of green tea on the long cushion next to the window, he said to me, "Let me tell you a story."

I was becoming a teenager by then, and was finding stories of my own. But I always had time to spend with Grandfather. I sat down beside him and looked into his old yet unwrinkled face.

"Mullah Nasruddin used to live in a village not far from here." I knew that was not true, of course. Mullah Nasruddin lives in folk tales throughout the Muslim world, but Grandfather always claimed he was our neighbor. I smiled at Grandfather as he put an arm around me and drew me close to him.

"Every morning, he rode his donkey out to a place where no one ever goes. Why would they? God had made it to show people the true meaning of a wasteland.

"After a while, his neighbor Ali Khan became very curious as to why the old man went back to that same spot day after day, but was too respectful to ask directly. He sent one of his sons to ask if there was anything he could do to make Mullah Nasruddin's life better.

"Mullah Nasruddin was delighted to see Ali Khan's son, and offered him a piece of hard candy that had bits of lint on it from where it had stuck to the inside of his pocket. The boy politely declined. Then, Mullah Nasruddin asked him, 'Why are you alone? Where are the others?'

"Ali Khan's son asked Mullah Nasruddin, 'Whom are you expecting?'

"'Well,' he said. 'Someday something good might happen here. And if it does, a large crowd will gather, and since I am here first,' he declared with his famous smile, 'I will have a good view of everything! Until then, I am waiting.'"

Grandfather raised a cup of tea to his lips, while I chuckled. Though I was too old for Mullah Nasruddin stories, and too young to understand how much wisdom has been distilled in them, I laughed, because I loved being with my grandfather. Now, however, these many years later, I finally understand it. If something good comes from all the foreign money in Afghanistan, like Mullah Nasruddin I will have a good view of it. Until that time, though, every day I am waiting, and waiting, and waiting.

When the Americans came, they needed interpreters. In six months, I taught myself enough English that I could work for them and earn dollars. They were desperate for anybody who could help them and were not concerned about proper grammar. I started listening to the BBC in English and watching American movies to practice the language even when I was not with the Americans. I was never shy about making mistakes when I spoke or wrote, and was always grateful when somebody pointed out my errors.

My first job was with American soldiers. I learned many interesting words from them. Later, when I was working with the United Nations, I discovered that I could not use these words in the office. A few times I did, and I saw shocked and puzzled faces.

Now that I could speak some English, I revived our family's carpet-selling business with my father. I never tried to restart my factory, at least not in the way that I had it. I had given away my looms and did not want to take them back, since many of my weavers had no other way of earning money. The flood of foreigners into Kabul created a large, new market for all the carpets that people had been making in their homes for years and now wanted to sell. I did not need to make my own carpets to have a business. Since I spoke English, I could sell other people's carpets to the foreigners. This gave me the chance to meet people from many countries.

The Americans are always very friendly. They buy a lot of carpets and pay me the price I ask. They always want to know everything they can about the carpets: where they were made, who made them, what the meaning of the pattern is. They have invited me to their embassy several times to make presentations on Afghan carpets. "Carpet makers are poets," I tell them. "And the carpets are like poems." I try to teach them how to read their verses.

The French come, look at carpets, throw them around in all directions, point out all their flaws, then do not want to pay what they are worth. They bargain for hours for even a small discount. Some of them have become my good friends, though, and bring me dark chocolate from France. Twice I went to France for short visits, and they invited me to their houses. They cooked meals for me that were so good that I had to wonder whether anything else I had eaten all my life could really be called food. I admire how they value their history, their traditions, and their old buildings in a way that Afghans do not.

The Italians are always loud. Before they look at carpets, they ask for a cup of tea. Then we talk for a long time about many things. Finally, we start discussing carpets while they go through the piles. They ask for more tea and start to bargain and make jokes. This can go on for hours. Suddenly, they pay the full price and leave in a hurry, because they are late for something. They are very much like Afghans, always friendly, dressing nicely, eating big meals, one minute laughing and the next minute shouting. When I went to Italy I saw all these things and I told myself, "I am at home."

When I had a chance to visit England, I was treated very well by everyone I met there. The countryside in England is so beautiful that I felt I was in paradise. But many of the English people I knew in Kabul lived up to the old reputation the English have in Afghanistan.

A skinny Englishman with a bony face rented part of the Qala-e-Noborja. He cut down all the large, old trees and the lilac bushes in the courtyard, even the towering acacia tree under which we laid Wakeel's body. He said they were in the wrong places.

I had kept those trees alive during the worst years of drought by carrying water twice every day in buckets strapped to my bicycle from the only place that had water, a pump more than a mile away up and over the hill by the Polytechnic.

This Englishman also decided he wanted more rooms at the Qala-e-Noborja. So, two very poor Afghan families who had lived for more than thirty years in their houses just beyond the courtyard were forced to leave. One of them was the Hazara family whose daughters had climbed over the wall to work in my factory. When they left, they had to sell their cow, whose milk gave them their only income. That meant that their daughters had to leave their schools and go find work.

My grandfather and his friends are somewhere nodding at one another knowingly about all that. Please, God, put some mercy in that Englishman's heart, and lead him to the right path.

Meanwhile, the Afghanistan that we had dreamed about during all those years of bombs, whips, and stonings still has not returned to us.

After we held our first presidential elections in 2004, we were very hopeful. For a couple of years, a lot of Afghans came back from the foreign countries where they had fled and started businesses. Some put up tall, modern buildings in Kabul and other provinces. There was a real feeling that finally Afghanistan was ours again.

But then things changed. Not everything, we soon learned, is the fault of the foreigners.

I went to the Ministry of Commerce to register my carpet business. I knew the special adviser to the minister. With her help, I finished all the necessary paperwork there within an hour. Then I had to take my papers to the Ministry of Finance, to the Ministry of Justice, and to police headquarters for more processing.

In all these places, I had to get stamps from many people, even though no one could tell me what the stamps were for. Every single person from whom I sought a stamp demanded a bribe. They did not ask directly for money, of course. They said, "Please, may I have some candy." I gave them a few afghanis, and they did what needed to be done.

As the day wore on, my money was nearly finished, and I was disgusted. I went out to a street vendor and used what money I had left to buy a bag of hard candy, the kind we put in our mouths when we drink tea. After that, whenever anybody asked me for candy, I gave them a piece from my pocket. They glared at me with one eyebrow up, one down. I acted stupid and smiled at them, as if I did not know what "candy" meant.

One said, "I don't want this. Give me real candy."

"This is real candy, and it is very good," I said, trying to sound innocent as I took out the bag and showed it to him. "Look, it comes all the way from Poland. And the ingredients are all healthy and organic. They used honey instead of sugar, and real milk. It tastes delicious!" Then I ate one, and yum-yummed.

"Idiot! I want money," he said sharply.

"Money? For what?" I asked, trying to sound surprised.

"For processing your papers," he said, somewhere between a shout and a whisper.

"But that is a bribe," I replied with my eyes wide with amazement. "And a bribe is a sin! In Islam it is forbidden! Are you trying to make us both sinners?"

"Are you stupid?" He looked at me in disbelief.

"Nobody has ever called me stupid before!" Then, more kindly, I added, "I'm just trying to explain to you the basic principles of Islam."

Soon he decided not to waste any more time on me, knowing he could get a bribe from the next person. He processed my papers and pressed the bell on the desk. A guard came bustling in and was told, "Get this psychopath out of here!"

"I'm not a psychopath! I'm not a sinner, either. I'm not a bribe taker, or angry all the time. Now, tell me who is a psychopath?" Then I walked out, smiling, without waiting to hear the answer.

More than ten years have passed since that night on the roof when we saw the first American bombs. From time to time, I think about some of the people—good and bad—whom I had known during the worst years, and I wonder what has become of them.

I have never seen Berar again, though I have looked for him in many places. If he is dead, please, God, keep his soul at peace. If he is alive, I pray to God to make us meet again one day.

The garden where Grandfather and I saw the skulls now has three houses covering the place where the fountain was.

Sometimes when I am riding in a taxi, the driver might take a shortcut on a street where a horrific memory comes back to life. I lean forward and ask him please to go another way, as being there reminds me of something from the war that I want to forget. Every driver understands this, and they always turn around and find another route.

I never again saw the young teacher who was forced to sell herself. I hope she earned enough money to go to another country and start a new life. I will always think of her with deep respect, despite the circumstances in which we met.

I have never seen the family in Tashkurghan from whom I stole the five pomegranates. Maybe they are living in America by now. I heard the garden was in ruins until five years ago, when somebody re-planted it. I went there once, but the people living there said they had never heard of Hamza or his family. I wonder how Hamza can be happy anywhere else.

Sometimes our Kuchi cousins call my father when they are pass-ing near Kabul with their sheep and camels in late spring, heading from their winter homes in Jalalabad to the central highlands. They are still Kuchis, but they all have cell phones now.

Omar Khan, once a herd boy with a flute, is now in Germany. He became a car mechanic. He is running a garage with another Afghan who was born there. He speaks German fluently. He has not returned to Afghanistan in the years since he left. He is waiting for the Ger-man government to give him a German passport, so he can travel to Afghanistan to visit his family.

Aaron Khan is living in Greece. He became a tailor. He got mar-ried to a pretty Greek woman. His parents are unhappy with him for marrying a Greek, because a Kuchi should marry another Kuchi and produce more Kuchis. They are not in touch with him, but know about him through Omar Khan.

Solomon Khan remained a Kuchi. He has two beautiful wives. He has three beautiful daughters from his first wife, and two hand-some sons from his second wife. He still does not talk very much, but he taught his wives and kids how to read and write.

Many of my classmates, including those with whom I celebrated our graduation by punching one another, are still in touch with me. A few of them went to India for a couple of years for education. A cou-ple of them got visas to European countries by marrying their cous-ins who were already there. Five of them are in Kabul, running good businesses. Three of them died in suicide bombings, two while they were walking toward their houses with bags of fruit for dinner. We carry their memories in our hearts.

One night at a party in Kabul, I heard that Zardad, the sadist, is in jail in England. He was hiding in London, but a journalist from the BBC found him, and he was arrested for crimes against humanity.

A foreigner, one of the few who truly has helped Afghanistan, told me in a garden full of music being performed by masters that he had been asked to testify against Zardad. It had taken two trials to convict him. The foreigner also said that Dog is dead, executed at Pul-e-Charkhi prison. Before that night, I had once tried to find out about Zardad and Dog using the Internet, but doing so made me feel violently sick. It reminded me too clearly of those days. I do not care whether they are dead or alive. If they are dead, I pray they are in the depths of hell.

For Gulbuddin Hekmatyar, whose rocket killed Wakeel, hell is too good a place, and eternity too short a time. He is still alive, still doing evil.

When the foreigners began to come to Kabul after the Taliban were driven out, Haji Noor Sher returned from India and reopened his carpet business at the heart of the Shahr-e-Naw shopping district. He came back to live in his rooms in the Qala-e-Noborja. No one had used them in all the years he had been away. One day he just appeared in the courtyard and yelled "Malem," the Dari word for "teacher," meaning my father. We had just finished lunch and my father was about to have his nap, but when we heard that familiar voice, we all quickly ran outside and were overjoyed to see him.

For the next couple of years he lived at Noborja, while his family remained in India. Sometimes he went to visit them, but he was happiest in Kabul among his carpets and his friends. He and my father spent hours together gathering and selling carpets again, and just enjoying each other's company after so many years apart.

He began to show signs of health problems, though he never said what they were. He went to India a couple of times to see doctors, and seemed to be sicker when he came back to Kabul. Then a few weeks after he had gone there again, we got a call telling us that he had died. A part of ourselves died with him. His kindness and generosity had made it possible for our whole family to survive the fighting.

Recently, I went to visit that Hazara baker, to thank him for saving me from the Talib rapist.

Three times I went to the baker's shop. Each time I could not bring myself to mention these things. There was no one else in the shop. He was always just sitting behind the counter, looking at the pedestrians and traffic on the road.

Somehow, for no particular reason, I felt weak, though I wanted very much to talk to him and tell him who I was. Instead, each time I got a plastic bag, went through trays of cookies, and filled it. Then I gave him the bag to weigh it. He did not look at me while he was putting it on the scale, even though I kept staring at his face, wanting to say something, but nothing came out. Then I would pay and walk out.

He was a little heavier than all those years ago, but otherwise he looked much the same. His shop was the same, too, except that the back room where he had hidden me was now filled by a large, modern oven. His son had become a tall man, with broad shoulders. He operated the oven with several other workers.

The fourth time I went, I said, "I'm not here to buy anything." I ran out of breath, and my heart was beating very fast. He could tell I was nervous about something.

"Slow down, young man," the baker said. He had a calm voice, very different from that afternoon, years before, but still deep. "What do you want, then?"

"I'm here to thank you," I said, still with no breath left, as if I had run for miles.

"Thank you to you!" he said with a smile. "I'm glad you like our cakes and cookies."

"Yes, they are delicious, but I want to thank you for saving my life several years ago," I said.

Suddenly, the smile disappeared from his round, Asiatic face, and he looked into my eyes with no expression. He narrowed his eyes. "What are you talking about?"

"I was arrested just across the road there by a Talib. To escape from them, I shouted 'Bomb, bomb, bomb, bomb under the Taliban car.' People ran everywhere to—"

He interrupted me: "And you came here, stood behind this window, and you said, 'There is no bomb. I created this chaos, because a Talib arrested me for no good reason.' And I pushed you out, because I was afraid for myself." He stopped for a moment. "Then I saw a look of despair in your eyes . . ." His voice trailed off.

"You pulled me back inside, and hid me behind the flour bags—"

He interrupted me again: "And you kept sneezing . . ."

The baker came out from behind his counter and gave me a long and big hug. Now we were the same height. His chest was soft and fleshy, and he smelled of bread and ovens. We held each other very tightly.

"I have thought about you many, many times. I didn't know what happened to you. You never came back," the baker said.

"I was very scared," I said.

"After that night when I dropped you off in front of your house, several months later I was arrested three times for no reason. But you know they hated us. What wild animals they were! I was a good prey for them. The bastards got all my money. The third time I had nothing left to give them. They beat me like a dusting machine beats a carpet," he said.

He had a broad smile on his face, as if he were telling a funny joke. That is what I love the most about my countrymen. He should have been scarred for life after experiencing so many horrible things, but he was talking about his past as if it were funny.

"Are you still living in that old fort?" he asked.

"We lived there for sixteen years, but not anymore," I said. "After the Taliban were driven out of Kabul, one of the widows of the owner, Haji Noor Sher, came back from India and wanted to rent the old fort to the foreigners to earn big money. She asked us to leave. We did not mind. We wanted to have a home of our own without a lot of other families sharing our courtyard. But we had no home to go to. The Taliban had forced us to sell our own house in Kot-e-Sangi to them, to give it to them, really. We could not afford to buy any property on the flat land. A squatter who had lived for a long time up on the Koh-e-Aliabad—what we used to call Sniper Mountain—across from Kabul University sold my father a small plot at a good price. We have built a house there. I hope you will come and meet my family."

"I shall," he said.

I wrote my address on a piece of paper. He wrote his address and gave it to me. It was lunchtime, but he could not serve me anything because it was Ramazan. He made me promise to visit him in Eid days, when we celebrated the end of our month of fasting with three days of visits to the homes of all our relatives and friends. We talked about other things. He was a great talker and a good storyteller, sophisticated and full of funny jokes.

He was not just a baker, I discovered. He had graduated from the Literature Faculty of Kabul University and had taught at Kabul University for two years. But he did not earn enough money there to support his big family. He stopped teaching and took over his family's baking business. He built up the business and now has three shops. He has three sons and two daughters. All of them are married and have their own kids, but they all live with him in one big courtyard, the way we did with Grandfather.

"Do you still have to be home on time for dinner, otherwise your wife will be worried?" I asked him.

"Oh, of course! She is the boss after all!" he said with a huge smile.

My older sister accomplished her dream: she finished her education and became an architect and an engineer. Then she got married, and has a sweet son, who was given the name I had chosen: Suleiman. It was a name I always liked. Suleiman was an important man in many folktales as well as in the Holy Koran and the Bible. More practically, it is a name that people rarely mispronounce. And when I was little, I often dreamed of Suleiman's magic carpet, on which I could fly to interesting places, and cut the most beautiful kites along the way.

Now my older sister can tease her husband instead of me. Her husband is a good man. He teases her right back. She complains about that. I smile and tell her, "What goes around comes around."

These days, she has become my best friend, even though sometimes she still says that when I eat I make noises like a cow. Maybe I do.

But I do not think I do. These words bring memories of our time in the garden of Hamza's father, and the stealing of the pomegranates.

One night about six months after their wedding, her husband asked her, "Tell me a few things about your brothers and sisters. I don't know much about them." He had been living in other countries for several years before they were married.

She told him about our childhood at Grandfather's house in Kot-e-Sangi, and how everything changed when the civil war started, how we took shelter at the Qala-e-Noborja as refugees, then tried so hard to get away from the madness that was destroying our country. Later he told me that as she started telling him how hard I had tried to help my father support us, her voice began to shake. She burst out sobbing and could not stop, though her husband held her in his arms.

Around midnight, I heard knocking on our door and I opened the window to see who had come at that late hour. I was very surprised to see my older sister and her husband. I went down the long flight of stairs to the door and opened it for them. Before I had a chance to greet them, my sister hugged me and kissed me many times, her face soaked with tears.

"What is wrong?" I asked with alarm.

"Nothing," her husband said. "She got talking about you, and suddenly said she needed to see you."

I led them upstairs. The rest of the family were asleep, except for my mother. She was surprised to see my sister, who by then had calmed down a little. Her husband found a blanket and a *toshak* and went to sleep, but my sister, my mother, and I stayed awake for hours while the muted TV flickered at us, having an unexpected tea party and talking about things of the past. We almost never do that. The wounds from those days are deep and can easily be opened. It is better to leave them in the past.

The crying machine is a big man now, handsomer than I am, taller than I am, stronger than I am. He is full of muscles and can beat me when we arm wrestle. He has not cried since he was a baby. In fact, he is like my father, and can always tell good jokes. But I like to remember his old name. It reminds me of the time when we were with the Kuchis. Now he studies law, and hopes to bring order to our country.

My four younger sisters are all being educated, even though some people in Afghanistan still say that educating girls is a bad thing. They have high ambitions. One of them studies management, another agriculture. Another wants to be a writer and reads any book she can find. The youngest says she will be a nurse. Afghanistan will benefit from having good managers, agriculturists who can plant trees, writers to record the joys and sorrows of our people, and nurses to cure our wounded hearts. The older two have married very good men.

My mother had never really quit her job at the bank. She just stopped going during the civil war when the fighting made it too dangerous. And then she was prevented from working by the Taliban. But after they were driven out, she went one day to see what was going on at the bank, and then the next day she started back at her old job. No one had been hired to fill it, because no one had been there to do any hiring. After a few years, she finally left the bank and took a job with the Afghanistan Disaster Management Authority, where she feels she can be more useful. She works very hard to get government assistance quickly to communities that suffer earthquakes or blizzards or other calamities.

My father is still teaching physics at Habibia High School. He is the only teacher from before the war who was not killed or did not flee the country. All the younger teachers respect him like they do their own fathers. The school has a gym, but no equipment. He is trying to find money to buy what is needed and to start training again. He is still in great shape, and very strong, except for the arthritis that is creeping into his knees.

After so many years of trying, my father did finally manage to leave Afghanistan, though only briefly. He achieved his lifelong ambition to make a pilgrimage to Mecca. Now we are proud to call him "Haji."

My cousin Jerk can still be a jerk sometimes, but despite that he has done very well for himself. He has always been kind to his siblings and parents, and has willingly shouldered his family's burdens, as I tried to do with mine.

After not having seen him for a couple of years, I went to his house one day to deliver my second sister's wedding invitation card. He had put on a little weight, and had a few white hairs on his temples, which made him look distinguished. I pointed those out to him, and said, "You are getting old." Suddenly I felt *I* was being a jerk, since he is the same age as I am.

He ran his right hand over his temple and said, "Well, that's the story of life. As Grandfather said, 'We are raw, we get cooked, and finally burned.' I'm in the process of being cooked."

"Will you stay in this country until you get burned?" I asked, trying to be funny.

"Yes, I will stay in this country and will do my best to fix things," he said, sounding serious. "Things that my father and his generation could not fix. I believe that there is a future for this country, but only if we do something about it now. If we don't do it, then who will?

"Somebody has to have the guts to step in. We know that no country is here to help us. They are here to help themselves. We have to tell the world that Afghanistan has a new owner, and that owner is our generation."

I gave him a big hug for the first time in many years—a lifetime— because I was so moved by what he said. I admire him for his determination.

A few years before Wakeel was killed, we received a letter from Russia. Who knows how it found us. But some friend of my grandfather's brought it to him. It was on a scrap of a Russian newspaper, stating, "I'm still alive. I can't write more. We're living in a dark hole. I'll come home one day." The handwriting belonged to Wakeel's father who had mysteriously disappeared all those years before. But we have never heard any more from him.

If he goes to look for us at Grandfather's house, he will not find us, or even the house. Most of it is completely destroyed. The part where my father and mother had our rooms is only a mound of dirt. Every one of Grandfather's beloved McIntosh apple trees is gone. There is no sign that once we had a good life there. Perhaps someday somebody will build a new house in Grandfather's garden. Perhaps they will find our gold.

There is one person I have never seen again, but I am determined to find her, because she has given my life its purpose. I now have my own carpet company called Kabul Carpets & Kilims. It is still small, but it will grow. Grandfather used to say, "Small streams make an ocean."

A few years ago, when I had a chance to go to Holland, I visited a Dutch woman who had once come to Kabul and has become my good friend. In her house in Haarlem, I saw one of my carpets that I had made in my factory in the worst days of the Taliban.

There is no way to describe the feelings I had when I saw that carpet again. It reminded me of my good memories, my hardships, my eagerness for a future, my factory, and eating lunch with my weavers around one cloth with everyone laughing, even though we knew terrible things would happen if the Taliban caught us. Now all of that history, my history, is being preserved in that faraway country.

None of this could have happened without my teacher.

I think she might be in Tajikistan. Maybe in a city. Maybe in a village. I have not dreamed about her in a long time. There is too much noise in my life now. But soon the time is coming when I shall set out to look for her.

I am sure she will know when I am coming. And, with her help and Allah's, I shall find her.

I have long carried this load of griefs in the cage of my heart.
Now I have given them to you. I hope you are strong enough to
hold them.

Qais Akbar Omar

Author's Note

A Fort of Nine Towers chronicles the past three tumultuous decades in Afghanistan. For part of that time, I was very young. Many things happened to my family and me, and for the first years of the fighting I cannot say exactly when they occurred—only that they did. I have included specific dates when I can be sure of them, and done my best to reconstruct them when I cannot.

Readers from outside Afghanistan may wonder why I have rarely included the names of my family in this account of our lives together. Afghans, however, will understand.

While this book focuses on my family's experience, every Afghan family has stories similar to ours. They all need to be told. They need to be heard. They must not happen again.

Acknowledgments

This book is dedicated to Afghanistan and its people, to the spirit of Grandfather, who still leads me in good and bad times like a guardian angel, to Wakeel, who visits me every three or four years in my dreams, to my parents, who mean everything in the world to me, to my sisters and brother, who will make their own families soon in Afghanistan or in other countries, to my uncles and aunts and cousins with whom I shared so much and whom I deeply love.

This book would not have been written if Stephen Landrigan had not come to Afghanistan, and I had not met him. He listened quietly when I spoke of the memories that haunted me, and encouraged me to write about them to ease their grip on my soul. His guidance helped me discover a love for writing. Someday I will write a book about all the good things he has done for Afghanistan. It will be a thick book.

A profound thanks to Janet Garcia and Linda Nicita of Colorado, who read an early draft before I knew so much about the English language, and who cleaned up all the grammatical errors and misspelled words. Thanks also to Laurence E. Landrigan, whose careful reading and editing of my manuscript provided many helpful insights. Their generosity has been deeply impressed on me, and I welcome the obligation of passing it on.

Khaled Hosseini and Michael Patrick MacDonald not only inspired me by their own writing, they were helpful in opening doors to agents and publishers, and to them I am grateful.

I am especially appreciative of the professionalism and kindness extended by Courtney Hodell, my editor at Farrar, Straus and Giroux, who nurtured this book through many drafts. Also, a big thanks to Jessica Papin, my agent with Dystel & Goderich Literary Management, for her positive energy and hard work that led me to the team at Farrar, Straus and Giroux, where Marion Duvert and Devon Mazzone helped this book find publishers in many other countries and languages, Lottchen Shivers spread the word as its publicist, and Mareike Grover made sure that everything in the text was as it should be.

And finally, thanks to Janie Harris, who gave me the first review long before *A Fort of Nine Towers* was even published. It was deeply moving to have somebody who lives on the other side of the world so excited by what I had written.

I hope this book will lead others to become curious about the many layers of Afghan culture that so unexpectedly and for so many of the wrong reasons have become the focus of the world's attention.

CPSIA information can be obtained
at www.ICGtesting.com
Printed in the USA
LVHW051536020322
712334LV00008B/1041